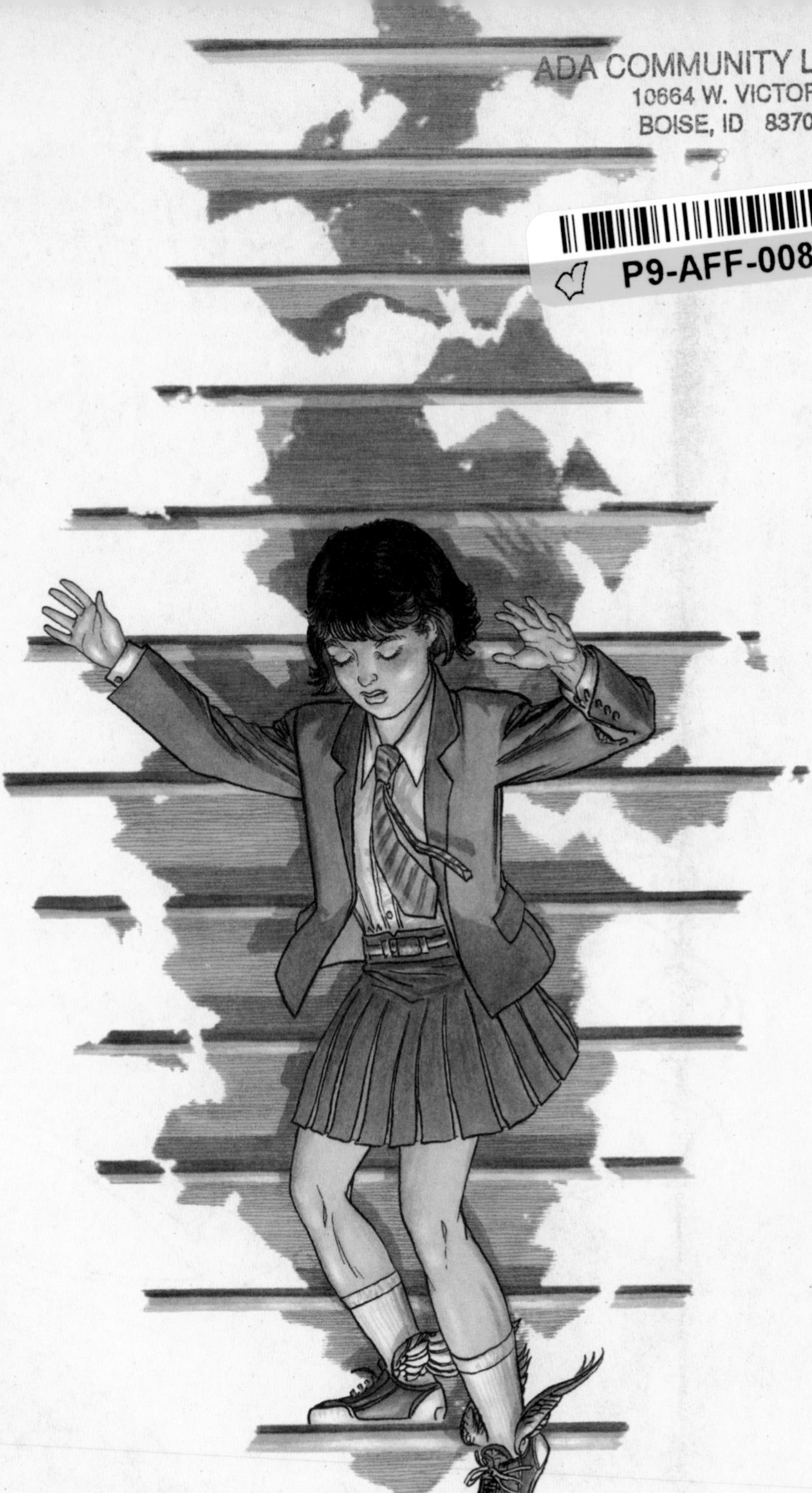

Lucifer
Morningstar

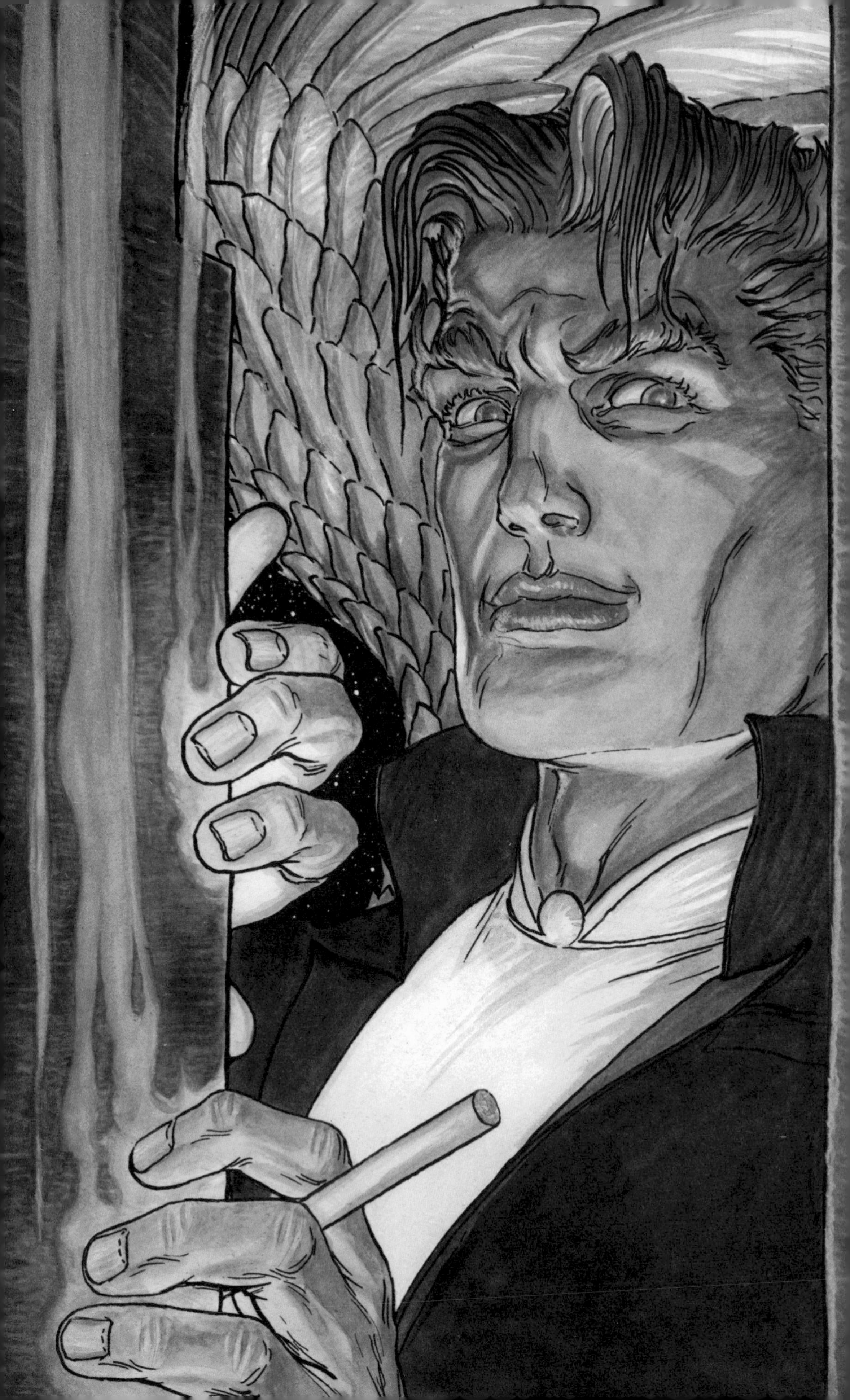

Morningstar

Mike Carey
Writer

Peter Gross
Ryan Kelly
Colleen Doran
Michael Wm. Kaluta
Artists

Daniel Vozzo
Colorist

Jared K. Fletcher
Letterer

Michael Wm. Kaluta
Original Series Covers

Based on characters created by
Neil Gaiman, Sam Kieth
and Mike Dringenberg

LUCIFER: MORNINGSTAR

Published by DC Comics. Cover and compilation Copyright
© 2006 DC Comics. All Rights Reserved.

Originally published in single magazine form as LUCIFER 62-69.
Copyright © 2005, 2006 DC Comics. All Rights Reserved.
All characters, their distinctive likenesses and related elements
featured in this publication are trademarks of DC Comics.
The stories, characters and incidents featured in this publication
are entirely fictional. DC Comics does not read or accept
unsolicited submissions of ideas, stories or artwork.

DC Comics, 1700 Broadway, New York, NY 10019
A Warner Bros. Entertainment Company
Printed in Canada. Second Printing.
ISBN: 978-1-4012-1006-9
Cover illustration by Christopher Moeller.
Logo design by Alex Jay.

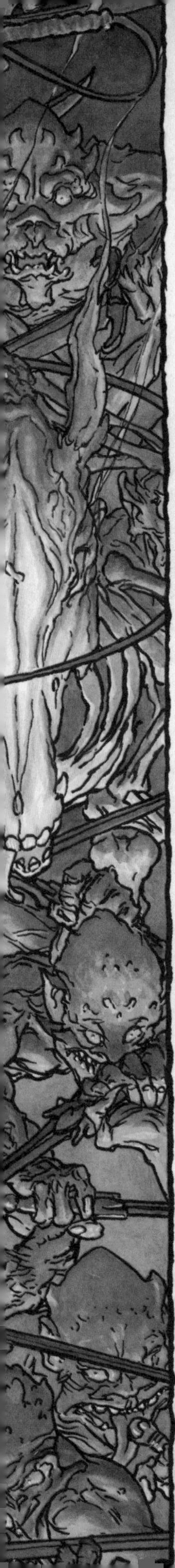

Table of Contents

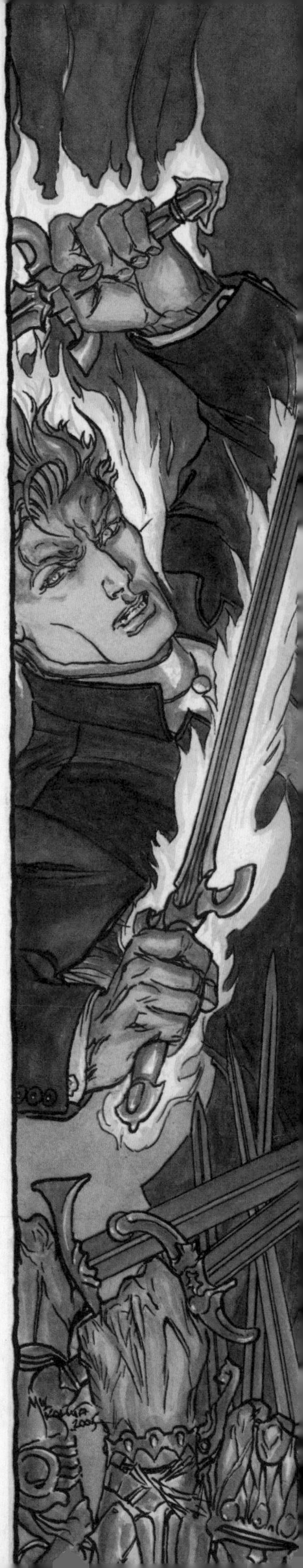

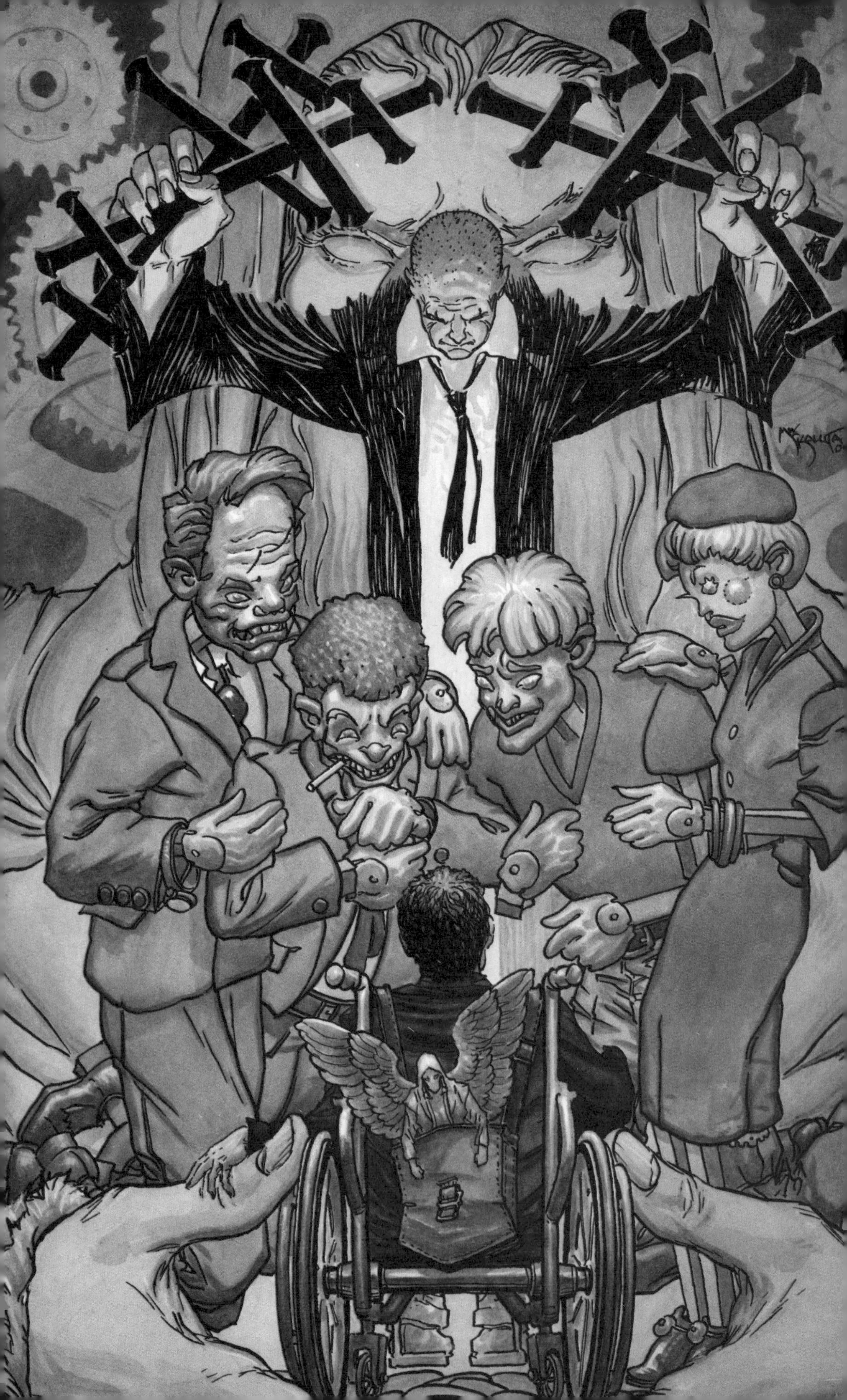

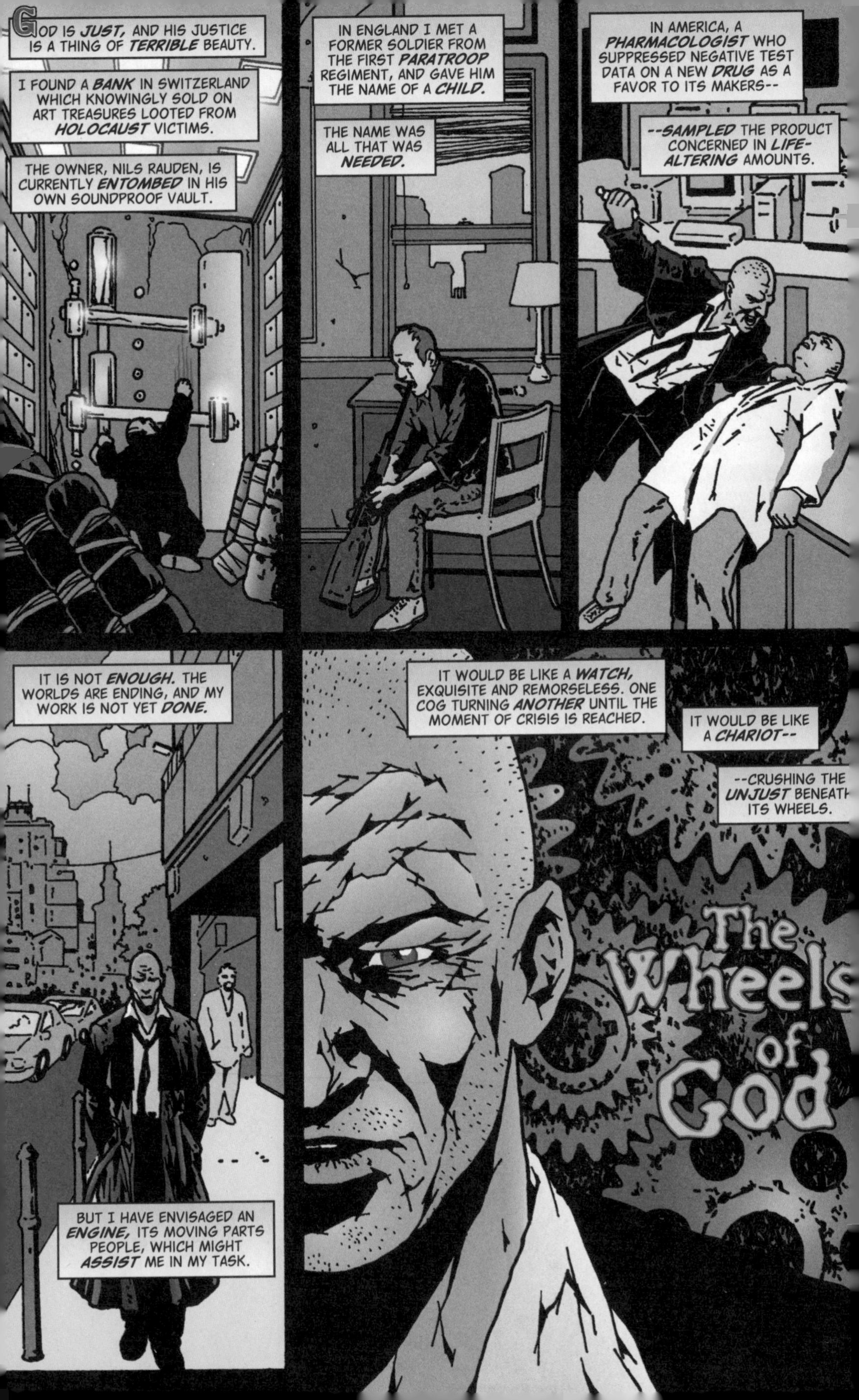
GOD IS JUST, AND HIS JUSTICE IS A THING OF TERRIBLE BEAUTY.
I FOUND A BANK IN SWITZERLAND WHICH KNOWINGLY SOLD ON ART TREASURES LOOTED FROM HOLOCAUST VICTIMS.
THE OWNER, NILS RAUDEN, IS CURRENTLY ENTOMBED IN HIS OWN SOUNDPROOF VAULT.
IN ENGLAND I MET A FORMER SOLDIER FROM THE FIRST PARATROOP REGIMENT, AND GAVE HIM THE NAME OF A CHILD.
THE NAME WAS ALL THAT WAS NEEDED.
IN AMERICA, A PHARMACOLOGIST WHO SUPPRESSED NEGATIVE TEST DATA ON A NEW DRUG AS A FAVOR TO ITS MAKERS--
--SAMPLED THE PRODUCT CONCERNED IN LIFE-ALTERING AMOUNTS.
IT IS NOT ENOUGH. THE WORLDS ARE ENDING, AND MY WORK IS NOT YET DONE.
BUT I HAVE ENVISAGED AN ENGINE, ITS MOVING PARTS PEOPLE, WHICH MIGHT ASSIST ME IN MY TASK.
IT WOULD BE LIKE A WATCH, EXQUISITE AND REMORSELESS. ONE COG TURNING ANOTHER UNTIL THE MOMENT OF CRISIS IS REACHED.
IT WOULD BE LIKE A CHARIOT--
--CRUSHING THE UNJUST BENEATH ITS WHEELS.
The Wheels of God

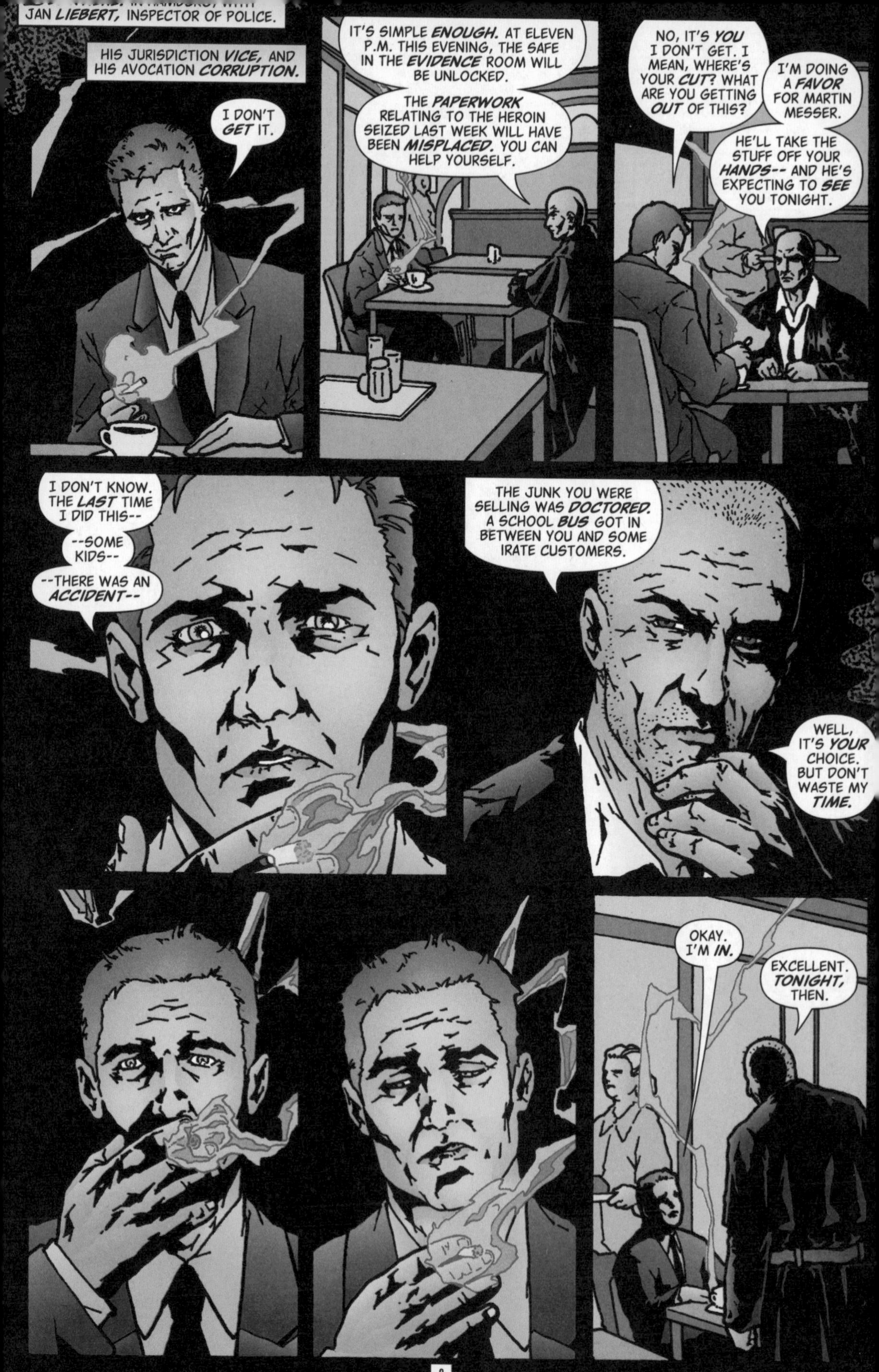

JAN LIEBERT, INSPECTOR OF POLICE.
HIS JURISDICTION VICE, AND HIS AVOCATION CORRUPTION.
I DON'T GET IT.
IT'S SIMPLE ENOUGH. AT ELEVEN P.M. THIS EVENING, THE SAFE IN THE EVIDENCE ROOM WILL BE UNLOCKED.
THE PAPERWORK RELATING TO THE HEROIN SEIZED LAST WEEK WILL HAVE BEEN MISPLACED. YOU CAN HELP YOURSELF.
NO, IT'S YOU I DON'T GET. I MEAN, WHERE'S YOUR CUT? WHAT ARE YOU GETTING OUT OF THIS?
I'M DOING A FAVOR FOR MARTIN MESSER.
HE'LL TAKE THE STUFF OFF YOUR HANDS-- AND HE'S EXPECTING TO SEE YOU TONIGHT.
I DON'T KNOW. THE LAST TIME I DID THIS--
--SOME KIDS--
--THERE WAS AN ACCIDENT--
THE JUNK YOU WERE SELLING WAS DOCTORED. A SCHOOL BUS GOT IN BETWEEN YOU AND SOME IRATE CUSTOMERS.
WELL, IT'S YOUR CHOICE. BUT DON'T WASTE MY TIME.
OKAY. I'M IN.
EXCELLENT. TONIGHT, THEN.

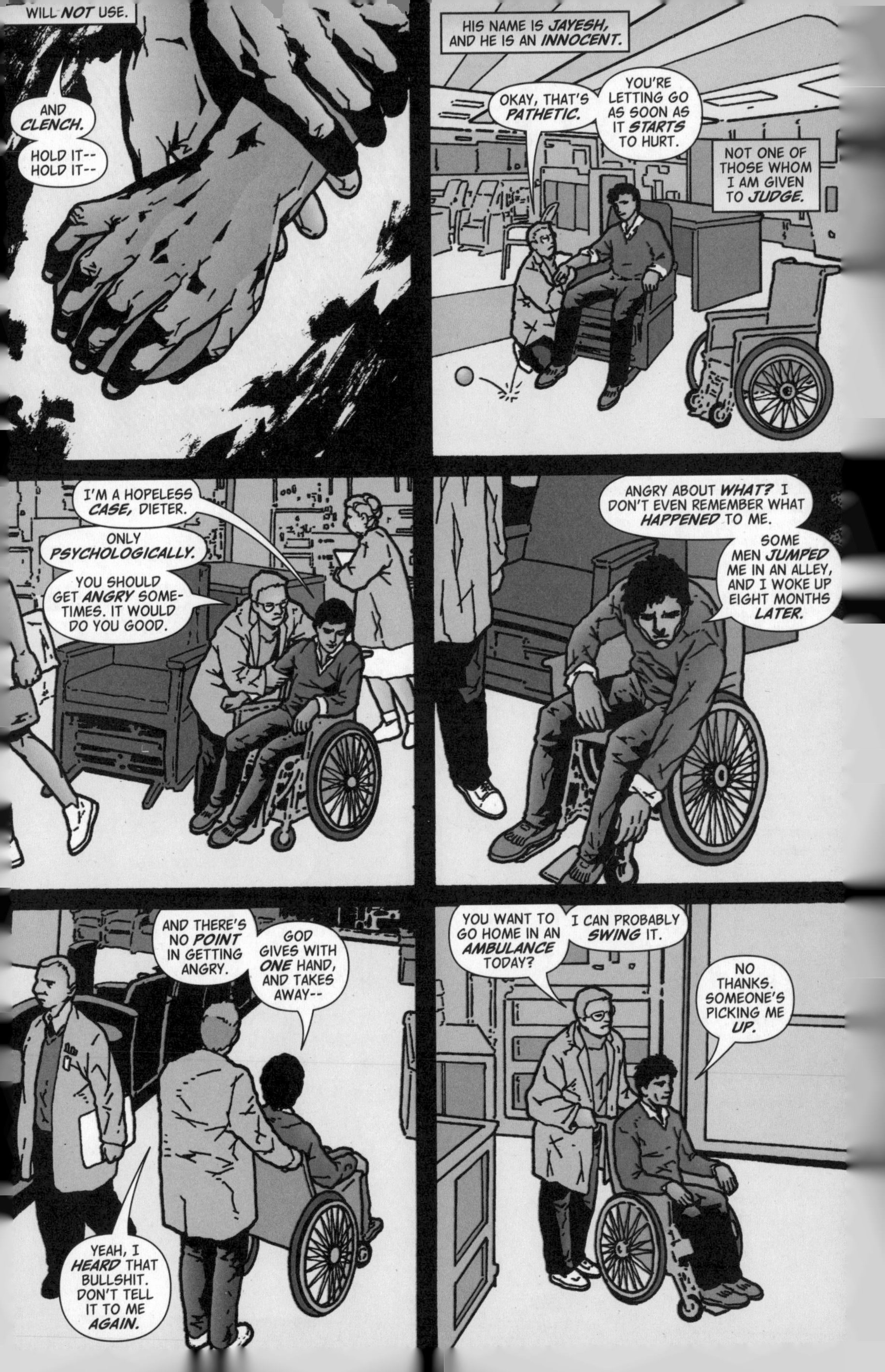
WILL NOT USE.
AND CLENCH.
HOLD IT-- HOLD IT--
HIS NAME IS JAYESH, AND HE IS AN INNOCENT.
OKAY, THAT'S PATHETIC.
YOU'RE LETTING GO AS SOON AS IT STARTS TO HURT.
NOT ONE OF THOSE WHOM I AM GIVEN TO JUDGE.
I'M A HOPELESS CASE, DIETER.
ONLY PSYCHOLOGICALLY.
YOU SHOULD GET ANGRY SOMETIMES. IT WOULD DO YOU GOOD.
ANGRY ABOUT WHAT? I DON'T EVEN REMEMBER WHAT HAPPENED TO ME.
SOME MEN JUMPED ME IN AN ALLEY, AND I WOKE UP EIGHT MONTHS LATER.
AND THERE'S NO POINT IN GETTING ANGRY.
GOD GIVES WITH ONE HAND, AND TAKES AWAY--
YEAH, I HEARD THAT BULLSHIT. DON'T TELL IT TO ME AGAIN.
YOU WANT TO GO HOME IN AN AMBULANCE TODAY?
I CAN PROBABLY SWING IT.
NO THANKS. SOMEONE'S PICKING ME UP.

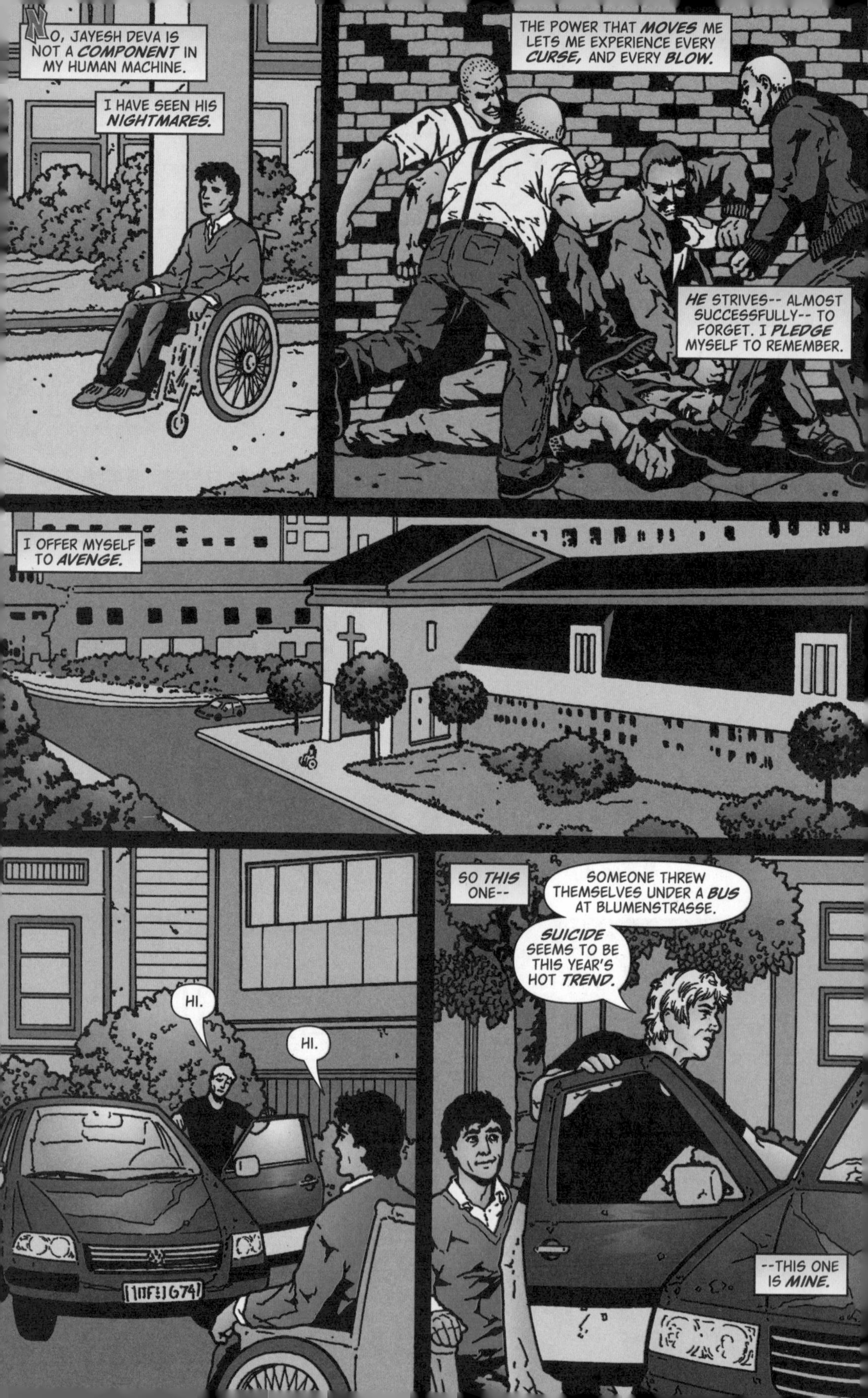
NO, JAYESH DEVA IS NOT A COMPONENT IN MY HUMAN MACHINE.
I HAVE SEEN HIS NIGHTMARES.
THE POWER THAT MOVES ME LETS ME EXPERIENCE EVERY CURSE, AND EVERY BLOW.
HE STRIVES-- ALMOST SUCCESSFULLY-- TO FORGET. I PLEDGE MYSELF TO REMEMBER.
I OFFER MYSELF TO AVENGE.
HI.
HI.
SO THIS ONE--
SOMEONE THREW THEMSELVES UNDER A BUS AT BLUMENSTRASSE.
SUICIDE SEEMS TO BE THIS YEAR'S HOT TREND.
--THIS ONE IS MINE.

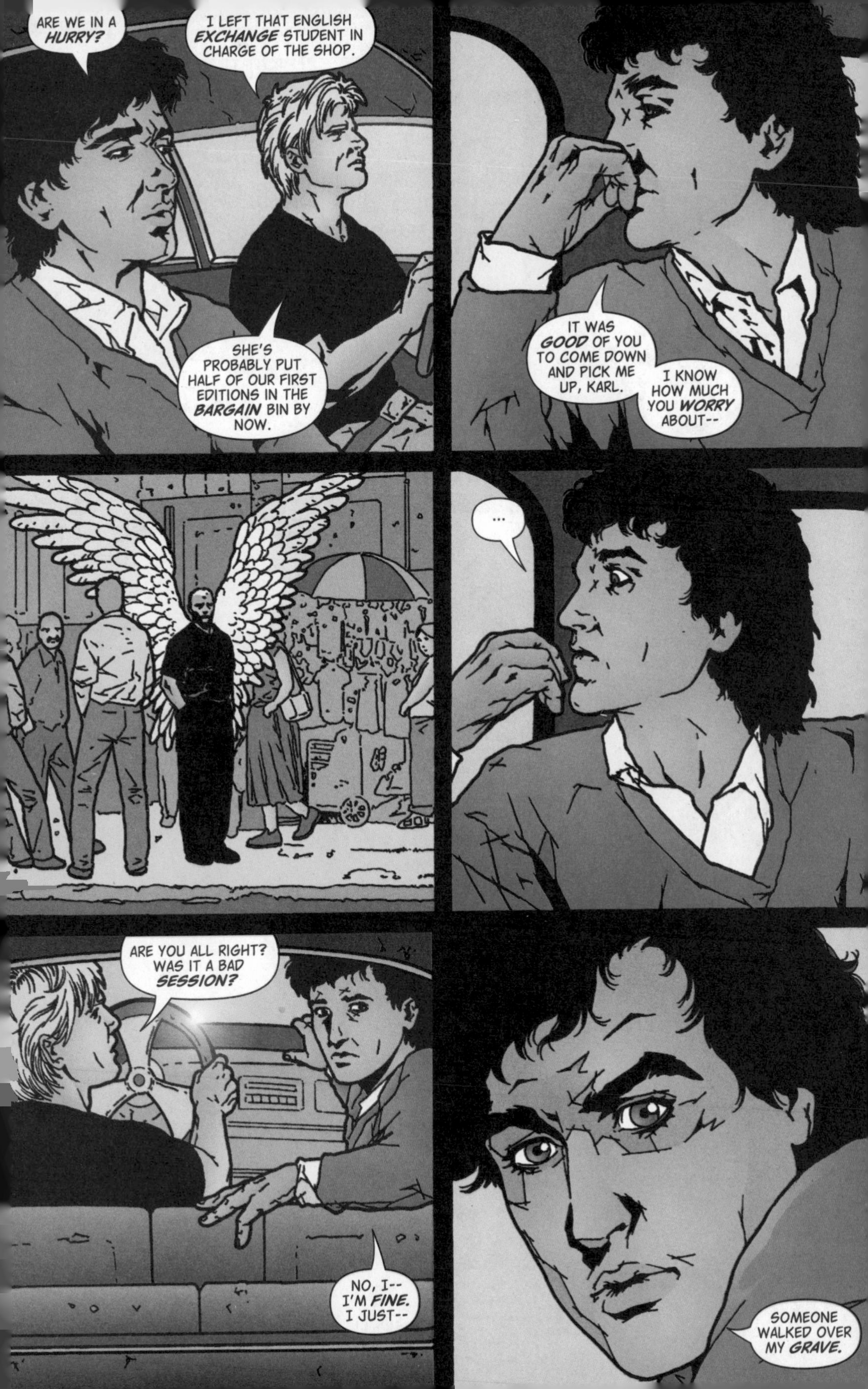
ARE WE IN A HURRY?
I LEFT THAT ENGLISH EXCHANGE STUDENT IN CHARGE OF THE SHOP.
SHE'S PROBABLY PUT HALF OF OUR FIRST EDITIONS IN THE BARGAIN BIN BY NOW.
IT WAS GOOD OF YOU TO COME DOWN AND PICK ME UP, KARL.
I KNOW HOW MUCH YOU WORRY ABOUT--
...
ARE YOU ALL RIGHT? WAS IT A BAD SESSION?
NO, I-- I'M FINE. I JUST--
SOMEONE WALKED OVER MY GRAVE.

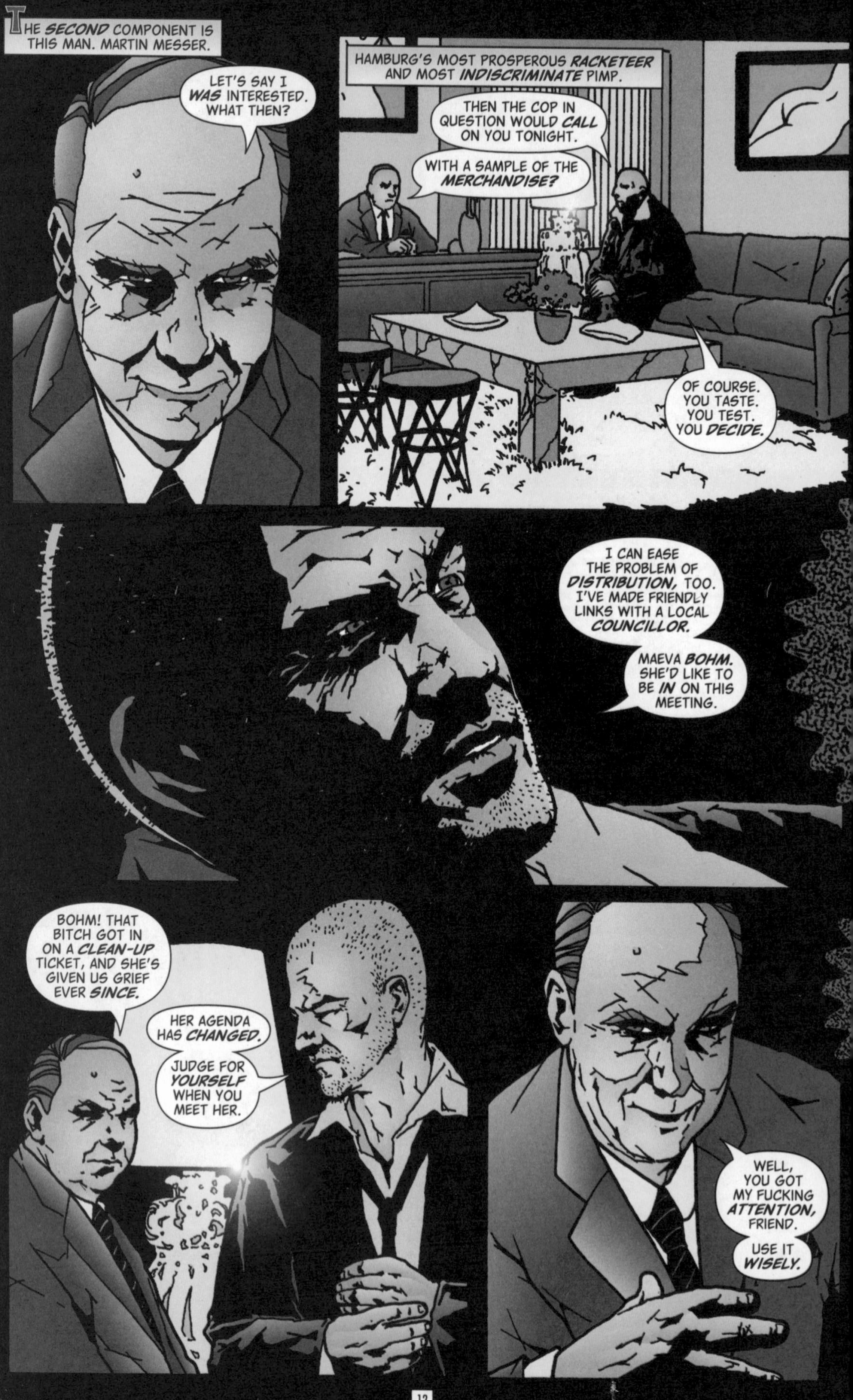
THE SECOND COMPONENT IS THIS MAN. MARTIN MESSER.
LET'S SAY I WAS INTERESTED. WHAT THEN?
HAMBURG'S MOST PROSPEROUS RACKETEER AND MOST INDISCRIMINATE PIMP.
THEN THE COP IN QUESTION WOULD CALL ON YOU TONIGHT.
WITH A SAMPLE OF THE MERCHANDISE?
OF COURSE. YOU TASTE. YOU TEST. YOU DECIDE.
I CAN EASE THE PROBLEM OF DISTRIBUTION, TOO. I'VE MADE FRIENDLY LINKS WITH A LOCAL COUNCILLOR.
MAEVA BOHM. SHE'D LIKE TO BE IN ON THIS MEETING.
BOHM! THAT BITCH GOT IN ON A CLEAN-UP TICKET, AND SHE'S GIVEN US GRIEF EVER SINCE.
HER AGENDA HAS CHANGED.
JUDGE FOR YOURSELF WHEN YOU MEET HER.
WELL, YOU GOT MY FUCKING ATTENTION, FRIEND.
USE IT WISELY.

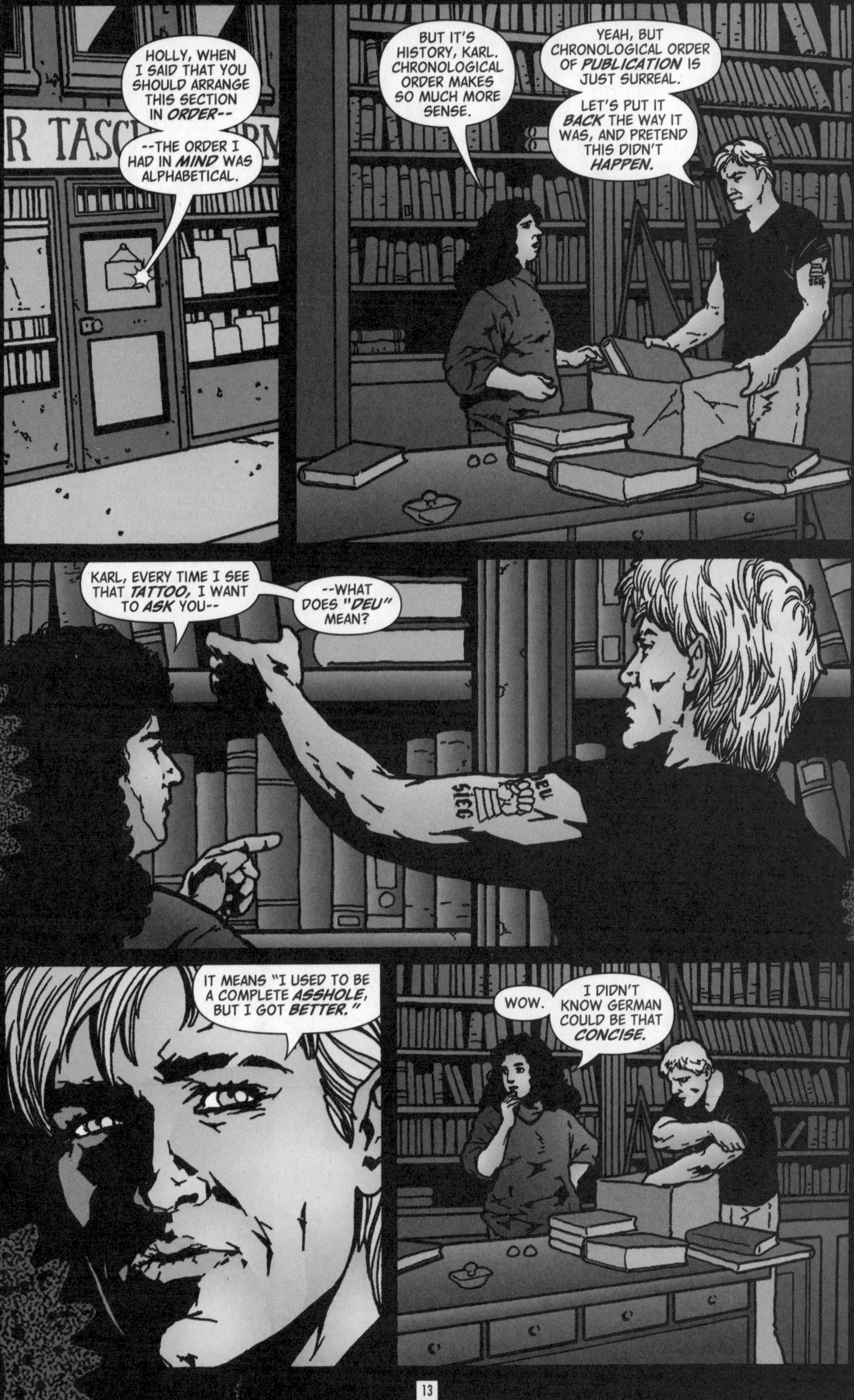
HOLLY, WHEN I SAID THAT YOU SHOULD ARRANGE THIS SECTION IN *ORDER*--
--THE ORDER I HAD IN *MIND* WAS ALPHABETICAL.
BUT IT'S HISTORY, KARL. CHRONOLOGICAL ORDER MAKES SO MUCH MORE SENSE.
YEAH, BUT CHRONOLOGICAL ORDER OF *PUBLICATION* IS JUST SURREAL.
LET'S PUT IT *BACK* THE WAY IT WAS, AND PRETEND THIS DIDN'T *HAPPEN.*
KARL, EVERY TIME I SEE THAT *TATTOO,* I WANT TO *ASK* YOU--
--WHAT DOES *"DEU"* MEAN?
DEU
SIEG
IT MEANS "I USED TO BE A COMPLETE *ASSHOLE,* BUT I GOT *BETTER."*
WOW.
I DIDN'T KNOW GERMAN COULD BE THAT *CONCISE.*

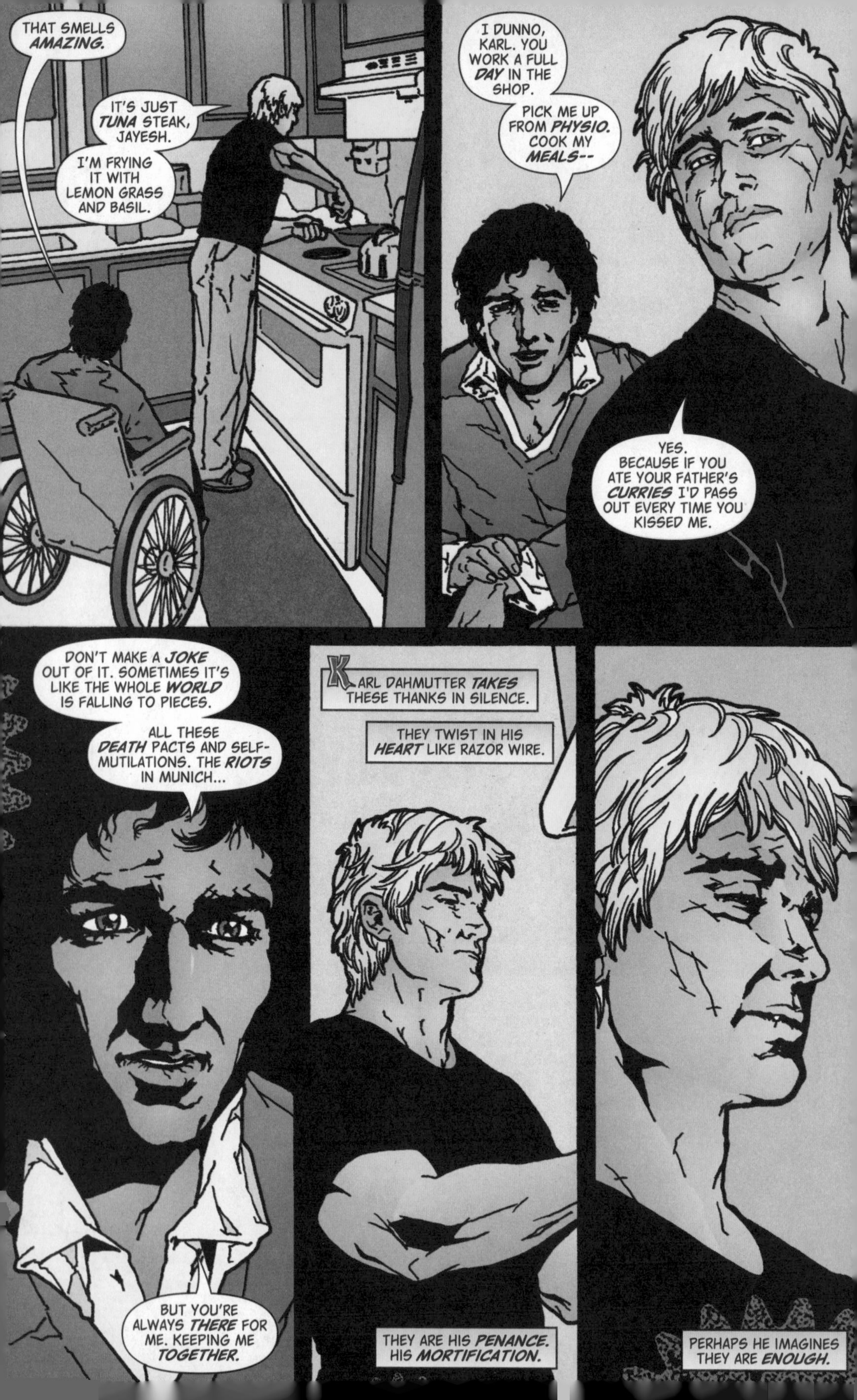

THAT SMELLS AMAZING.
IT'S JUST TUNA STEAK, JAYESH.
I'M FRYING IT WITH LEMON GRASS AND BASIL.
I DUNNO, KARL. YOU WORK A FULL DAY IN THE SHOP.
PICK ME UP FROM PHYSIO. COOK MY MEALS--
YES. BECAUSE IF YOU ATE YOUR FATHER'S CURRIES I'D PASS OUT EVERY TIME YOU KISSED ME.
DON'T MAKE A JOKE OUT OF IT. SOMETIMES IT'S LIKE THE WHOLE WORLD IS FALLING TO PIECES.
ALL THESE DEATH PACTS AND SELF-MUTILATIONS. THE RIOTS IN MUNICH...
BUT YOU'RE ALWAYS THERE FOR ME. KEEPING ME TOGETHER.
KARL DAHMUTTER TAKES THESE THANKS IN SILENCE.
THEY TWIST IN HIS HEART LIKE RAZOR WIRE.
THEY ARE HIS PENANCE. HIS MORTIFICATION.
PERHAPS HE IMAGINES THEY ARE ENOUGH.

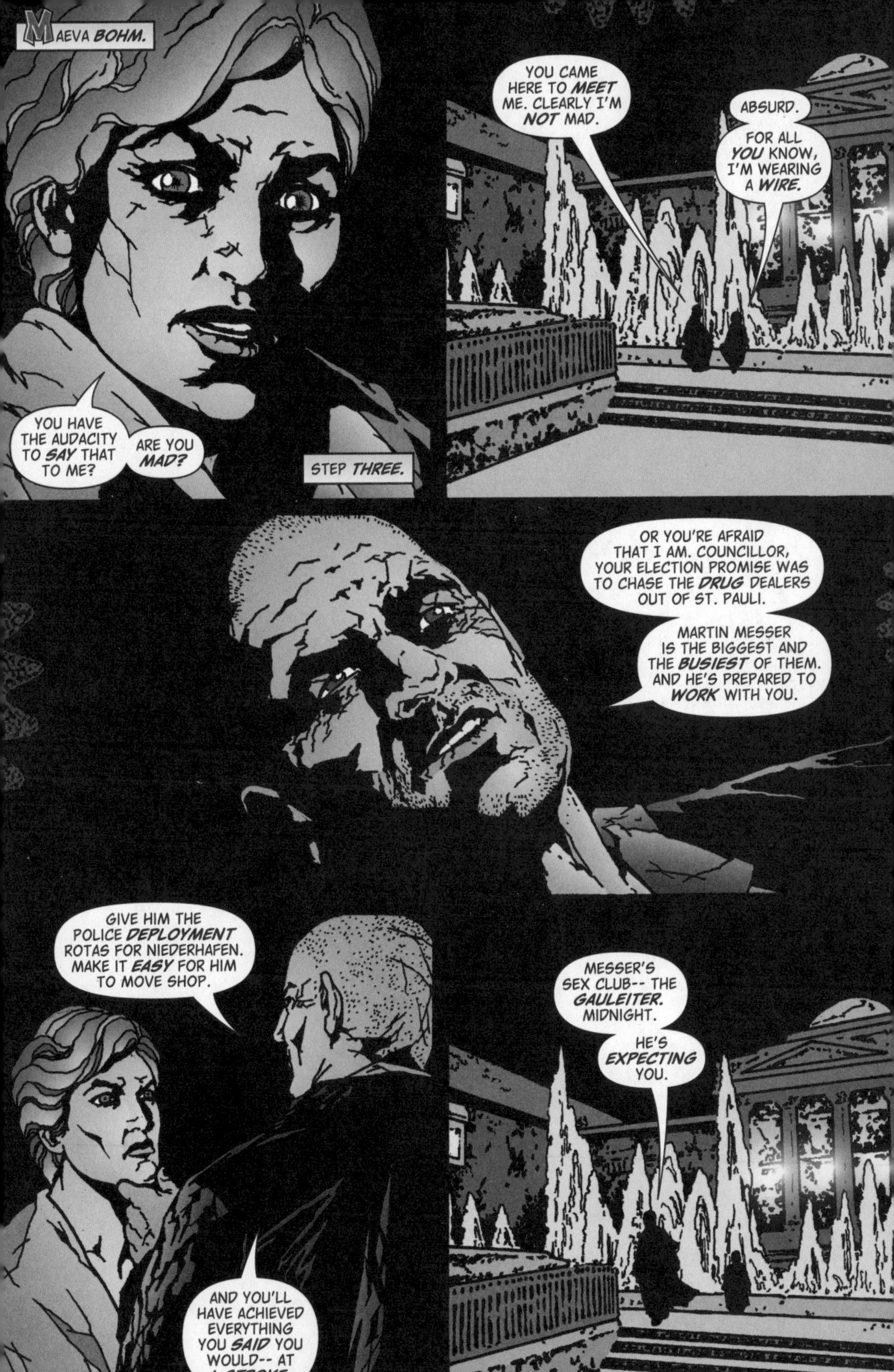
MAEVA BOHM.
YOU HAVE THE AUDACITY TO SAY THAT TO ME?
ARE YOU MAD?
STEP THREE.
YOU CAME HERE TO MEET ME. CLEARLY I'M NOT MAD.
ABSURD.
FOR ALL YOU KNOW, I'M WEARING A WIRE.
OR YOU'RE AFRAID THAT I AM. COUNCILLOR, YOUR ELECTION PROMISE WAS TO CHASE THE DRUG DEALERS OUT OF ST. PAULI.
MARTIN MESSER IS THE BIGGEST AND THE BUSIEST OF THEM. AND HE'S PREPARED TO WORK WITH YOU.
GIVE HIM THE POLICE DEPLOYMENT ROTAS FOR NIEDERHAFEN. MAKE IT EASY FOR HIM TO MOVE SHOP.
AND YOU'LL HAVE ACHIEVED EVERYTHING YOU SAID YOU WOULD-- AT A STROKE.
MESSER'S SEX CLUB-- THE GAULEITER. MIDNIGHT.
HE'S EXPECTING YOU.

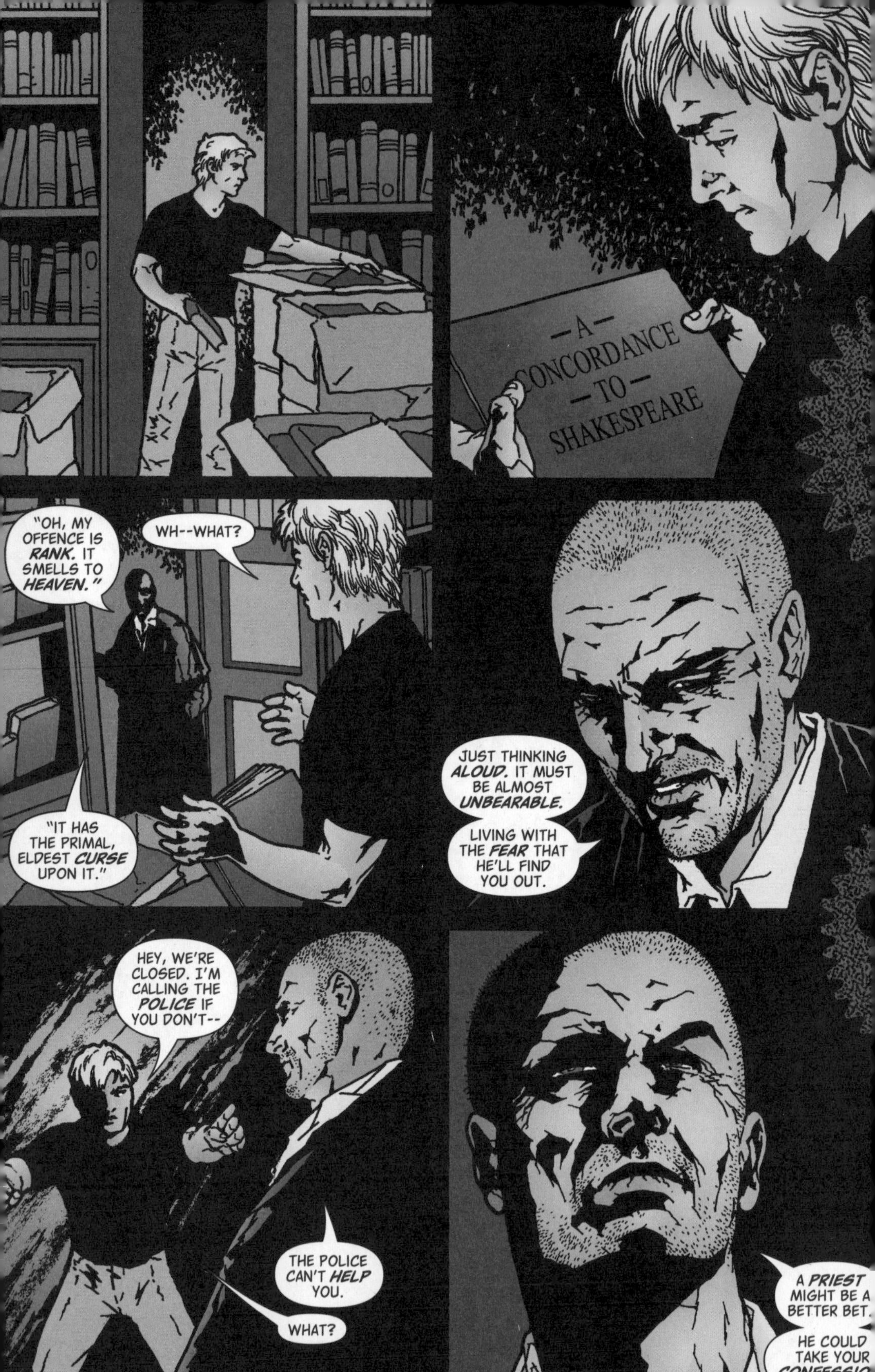

-A- CONCORDANCE -TO- SHAKESPEARE
"OH, MY OFFENCE IS RANK. IT SMELLS TO HEAVEN."
WH--WHAT?
"IT HAS THE PRIMAL, ELDEST CURSE UPON IT."
JUST THINKING ALOUD. IT MUST BE ALMOST UNBEARABLE.
LIVING WITH THE FEAR THAT HE'LL FIND YOU OUT.
HEY, WE'RE CLOSED. I'M CALLING THE POLICE IF YOU DON'T--
THE POLICE CAN'T HELP YOU.
WHAT?
A PRIEST MIGHT BE A BETTER BET.
HE COULD TAKE YOUR CONFESSIO

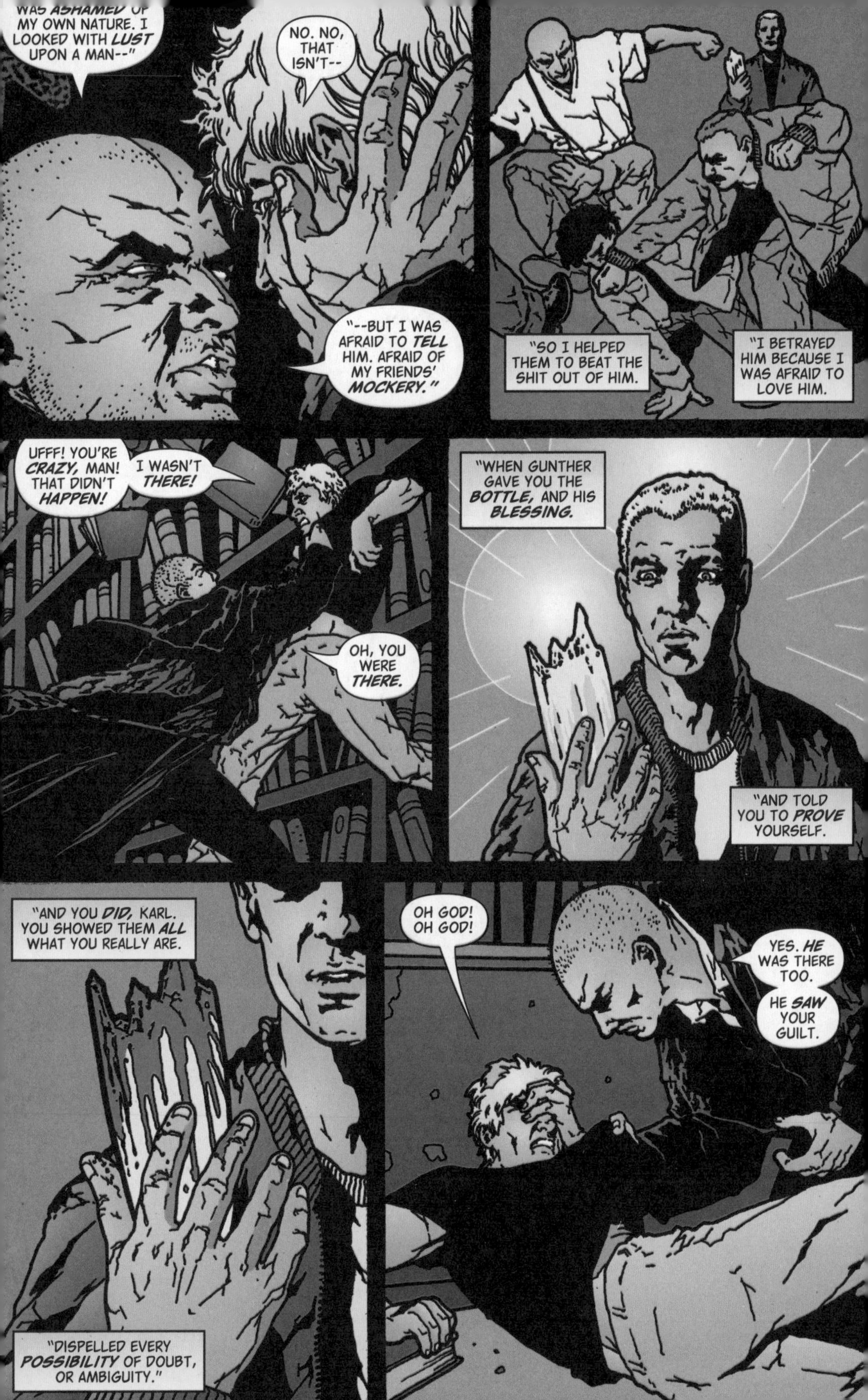
WAS ASHAMED OF MY OWN NATURE. I LOOKED WITH LUST UPON A MAN--"
NO. NO, THAT ISN'T--
"--BUT I WAS AFRAID TO TELL HIM. AFRAID OF MY FRIENDS' MOCKERY."
"SO I HELPED THEM TO BEAT THE SHIT OUT OF HIM.
"I BETRAYED HIM BECAUSE I WAS AFRAID TO LOVE HIM.
UFFF! YOU'RE CRAZY, MAN! THAT DIDN'T HAPPEN!
I WASN'T THERE!
OH, YOU WERE THERE.
"WHEN GUNTHER GAVE YOU THE BOTTLE, AND HIS BLESSING.
"AND TOLD YOU TO PROVE YOURSELF.
"AND YOU DID, KARL. YOU SHOWED THEM ALL WHAT YOU REALLY ARE.
"DISPELLED EVERY POSSIBILITY OF DOUBT, OR AMBIGUITY."
OH GOD! OH GOD!
YES. HE WAS THERE TOO.
HE SAW YOUR GUILT.

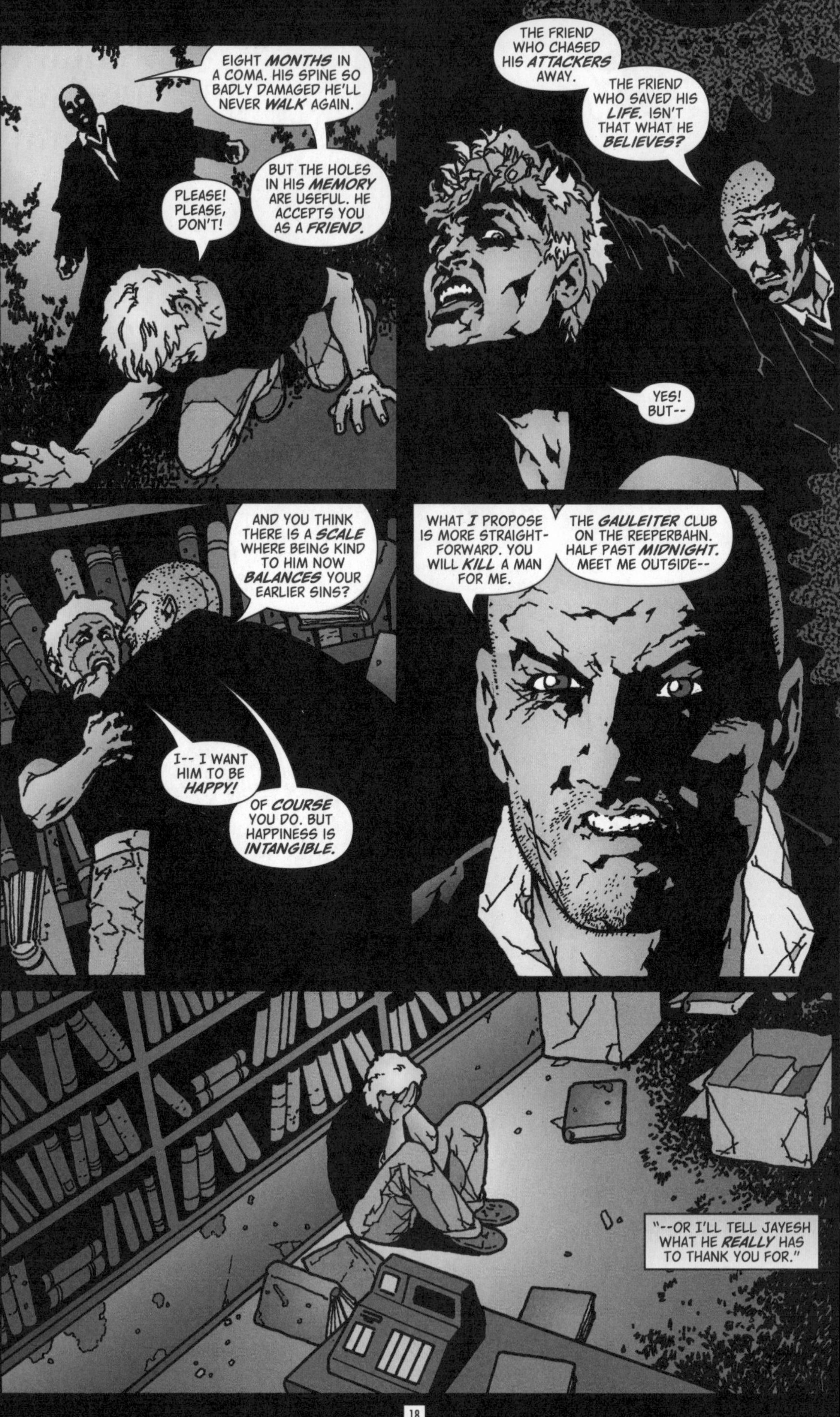

EIGHT MONTHS IN A COMA. HIS SPINE SO BADLY DAMAGED HE'LL NEVER WALK AGAIN.
PLEASE! PLEASE, DON'T!
BUT THE HOLES IN HIS MEMORY ARE USEFUL. HE ACCEPTS YOU AS A FRIEND.
THE FRIEND WHO CHASED HIS ATTACKERS AWAY.
THE FRIEND WHO SAVED HIS LIFE. ISN'T THAT WHAT HE BELIEVES?
YES! BUT--
AND YOU THINK THERE IS A SCALE WHERE BEING KIND TO HIM NOW BALANCES YOUR EARLIER SINS?
I-- I WANT HIM TO BE HAPPY!
OF COURSE YOU DO. BUT HAPPINESS IS INTANGIBLE.
WHAT I PROPOSE IS MORE STRAIGHT-FORWARD. YOU WILL KILL A MAN FOR ME.
THE GAULEITER CLUB ON THE REEPERBAHN. HALF PAST MIDNIGHT. MEET ME OUTSIDE--
"--OR I'LL TELL JAYESH WHAT HE REALLY HAS TO THANK YOU FOR."

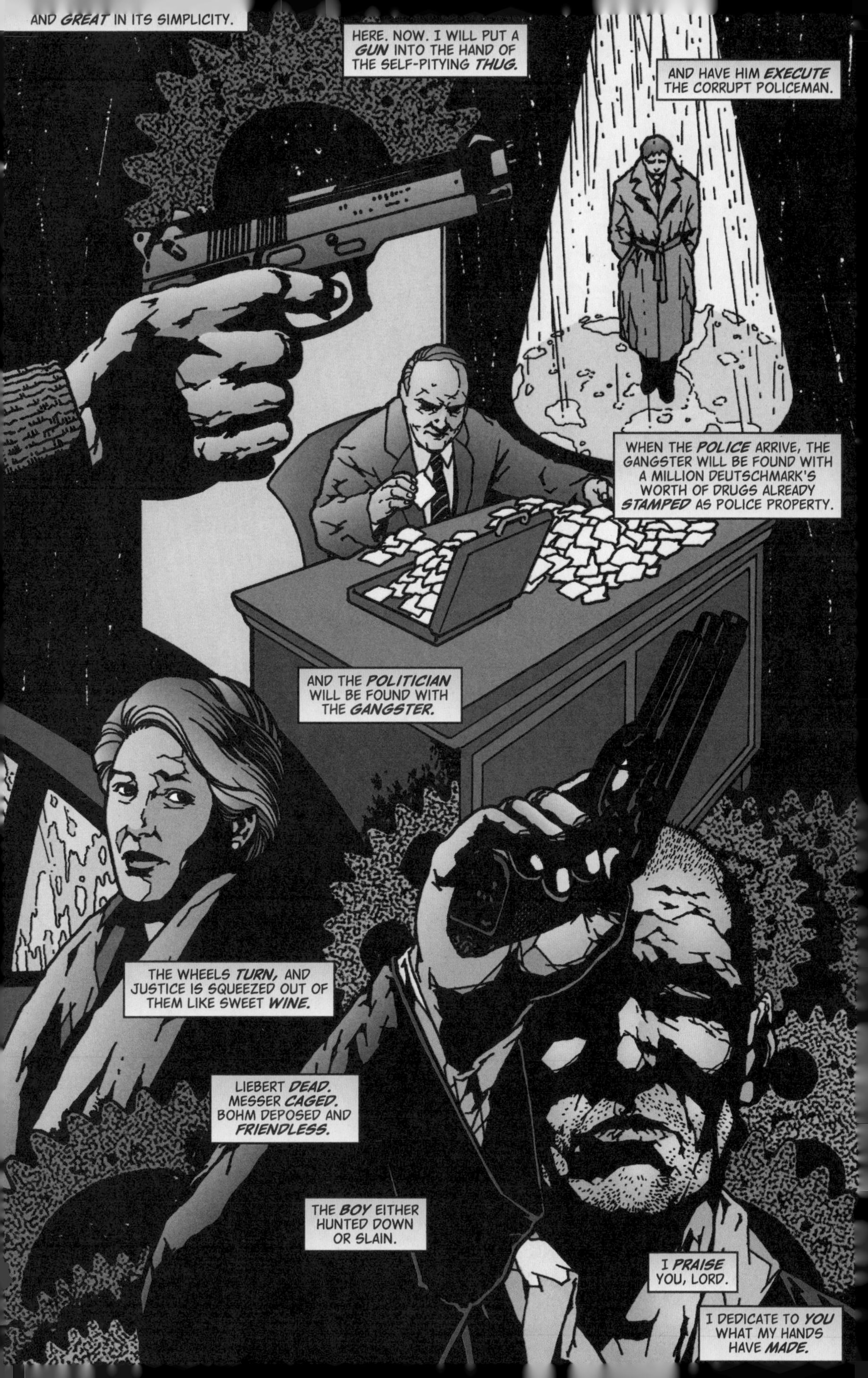
AND GREAT IN ITS SIMPLICITY.
HERE. NOW. I WILL PUT A GUN INTO THE HAND OF THE SELF-PITYING THUG.
AND HAVE HIM EXECUTE THE CORRUPT POLICEMAN.
WHEN THE POLICE ARRIVE, THE GANGSTER WILL BE FOUND WITH A MILLION DEUTSCHMARK'S WORTH OF DRUGS ALREADY STAMPED AS POLICE PROPERTY.
AND THE POLITICIAN WILL BE FOUND WITH THE GANGSTER.
THE WHEELS TURN, AND JUSTICE IS SQUEEZED OUT OF THEM LIKE SWEET WINE.
LIEBERT DEAD. MESSER CAGED. BOHM DEPOSED AND FRIENDLESS.
THE BOY EITHER HUNTED DOWN OR SLAIN.
I PRAISE YOU, LORD.
I DEDICATE TO YOU WHAT MY HANDS HAVE MADE.

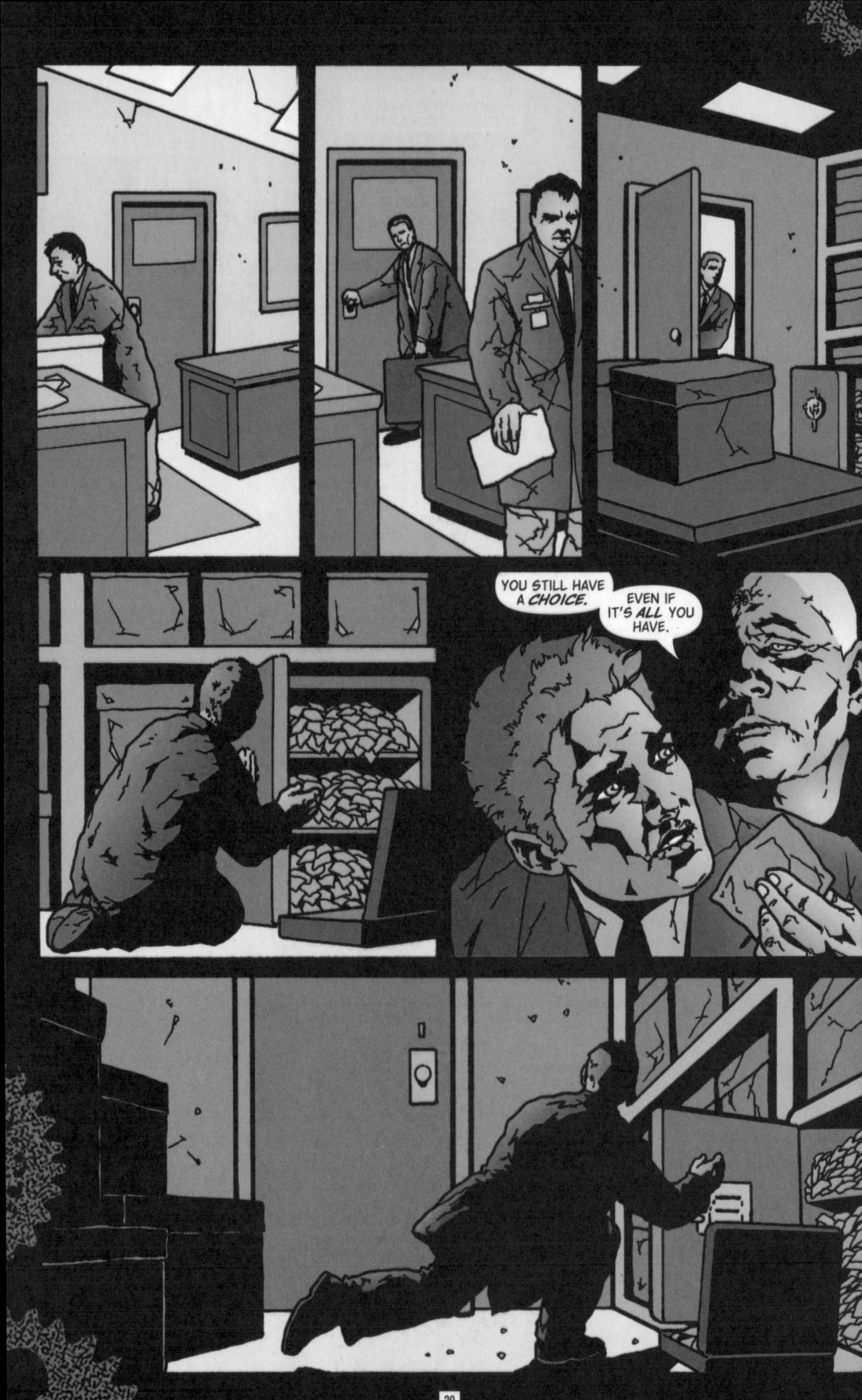
YOU STILL HAVE A *CHOICE.*
EVEN IF IT'S *ALL* YOU HAVE.

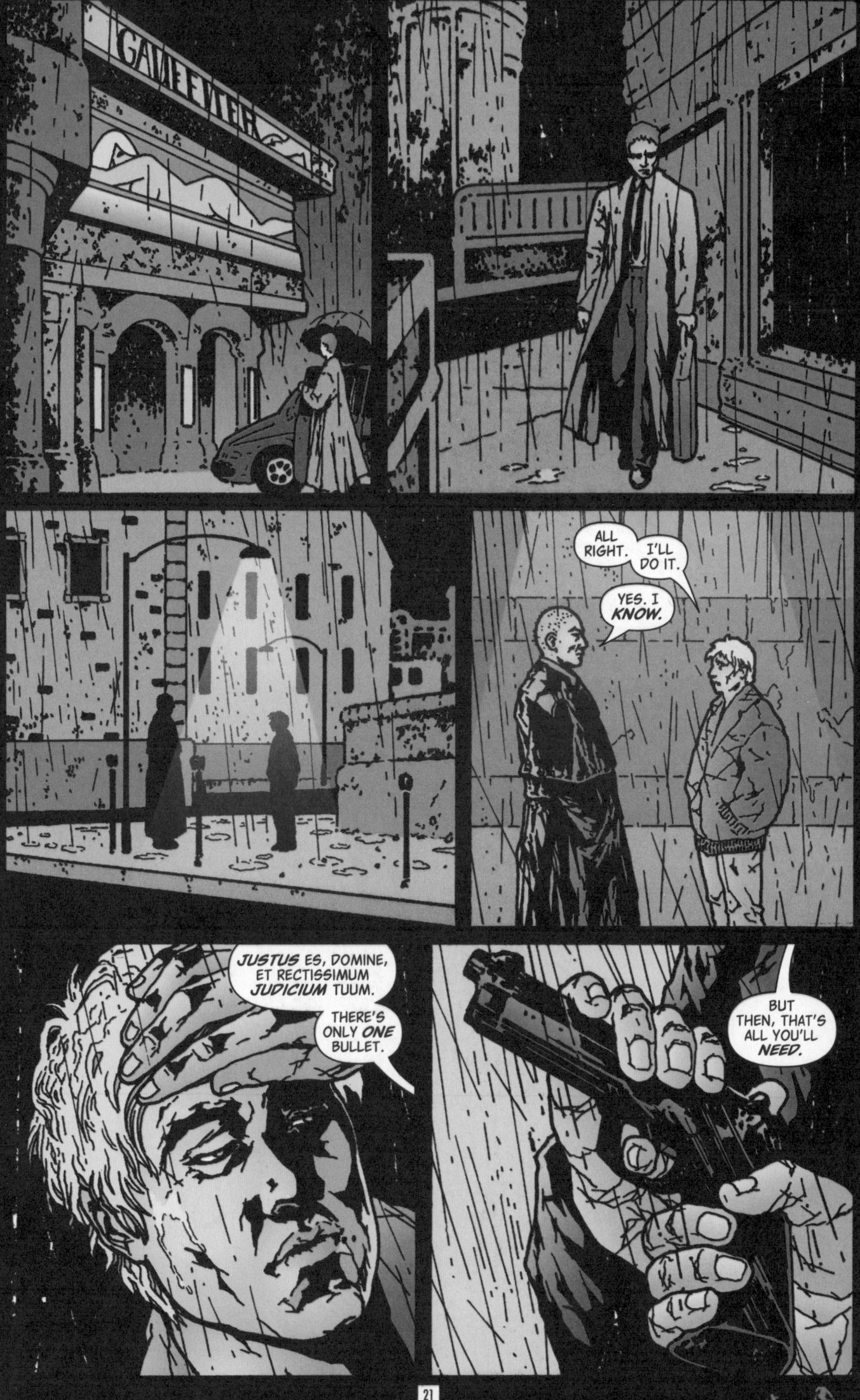
GAULEITER
ALL RIGHT. I'LL DO IT.
YES. I KNOW.
JUSTUS ES, DOMINE, ET RECTISSIMUM JUDICIUM TUUM.
THERE'S ONLY ONE BULLET.
BUT THEN, THAT'S ALL YOU'LL NEED.

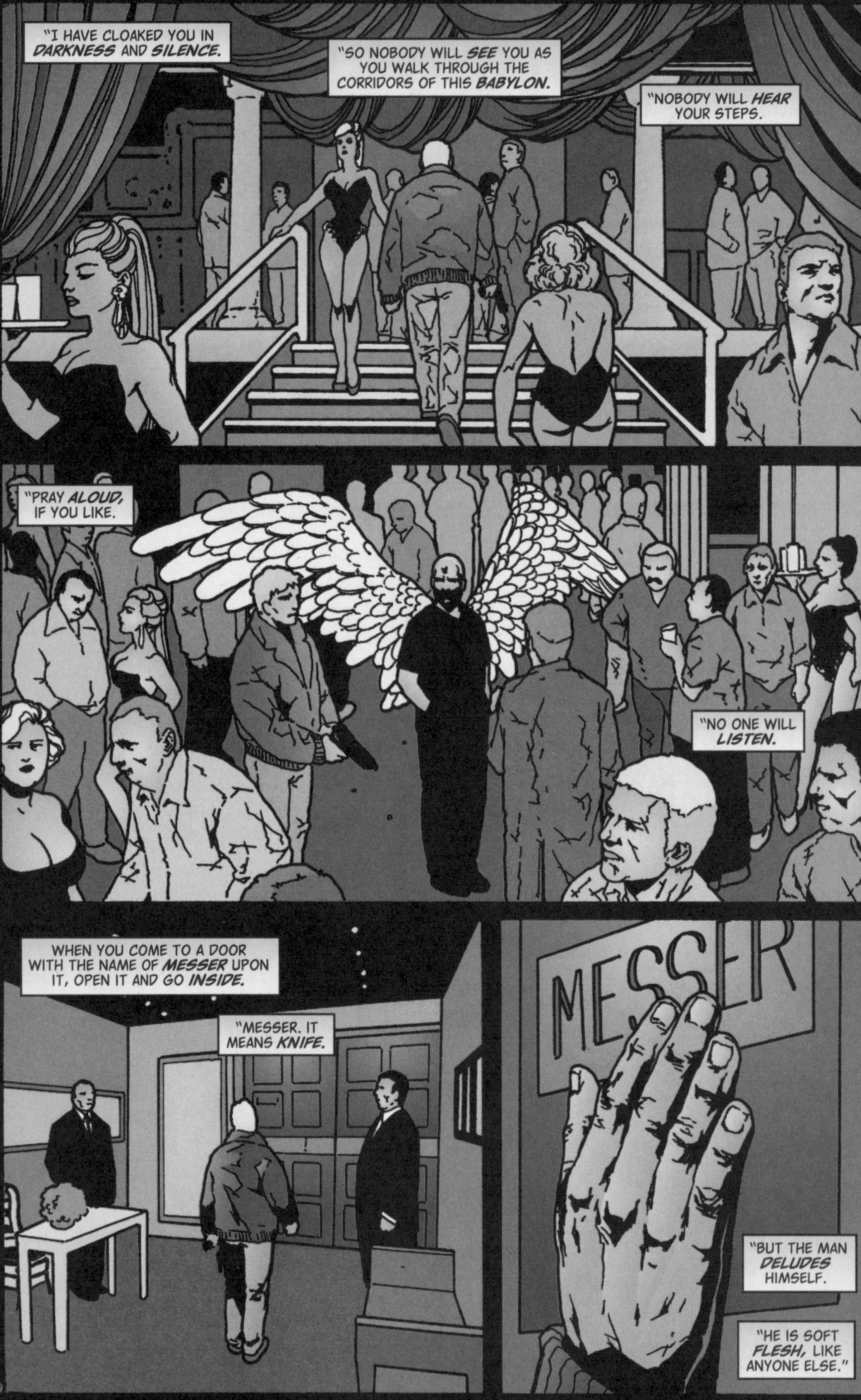
"I HAVE CLOAKED YOU IN DARKNESS AND SILENCE.
"SO NOBODY WILL SEE YOU AS YOU WALK THROUGH THE CORRIDORS OF THIS BABYLON.
"NOBODY WILL HEAR YOUR STEPS.
"PRAY ALOUD, IF YOU LIKE.
"NO ONE WILL LISTEN.
WHEN YOU COME TO A DOOR WITH THE NAME OF MESSER UPON IT, OPEN IT AND GO INSIDE.
"MESSER. IT MEANS KNIFE.
MESSER
"BUT THE MAN DELUDES HIMSELF.
"HE IS SOFT FLESH, LIKE ANYONE ELSE."

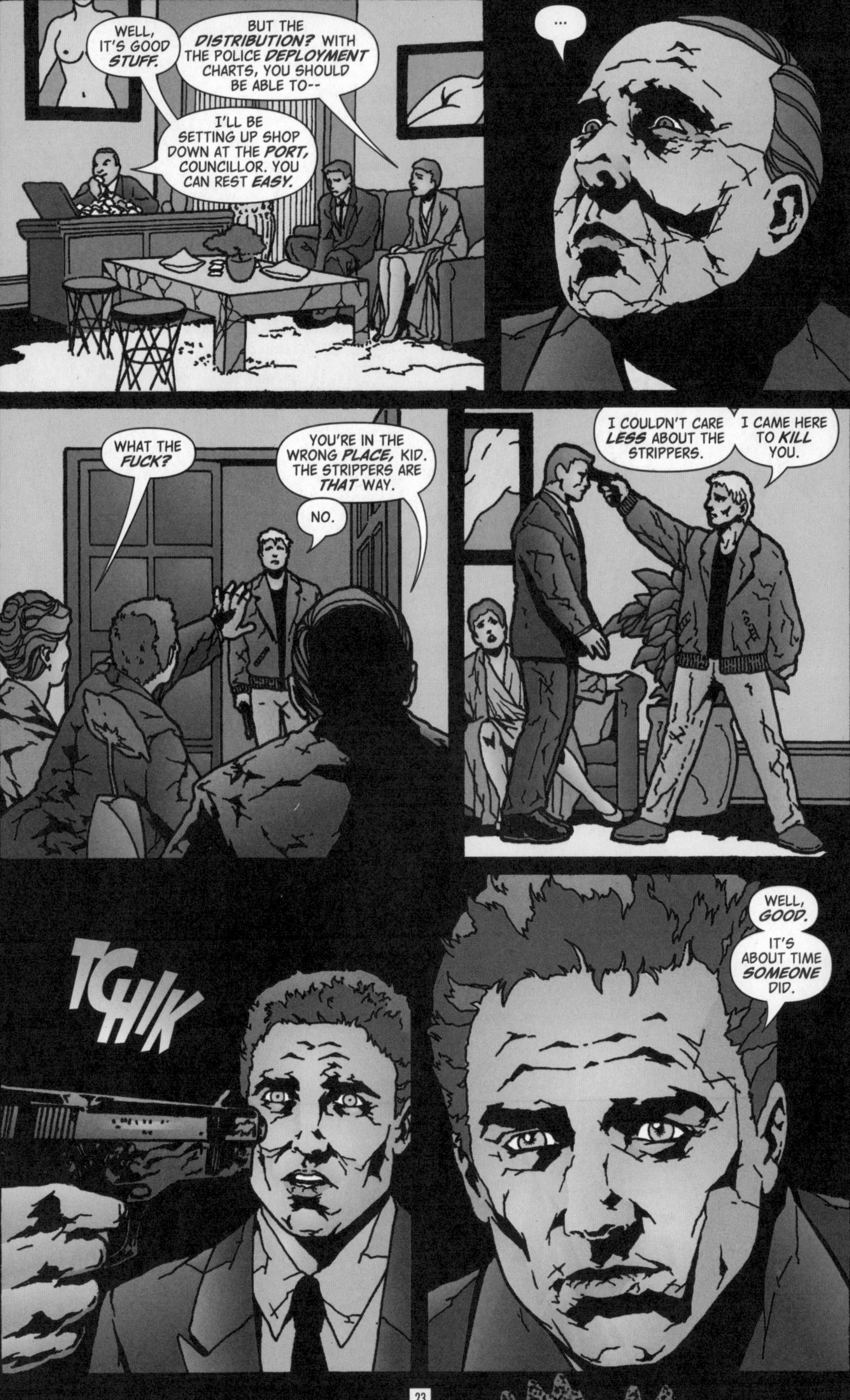
WELL, IT'S GOOD STUFF.
BUT THE DISTRIBUTION? WITH THE POLICE DEPLOYMENT CHARTS, YOU SHOULD BE ABLE TO--
I'LL BE SETTING UP SHOP DOWN AT THE PORT, COUNCILLOR. YOU CAN REST EASY.
...
WHAT THE FUCK?
YOU'RE IN THE WRONG PLACE, KID. THE STRIPPERS ARE THAT WAY.
NO.
I COULDN'T CARE LESS ABOUT THE STRIPPERS.
I CAME HERE TO KILL YOU.
TCHIK
WELL, GOOD.
IT'S ABOUT TIME SOMEONE DID.

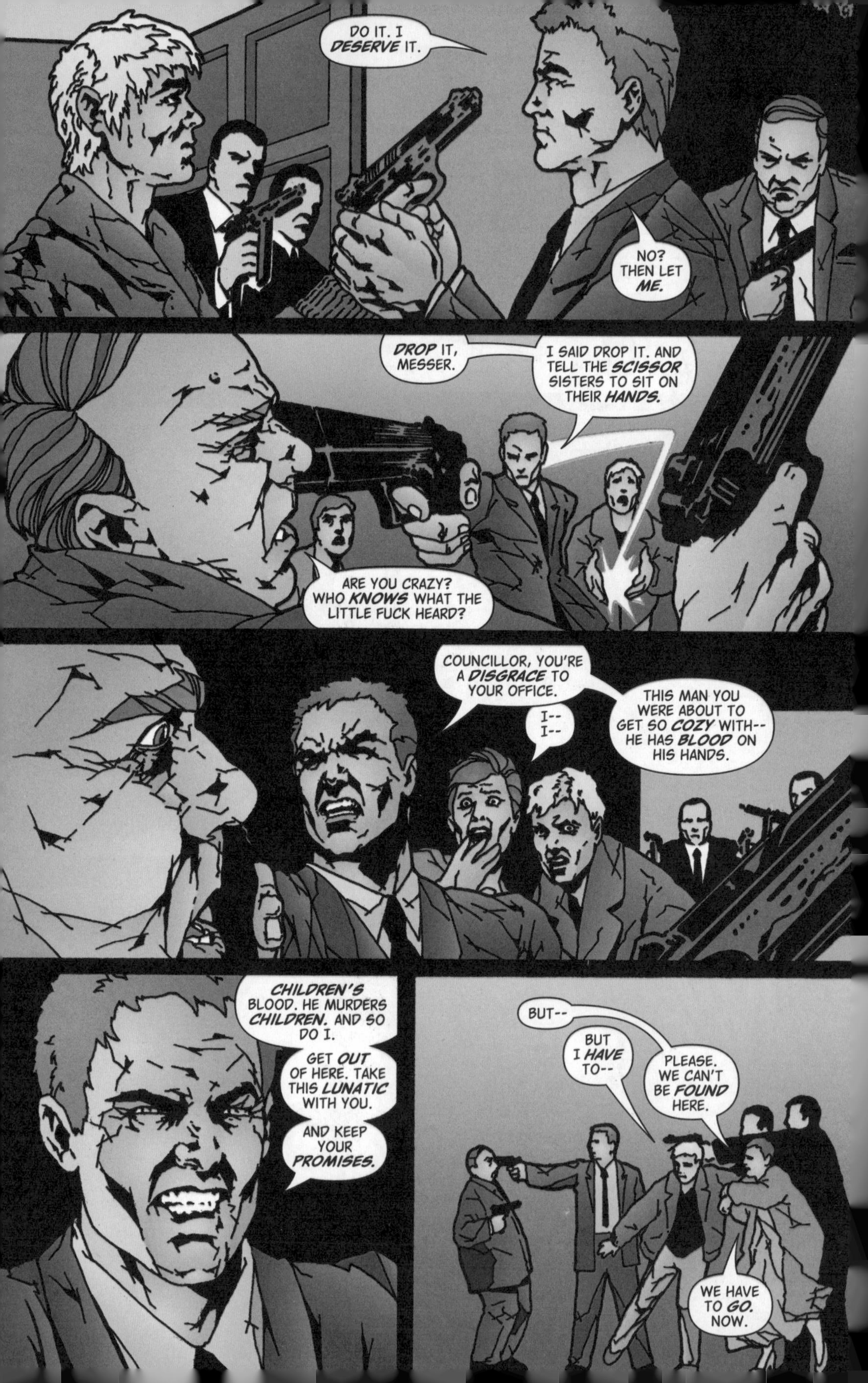
DO IT. I DESERVE IT.
NO? THEN LET ME.
DROP IT, MESSER.
I SAID DROP IT. AND TELL THE SCISSOR SISTERS TO SIT ON THEIR HANDS.
ARE YOU CRAZY? WHO KNOWS WHAT THE LITTLE FUCK HEARD?
COUNCILLOR, YOU'RE A DISGRACE TO YOUR OFFICE.
I-- I--
THIS MAN YOU WERE ABOUT TO GET SO COZY WITH-- HE HAS BLOOD ON HIS HANDS.
CHILDREN'S BLOOD. HE MURDERS CHILDREN. AND SO DO I.
GET OUT OF HERE. TAKE THIS LUNATIC WITH YOU.
AND KEEP YOUR PROMISES.
BUT--
BUT I HAVE TO--
PLEASE. WE CAN'T BE FOUND HERE.
WE HAVE TO GO. NOW.

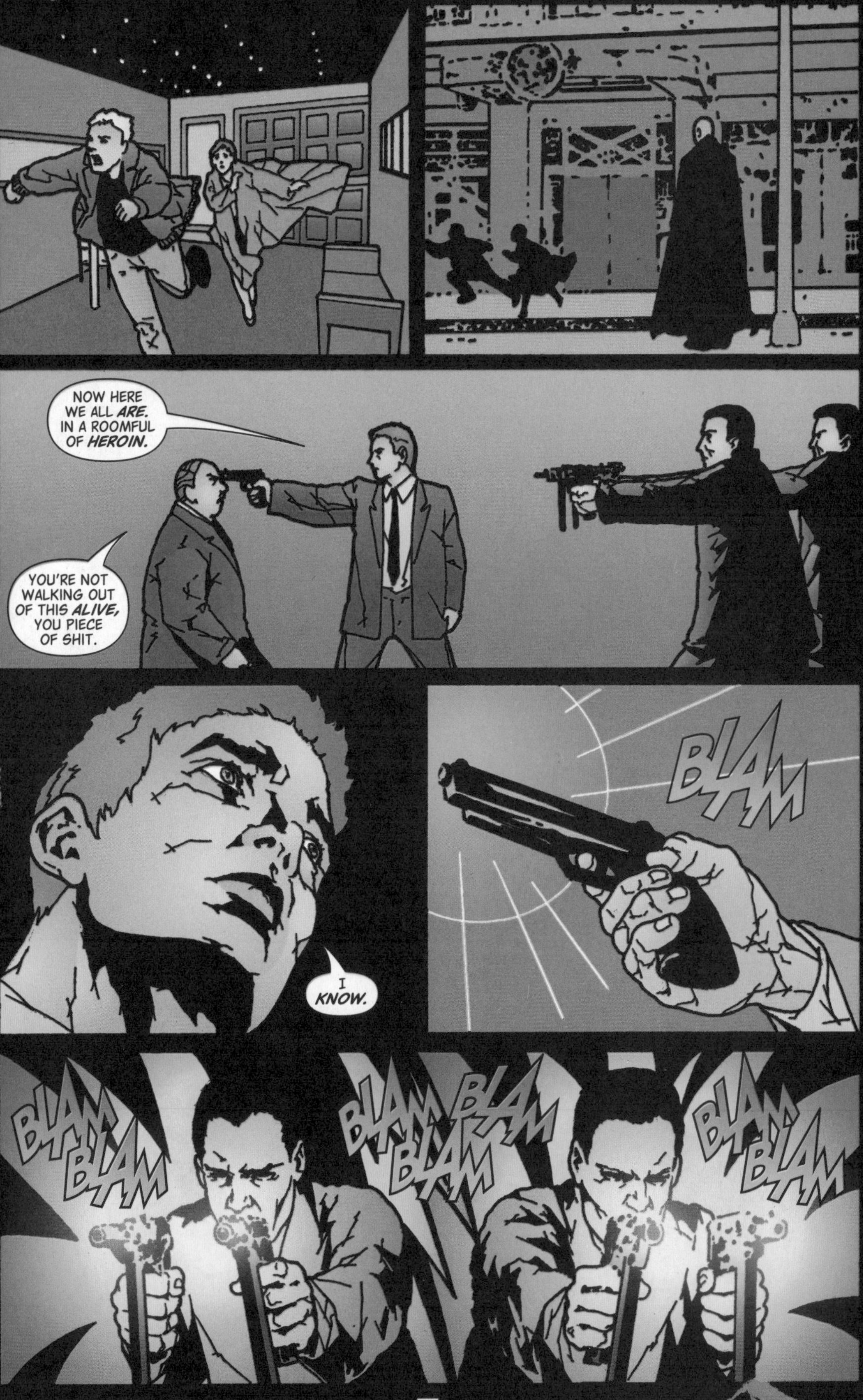
NOW HERE WE ALL ARE. IN A ROOMFUL OF HEROIN.
YOU'RE NOT WALKING OUT OF THIS ALIVE, YOU PIECE OF SHIT.
I KNOW.
BLAM
BLAM BLAM
BLAM BLAM BLAM BLAM
BLAM BLAM BLAM

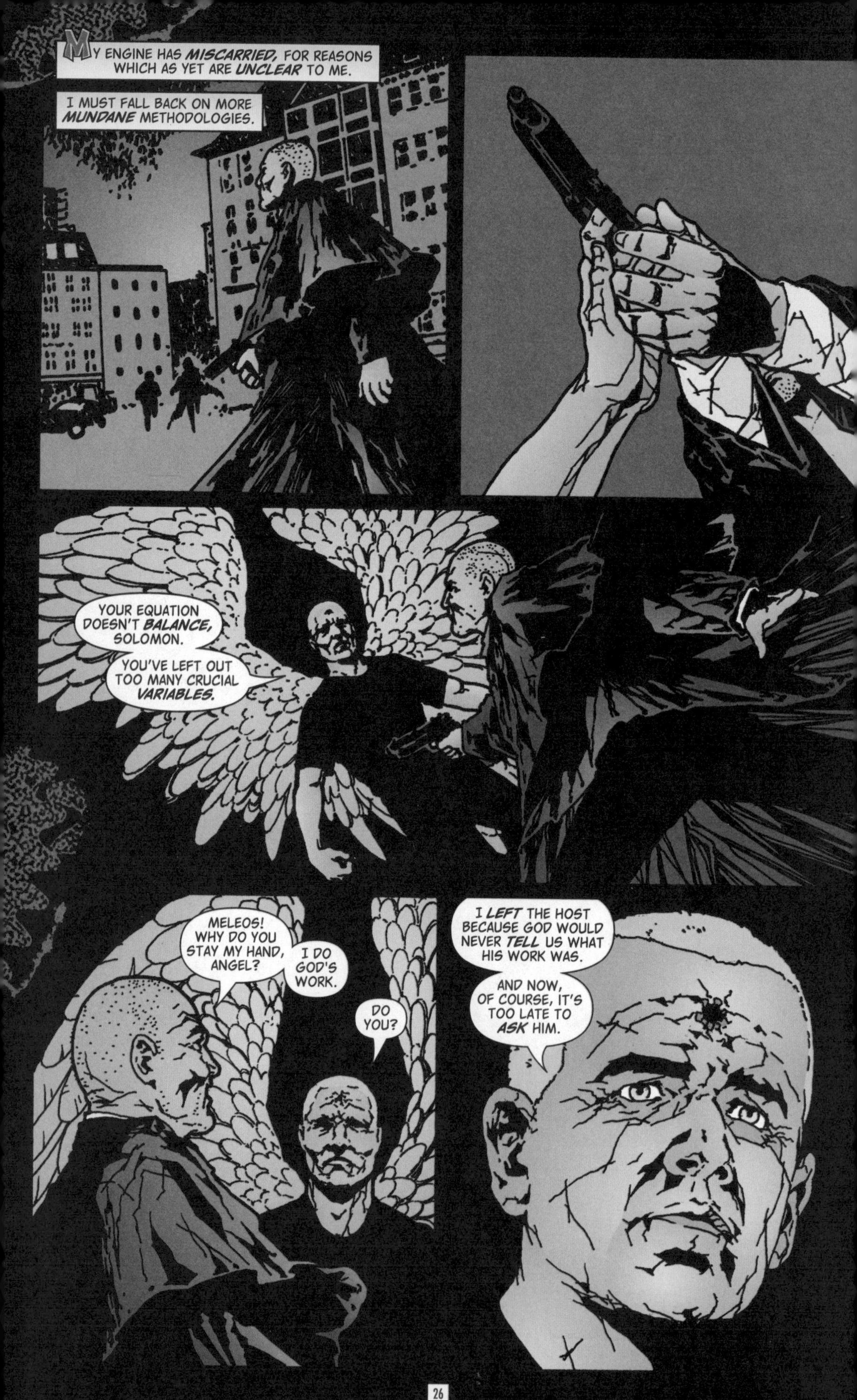
MY ENGINE HAS MISCARRIED, FOR REASONS WHICH AS YET ARE UNCLEAR TO ME.
I MUST FALL BACK ON MORE MUNDANE METHODOLOGIES.
YOUR EQUATION DOESN'T BALANCE, SOLOMON.
YOU'VE LEFT OUT TOO MANY CRUCIAL VARIABLES.
MELEOS! WHY DO YOU STAY MY HAND, ANGEL?
I DO GOD'S WORK.
DO YOU?
I LEFT THE HOST BECAUSE GOD WOULD NEVER TELL US WHAT HIS WORK WAS.
AND NOW, OF COURSE, IT'S TOO LATE TO ASK HIM.

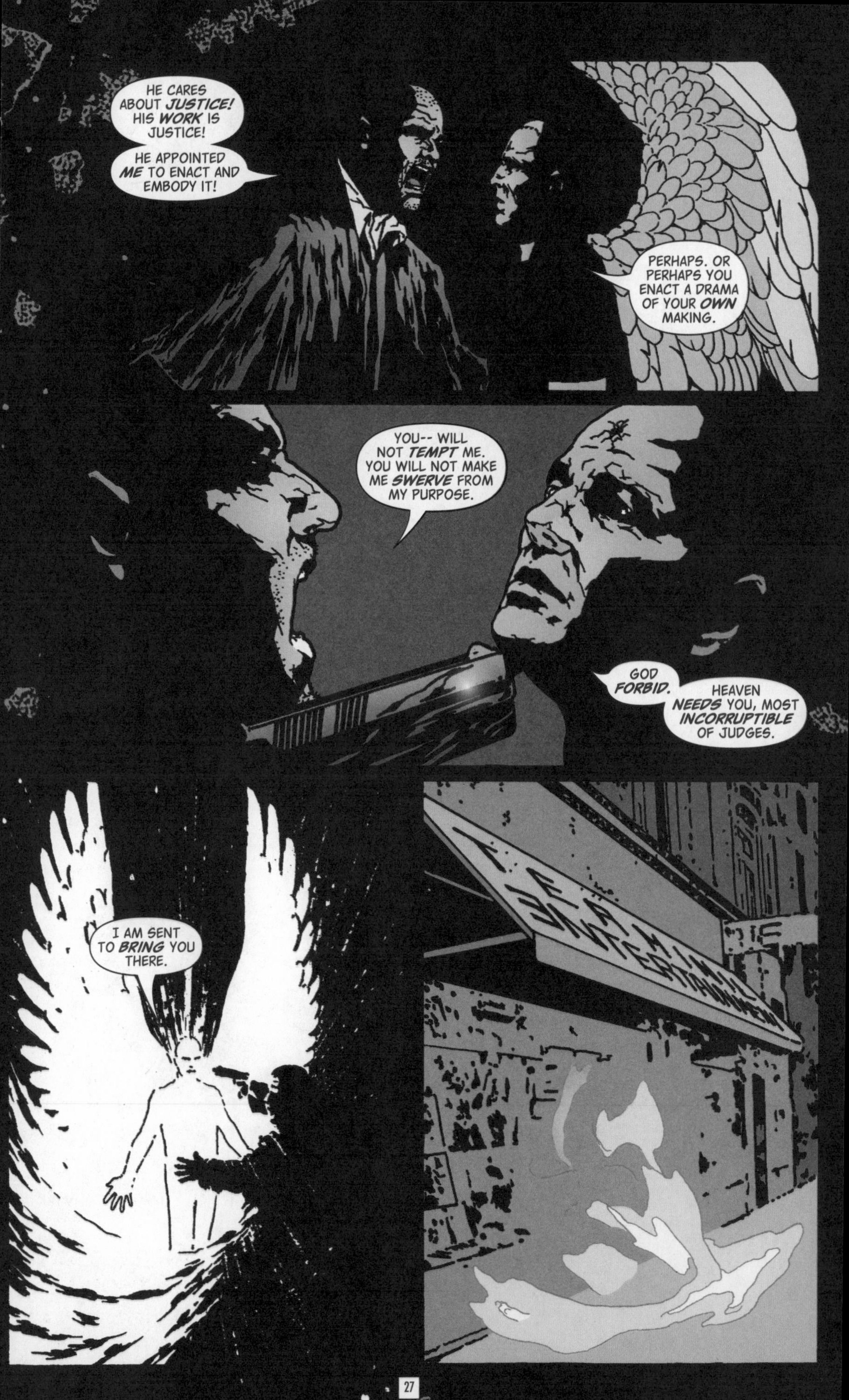
HE CARES ABOUT JUSTICE! HIS WORK IS JUSTICE!
HE APPOINTED ME TO ENACT AND EMBODY IT!
PERHAPS. OR PERHAPS YOU ENACT A DRAMA OF YOUR OWN MAKING.
YOU-- WILL NOT TEMPT ME. YOU WILL NOT MAKE ME SWERVE FROM MY PURPOSE.
GOD FORBID.
HEAVEN NEEDS YOU, MOST INCORRUPTIBLE OF JUDGES.
I AM SENT TO BRING YOU THERE.

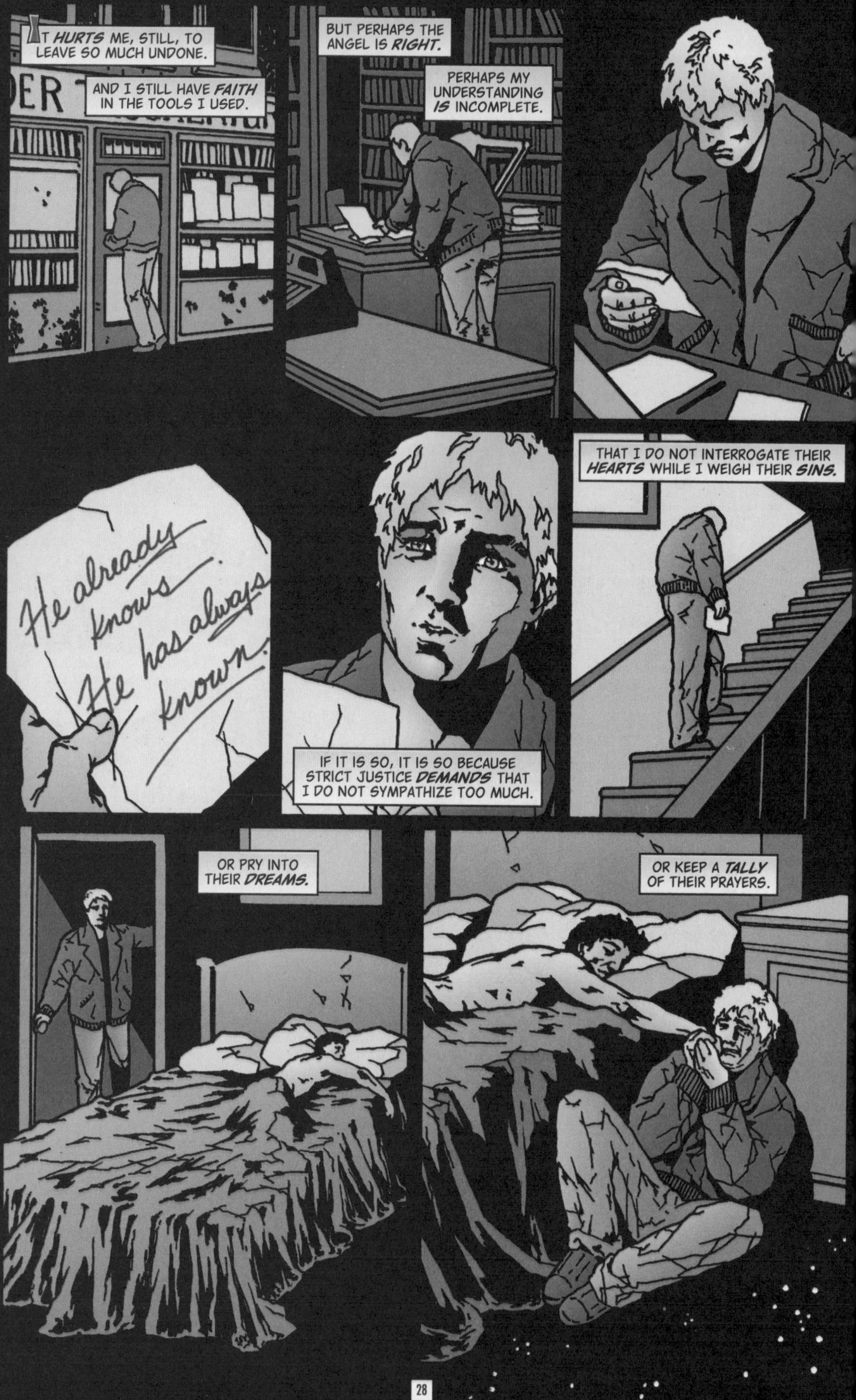
IT HURTS ME, STILL, TO LEAVE SO MUCH UNDONE.
AND I STILL HAVE FAITH IN THE TOOLS I USED.
BUT PERHAPS THE ANGEL IS RIGHT.
PERHAPS MY UNDERSTANDING IS INCOMPLETE.
He already knows. He has always known.
IF IT IS SO, IT IS SO BECAUSE STRICT JUSTICE DEMANDS THAT I DO NOT SYMPATHIZE TOO MUCH.
THAT I DO NOT INTERROGATE THEIR HEARTS WHILE I WEIGH THEIR SINS.
OR PRY INTO THEIR DREAMS.
OR KEEP A TALLY OF THEIR PRAYERS.

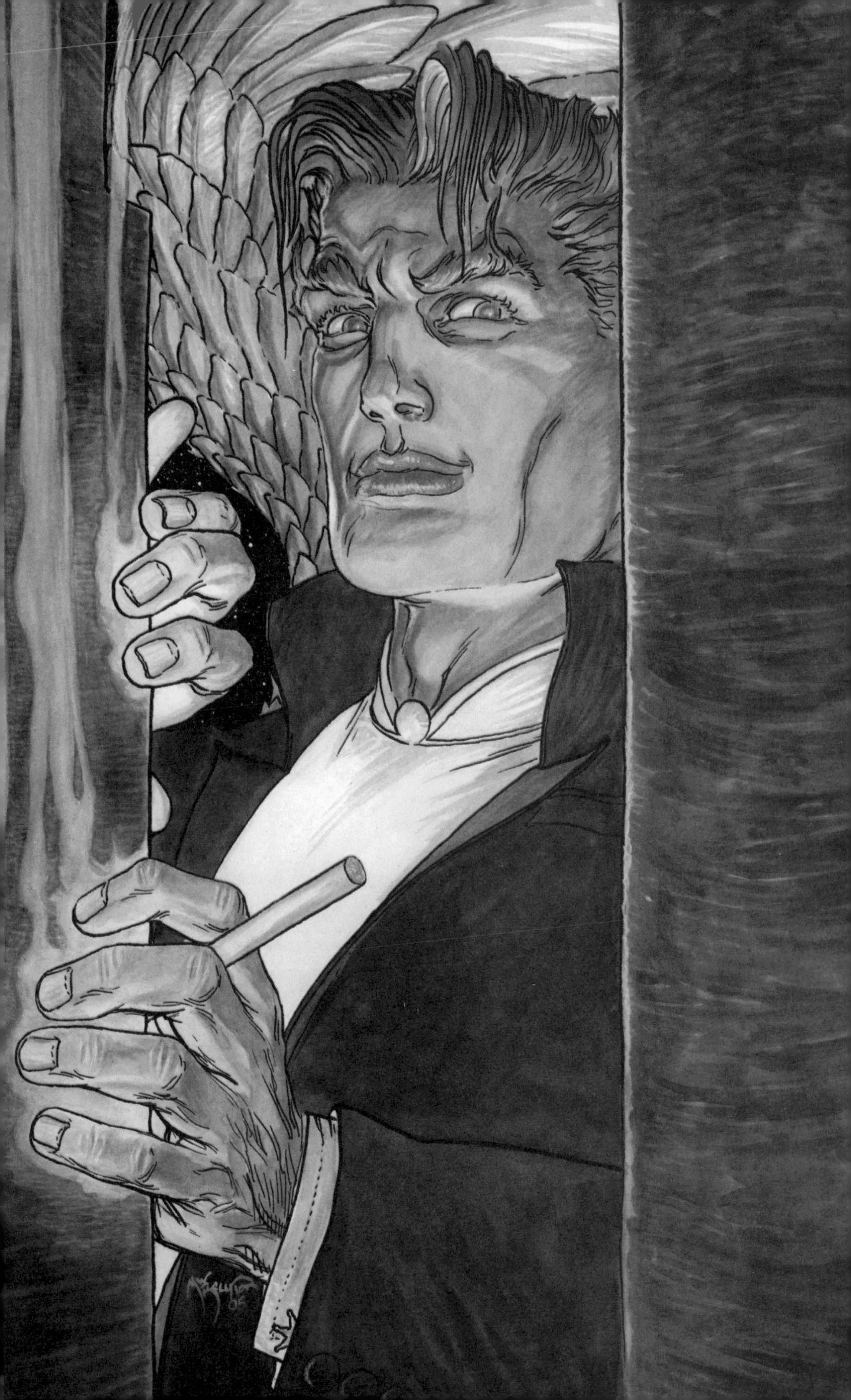

ELAINE:

IT'S EASY TO SAY WHAT WENT *WRONG*, BUT IT'S A LOT HARDER TO EXPLAIN *WHY*. GOD-- YAHWEH-- STARTED THE BALL ROLLING WHEN HE *DISAPPEARED*, LEAVING THE THRONE OF HEAVEN EMPTY. BEFORE HE WENT, HE SAID *GOODBYE* TO HIS SONS, MICHAEL AND LUCIFER. BUT HE DIDN'T REALLY EXPLAIN *WHY* HE WAS LEAVING, OR WHETHER HE EVER INTENDED TO COME *BACK*.

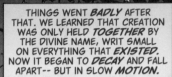
THINGS WENT *BADLY* AFTER THAT. WE LEARNED THAT CREATION WAS ONLY HELD *TOGETHER* BY THE DIVINE NAME, WRIT SMALL ON EVERYTHING THAT *EXISTED*. NOW IT BEGAN TO *DECAY* AND FALL APART-- BUT IN SLOW *MOTION*.

TO SPEED THINGS UP, *FENRIS* THE WOLF TRICKED MICHAEL AND LUCIFER INTO *FIGHTING* EACH OTHER ABOVE THE WORLD-TREE, *YGGDRASIL*. MICHAEL DIED, AND HIS BLOOD SPILLED OVER THE ROOTS OF THE TREE, ADDING UNSTOPPABLE *MOMENTUM* TO THE DISSOLUTION.

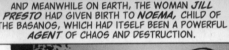
AND MEANWHILE ON EARTH, THE WOMAN *JILL PRESTO* HAD GIVEN BIRTH TO *NOEMA*, CHILD OF THE BASANOS, WHICH HAD ITSELF BEEN A POWERFUL *AGENT* OF CHAOS AND DESTRUCTION.

CAN SOMETHING STILL BE *DONE?* PROBABLY NOT.

BUT AS THINGS FALL APART, A CONSPIRACY OF OLD *POWERS* HAS EMERGED TO CHALLENGE HEAVEN AND SMASH THE THRONE OF *PRIMUM MOBILE*-- SO THAT IF YAHWEH CHANGES HIS MIND, HE WON'T BE ABLE TO COME *HOME* AGAIN.

THEY'VE ENLISTED *LILITH*, WHO BUILT THE CITY OF HEAVEN, TO HELP THEM TEAR IT DOWN.

AND SHE'S RAISED AN ARMY OF HER CHILDREN, THE *LILIM*-- OUSTING AND EXILING THEIR LEADER, *MAZIKEEN*. SO FAR THEY'VE DONE ALL THE THINGS THEY SET OUT TO DO.

WELL, ALL EXCEPT *ONE*. THEY TRIED TO KILL *LUCIFER*. AND HE'S STILL *ALIVE*.

MORNINGSTAR

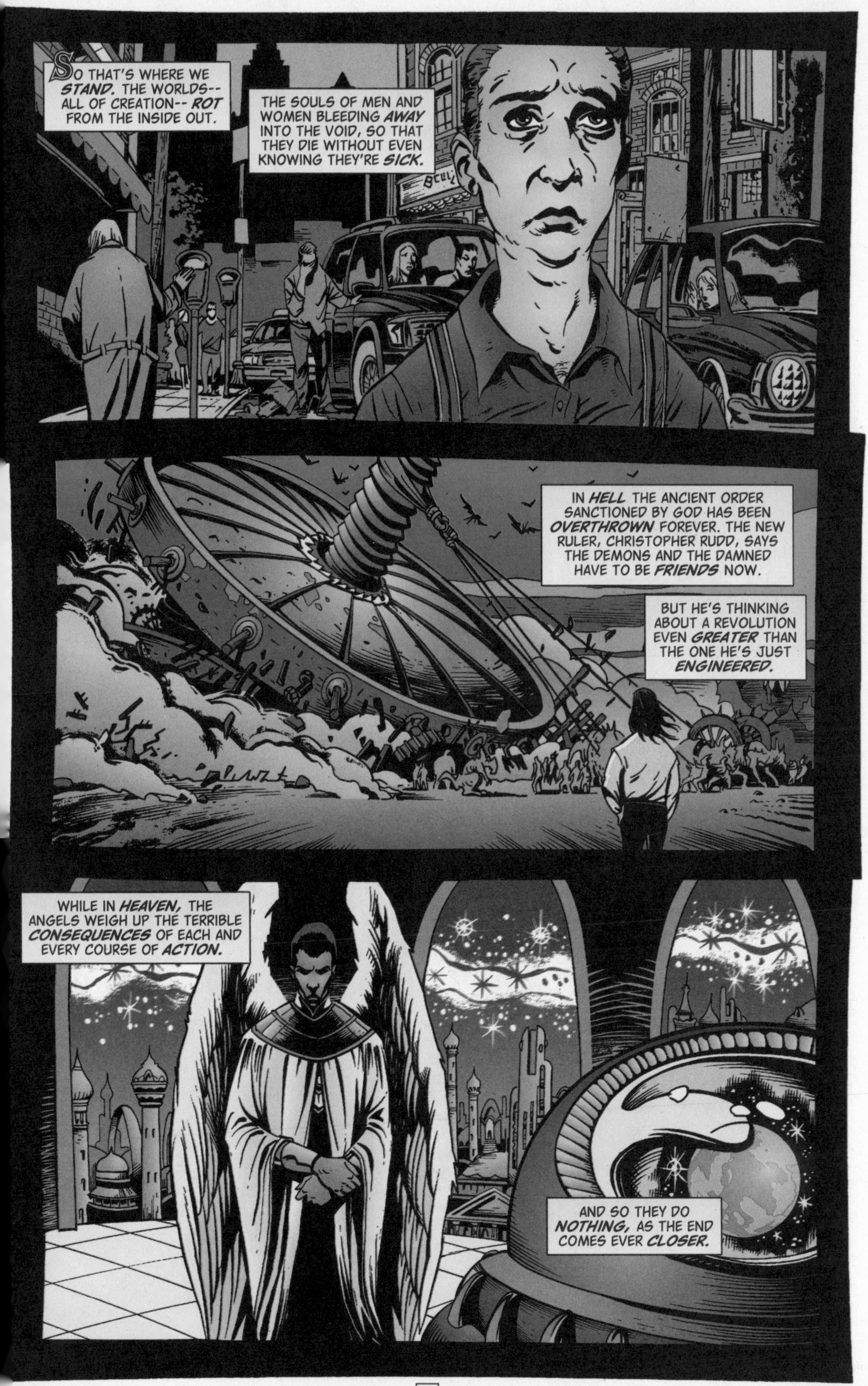
SO THAT'S WHERE WE STAND. THE WORLDS-- ALL OF CREATION-- ROT FROM THE INSIDE OUT.
THE SOULS OF MEN AND WOMEN BLEEDING AWAY INTO THE VOID, SO THAT THEY DIE WITHOUT EVEN KNOWING THEY'RE SICK.
IN HELL THE ANCIENT ORDER SANCTIONED BY GOD HAS BEEN OVERTHROWN FOREVER. THE NEW RULER, CHRISTOPHER RUDD, SAYS THE DEMONS AND THE DAMNED HAVE TO BE FRIENDS NOW.
BUT HE'S THINKING ABOUT A REVOLUTION EVEN GREATER THAN THE ONE HE'S JUST ENGINEERED.
WHILE IN HEAVEN, THE ANGELS WEIGH UP THE TERRIBLE CONSEQUENCES OF EACH AND EVERY COURSE OF ACTION.
AND SO THEY DO NOTHING, AS THE END COMES EVER CLOSER.

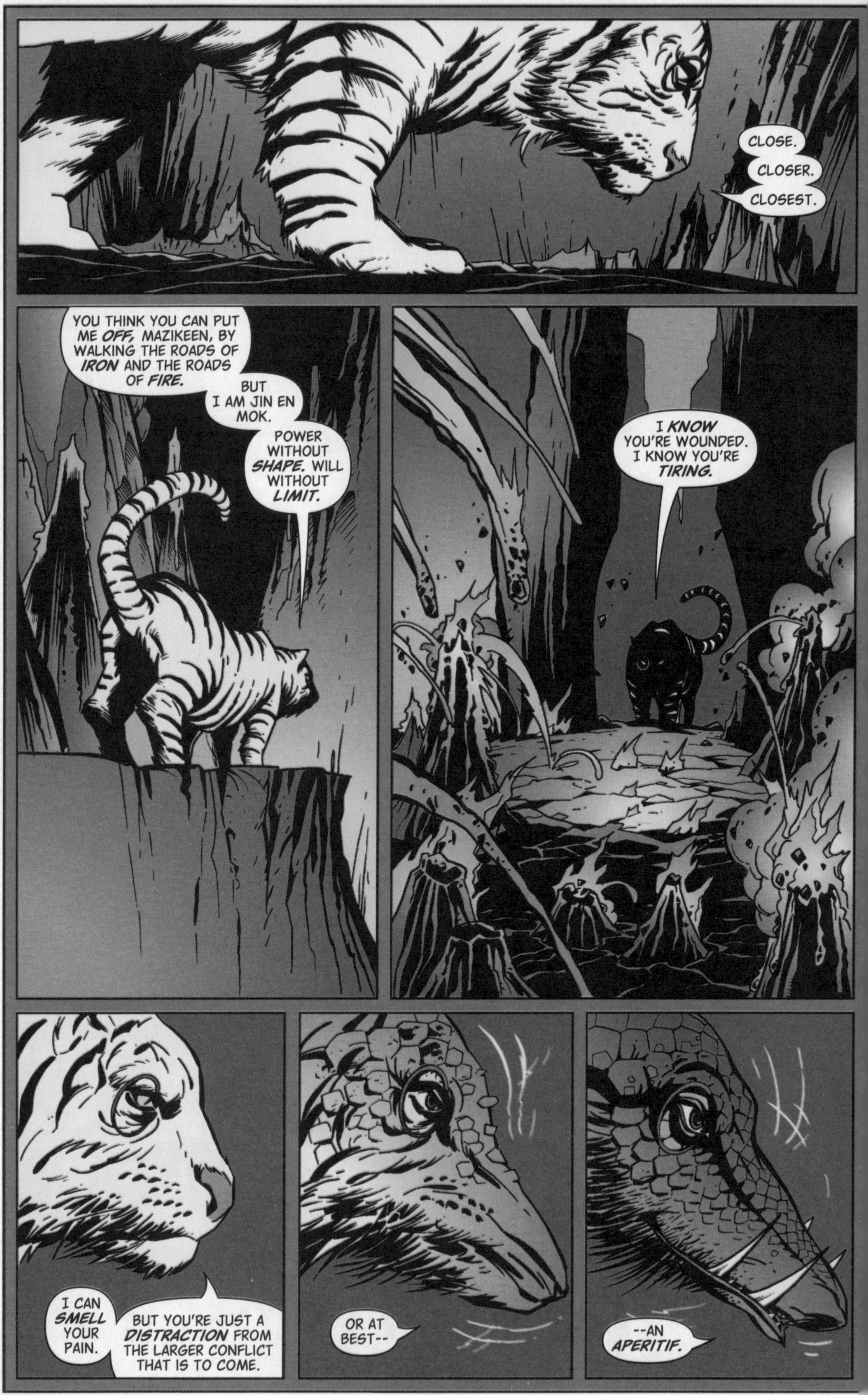
CLOSE.
CLOSER.
CLOSEST.
YOU THINK YOU CAN PUT ME OFF, MAZIKEEN, BY WALKING THE ROADS OF IRON AND THE ROADS OF FIRE.
BUT I AM JIN EN MOK.
POWER WITHOUT SHAPE. WILL WITHOUT LIMIT.
I KNOW YOU'RE WOUNDED. I KNOW YOU'RE TIRING.
I CAN SMELL YOUR PAIN.
BUT YOU'RE JUST A DISTRACTION FROM THE LARGER CONFLICT THAT IS TO COME.
OR AT BEST--
--AN APERITIF.

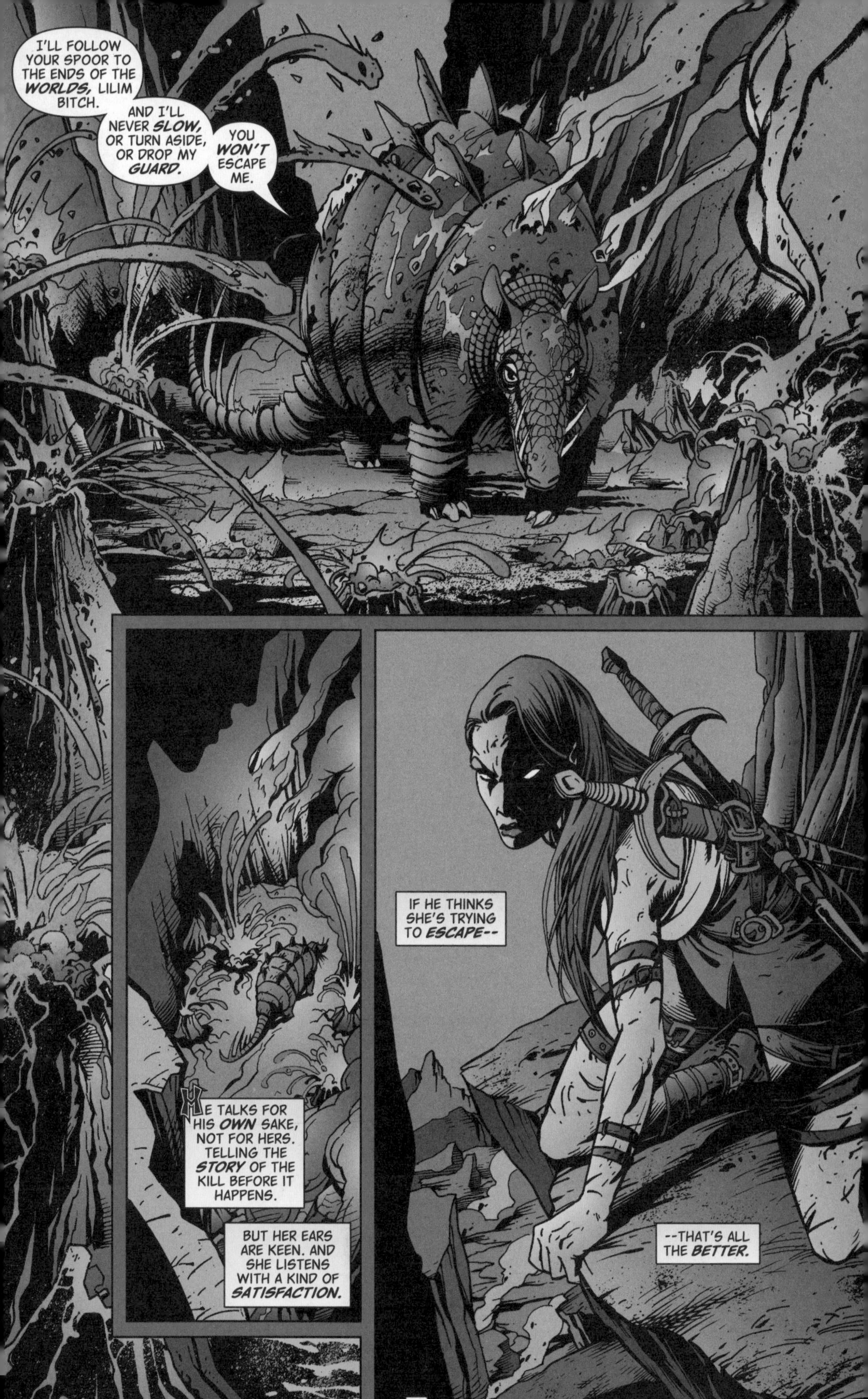

I'LL FOLLOW YOUR SPOOR TO THE ENDS OF THE WORLDS, LILIM BITCH.
AND I'LL NEVER SLOW, OR TURN ASIDE, OR DROP MY GUARD.
YOU WON'T ESCAPE ME.
HE TALKS FOR HIS OWN SAKE, NOT FOR HERS. TELLING THE STORY OF THE KILL BEFORE IT HAPPENS.
BUT HER EARS ARE KEEN. AND SHE LISTENS WITH A KIND OF SATISFACTION.
IF HE THINKS SHE'S TRYING TO ESCAPE--
--THAT'S ALL THE BETTER.

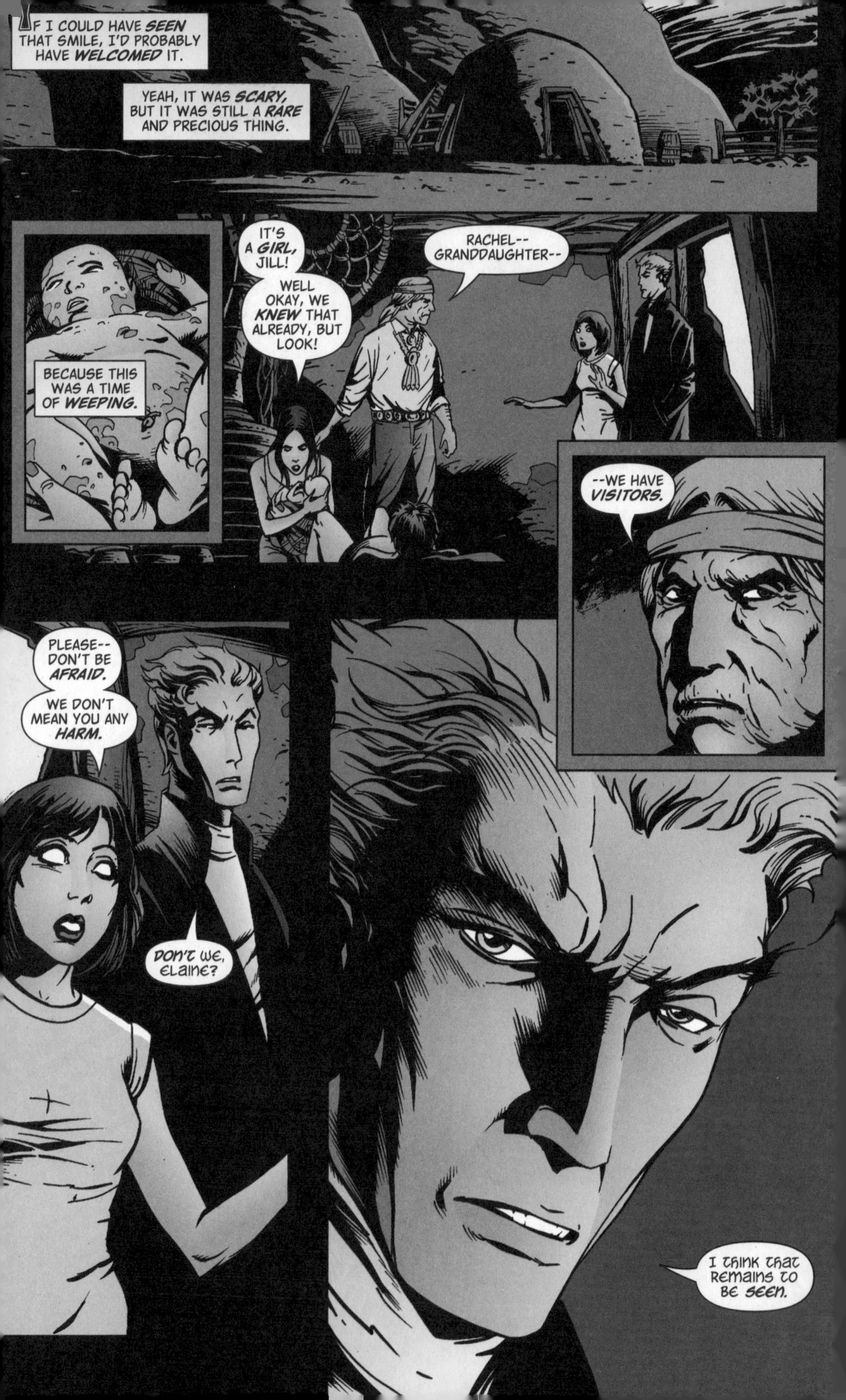
IF I COULD HAVE SEEN THAT SMILE, I'D PROBABLY HAVE WELCOMED IT.
YEAH, IT WAS SCARY, BUT IT WAS STILL A RARE AND PRECIOUS THING.
BECAUSE THIS WAS A TIME OF WEEPING.
IT'S A GIRL, JILL!
WELL OKAY, WE KNEW THAT ALREADY, BUT LOOK!
RACHEL-- GRANDDAUGHTER--
--WE HAVE VISITORS.
PLEASE-- DON'T BE AFRAID.
WE DON'T MEAN YOU ANY HARM.
DON'T WE, ELAINE?
I THINK THAT REMAINS TO BE SEEN.

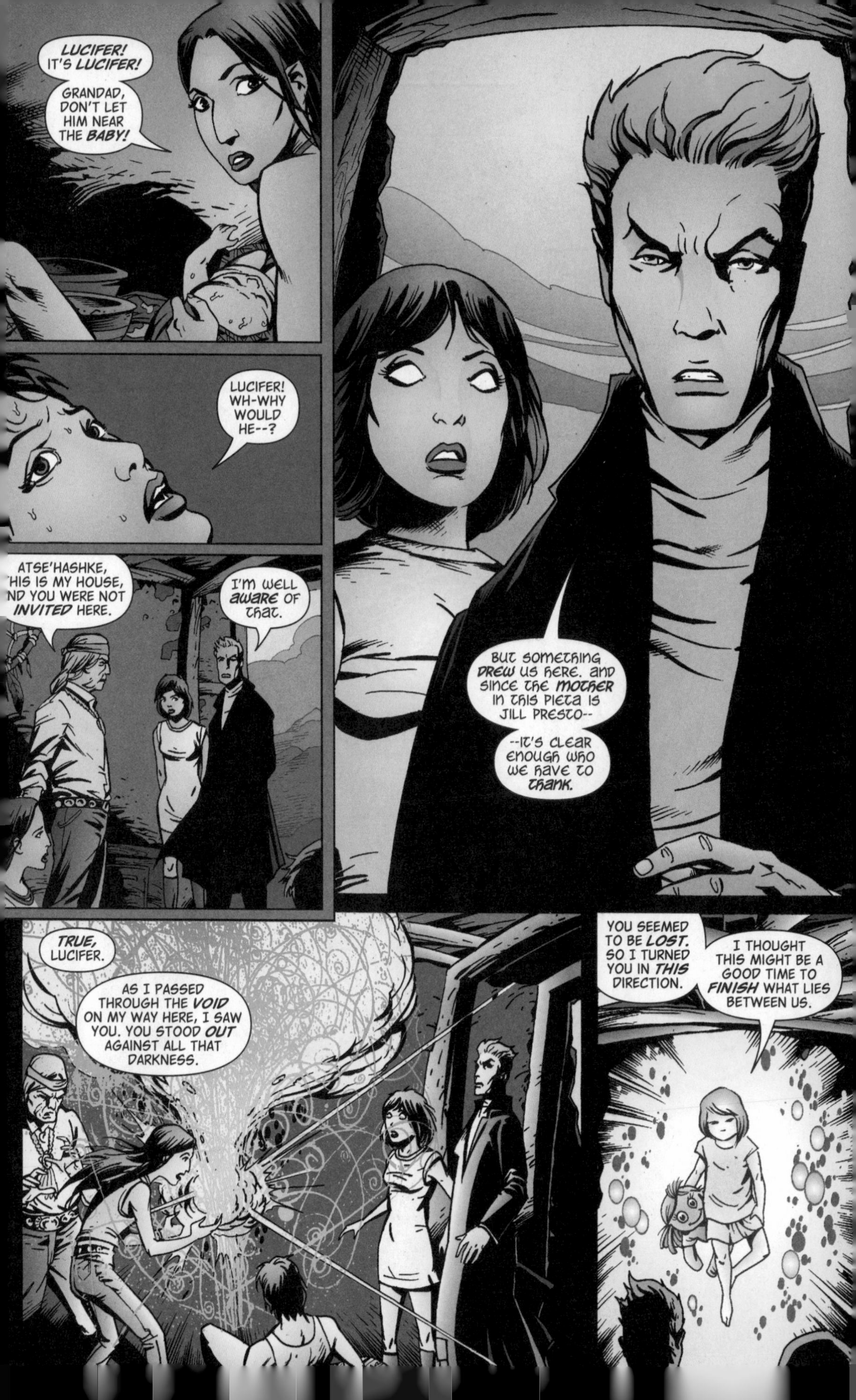
LUCIFER! IT'S LUCIFER!
GRANDAD, DON'T LET HIM NEAR THE BABY!
LUCIFER! WH-WHY WOULD HE--?
ATSE'HASHKE, THIS IS MY HOUSE, AND YOU WERE NOT INVITED HERE.
I'M WELL AWARE OF THAT.
BUT SOMETHING DREW US HERE. AND SINCE THE MOTHER IN THIS PIETA IS JILL PRESTO--
--IT'S CLEAR ENOUGH WHO WE HAVE TO THANK.
TRUE, LUCIFER.
AS I PASSED THROUGH THE VOID ON MY WAY HERE, I SAW YOU. YOU STOOD OUT AGAINST ALL THAT DARKNESS.
YOU SEEMED TO BE LOST. SO I TURNED YOU IN THIS DIRECTION.
I THOUGHT THIS MIGHT BE A GOOD TIME TO FINISH WHAT LIES BETWEEN US.

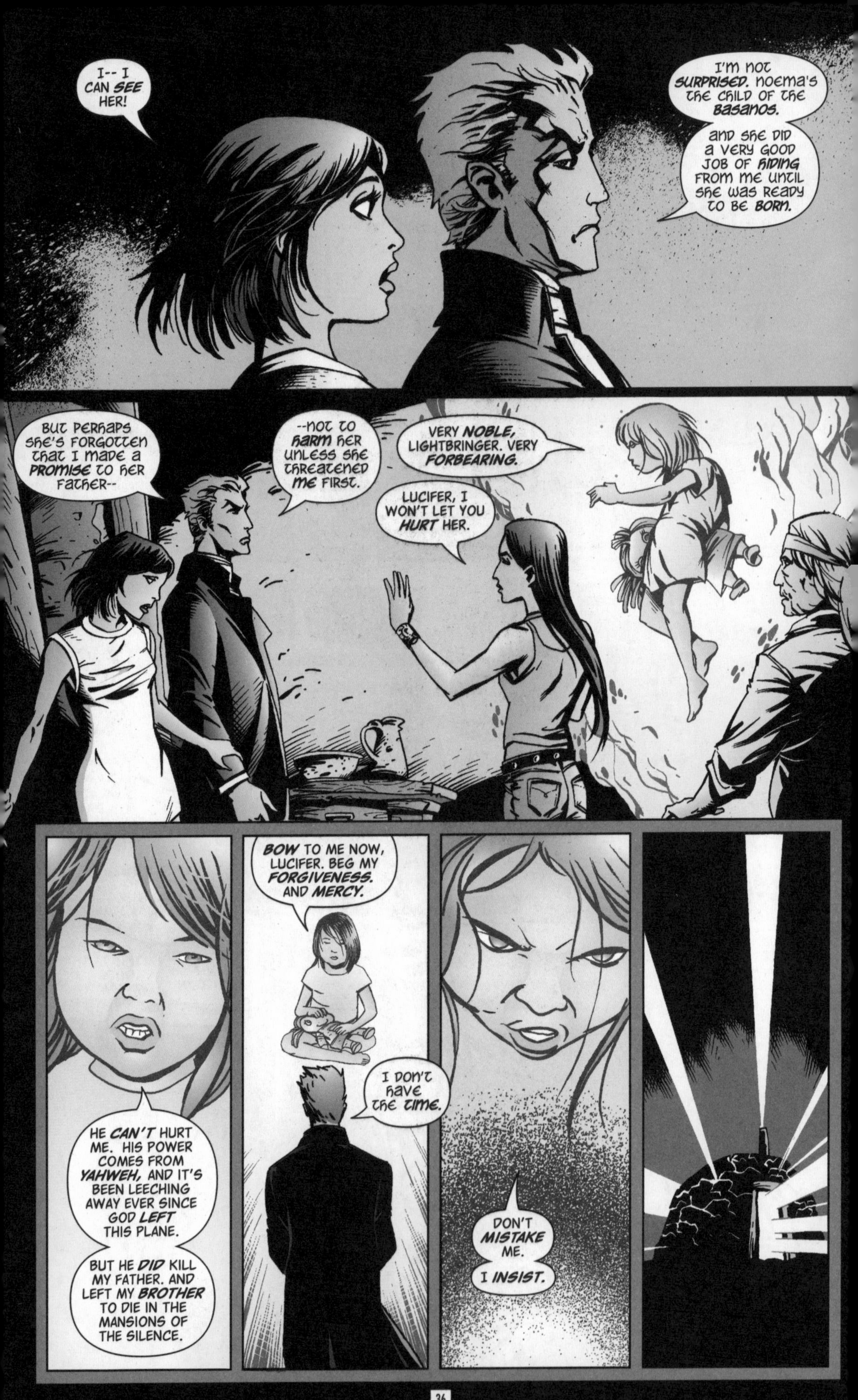

I-- I CAN SEE HER!
I'M NOT SURPRISED. NOEMA'S THE CHILD OF THE BASANOS.
AND SHE DID A VERY GOOD JOB OF HIDING FROM ME UNTIL SHE WAS READY TO BE BORN.
BUT PERHAPS SHE'S FORGOTTEN THAT I MADE A PROMISE TO HER FATHER--
--NOT TO HARM HER UNLESS SHE THREATENED ME FIRST.
VERY NOBLE, LIGHTBRINGER. VERY FORBEARING.
LUCIFER, I WON'T LET YOU HURT HER.
HE CAN'T HURT ME. HIS POWER COMES FROM YAHWEH, AND IT'S BEEN LEECHING AWAY EVER SINCE GOD LEFT THIS PLANE.
BUT HE DID KILL MY FATHER. AND LEFT MY BROTHER TO DIE IN THE MANSIONS OF THE SILENCE.
BOW TO ME NOW, LUCIFER. BEG MY FORGIVENESS. AND MERCY.
I DON'T HAVE THE TIME.
DON'T MISTAKE ME.
I INSIST.

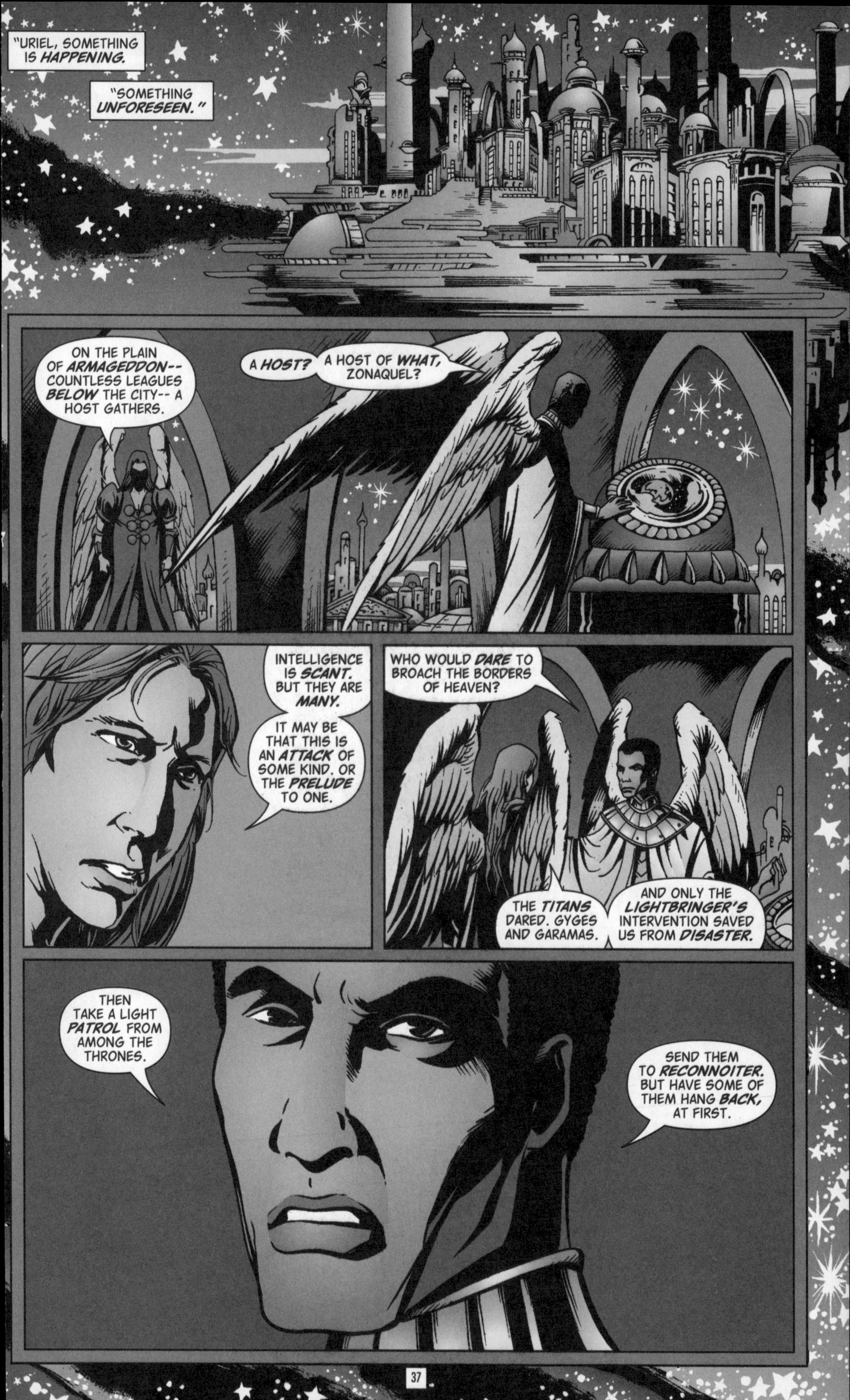

"URIEL, SOMETHING IS HAPPENING.
"SOMETHING UNFORESEEN."
ON THE PLAIN OF ARMAGEDDON-- COUNTLESS LEAGUES BELOW THE CITY-- A HOST GATHERS.
A HOST?
A HOST OF WHAT, ZONAQUEL?
INTELLIGENCE IS SCANT. BUT THEY ARE MANY.
IT MAY BE THAT THIS IS AN ATTACK OF SOME KIND. OR THE PRELUDE TO ONE.
WHO WOULD DARE TO BROACH THE BORDERS OF HEAVEN?
THE TITANS DARED. GYGES AND GARAMAS.
AND ONLY THE LIGHTBRINGER'S INTERVENTION SAVED US FROM DISASTER.
THEN TAKE A LIGHT PATROL FROM AMONG THE THRONES.
SEND THEM TO RECONNOITER. BUT HAVE SOME OF THEM HANG BACK, AT FIRST.

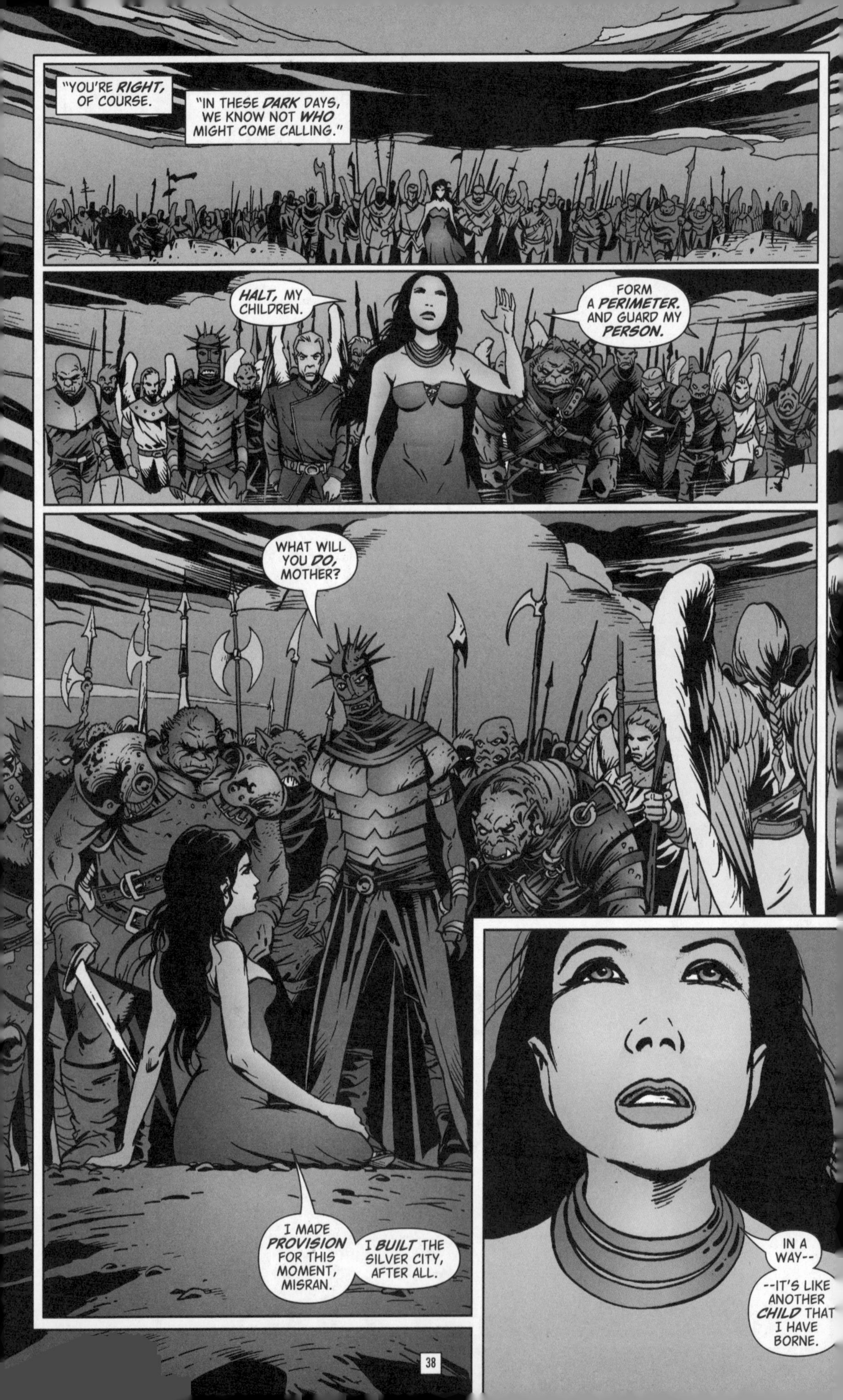

"YOU'RE RIGHT, OF COURSE.
"IN THESE DARK DAYS, WE KNOW NOT WHO MIGHT COME CALLING."
HALT, MY CHILDREN.
FORM A PERIMETER. AND GUARD MY PERSON.
WHAT WILL YOU DO, MOTHER?
I MADE PROVISION FOR THIS MOMENT, MISRAN.
I BUILT THE SILVER CITY, AFTER ALL.
IN A WAY--
--IT'S LIKE ANOTHER CHILD THAT I HAVE BORNE.

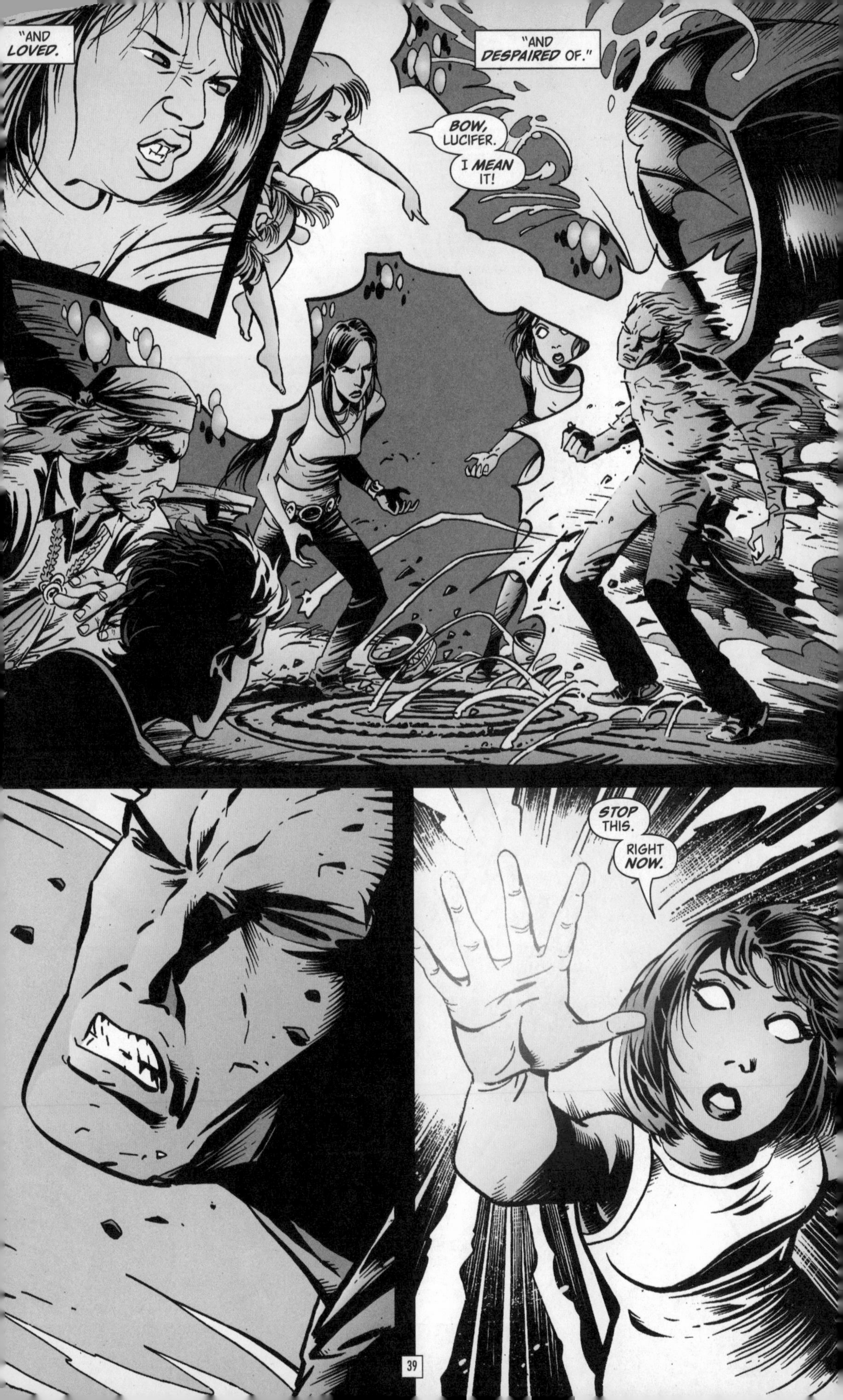
"AND
LOVED.
"AND
DESPAIRED OF."
BOW,
LUCIFER.
I MEAN
IT!
STOP
THIS.
RIGHT
NOW.

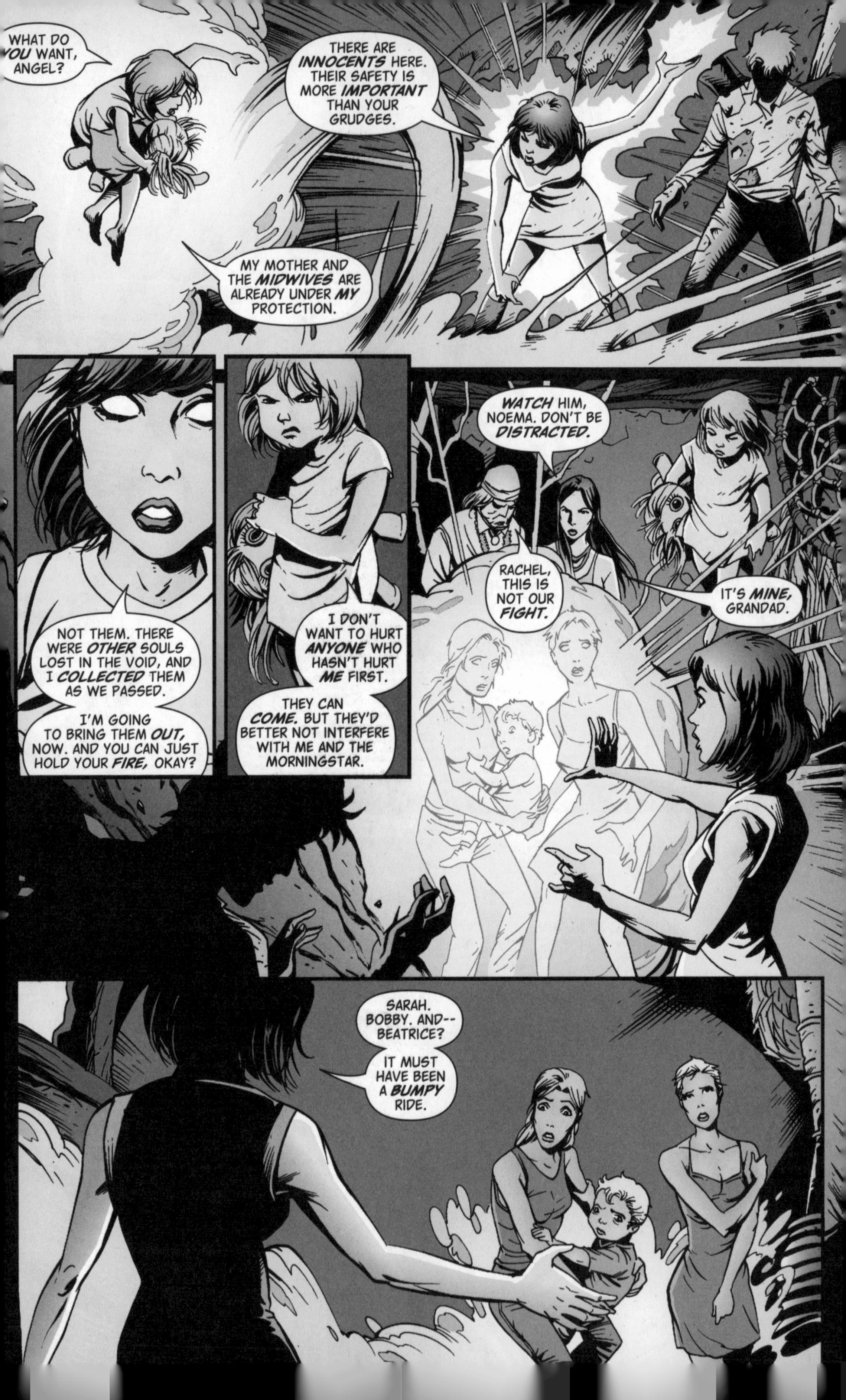
WHAT DO YOU WANT, ANGEL?
THERE ARE INNOCENTS HERE. THEIR SAFETY IS MORE IMPORTANT THAN YOUR GRUDGES.
MY MOTHER AND THE MIDWIVES ARE ALREADY UNDER MY PROTECTION.
NOT THEM. THERE WERE OTHER SOULS LOST IN THE VOID, AND I COLLECTED THEM AS WE PASSED.
I'M GOING TO BRING THEM OUT, NOW. AND YOU CAN JUST HOLD YOUR FIRE, OKAY?
I DON'T WANT TO HURT ANYONE WHO HASN'T HURT ME FIRST.
THEY CAN COME. BUT THEY'D BETTER NOT INTERFERE WITH ME AND THE MORNINGSTAR.
WATCH HIM, NOEMA. DON'T BE DISTRACTED.
RACHEL, THIS IS NOT OUR FIGHT.
IT'S MINE, GRANDAD.
SARAH. BOBBY. AND-- BEATRICE?
IT MUST HAVE BEEN A BUMPY RIDE.

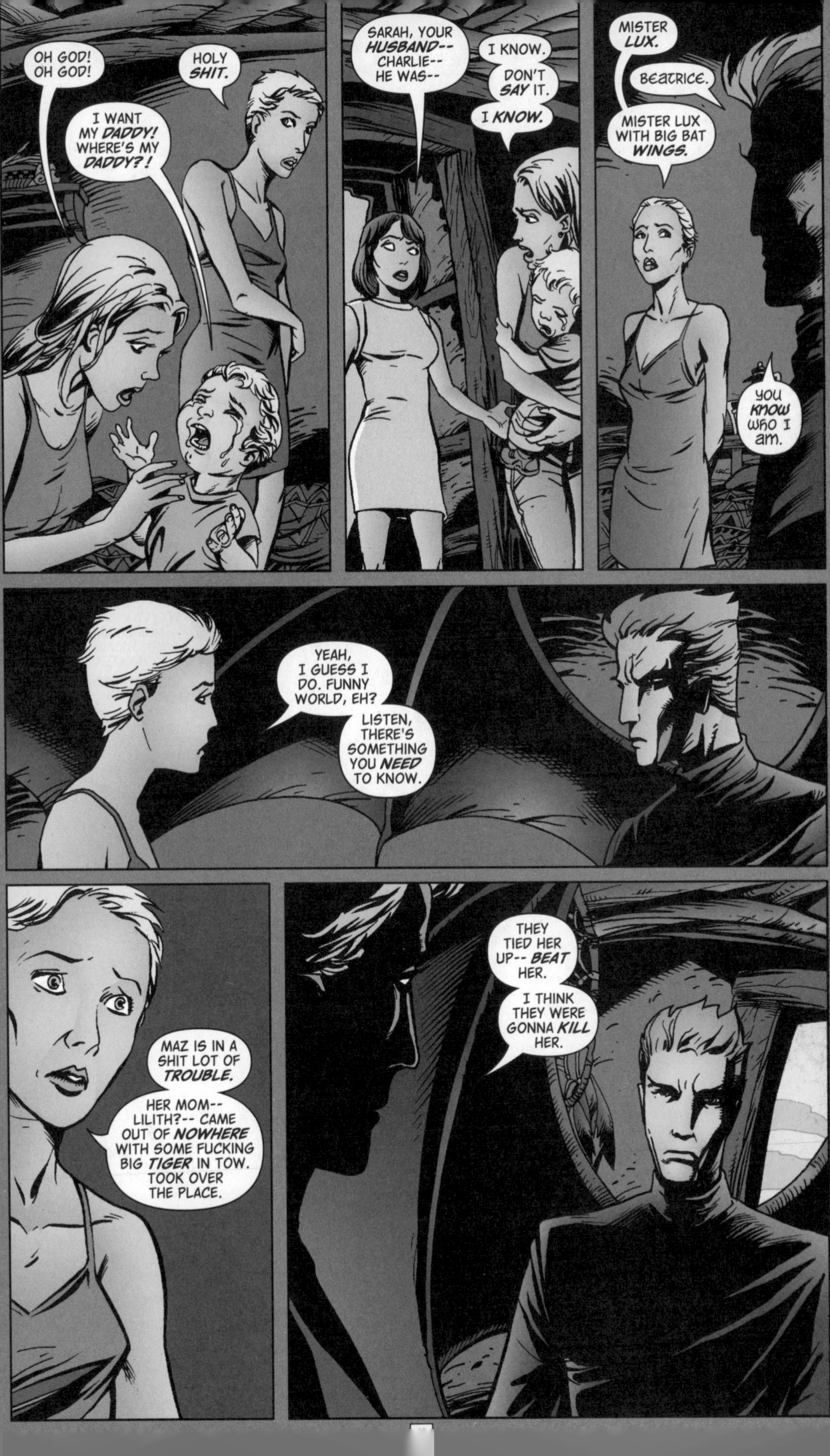
OH GOD! OH GOD!
HOLY SHIT.
I WANT MY DADDY! WHERE'S MY DADDY?!
SARAH, YOUR HUSBAND-- CHARLIE-- HE WAS--
I KNOW.
DON'T SAY IT.
I KNOW.
MISTER LUX.
BEATRICE.
MISTER LUX WITH BIG BAT WINGS.
YOU KNOW WHO I AM.
YEAH, I GUESS I DO. FUNNY WORLD, EH?
LISTEN, THERE'S SOMETHING YOU NEED TO KNOW.
MAZ IS IN A SHIT LOT OF TROUBLE.
HER MOM-- LILITH?-- CAME OUT OF NOWHERE WITH SOME FUCKING BIG TIGER IN TOW. TOOK OVER THE PLACE.
THEY TIED HER UP-- BEAT HER.
I THINK THEY WERE GONNA KILL HER.

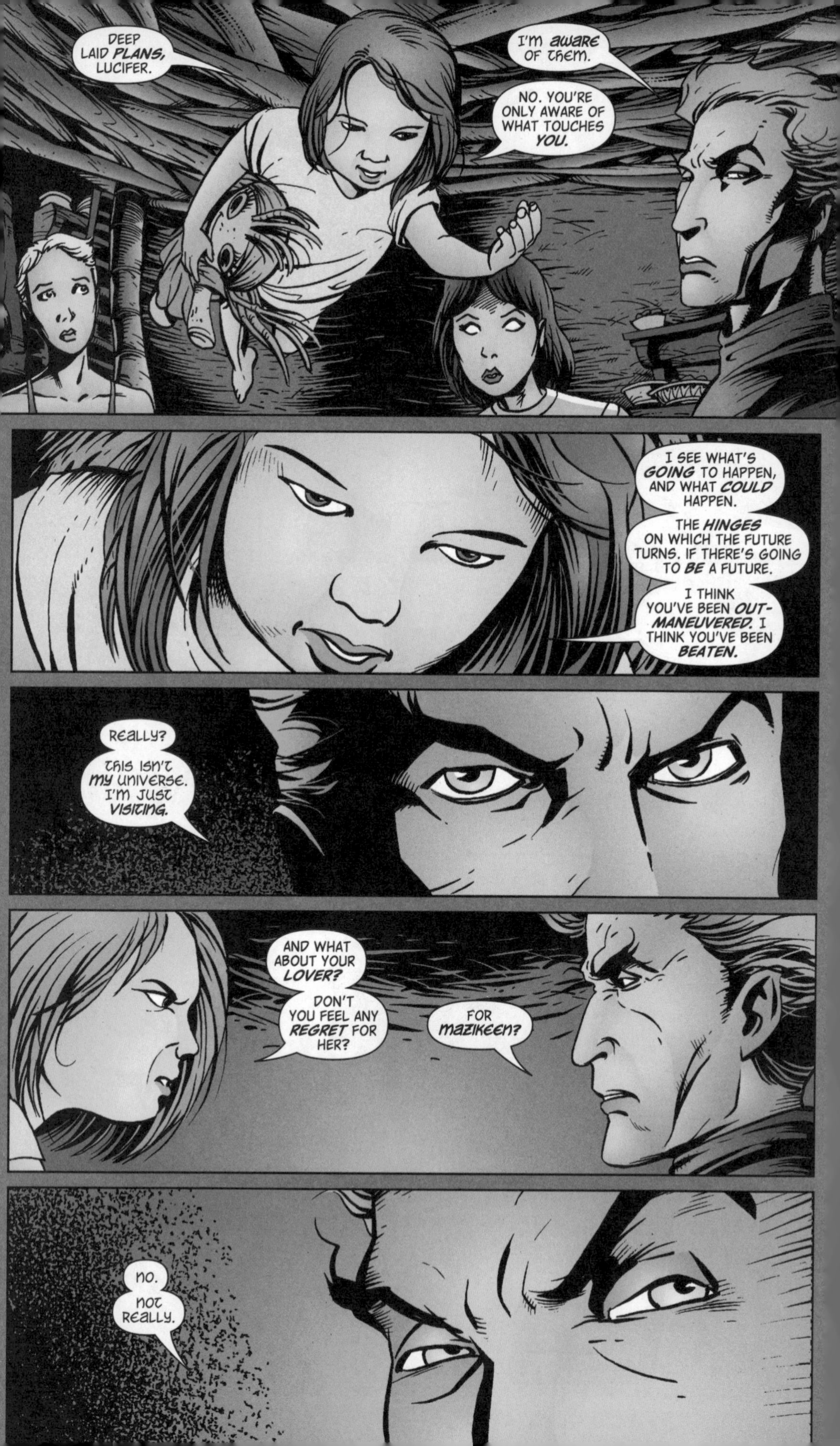
DEEP LAID PLANS, LUCIFER.
I'M AWARE OF THEM.
NO. YOU'RE ONLY AWARE OF WHAT TOUCHES YOU.
I SEE WHAT'S GOING TO HAPPEN, AND WHAT COULD HAPPEN.
THE HINGES ON WHICH THE FUTURE TURNS. IF THERE'S GOING TO BE A FUTURE.
I THINK YOU'VE BEEN OUT-MANEUVERED. I THINK YOU'VE BEEN BEATEN.
REALLY?
THIS ISN'T MY UNIVERSE. I'M JUST VISITING.
AND WHAT ABOUT YOUR LOVER?
DON'T YOU FEEL ANY REGRET FOR HER?
FOR MAZIKEEN?
NO.
NOT REALLY.

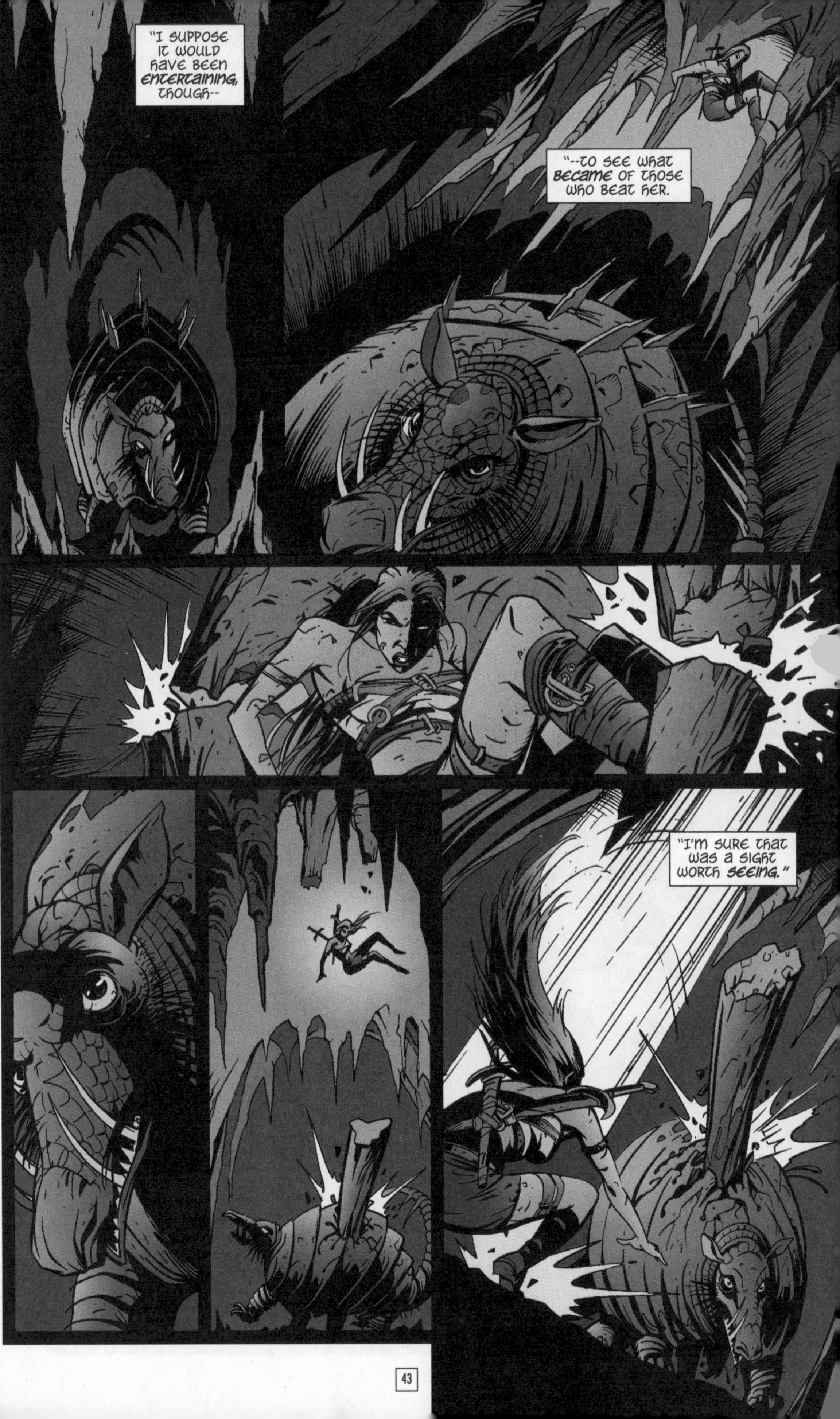
"I SUPPOSE IT WOULD HAVE BEEN ENTERTAINING, THOUGH--
"--TO SEE WHAT BECAME OF THOSE WHO BEAT HER.
"I'M SURE THAT WAS A SIGHT WORTH SEEING."

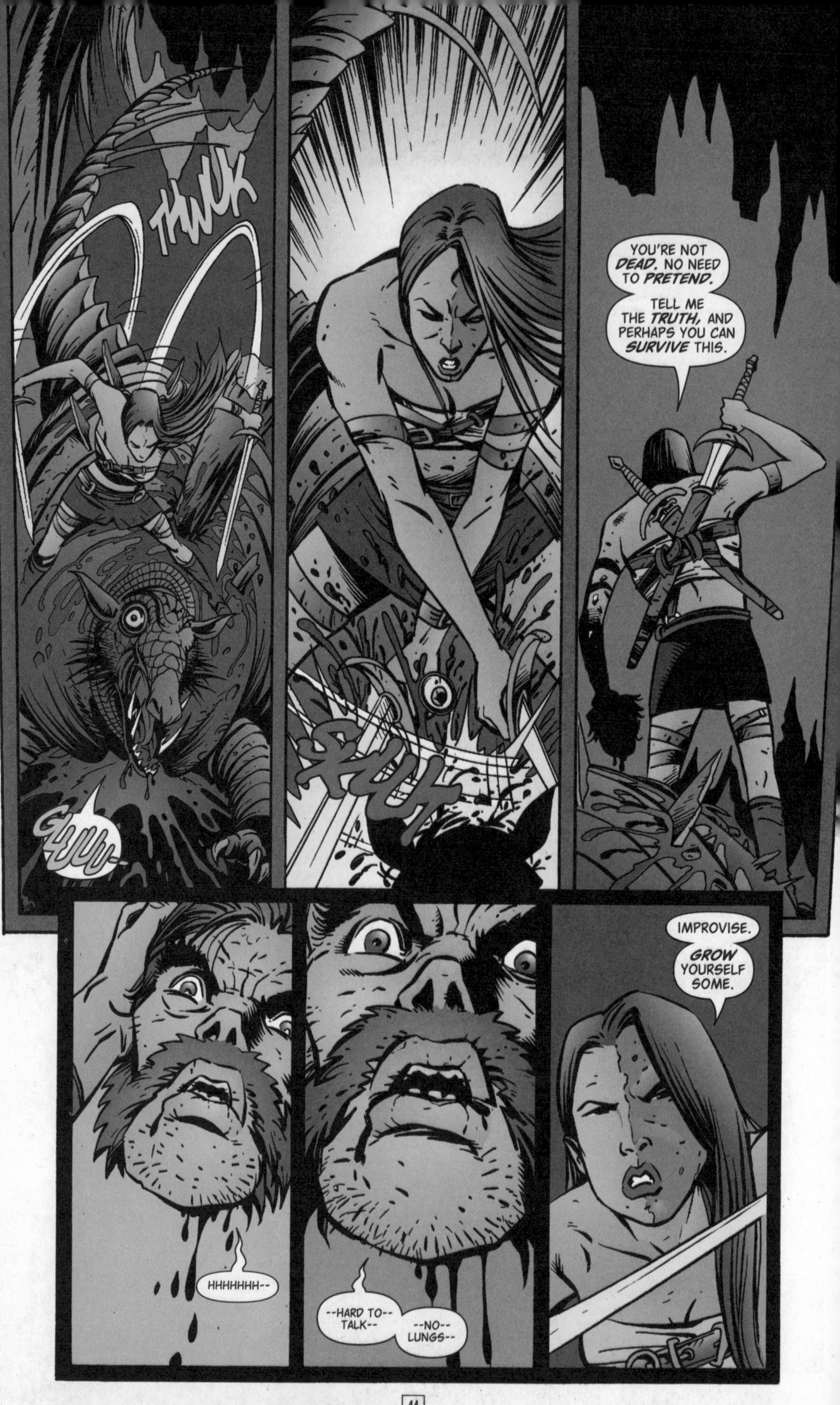
THUK
GLUUU--
SHUK
YOU'RE NOT DEAD. NO NEED TO PRETEND.
TELL ME THE TRUTH, AND PERHAPS YOU CAN SURVIVE THIS.
HHHHHHH--
--HARD TO-- TALK--
--NO-- LUNGS--
IMPROVISE.
GROW YOURSELF SOME.

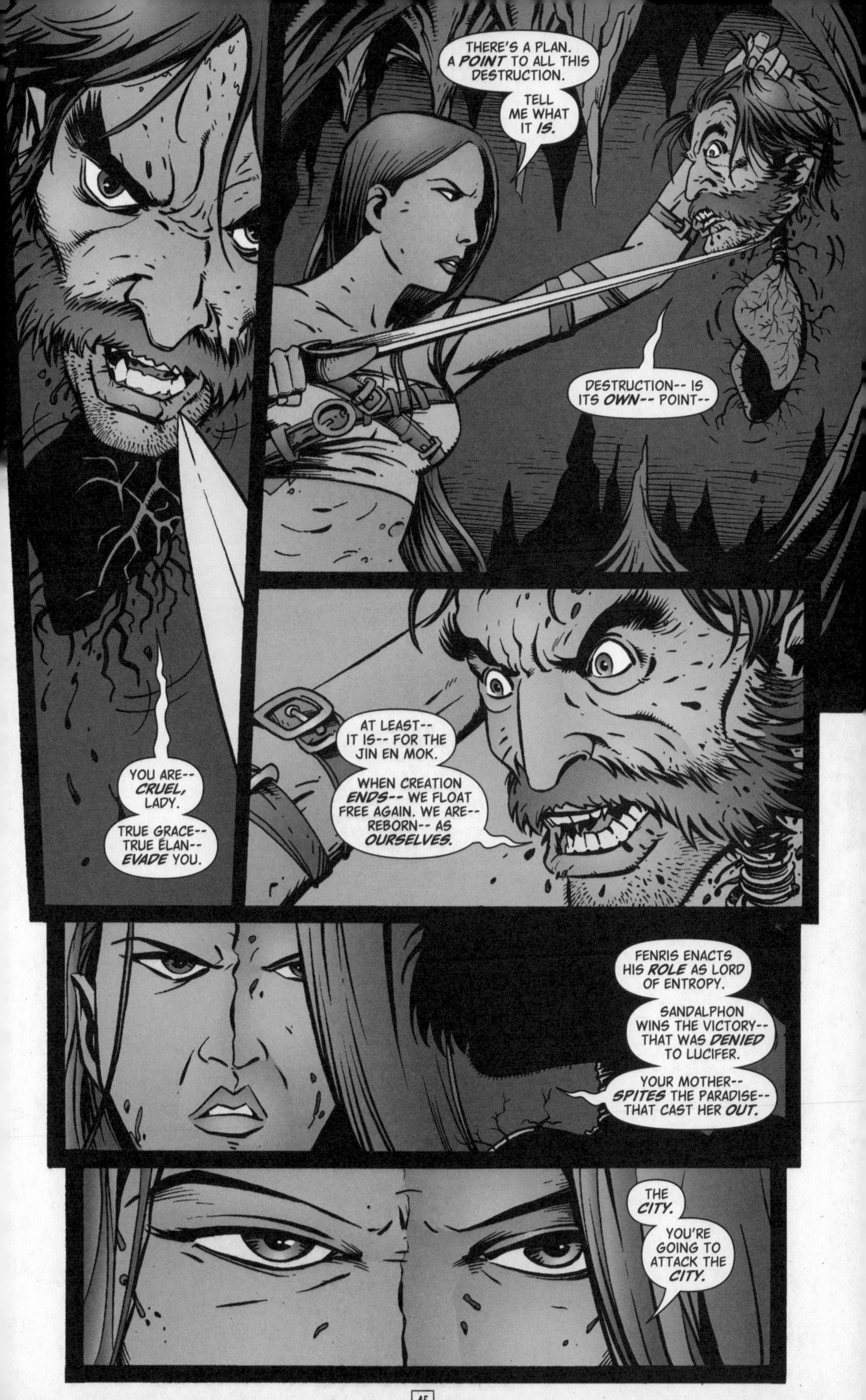
THERE'S A PLAN. A POINT TO ALL THIS DESTRUCTION.
TELL ME WHAT IT IS.
DESTRUCTION-- IS ITS OWN-- POINT--
YOU ARE-- CRUEL, LADY.
TRUE GRACE-- TRUE ÉLAN-- EVADE YOU.
AT LEAST-- IT IS-- FOR THE JIN EN MOK.
WHEN CREATION ENDS-- WE FLOAT FREE AGAIN. WE ARE-- REBORN-- AS OURSELVES.
FENRIS ENACTS HIS ROLE AS LORD OF ENTROPY.
SANDALPHON WINS THE VICTORY-- THAT WAS DENIED TO LUCIFER.
YOUR MOTHER-- SPITES THE PARADISE-- THAT CAST HER OUT.
THE CITY.
YOU'RE GOING TO ATTACK THE CITY.

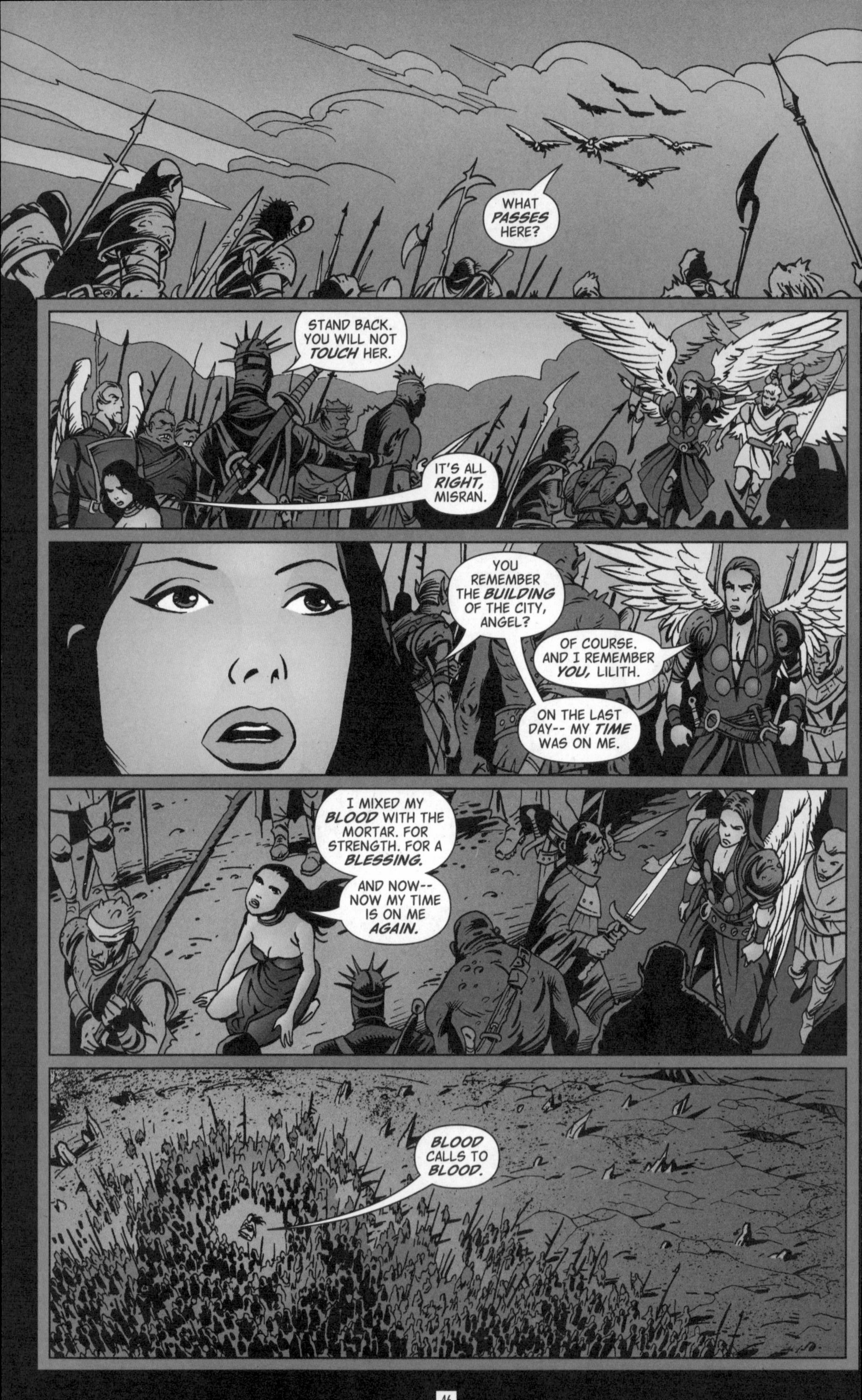
WHAT PASSES HERE?
STAND BACK. YOU WILL NOT TOUCH HER.
IT'S ALL RIGHT, MISRAN.
YOU REMEMBER THE BUILDING OF THE CITY, ANGEL?
OF COURSE. AND I REMEMBER YOU, LILITH.
ON THE LAST DAY-- MY TIME WAS ON ME.
I MIXED MY BLOOD WITH THE MORTAR. FOR STRENGTH. FOR A BLESSING.
AND NOW-- NOW MY TIME IS ON ME AGAIN.
BLOOD CALLS TO BLOOD.

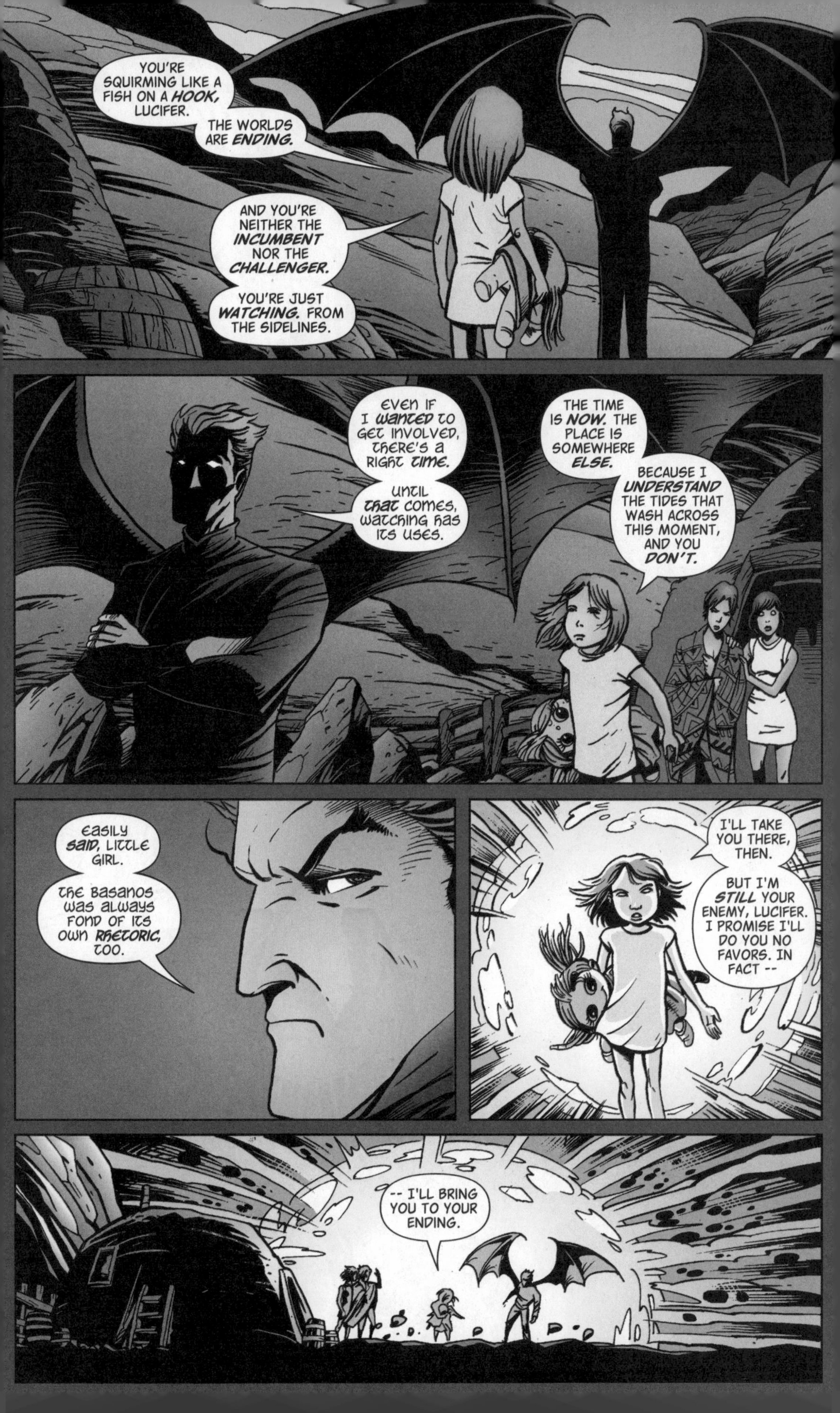
YOU'RE SQUIRMING LIKE A FISH ON A *HOOK,* LUCIFER.
THE WORLDS ARE *ENDING.*
AND YOU'RE NEITHER THE *INCUMBENT* NOR THE *CHALLENGER.*
YOU'RE JUST *WATCHING.* FROM THE SIDELINES.
EVEN IF I *WANTED* TO GET INVOLVED, THERE'S A RIGHT *TIME.*
UNTIL *THAT* COMES, WATCHING HAS ITS USES.
THE TIME IS *NOW.* THE PLACE IS SOMEWHERE *ELSE.*
BECAUSE I *UNDERSTAND* THE TIDES THAT WASH ACROSS THIS MOMENT, AND YOU *DON'T.*
EASILY *SAID,* LITTLE GIRL.
THE BASANOS WAS ALWAYS FOND OF ITS OWN *RHETORIC,* TOO.
I'LL TAKE YOU THERE, THEN.
BUT I'M *STILL* YOUR ENEMY, LUCIFER. I PROMISE I'LL DO YOU NO FAVORS. IN FACT --
-- I'LL BRING YOU TO YOUR ENDING.

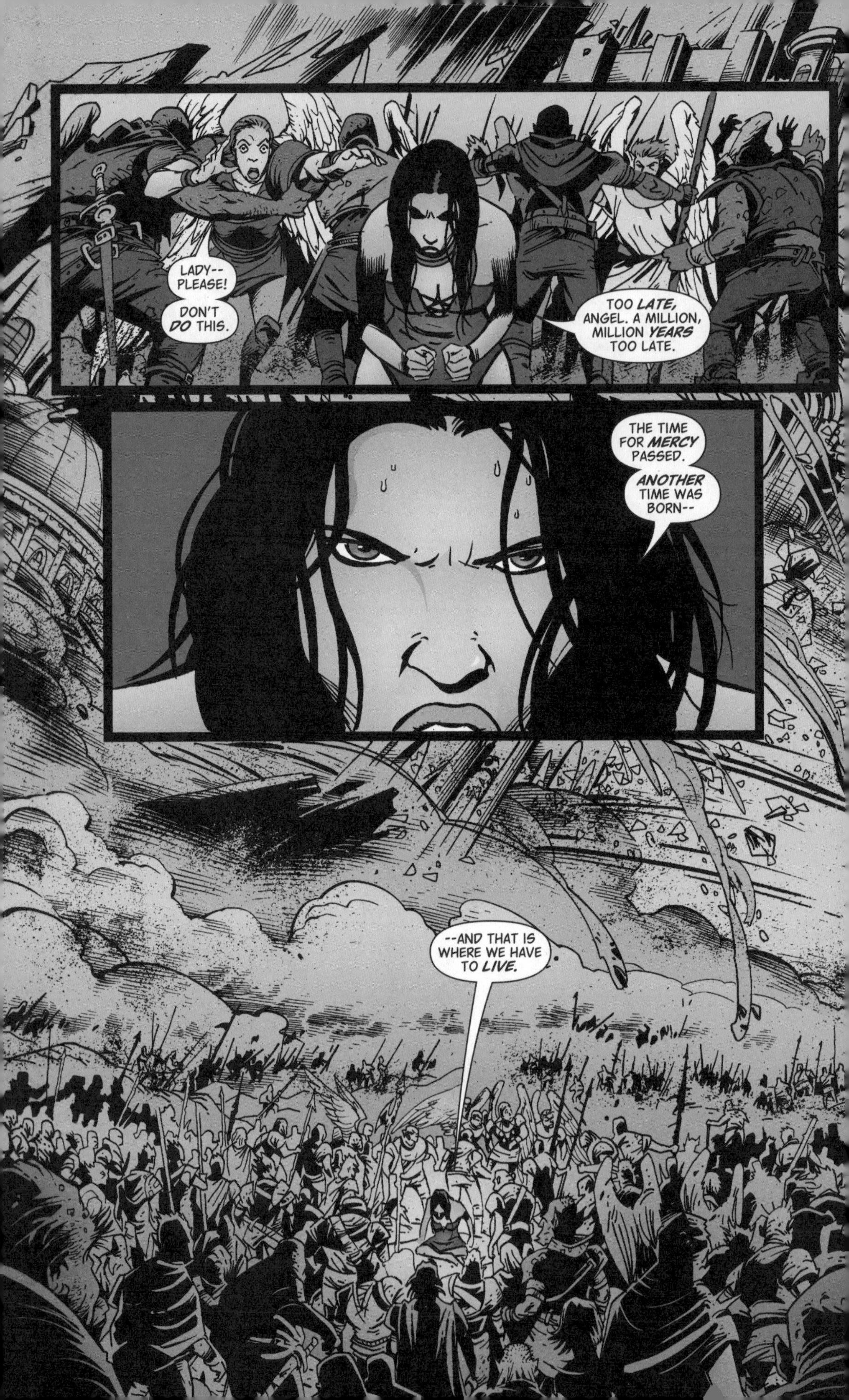
LADY-- PLEASE!
DON'T DO THIS.
TOO LATE, ANGEL. A MILLION, MILLION YEARS TOO LATE.
THE TIME FOR MERCY PASSED.
ANOTHER TIME WAS BORN--
--AND THAT IS WHERE WE HAVE TO LIVE.

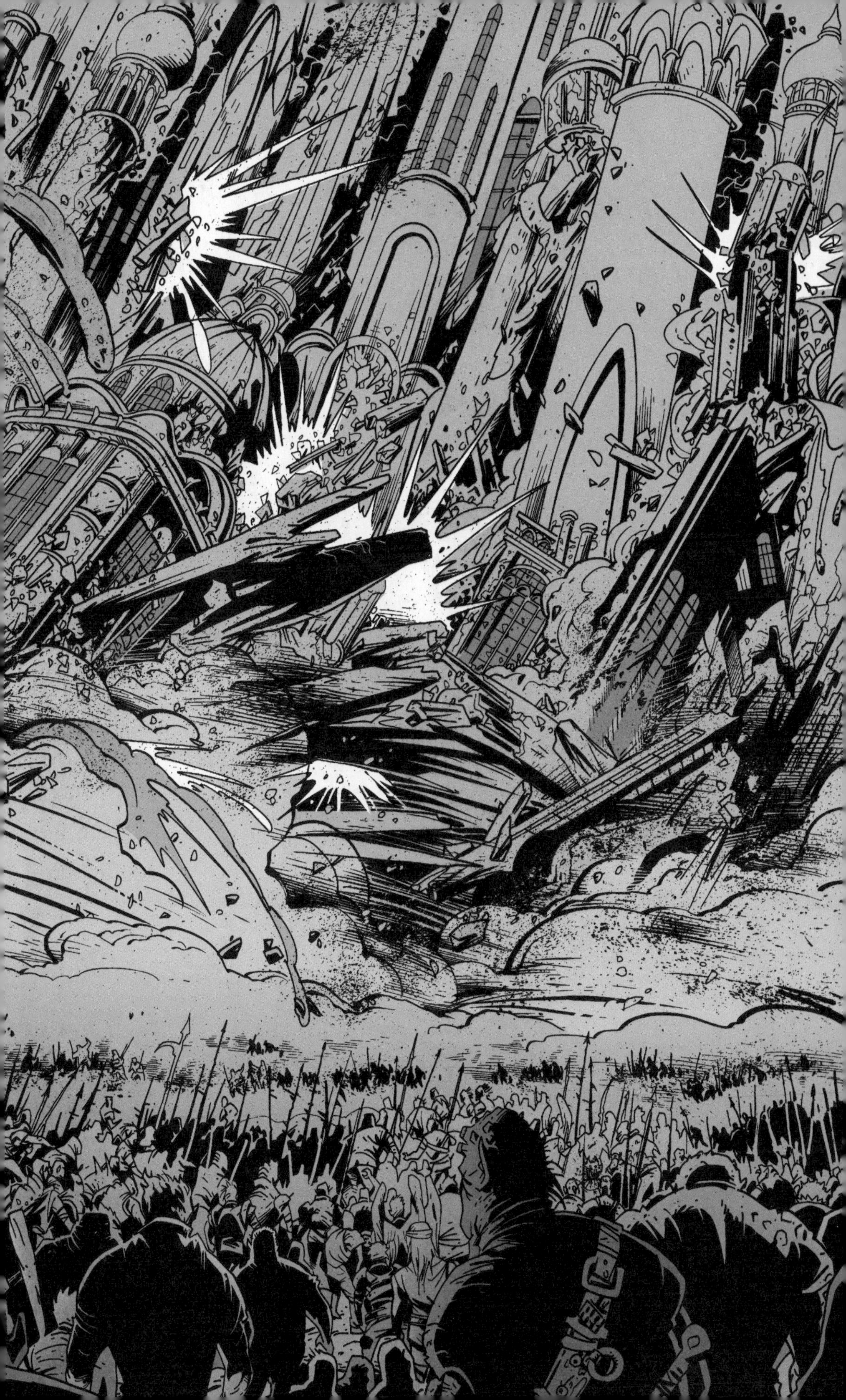

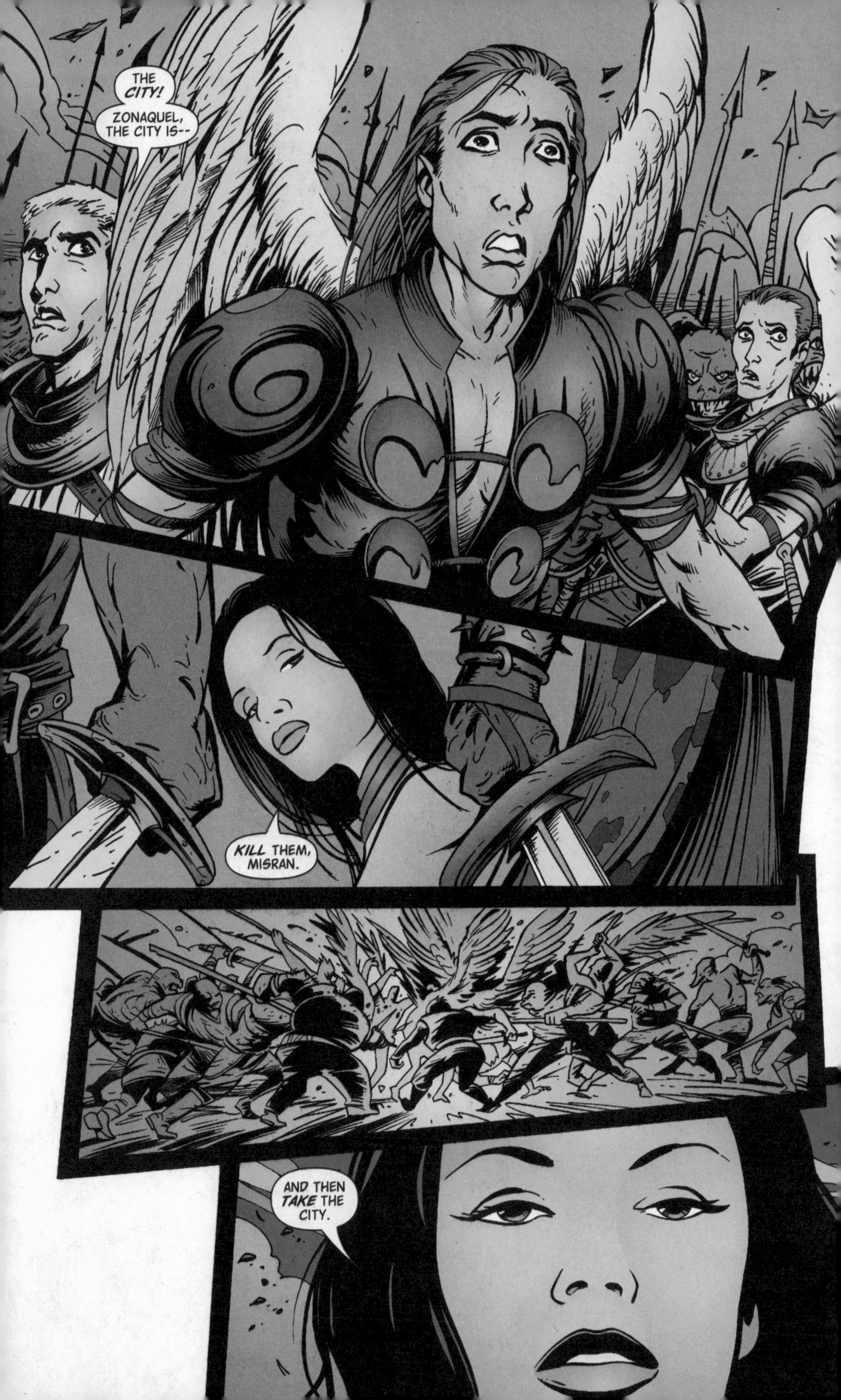
THE CITY!
ZONAQUEL, THE CITY IS--
KILL THEM, MISRAN.
AND THEN TAKE THE CITY.

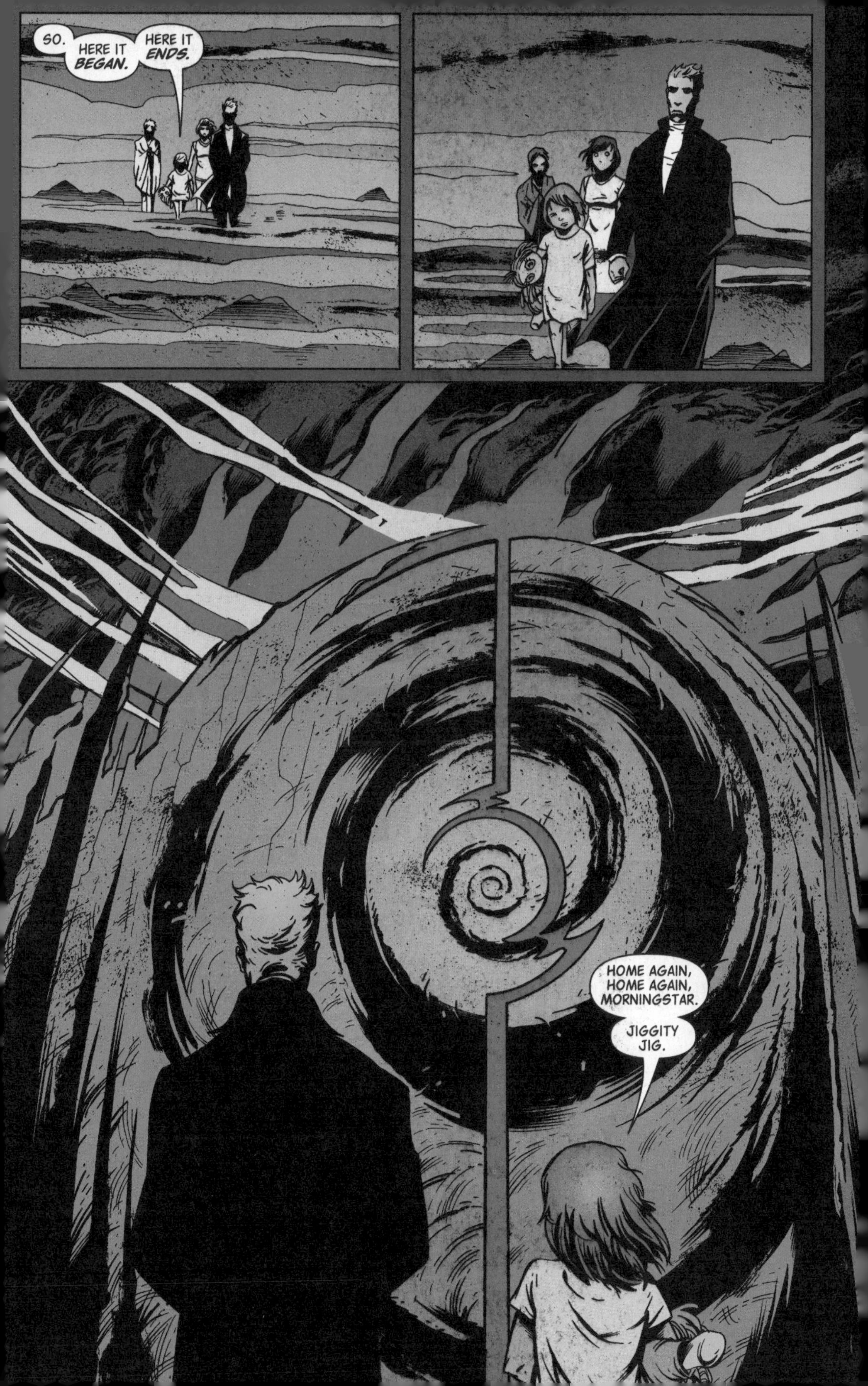
SO.
HERE IT BEGAN.
HERE IT ENDS.
HOME AGAIN, HOME AGAIN, MORNINGSTAR.
JIGGITY JIG.

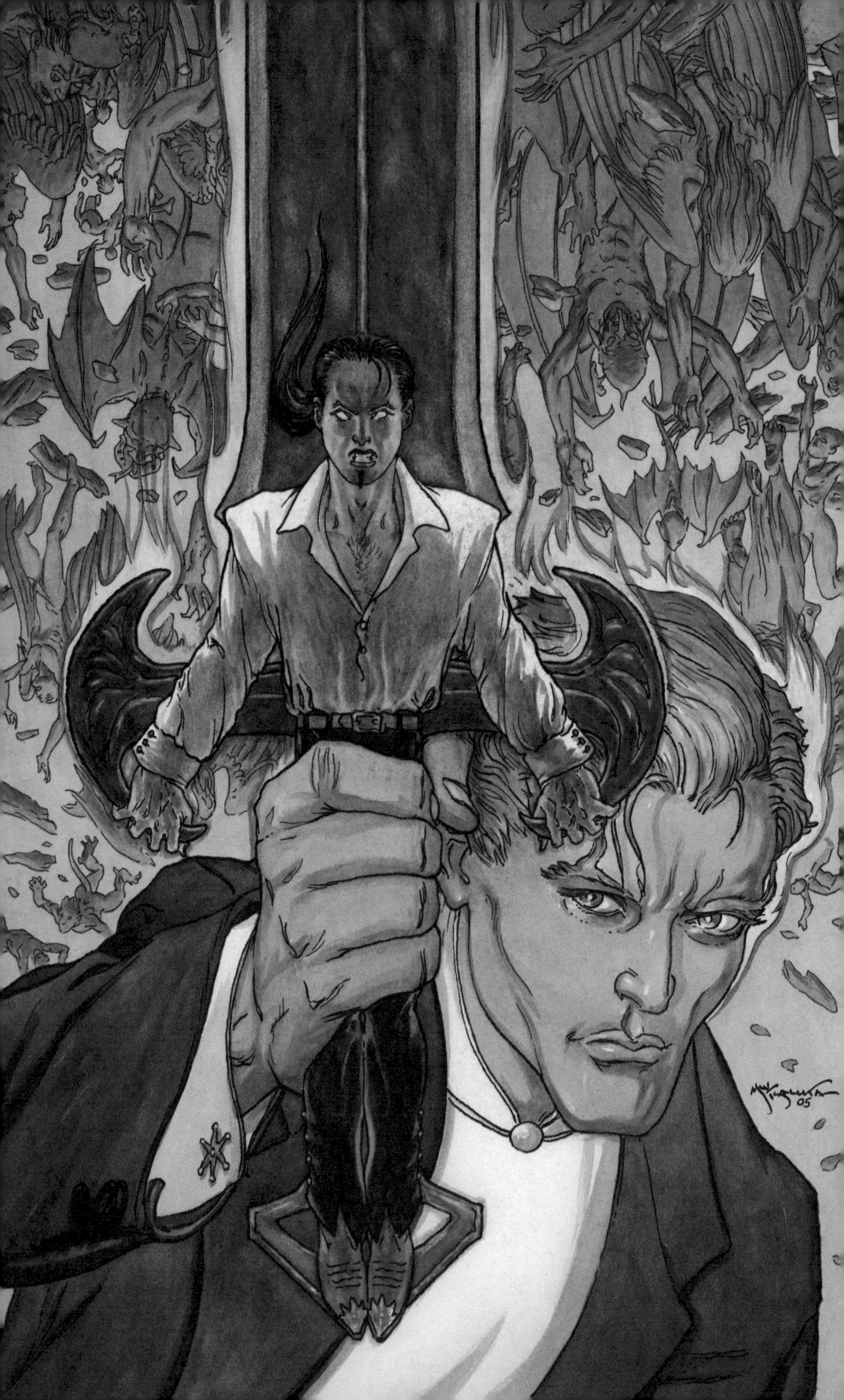

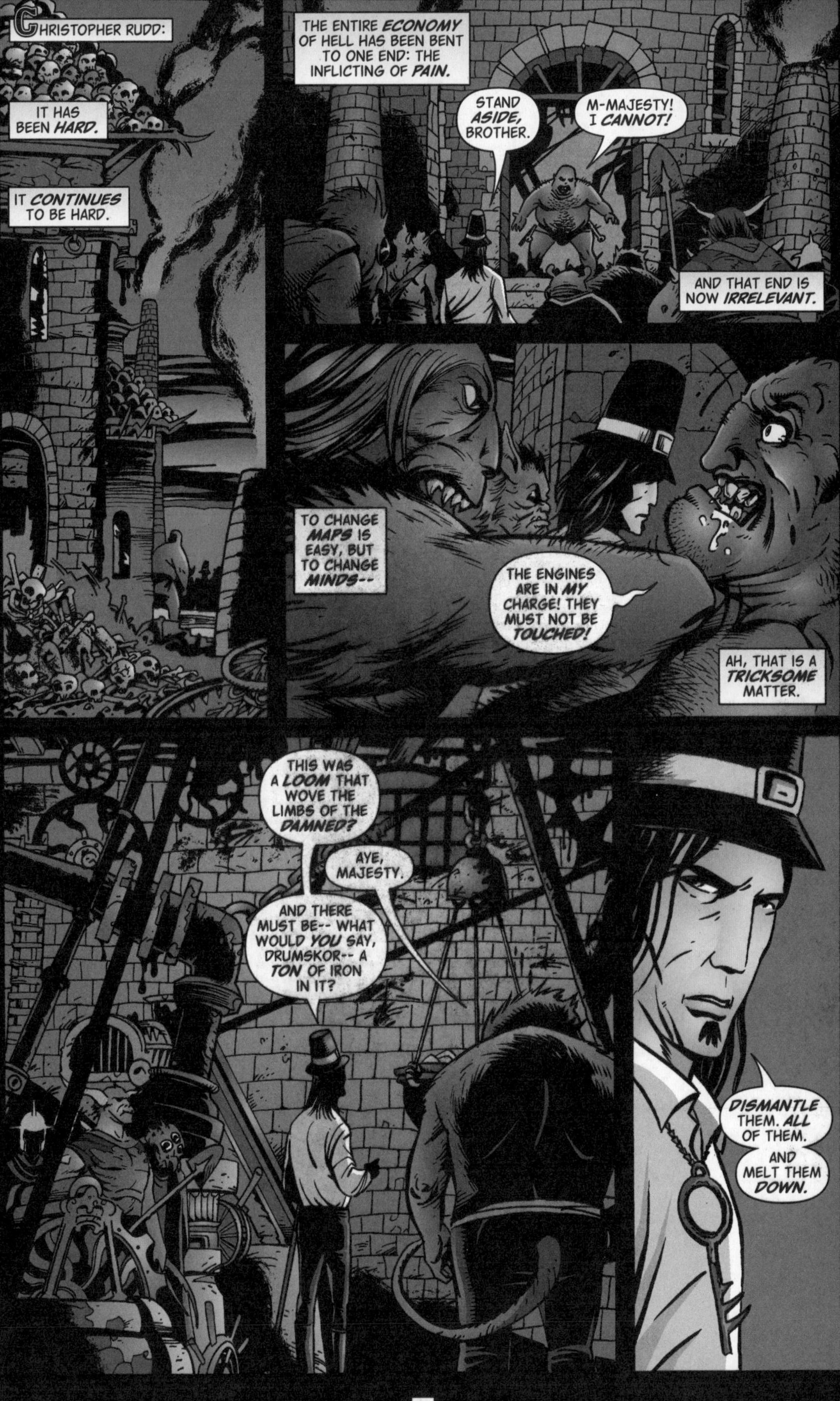
CHRISTOPHER RUDD:
IT HAS BEEN HARD.
IT CONTINUES TO BE HARD.
THE ENTIRE ECONOMY OF HELL HAS BEEN BENT TO ONE END: THE INFLICTING OF PAIN.
STAND ASIDE, BROTHER.
M-MAJESTY! I CANNOT!
AND THAT END IS NOW IRRELEVANT.
TO CHANGE MAPS IS EASY, BUT TO CHANGE MINDS--
THE ENGINES ARE IN MY CHARGE! THEY MUST NOT BE TOUCHED!
AH, THAT IS A TRICKSOME MATTER.
THIS WAS A LOOM THAT WOVE THE LIMBS OF THE DAMNED?
AYE, MAJESTY.
AND THERE MUST BE-- WHAT WOULD YOU SAY, DRUMSKOR-- A TON OF IRON IN IT?
DISMANTLE THEM. ALL OF THEM.
AND MELT THEM DOWN.

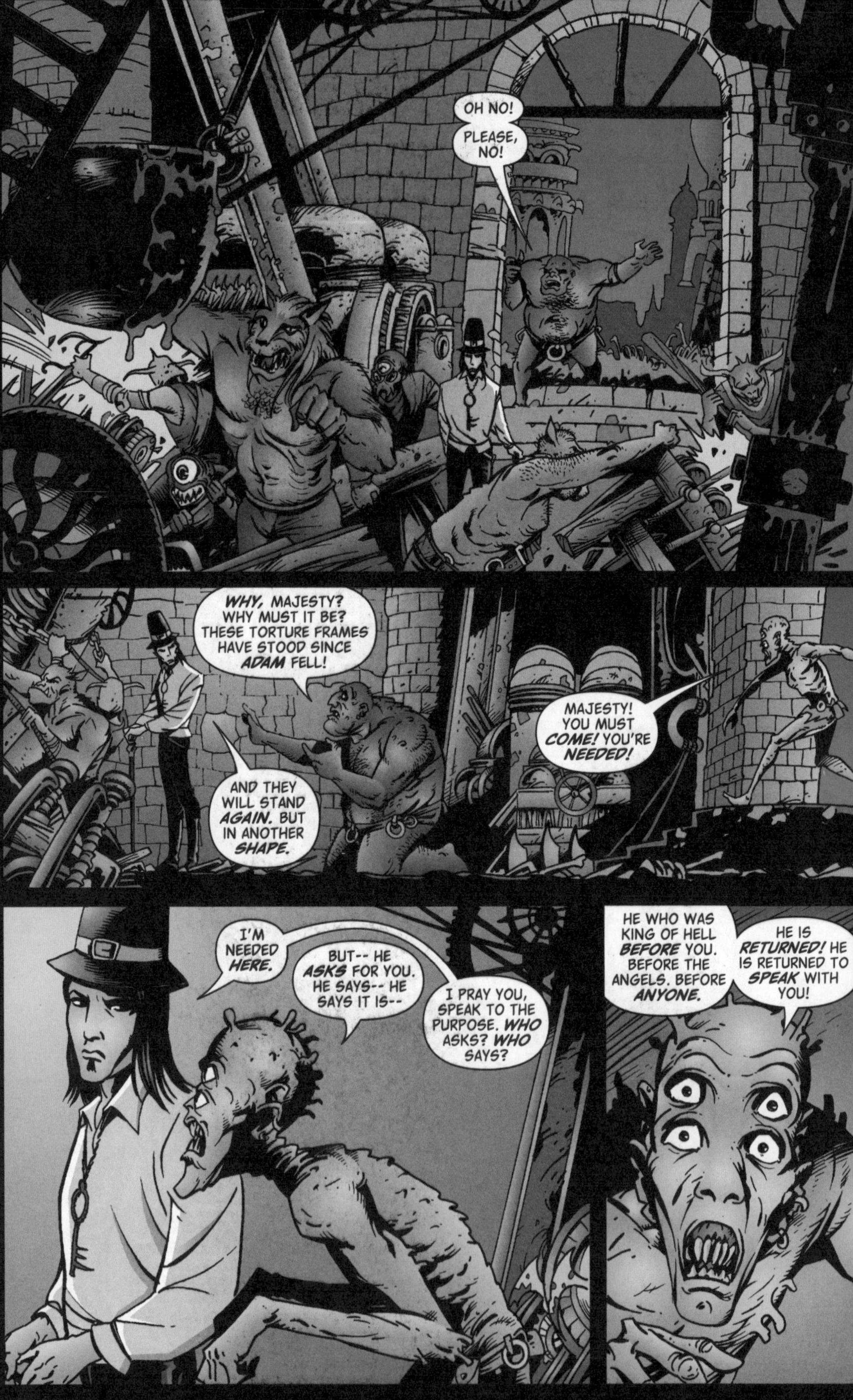
OH NO!
PLEASE, NO!
WHY, MAJESTY? WHY MUST IT BE? THESE TORTURE FRAMES HAVE STOOD SINCE ADAM FELL!
AND THEY WILL STAND AGAIN. BUT IN ANOTHER SHAPE.
MAJESTY! YOU MUST COME! YOU'RE NEEDED!
I'M NEEDED HERE.
BUT-- HE ASKS FOR YOU. HE SAYS-- HE SAYS IT IS--
I PRAY YOU, SPEAK TO THE PURPOSE. WHO ASKS? WHO SAYS?
HE WHO WAS KING OF HELL BEFORE YOU. BEFORE THE ANGELS. BEFORE ANYONE.
HE IS RETURNED! HE IS RETURNED TO SPEAK WITH YOU!

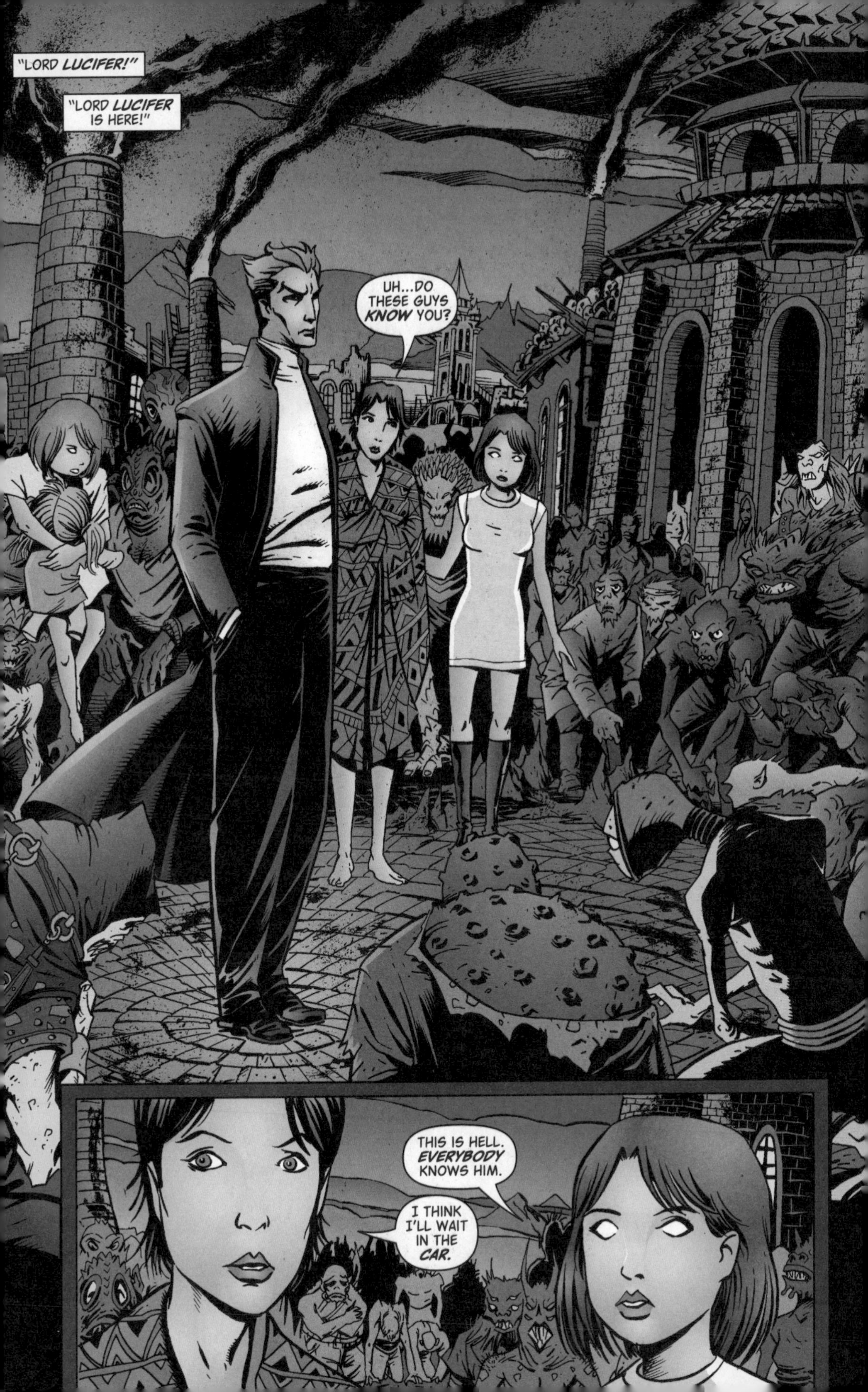
"LORD LUCIFER!"
"LORD LUCIFER IS HERE!"
UH...DO THESE GUYS KNOW YOU?
THIS IS HELL. EVERYBODY KNOWS HIM.
I THINK I'LL WAIT IN THE CAR.

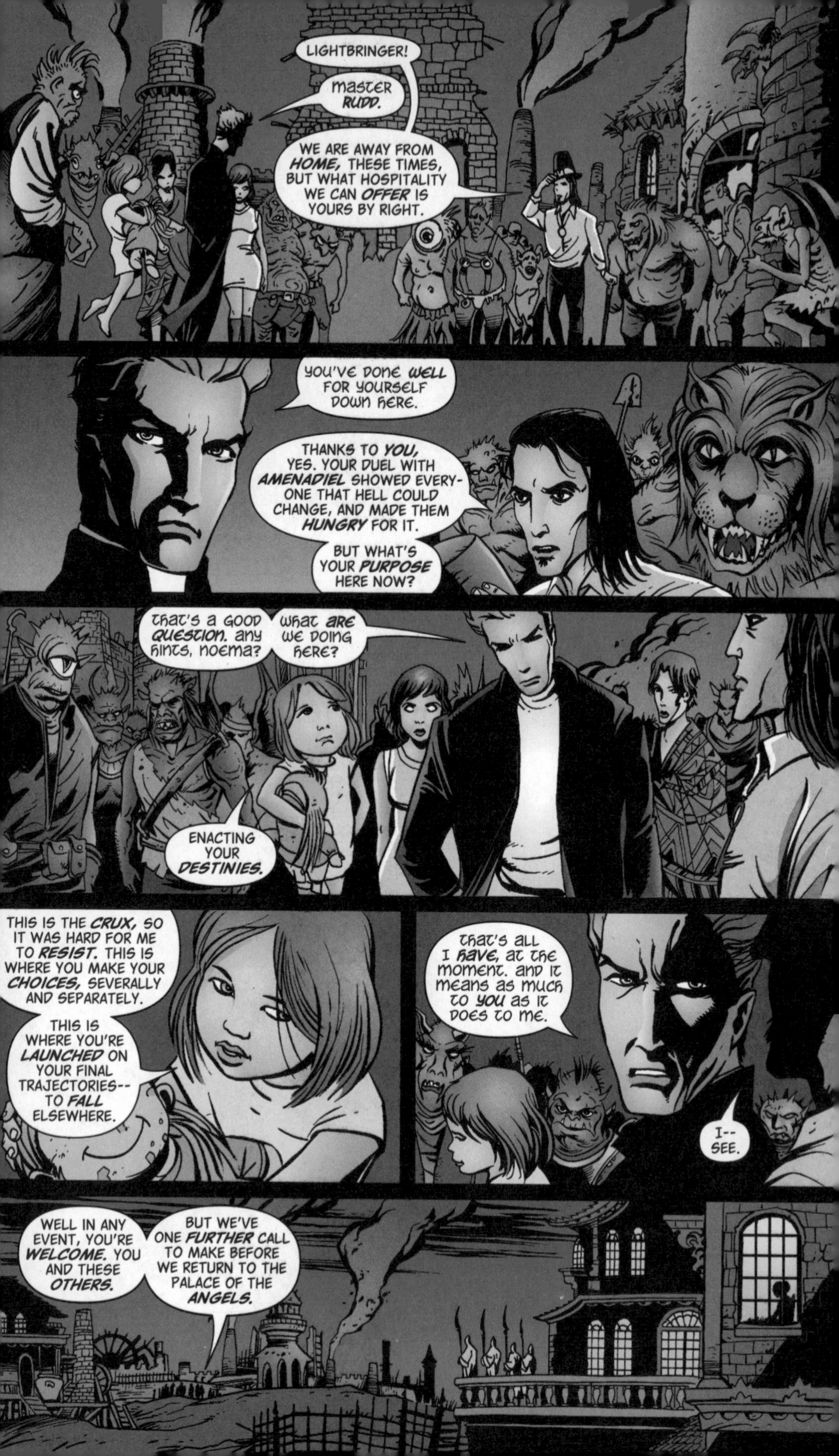
LIGHTBRINGER!
MASTER RUDD.
WE ARE AWAY FROM HOME, THESE TIMES, BUT WHAT HOSPITALITY WE CAN OFFER IS YOURS BY RIGHT.
YOU'VE DONE WELL FOR YOURSELF DOWN HERE.
THANKS TO YOU, YES. YOUR DUEL WITH AMENADIEL SHOWED EVERY-ONE THAT HELL COULD CHANGE, AND MADE THEM HUNGRY FOR IT.
BUT WHAT'S YOUR PURPOSE HERE NOW?
THAT'S A GOOD QUESTION. ANY HINTS, NOEMA?
WHAT ARE WE DOING HERE?
ENACTING YOUR DESTINIES.
THIS IS THE CRUX, SO IT WAS HARD FOR ME TO RESIST. THIS IS WHERE YOU MAKE YOUR CHOICES, SEVERALLY AND SEPARATELY.
THIS IS WHERE YOU'RE LAUNCHED ON YOUR FINAL TRAJECTORIES-- TO FALL ELSEWHERE.
THAT'S ALL I HAVE, AT THE MOMENT. AND IT MEANS AS MUCH TO YOU AS IT DOES TO ME.
I-- SEE.
WELL IN ANY EVENT, YOU'RE WELCOME. YOU AND THESE OTHERS.
BUT WE'VE ONE FURTHER CALL TO MAKE BEFORE WE RETURN TO THE PALACE OF THE ANGELS.

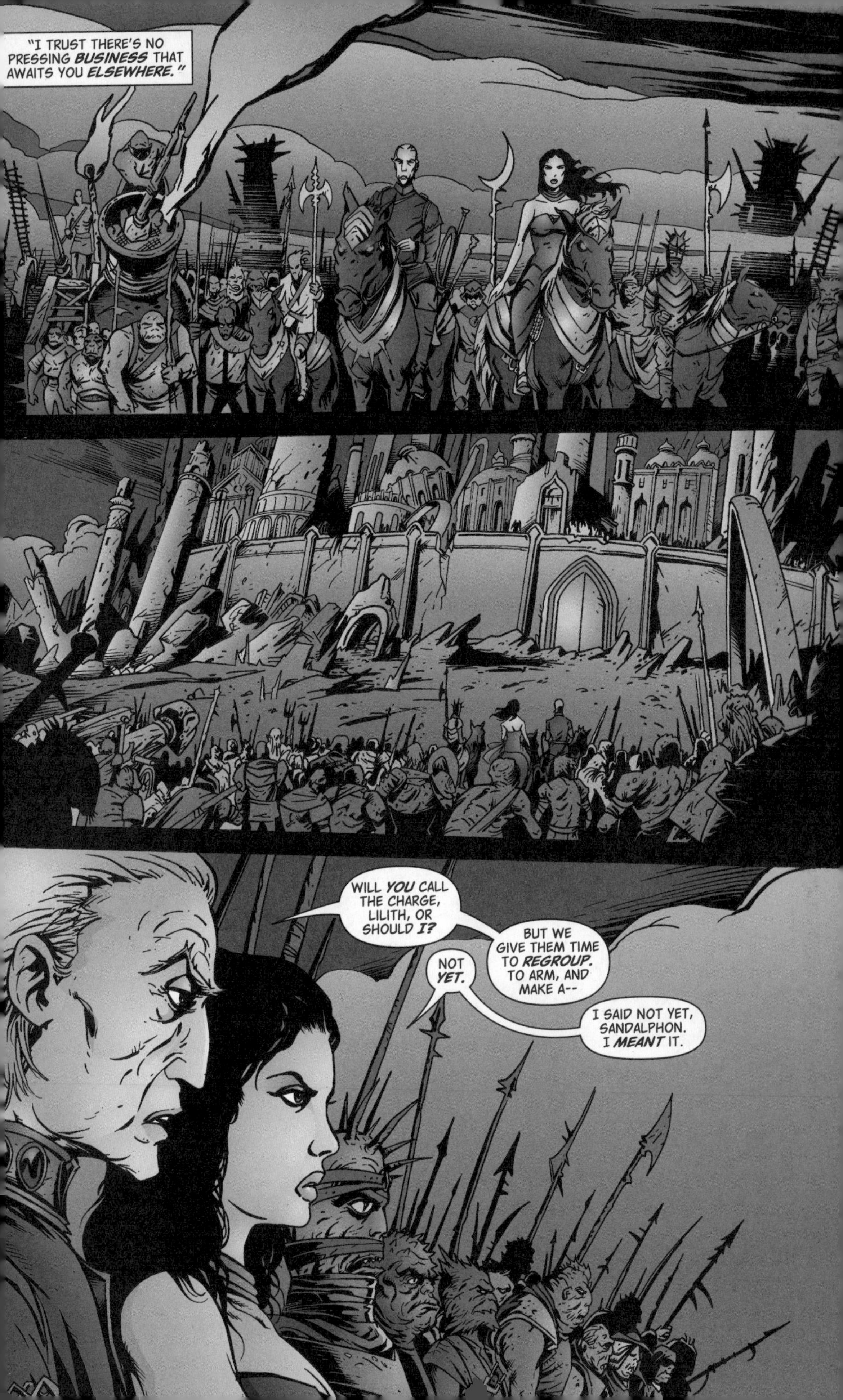
"I TRUST THERE'S NO PRESSING BUSINESS THAT AWAITS YOU ELSEWHERE."
WILL YOU CALL THE CHARGE, LILITH, OR SHOULD I?
NOT YET.
BUT WE GIVE THEM TIME TO REGROUP. TO ARM, AND MAKE A--
I SAID NOT YET, SANDALPHON. I MEANT IT.

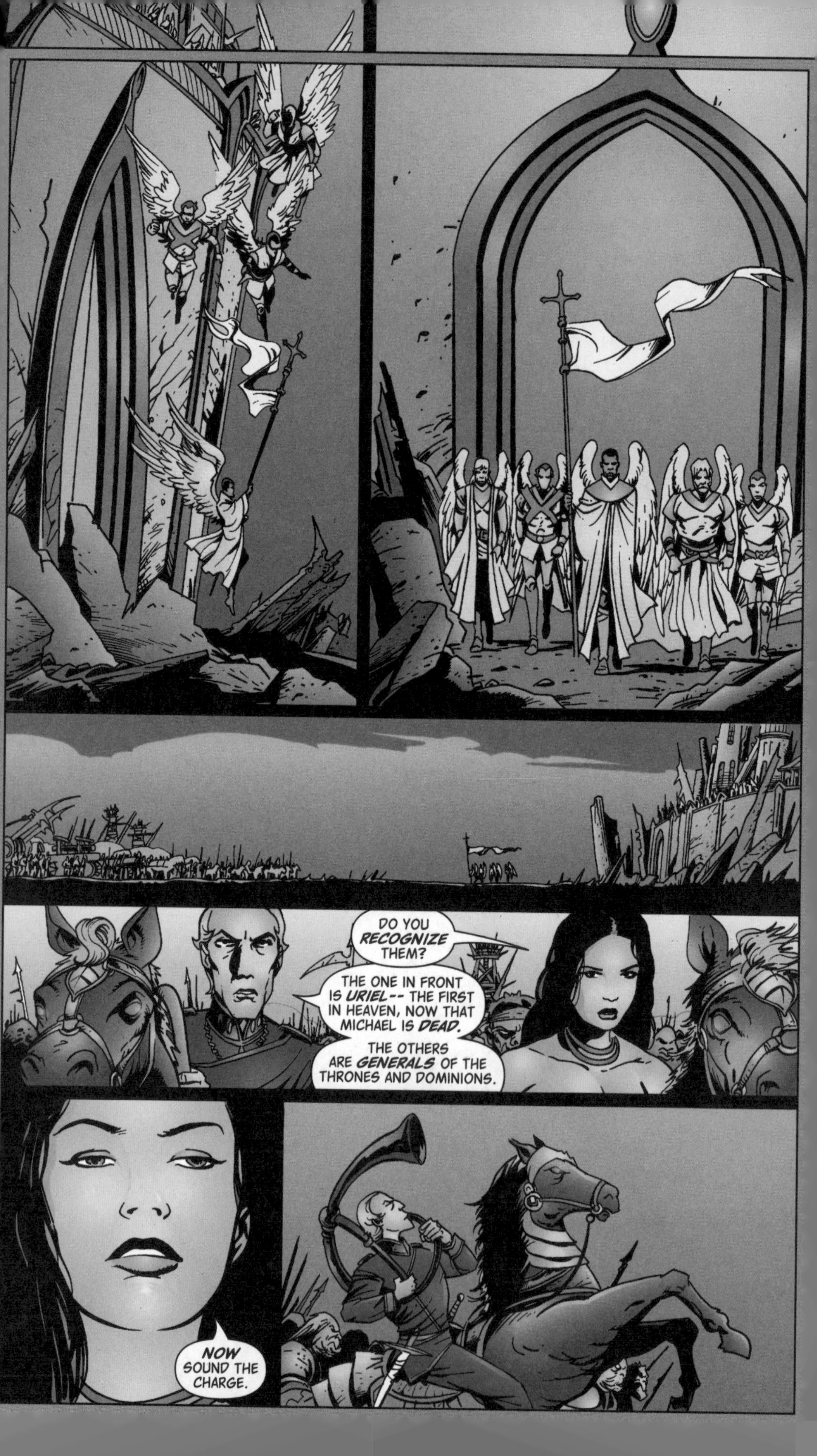
DO YOU RECOGNIZE THEM?
THE ONE IN FRONT IS URIEL-- THE FIRST IN HEAVEN, NOW THAT MICHAEL IS DEAD.
THE OTHERS ARE GENERALS OF THE THRONES AND DOMINIONS.
NOW SOUND THE CHARGE.

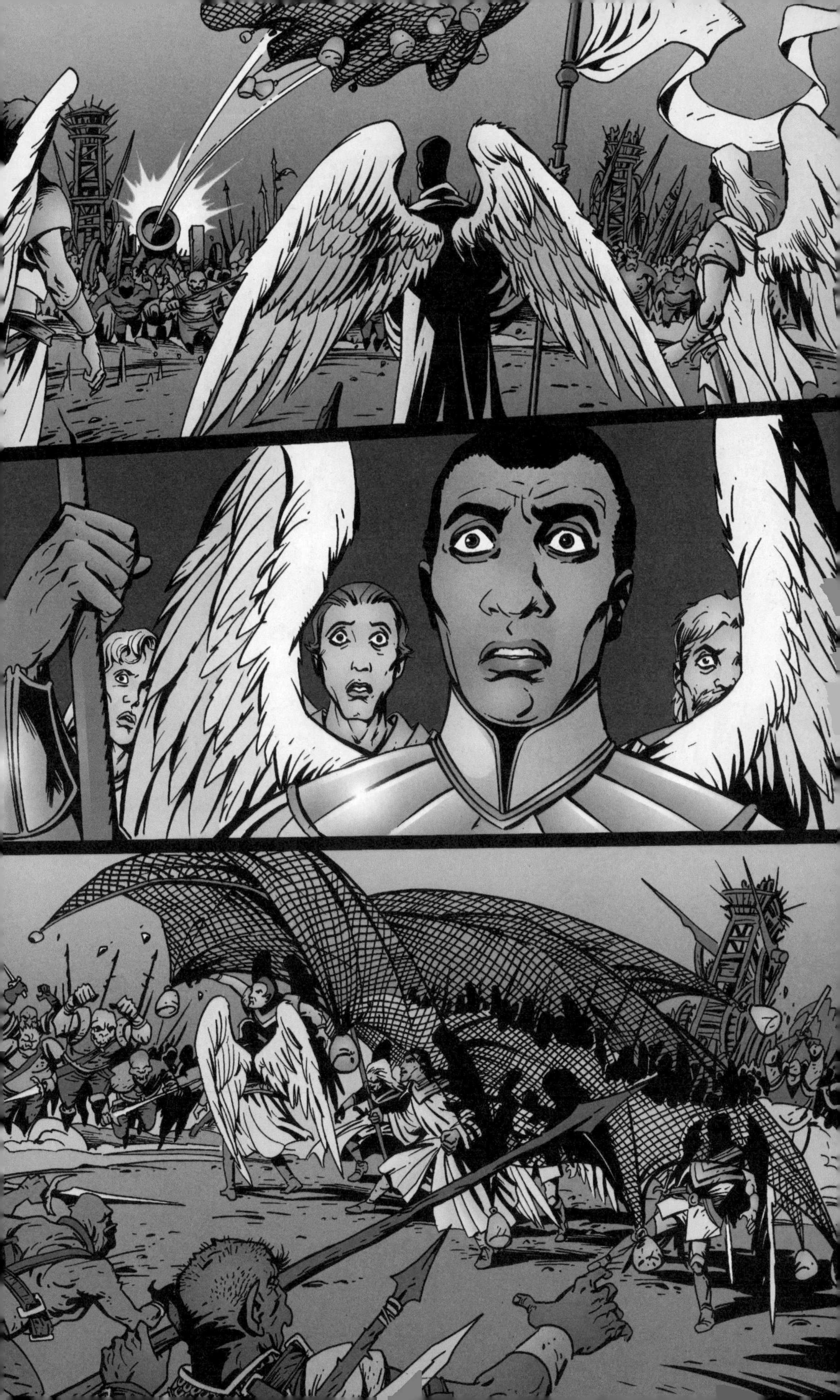

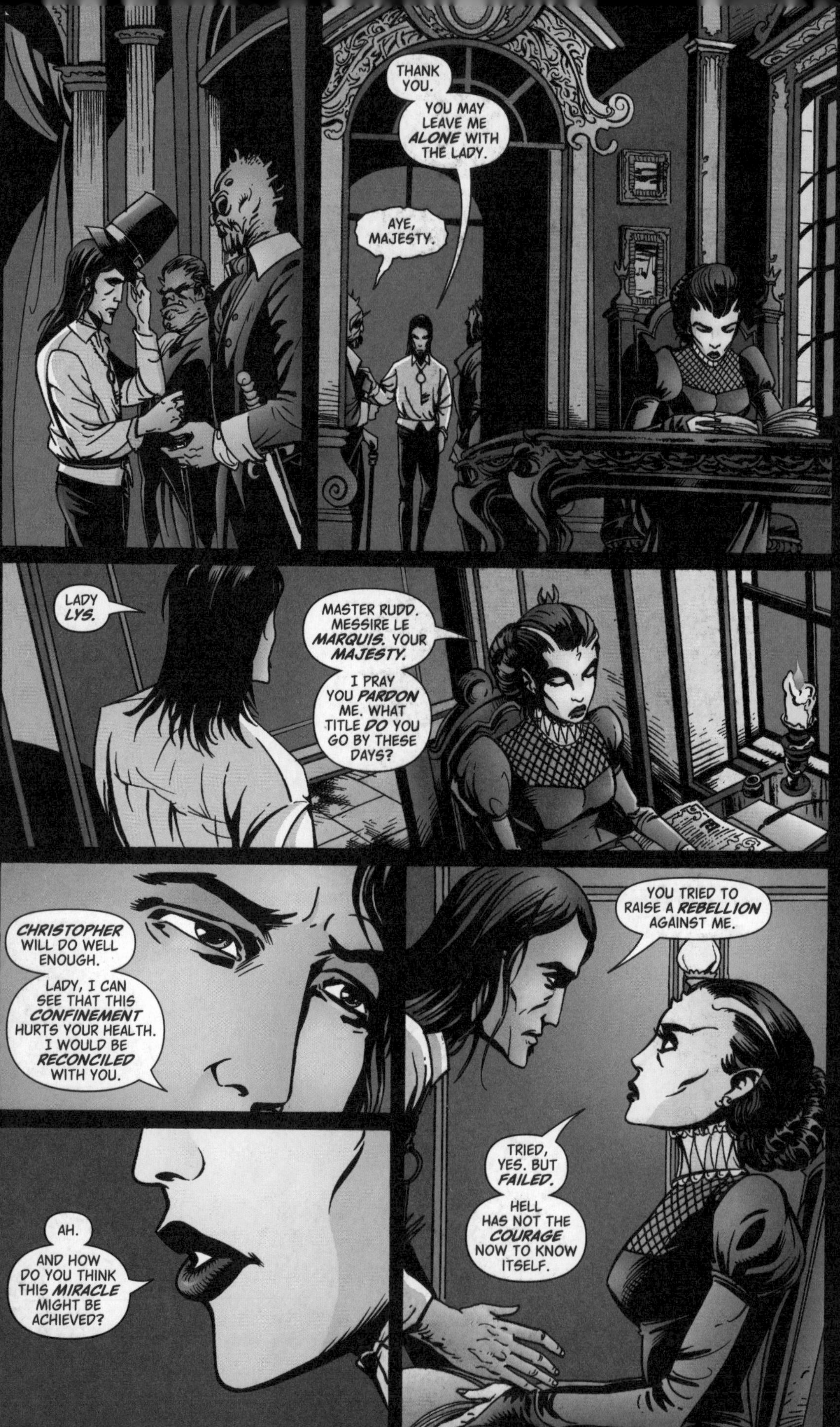
THANK YOU.
YOU MAY LEAVE ME ALONE WITH THE LADY.
AYE, MAJESTY.
LADY LYS.
MASTER RUDD. MESSIRE LE MARQUIS. YOUR MAJESTY.
I PRAY YOU PARDON ME. WHAT TITLE DO YOU GO BY THESE DAYS?
CHRISTOPHER WILL DO WELL ENOUGH.
LADY, I CAN SEE THAT THIS CONFINEMENT HURTS YOUR HEALTH. I WOULD BE RECONCILED WITH YOU.
AH.
AND HOW DO YOU THINK THIS MIRACLE MIGHT BE ACHIEVED?
YOU TRIED TO RAISE A REBELLION AGAINST ME.
TRIED, YES. BUT FAILED.
HELL HAS NOT THE COURAGE NOW TO KNOW ITSELF.

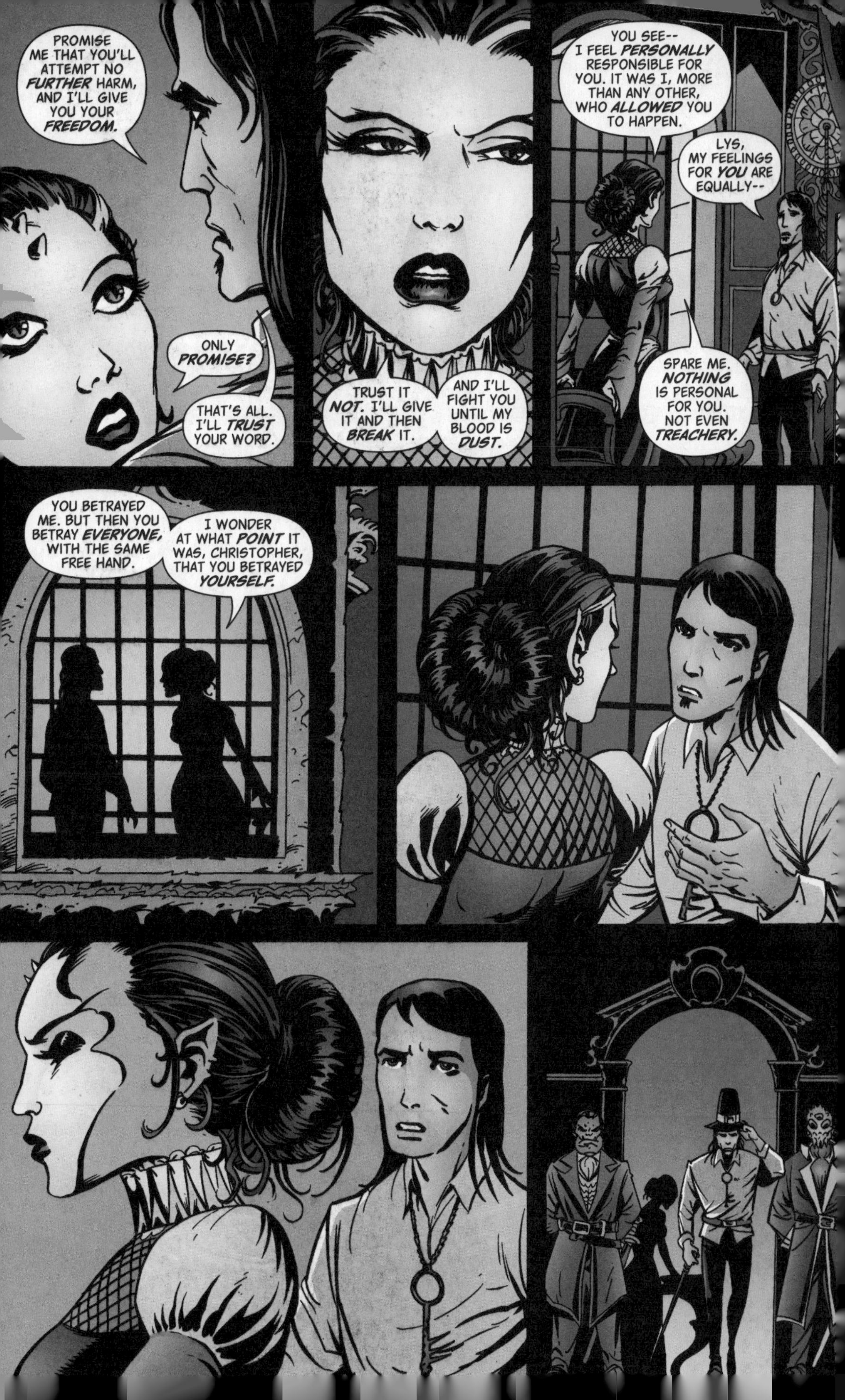
PROMISE ME THAT YOU'LL ATTEMPT NO FURTHER HARM, AND I'LL GIVE YOU YOUR FREEDOM.
ONLY PROMISE?
THAT'S ALL. I'LL TRUST YOUR WORD.
TRUST IT NOT. I'LL GIVE IT AND THEN BREAK IT.
AND I'LL FIGHT YOU UNTIL MY BLOOD IS DUST.
YOU SEE-- I FEEL PERSONALLY RESPONSIBLE FOR YOU. IT WAS I, MORE THAN ANY OTHER, WHO ALLOWED YOU TO HAPPEN.
LYS, MY FEELINGS FOR YOU ARE EQUALLY--
SPARE ME. NOTHING IS PERSONAL FOR YOU. NOT EVEN TREACHERY.
YOU BETRAYED ME. BUT THEN YOU BETRAY EVERYONE, WITH THE SAME FREE HAND.
I WONDER AT WHAT POINT IT WAS, CHRISTOPHER, THAT YOU BETRAYED YOURSELF.

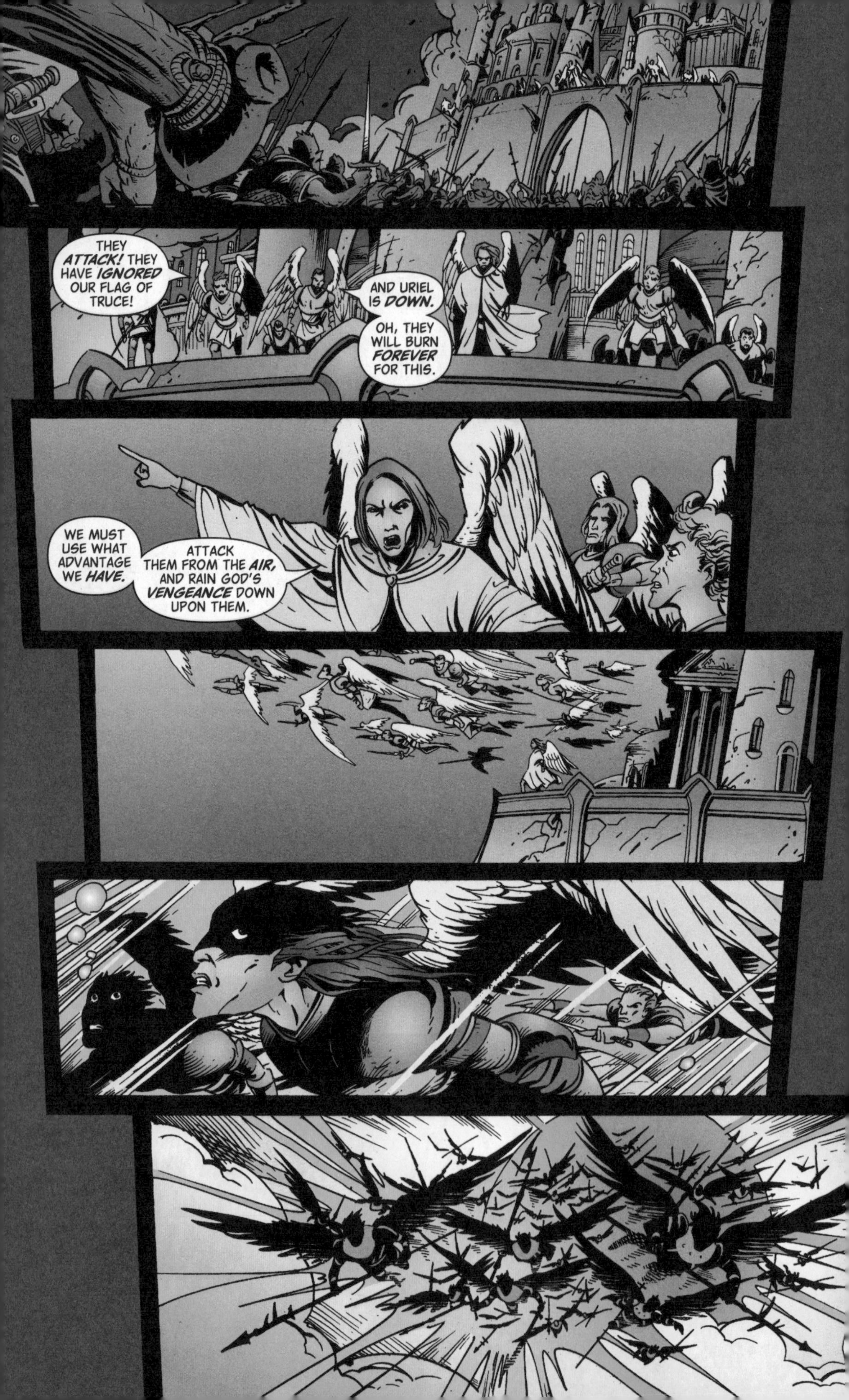
THEY ATTACK! THEY HAVE IGNORED OUR FLAG OF TRUCE!
AND URIEL IS DOWN.
OH, THEY WILL BURN FOREVER FOR THIS.
WE MUST USE WHAT ADVANTAGE WE HAVE.
ATTACK THEM FROM THE AIR, AND RAIN GOD'S VENGEANCE DOWN UPON THEM.

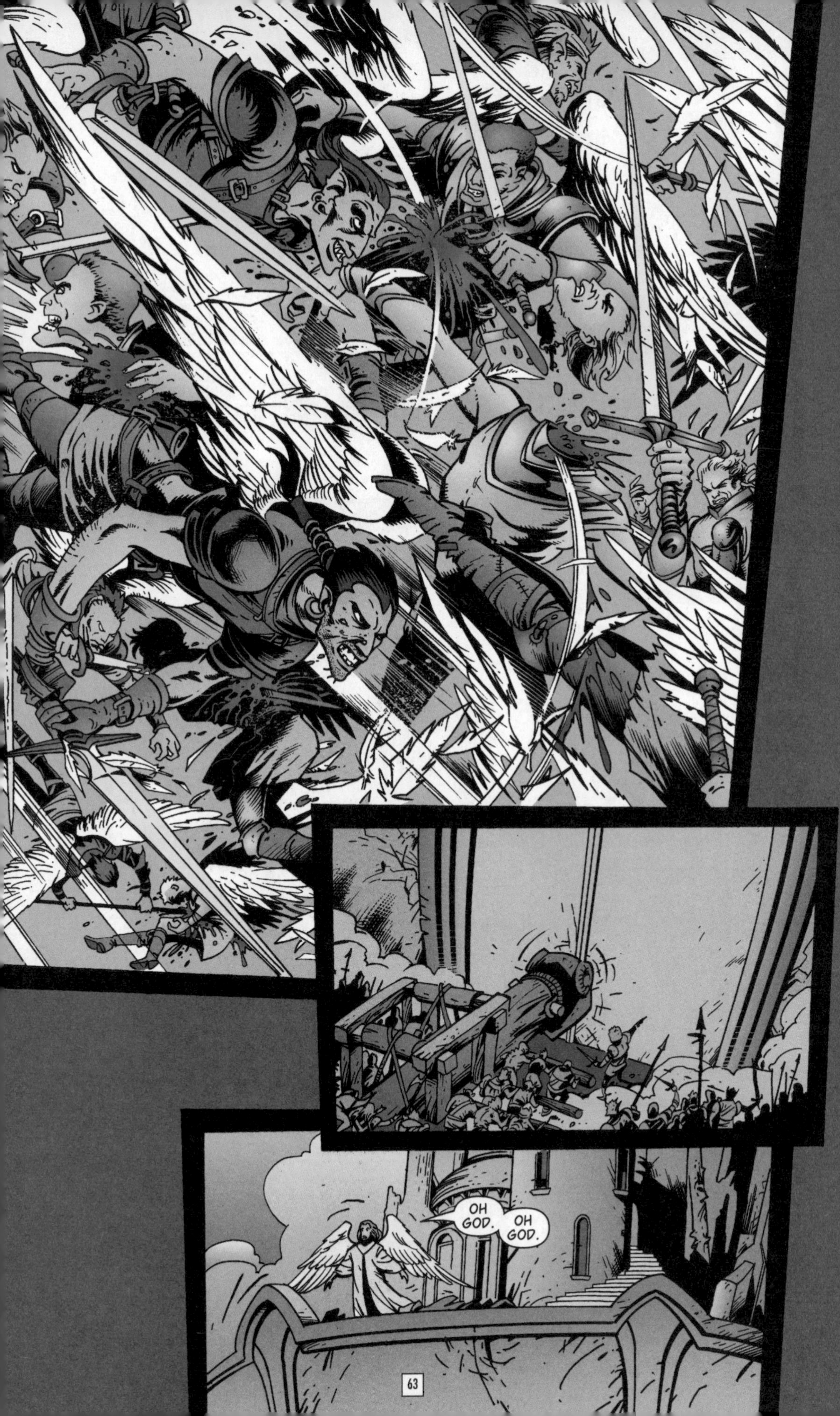
OH GOD.
OH GOD.

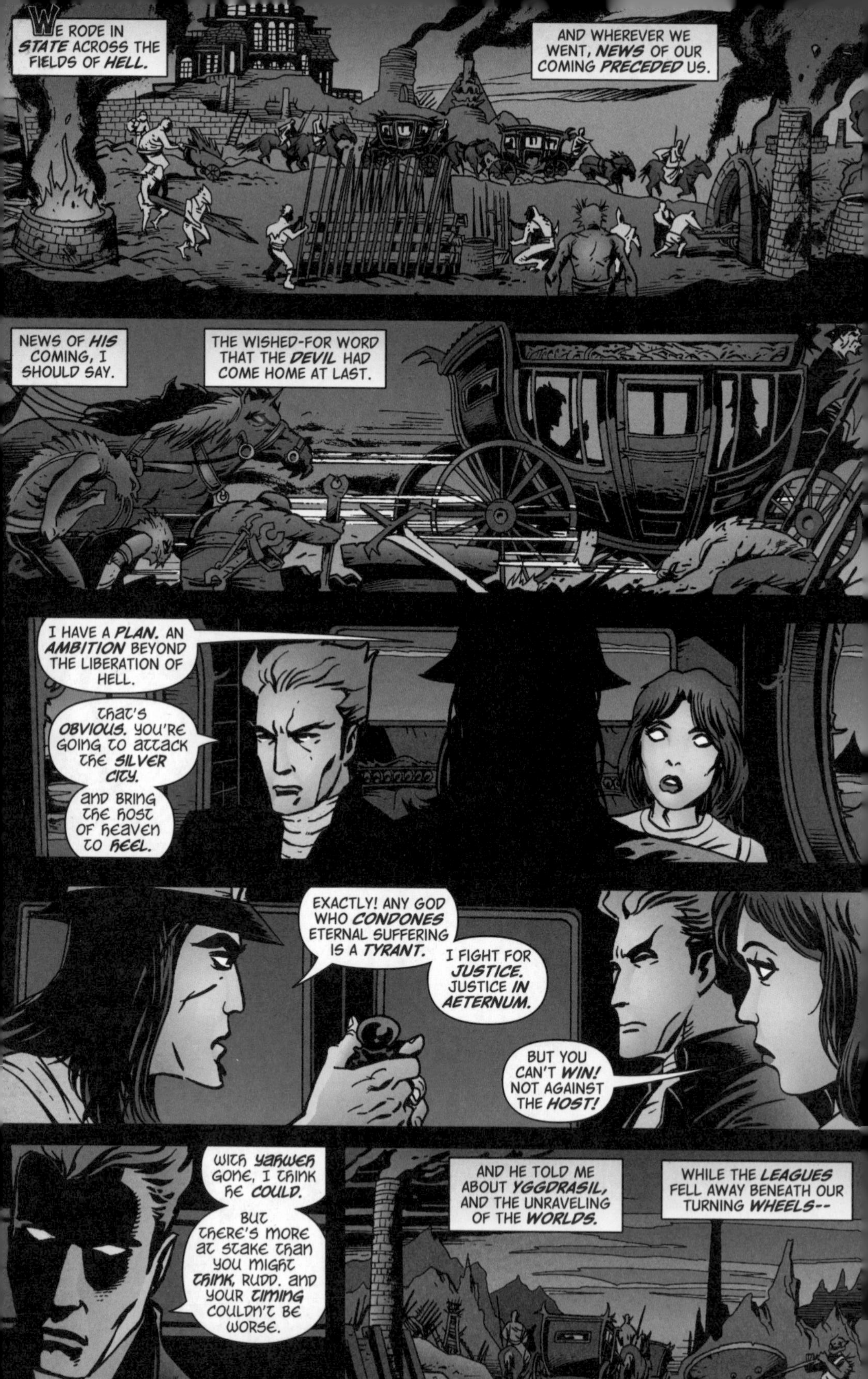

WE RODE IN STATE ACROSS THE FIELDS OF HELL.
AND WHEREVER WE WENT, NEWS OF OUR COMING PRECEDED US.
NEWS OF HIS COMING, I SHOULD SAY.
THE WISHED-FOR WORD THAT THE DEVIL HAD COME HOME AT LAST.
I HAVE A PLAN. AN AMBITION BEYOND THE LIBERATION OF HELL.
THAT'S OBVIOUS. YOU'RE GOING TO ATTACK THE SILVER CITY.
AND BRING THE HOST OF HEAVEN TO HEEL.
EXACTLY! ANY GOD WHO CONDONES ETERNAL SUFFERING IS A TYRANT.
I FIGHT FOR JUSTICE. JUSTICE IN AETERNUM.
BUT YOU CAN'T WIN! NOT AGAINST THE HOST!
WITH YAHWEH GONE, I THINK HE COULD.
BUT THERE'S MORE AT STAKE THAN YOU MIGHT THINK, RUDD. AND YOUR TIMING COULDN'T BE WORSE.
AND HE TOLD ME ABOUT YGGDRASIL, AND THE UNRAVELING OF THE WORLDS.
WHILE THE LEAGUES FELL AWAY BENEATH OUR TURNING WHEELS--

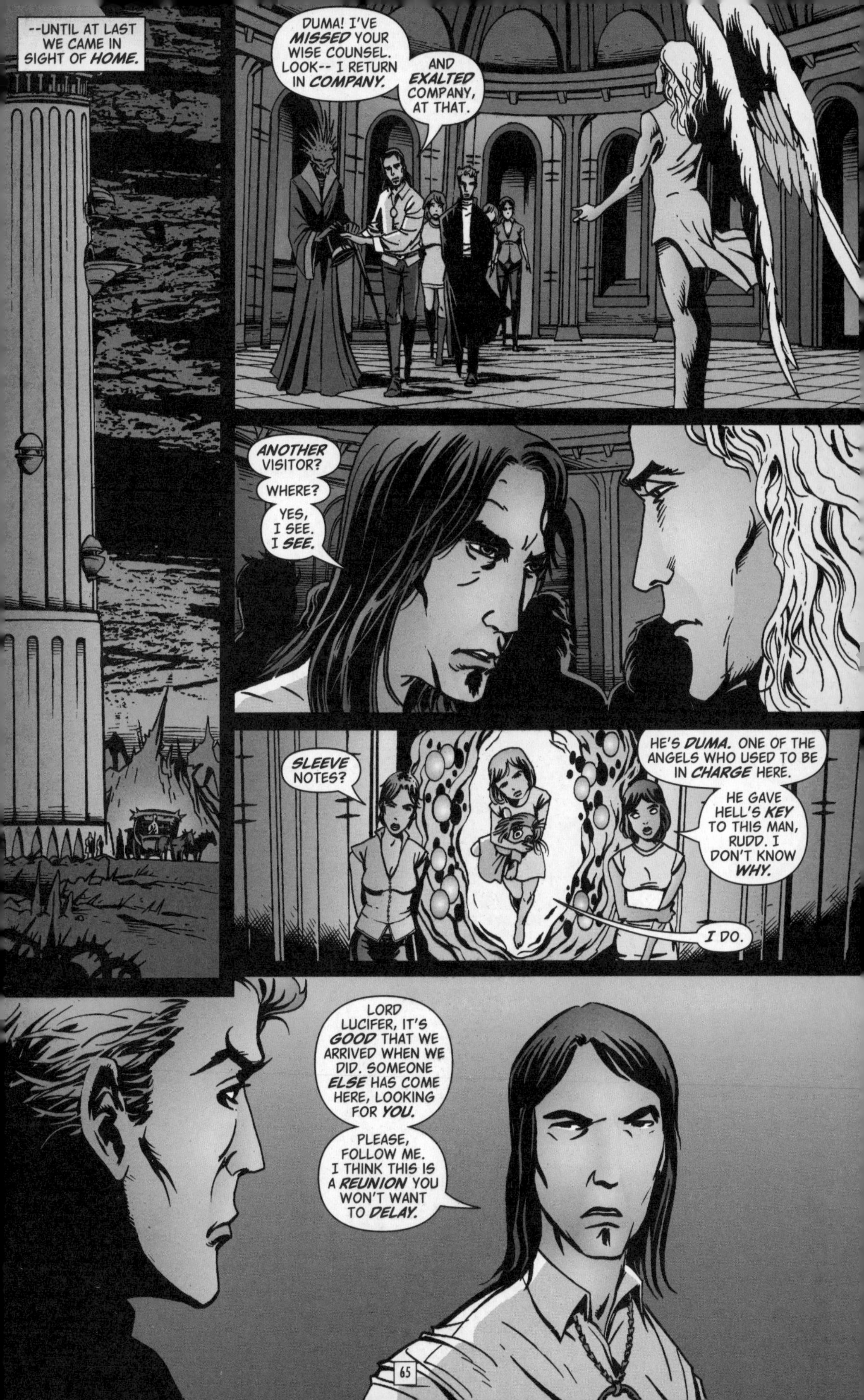
--UNTIL AT LAST WE CAME IN SIGHT OF HOME.
DUMA! I'VE MISSED YOUR WISE COUNSEL. LOOK-- I RETURN IN COMPANY.
AND EXALTED COMPANY, AT THAT.
ANOTHER VISITOR?
WHERE?
YES, I SEE. I SEE.
SLEEVE NOTES?
HE'S DUMA. ONE OF THE ANGELS WHO USED TO BE IN CHARGE HERE.
HE GAVE HELL'S KEY TO THIS MAN, RUDD. I DON'T KNOW WHY.
I DO.
LORD LUCIFER, IT'S GOOD THAT WE ARRIVED WHEN WE DID. SOMEONE ELSE HAS COME HERE, LOOKING FOR YOU.
PLEASE, FOLLOW ME. I THINK THIS IS A REUNION YOU WON'T WANT TO DELAY.

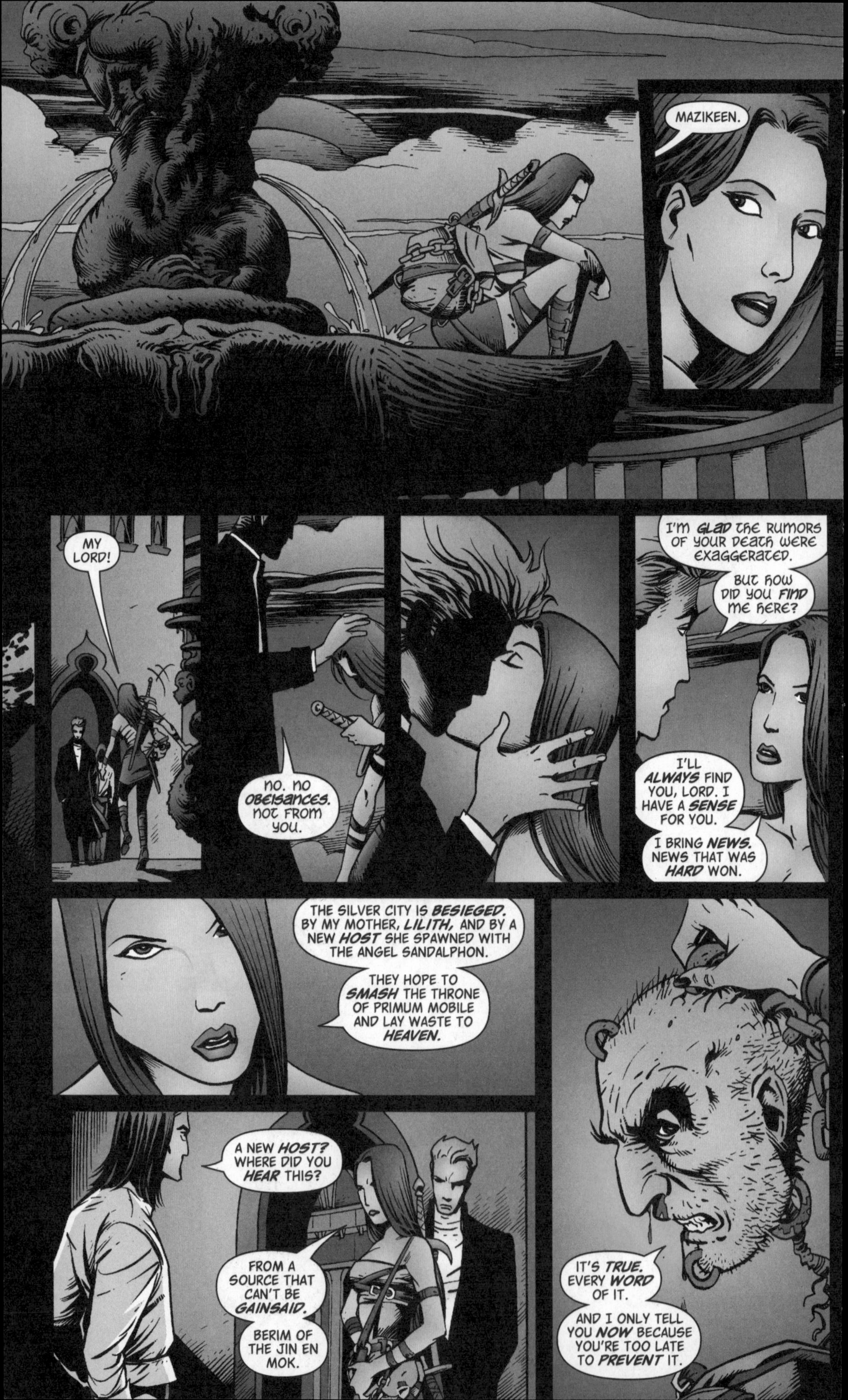
MAZIKEEN.
MY LORD!
NO. NO OBEISANCES. NOT FROM YOU.
I'M GLAD THE RUMORS OF YOUR DEATH WERE EXAGGERATED.
BUT HOW DID YOU FIND ME HERE?
I'LL ALWAYS FIND YOU, LORD. I HAVE A SENSE FOR YOU.
I BRING NEWS. NEWS THAT WAS HARD WON.
THE SILVER CITY IS BESIEGED. BY MY MOTHER, LILITH, AND BY A NEW HOST SHE SPAWNED WITH THE ANGEL SANDALPHON.
THEY HOPE TO SMASH THE THRONE OF PRIMUM MOBILE AND LAY WASTE TO HEAVEN.
A NEW HOST? WHERE DID YOU HEAR THIS?
FROM A SOURCE THAT CAN'T BE GAINSAID.
BERIM OF THE JIN EN MOK.
IT'S TRUE. EVERY WORD OF IT.
AND I ONLY TELL YOU NOW BECAUSE YOU'RE TOO LATE TO PREVENT IT.

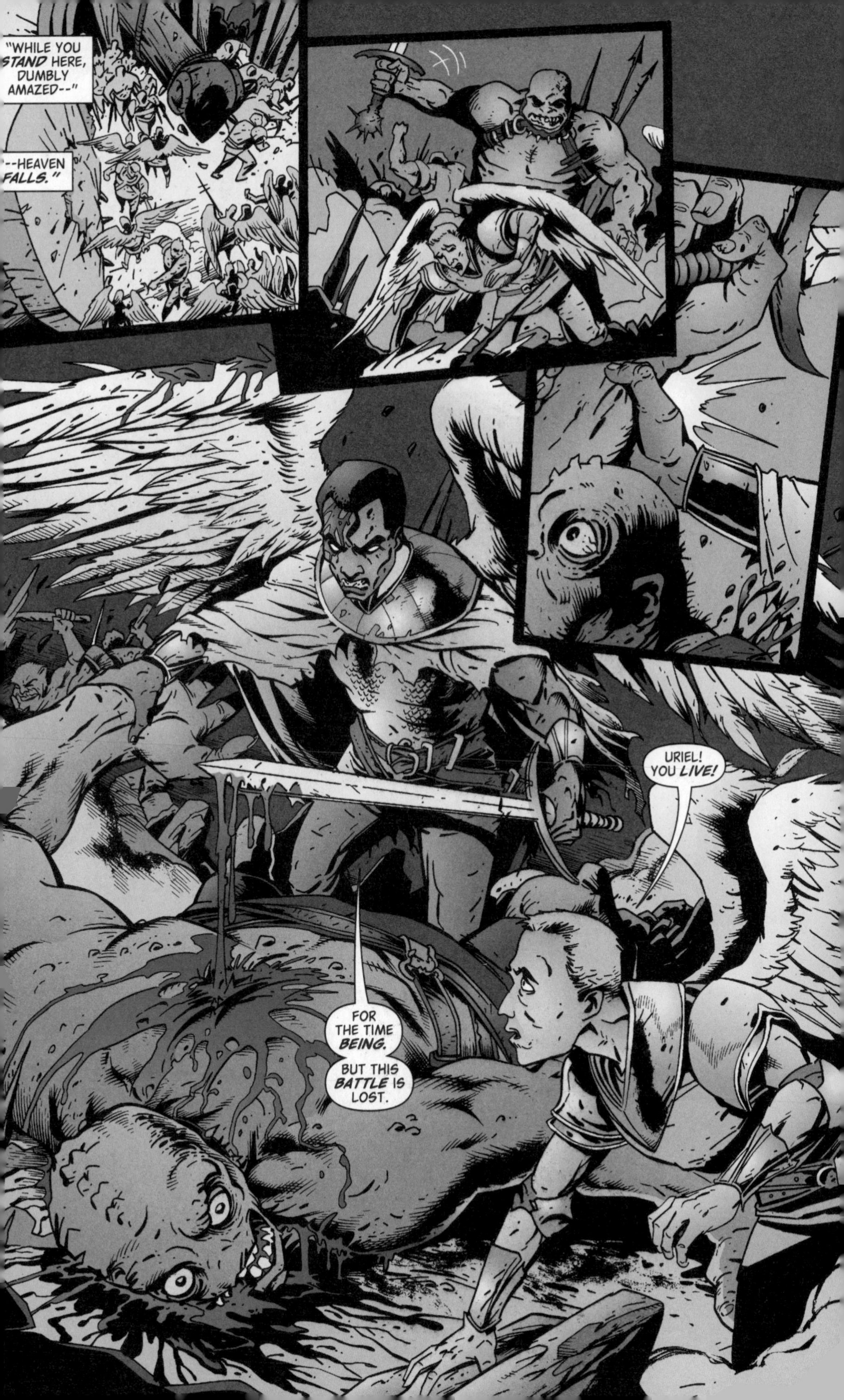
"WHILE YOU STAND HERE, DUMBLY AMAZED--"
--HEAVEN FALLS."
URIEL! YOU LIVE!
FOR THE TIME BEING.
BUT THIS BATTLE IS LOST.

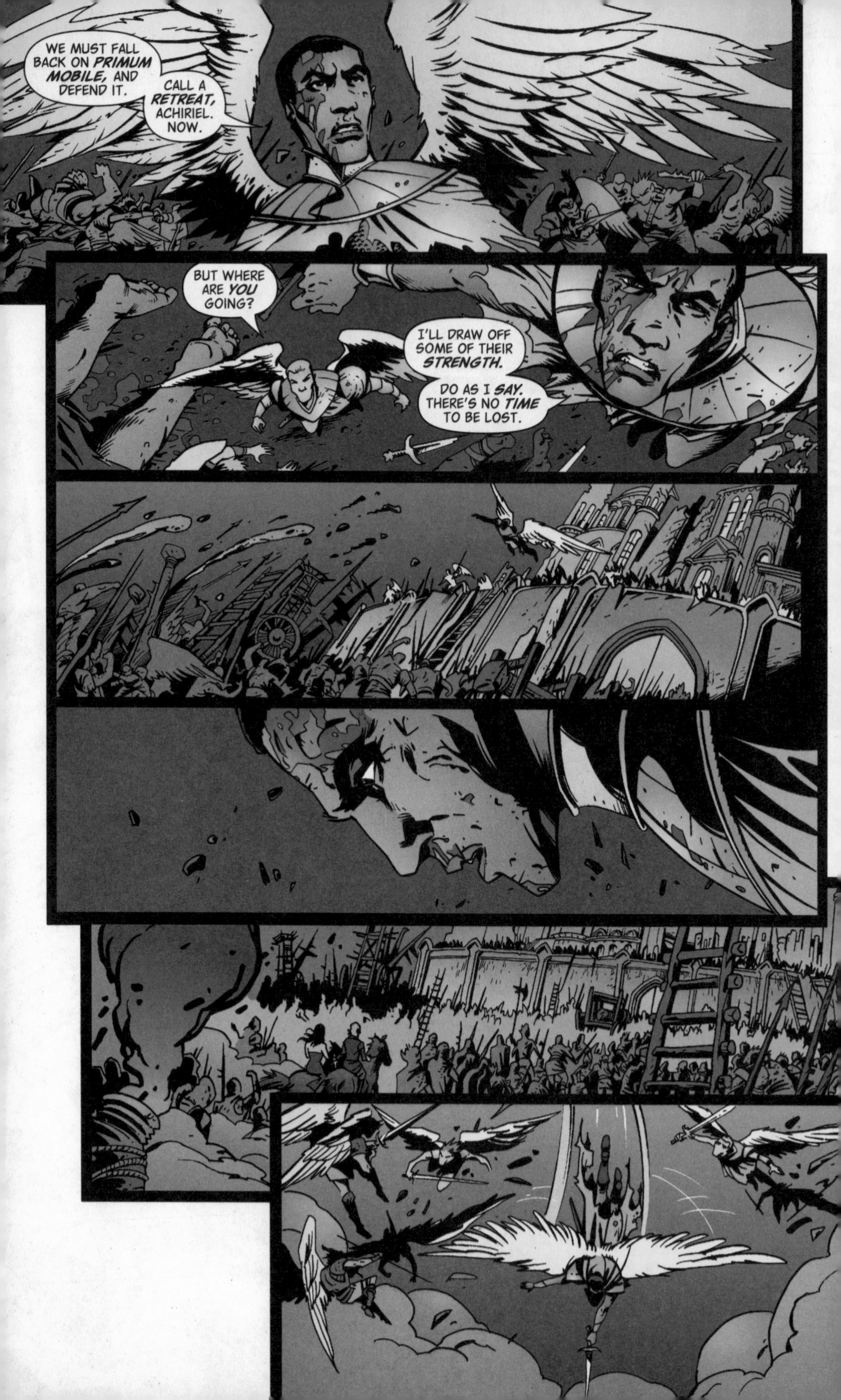
WE MUST FALL BACK ON PRIMUM MOBILE, AND DEFEND IT.
CALL A RETREAT, ACHIRIEL. NOW.
BUT WHERE ARE YOU GOING?
I'LL DRAW OFF SOME OF THEIR STRENGTH.
DO AS I SAY. THERE'S NO TIME TO BE LOST.

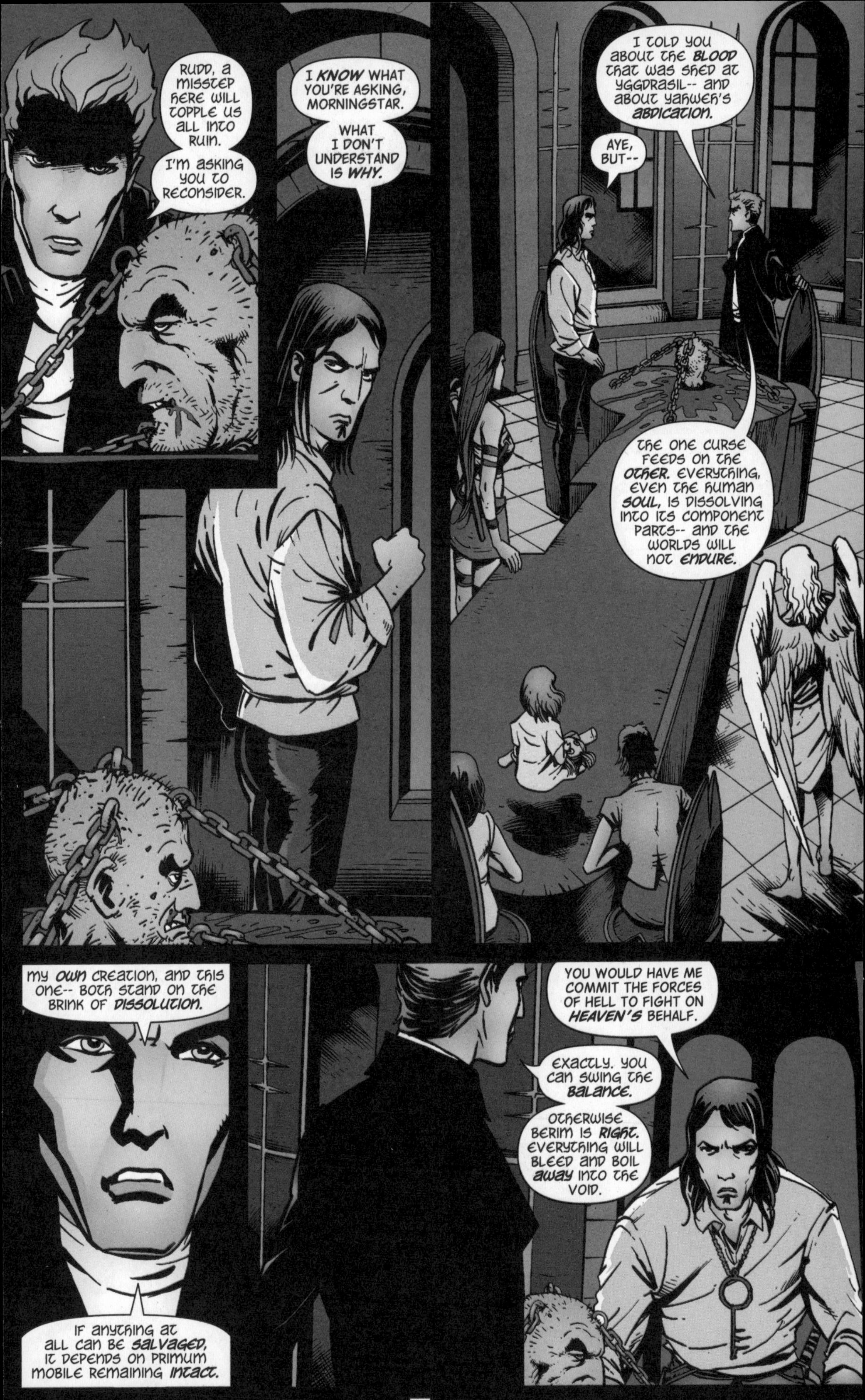

RUDD, A MISSTEP HERE WILL TOPPLE US ALL INTO RUIN.
I'M ASKING YOU TO RECONSIDER.
I KNOW WHAT YOU'RE ASKING, MORNINGSTAR.
WHAT I DON'T UNDERSTAND IS WHY.
I TOLD YOU ABOUT THE BLOOD THAT WAS SHED AT YGGDRASIL-- AND ABOUT YAHWEH'S ABDICATION.
AYE, BUT--
THE ONE CURSE FEEDS ON THE OTHER. EVERYTHING, EVEN THE HUMAN SOUL, IS DISSOLVING INTO ITS COMPONENT PARTS-- AND THE WORLDS WILL NOT ENDURE.
MY OWN CREATION, AND THIS ONE-- BOTH STAND ON THE BRINK OF DISSOLUTION.
IF ANYTHING AT ALL CAN BE SALVAGED, IT DEPENDS ON PRIMUM MOBILE REMAINING INTACT.
YOU WOULD HAVE ME COMMIT THE FORCES OF HELL TO FIGHT ON HEAVEN'S BEHALF.
EXACTLY. YOU CAN SWING THE BALANCE.
OTHERWISE BERIM IS RIGHT. EVERYTHING WILL BLEED AND BOIL AWAY INTO THE VOID.

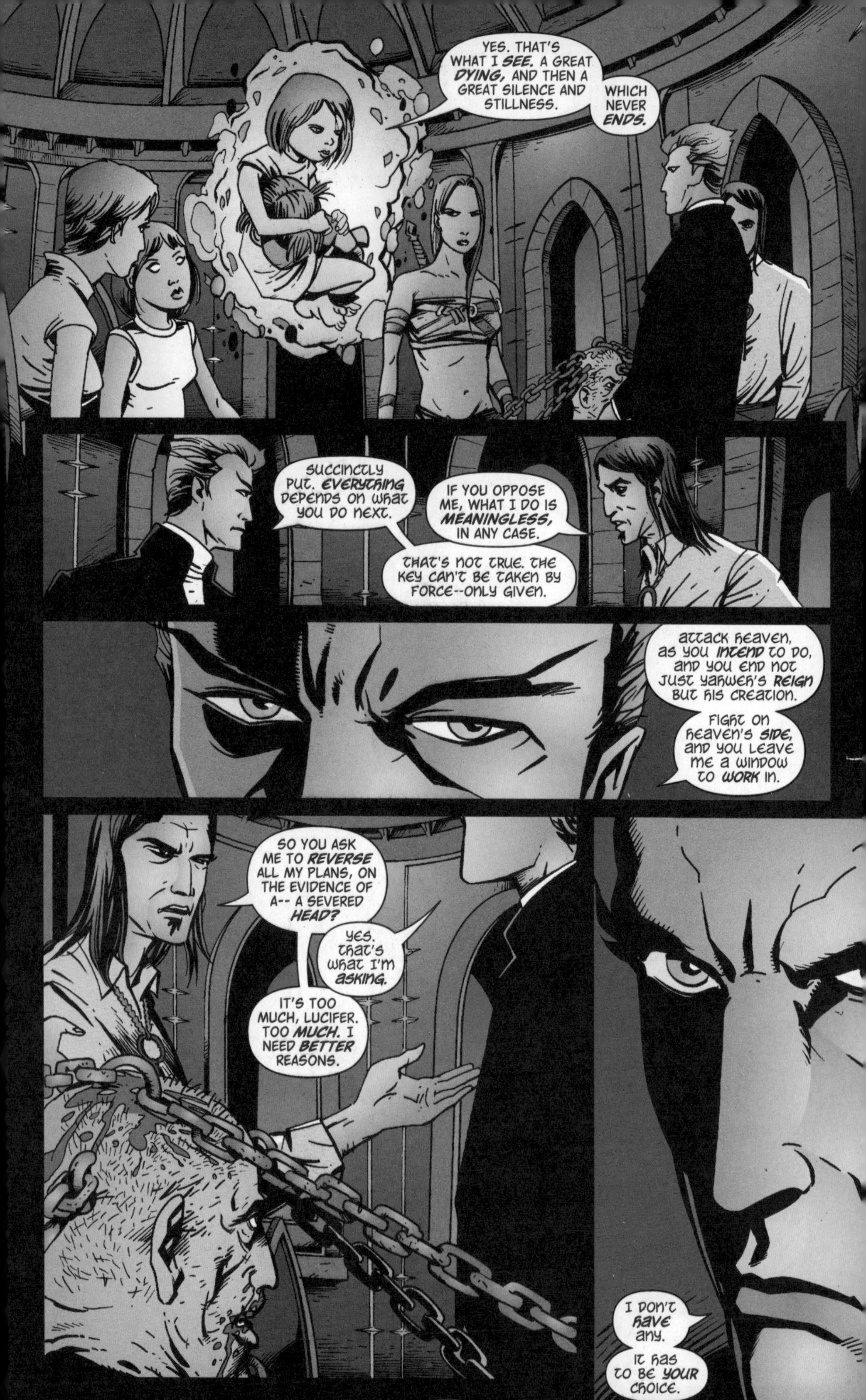
YES. THAT'S WHAT I SEE. A GREAT DYING, AND THEN A GREAT SILENCE AND STILLNESS.
WHICH NEVER ENDS.
SUCCINCTLY PUT. EVERYTHING DEPENDS ON WHAT YOU DO NEXT.
IF YOU OPPOSE ME, WHAT I DO IS MEANINGLESS, IN ANY CASE.
THAT'S NOT TRUE. THE KEY CAN'T BE TAKEN BY FORCE--ONLY GIVEN.
ATTACK HEAVEN, AS YOU INTEND TO DO, AND YOU END NOT JUST YAHWEH'S REIGN BUT HIS CREATION.
FIGHT ON HEAVEN'S SIDE, AND YOU LEAVE ME A WINDOW TO WORK IN.
SO YOU ASK ME TO REVERSE ALL MY PLANS, ON THE EVIDENCE OF A-- A SEVERED HEAD?
YES. THAT'S WHAT I'M ASKING.
IT'S TOO MUCH, LUCIFER. TOO MUCH. I NEED BETTER REASONS.
I DON'T HAVE ANY.
IT HAS TO BE YOUR CHOICE.

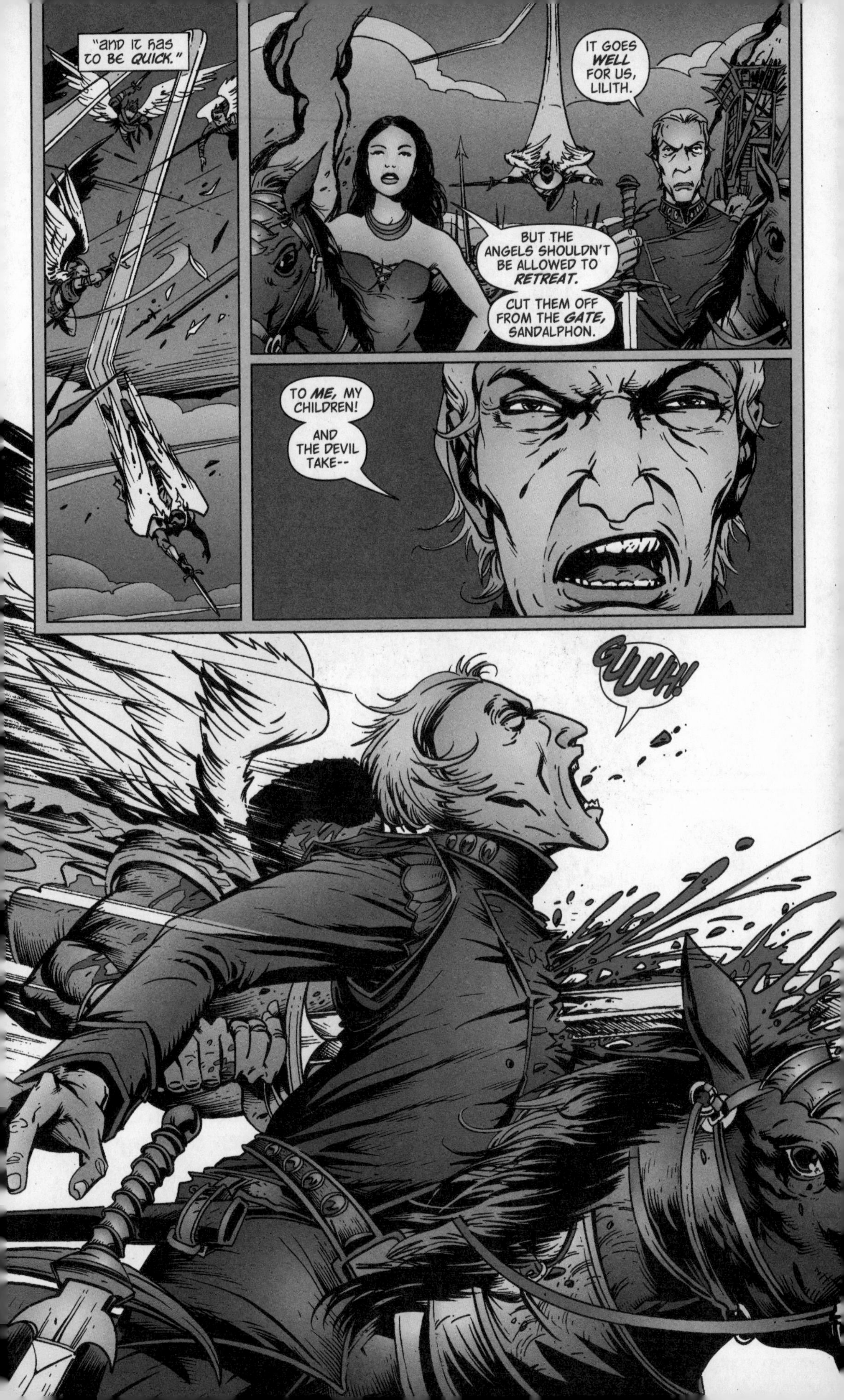
"and it has to be QUICK."
IT GOES WELL FOR US, LILITH.
BUT THE ANGELS SHOULDN'T BE ALLOWED TO RETREAT.
CUT THEM OFF FROM THE GATE, SANDALPHON.
TO ME, MY CHILDREN!
AND THE DEVIL TAKE--
GUUUH!

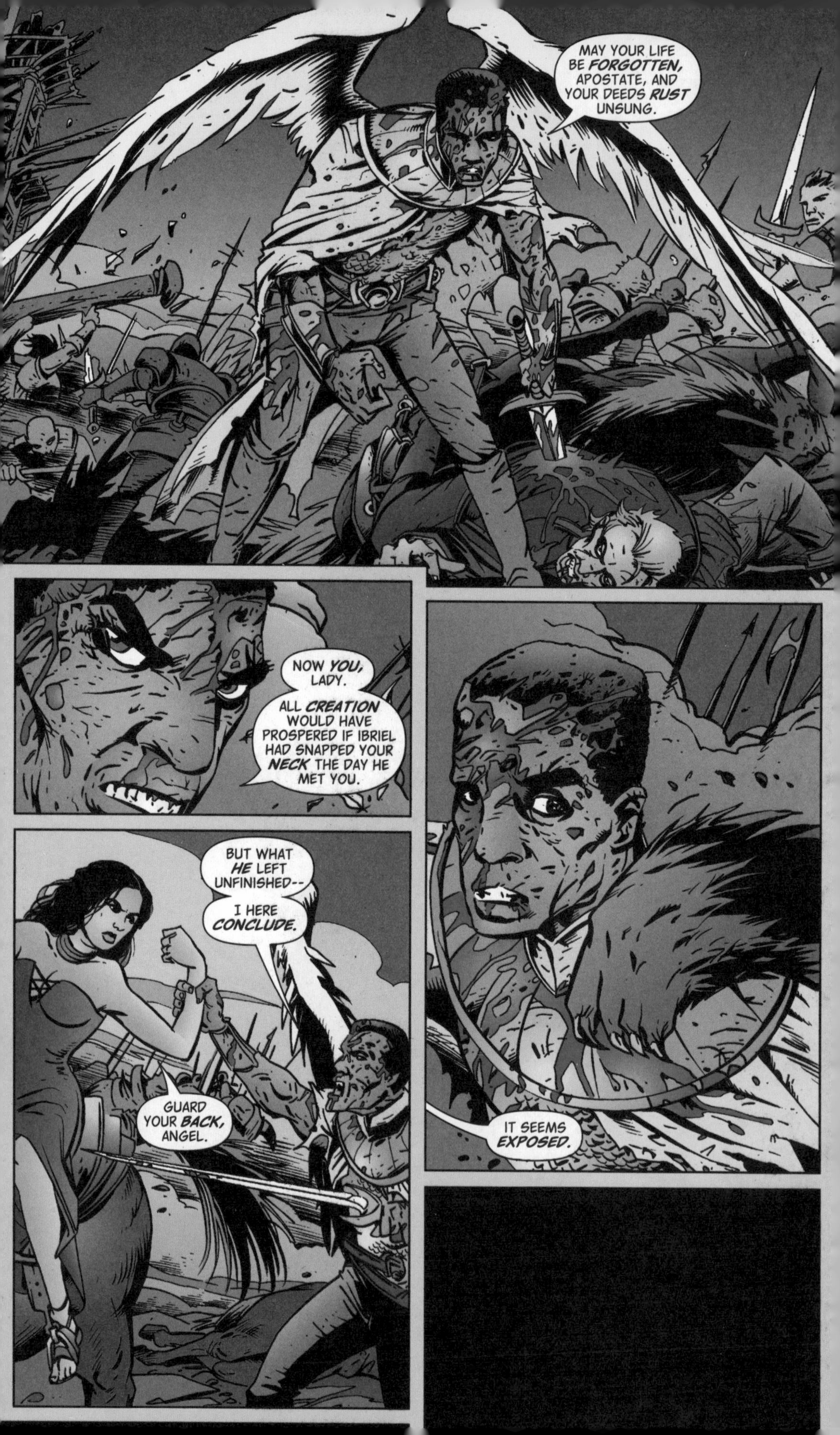
MAY YOUR LIFE BE FORGOTTEN, APOSTATE, AND YOUR DEEDS RUST UNSUNG.
NOW YOU, LADY.
ALL CREATION WOULD HAVE PROSPERED IF IBRIEL HAD SNAPPED YOUR NECK THE DAY HE MET YOU.
BUT WHAT HE LEFT UNFINISHED--
I HERE CONCLUDE.
GUARD YOUR BACK, ANGEL.
IT SEEMS EXPOSED.

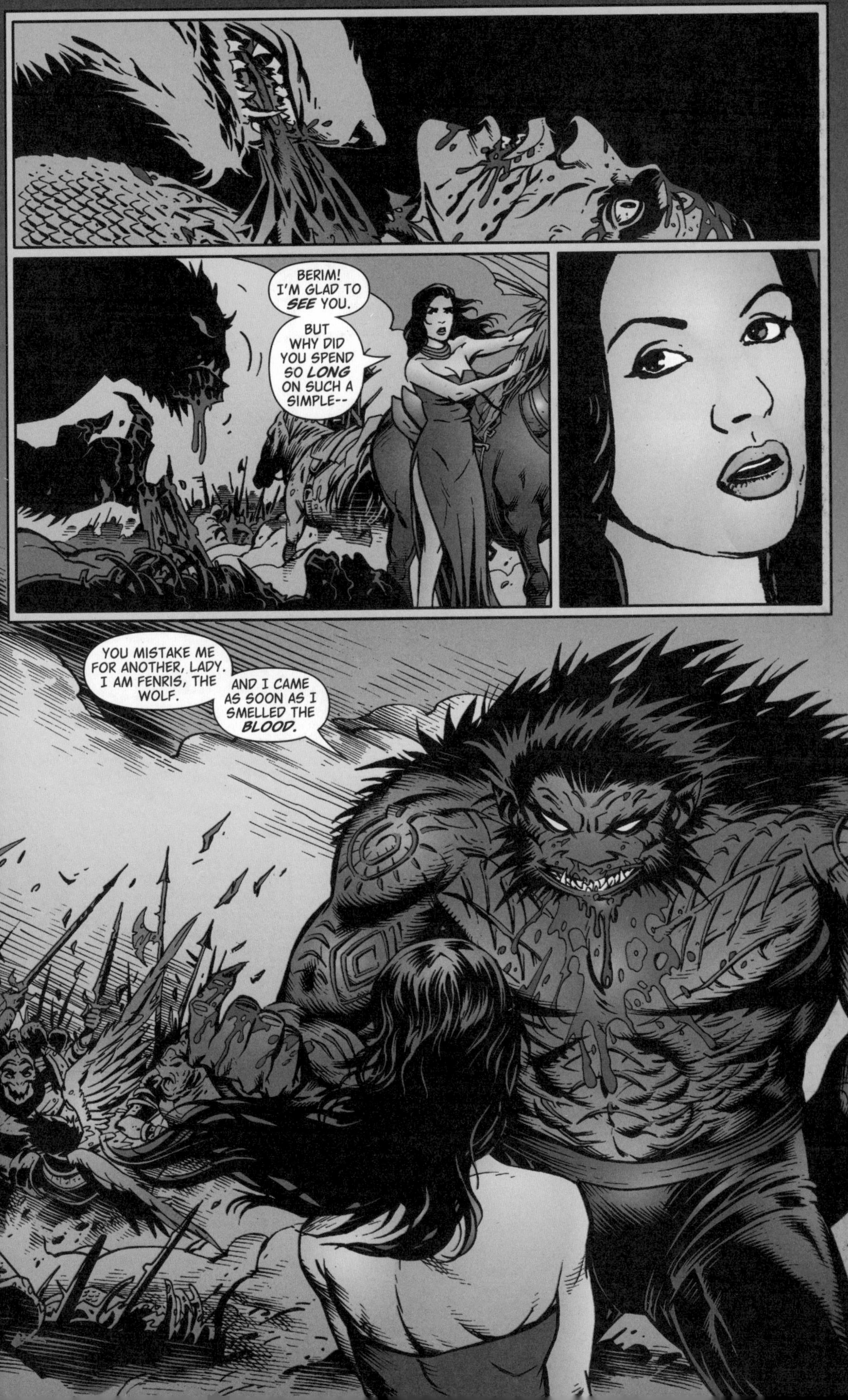
BERIM! I'M GLAD TO SEE YOU.
BUT WHY DID YOU SPEND SO LONG ON SUCH A SIMPLE--
YOU MISTAKE ME FOR ANOTHER, LADY. I AM FENRIS, THE WOLF.
AND I CAME AS SOON AS I SMELLED THE BLOOD.

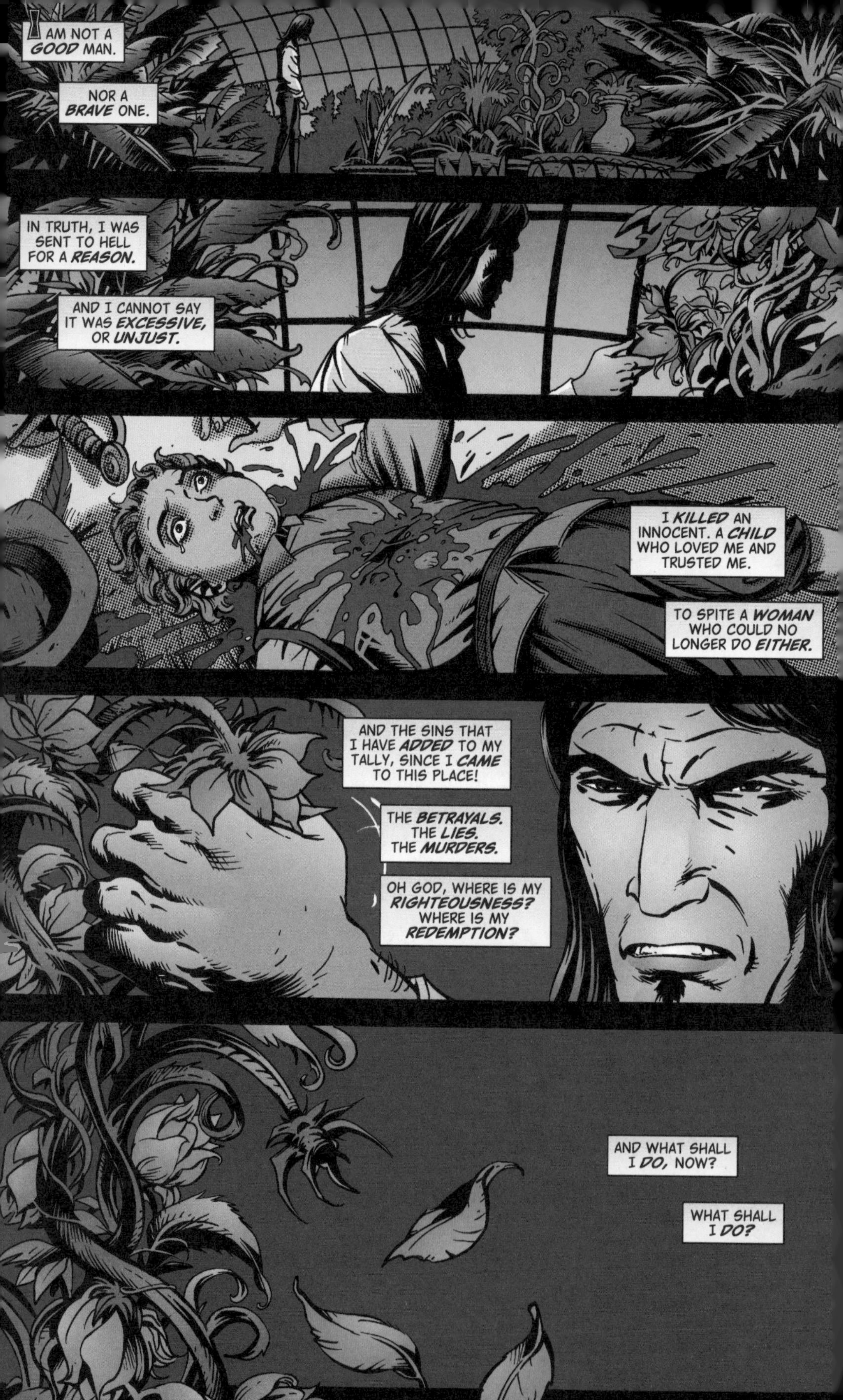
I AM NOT A GOOD MAN.
NOR A BRAVE ONE.
IN TRUTH, I WAS SENT TO HELL FOR A REASON.
AND I CANNOT SAY IT WAS EXCESSIVE, OR UNJUST.
I KILLED AN INNOCENT. A CHILD WHO LOVED ME AND TRUSTED ME.
TO SPITE A WOMAN WHO COULD NO LONGER DO EITHER.
AND THE SINS THAT I HAVE ADDED TO MY TALLY, SINCE I CAME TO THIS PLACE!
THE BETRAYALS. THE LIES. THE MURDERS.
OH GOD, WHERE IS MY RIGHTEOUSNESS? WHERE IS MY REDEMPTION?
AND WHAT SHALL I DO, NOW?
WHAT SHALL I DO?

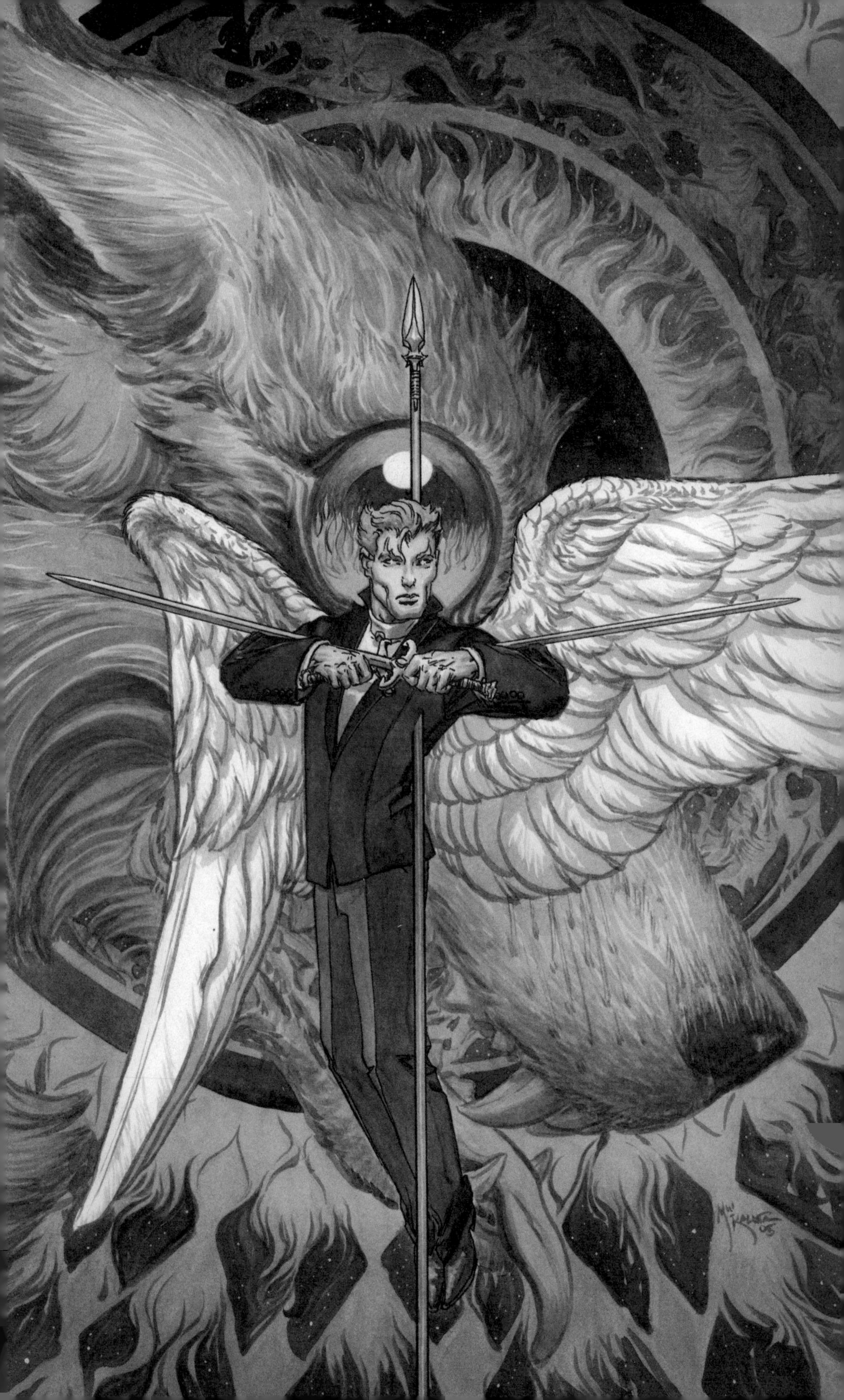

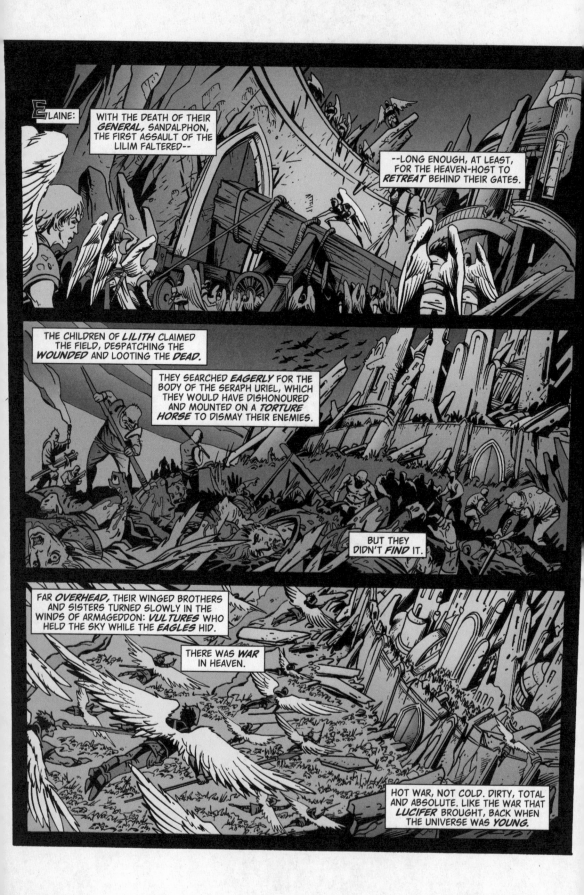

ELAINE: WITH THE DEATH OF THEIR *GENERAL*, SANDALPHON, THE FIRST ASSAULT OF THE LILIM FALTERED--

--LONG ENOUGH, AT LEAST, FOR THE HEAVEN-HOST TO *RETREAT* BEHIND THEIR GATES.

THE CHILDREN OF *LILITH* CLAIMED THE FIELD, DESPATCHING THE *WOUNDED* AND LOOTING THE *DEAD*.

THEY SEARCHED *EAGERLY* FOR THE BODY OF THE SERAPH URIEL, WHICH THEY WOULD HAVE DISHONOURED AND MOUNTED ON A *TORTURE HORSE* TO DISMAY THEIR ENEMIES.

BUT THEY DIDN'T *FIND* IT.

FAR *OVERHEAD,* THEIR WINGED BROTHERS AND SISTERS TURNED SLOWLY IN THE WINDS OF ARMAGEDDON: *VULTURES* WHO HELD THE SKY WHILE THE *EAGLES* HID.

THERE WAS *WAR* IN HEAVEN.

HOT WAR, NOT COLD. DIRTY, TOTAL AND ABSOLUTE. LIKE THE WAR THAT *LUCIFER* BROUGHT, BACK WHEN THE UNIVERSE WAS *YOUNG.*

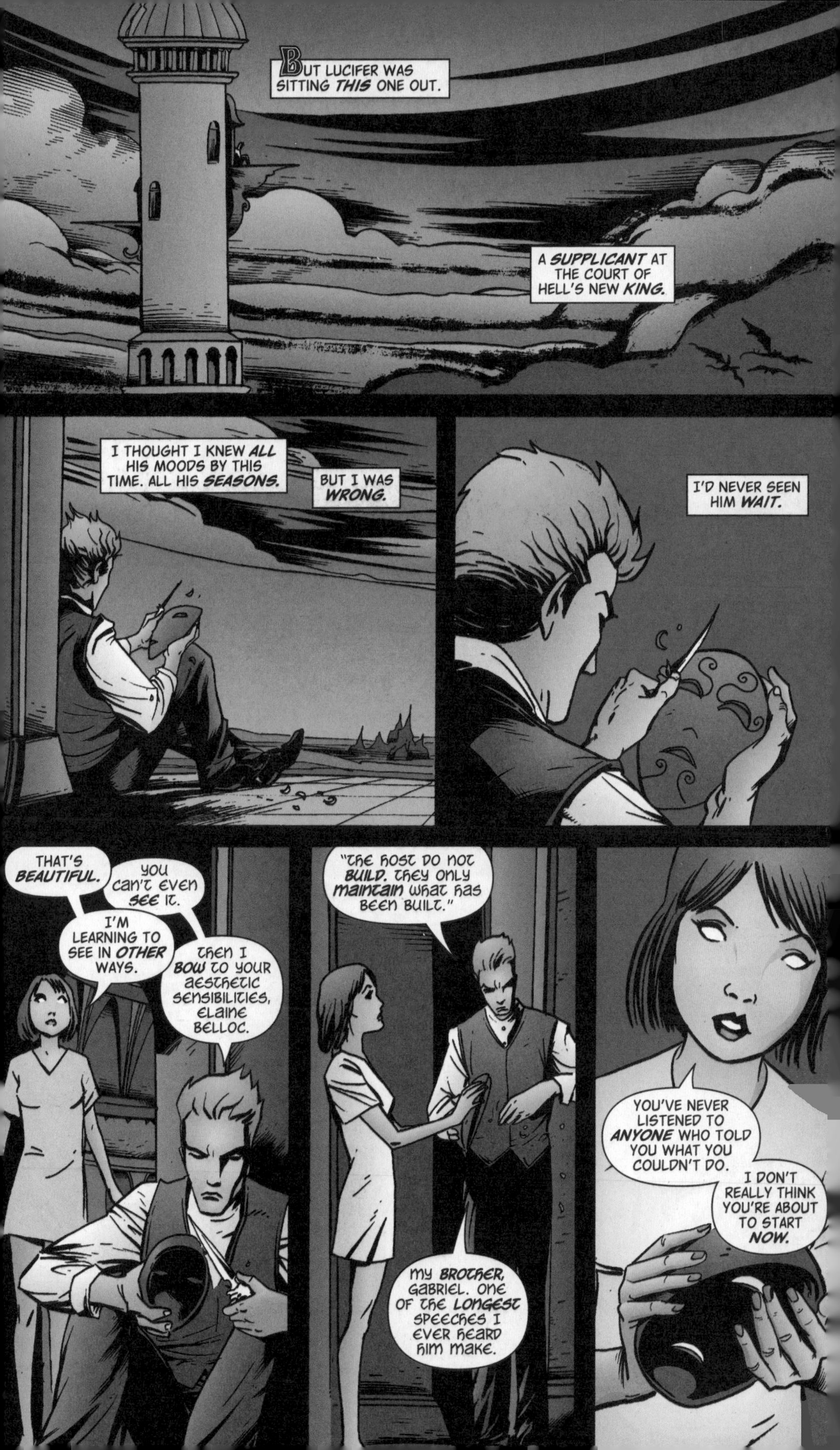

BUT LUCIFER WAS SITTING THIS ONE OUT.
A SUPPLICANT AT THE COURT OF HELL'S NEW KING.
I THOUGHT I KNEW ALL HIS MOODS BY THIS TIME. ALL HIS SEASONS.
BUT I WAS WRONG.
I'D NEVER SEEN HIM WAIT.
THAT'S BEAUTIFUL.
YOU CAN'T EVEN SEE IT.
I'M LEARNING TO SEE IN OTHER WAYS.
THEN I BOW TO YOUR AESTHETIC SENSIBILITIES, ELAINE BELLOC.
"THE HOST DO NOT BUILD. THEY ONLY MAINTAIN WHAT HAS BEEN BUILT."
MY BROTHER, GABRIEL. ONE OF THE LONGEST SPEECHES I EVER HEARD HIM MAKE.
YOU'VE NEVER LISTENED TO ANYONE WHO TOLD YOU WHAT YOU COULDN'T DO.
I DON'T REALLY THINK YOU'RE ABOUT TO START NOW.

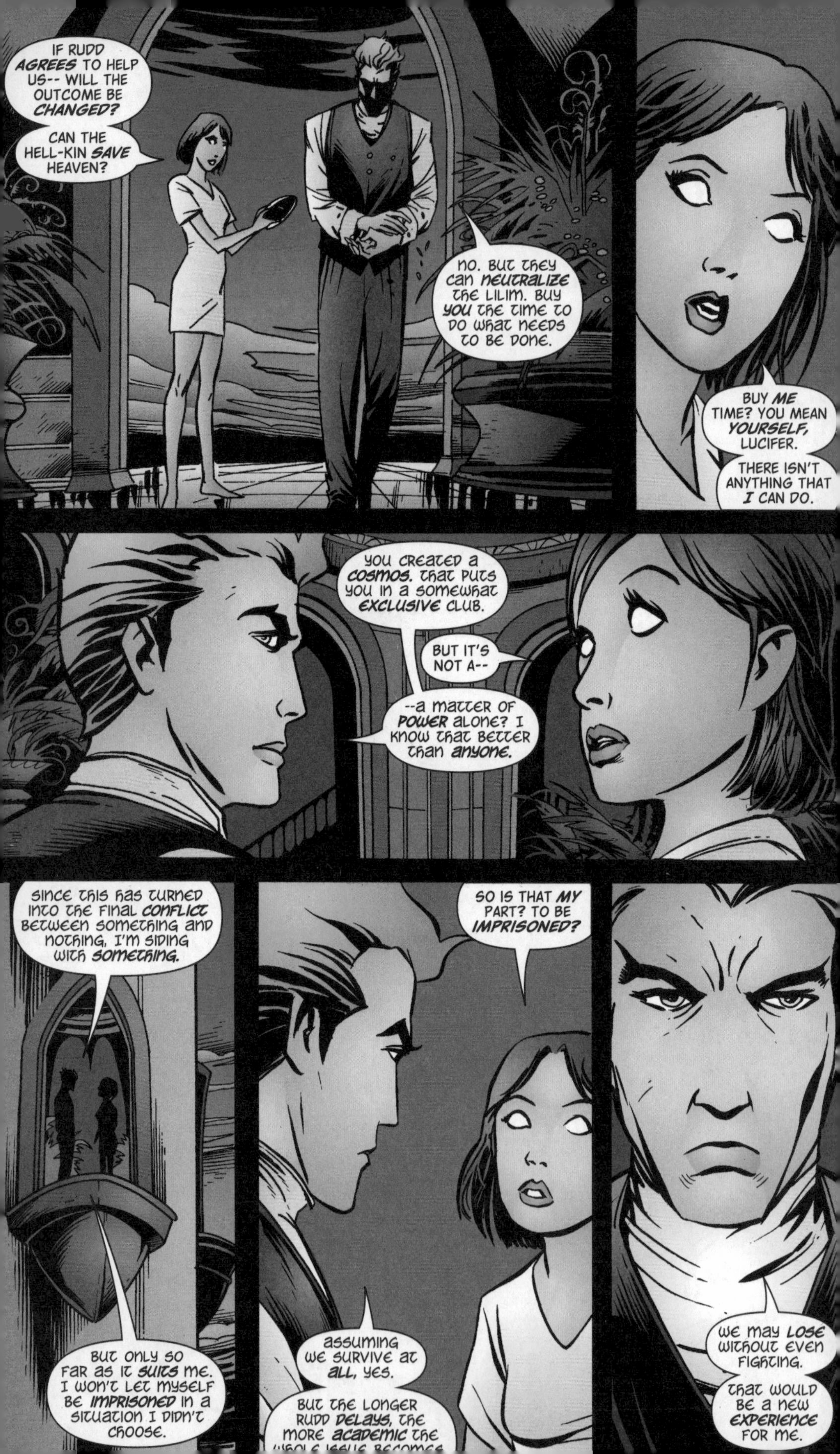
IF RUDD AGREES TO HELP US-- WILL THE OUTCOME BE CHANGED?
CAN THE HELL-KIN SAVE HEAVEN?
NO. BUT THEY CAN NEUTRALIZE THE LILIM. BUY YOU THE TIME TO DO WHAT NEEDS TO BE DONE.
BUY ME TIME? YOU MEAN YOURSELF, LUCIFER.
THERE ISN'T ANYTHING THAT I CAN DO.
YOU CREATED A COSMOS. THAT PUTS YOU IN A SOMEWHAT EXCLUSIVE CLUB.
BUT IT'S NOT A--
--A MATTER OF POWER ALONE? I KNOW THAT BETTER THAN ANYONE.
SINCE THIS HAS TURNED INTO THE FINAL CONFLICT BETWEEN SOMETHING AND NOTHING, I'M SIDING WITH SOMETHING.
BUT ONLY SO FAR AS IT SUITS ME. I WON'T LET MYSELF BE IMPRISONED IN A SITUATION I DIDN'T CHOOSE.
SO IS THAT MY PART? TO BE IMPRISONED?
ASSUMING WE SURVIVE AT ALL, YES.
BUT THE LONGER RUDD DELAYS, THE MORE ACADEMIC THE
WE MAY LOSE WITHOUT EVEN FIGHTING.
THAT WOULD BE A NEW EXPERIENCE FOR ME.

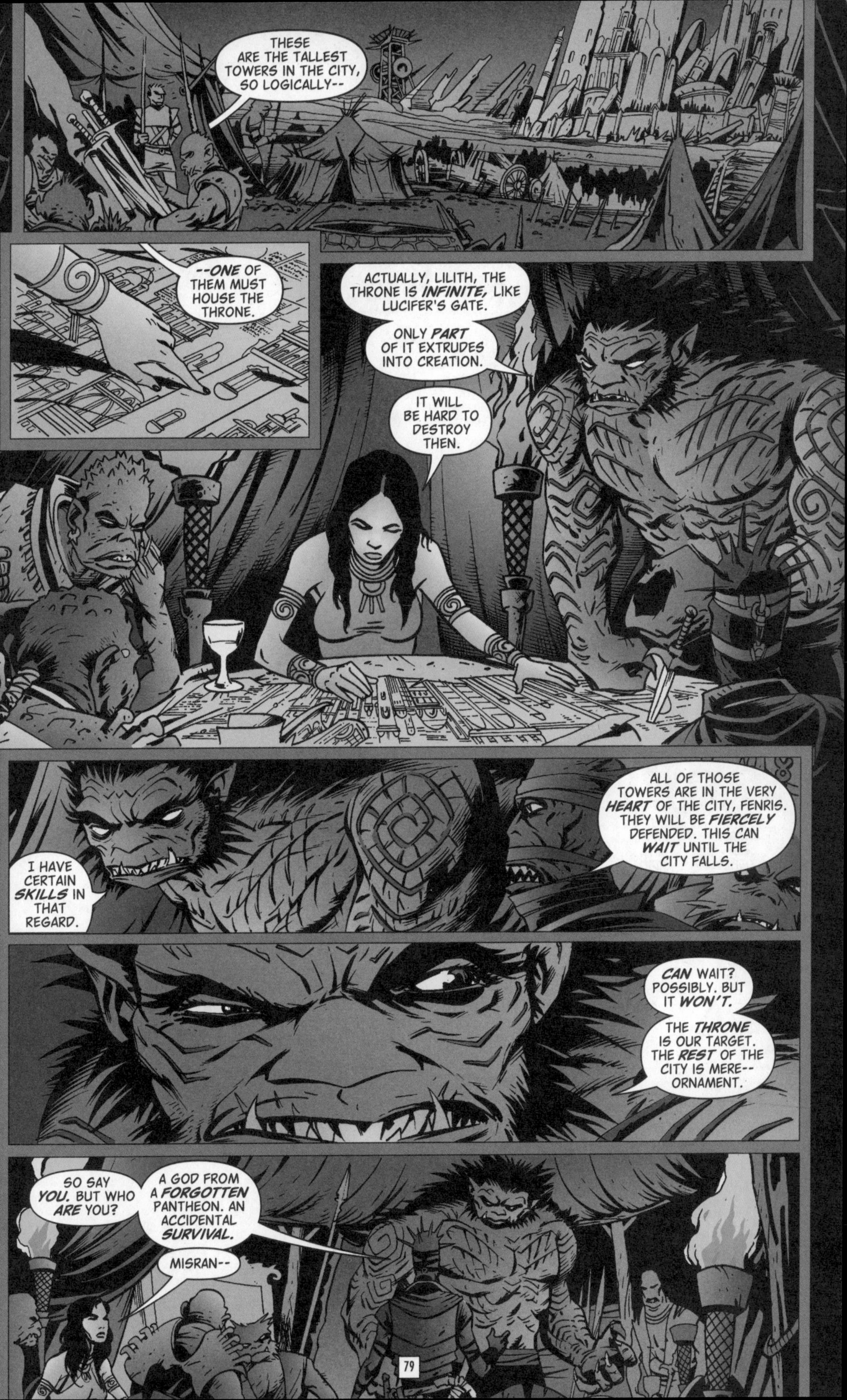
THESE ARE THE TALLEST TOWERS IN THE CITY, SO LOGICALLY--
--ONE OF THEM MUST HOUSE THE THRONE.
ACTUALLY, LILITH, THE THRONE IS INFINITE, LIKE LUCIFER'S GATE.
ONLY PART OF IT EXTRUDES INTO CREATION.
IT WILL BE HARD TO DESTROY THEN.
I HAVE CERTAIN SKILLS IN THAT REGARD.
ALL OF THOSE TOWERS ARE IN THE VERY HEART OF THE CITY, FENRIS. THEY WILL BE FIERCELY DEFENDED. THIS CAN WAIT UNTIL THE CITY FALLS.
CAN WAIT? POSSIBLY. BUT IT WON'T.
THE THRONE IS OUR TARGET. THE REST OF THE CITY IS MERE-- ORNAMENT.
SO SAY YOU. BUT WHO ARE YOU?
A GOD FROM A FORGOTTEN PANTHEON. AN ACCIDENTAL SURVIVAL.
MISRAN--

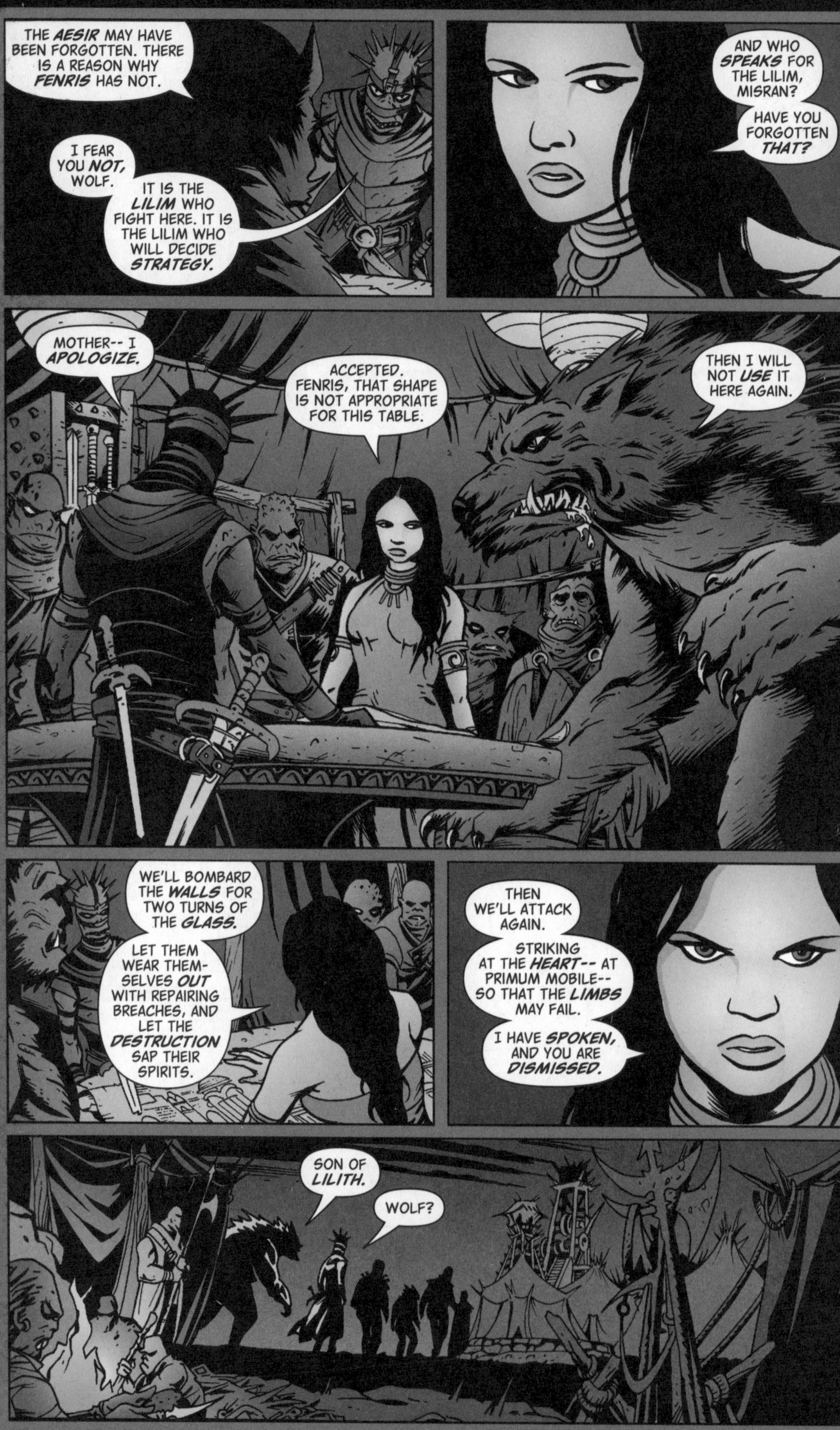
THE AESIR MAY HAVE BEEN FORGOTTEN. THERE IS A REASON WHY FENRIS HAS NOT.
I FEAR YOU NOT, WOLF.
IT IS THE LILIM WHO FIGHT HERE. IT IS THE LILIM WHO WILL DECIDE STRATEGY.
AND WHO SPEAKS FOR THE LILIM, MISRAN?
HAVE YOU FORGOTTEN THAT?
MOTHER-- I APOLOGIZE.
ACCEPTED. FENRIS, THAT SHAPE IS NOT APPROPRIATE FOR THIS TABLE.
THEN I WILL NOT USE IT HERE AGAIN.
WE'LL BOMBARD THE WALLS FOR TWO TURNS OF THE GLASS.
LET THEM WEAR THEMSELVES OUT WITH REPAIRING BREACHES, AND LET THE DESTRUCTION SAP THEIR SPIRITS.
THEN WE'LL ATTACK AGAIN.
STRIKING AT THE HEART-- AT PRIMUM MOBILE-- SO THAT THE LIMBS MAY FAIL.
I HAVE SPOKEN, AND YOU ARE DISMISSED.
SON OF LILITH.
WOLF?

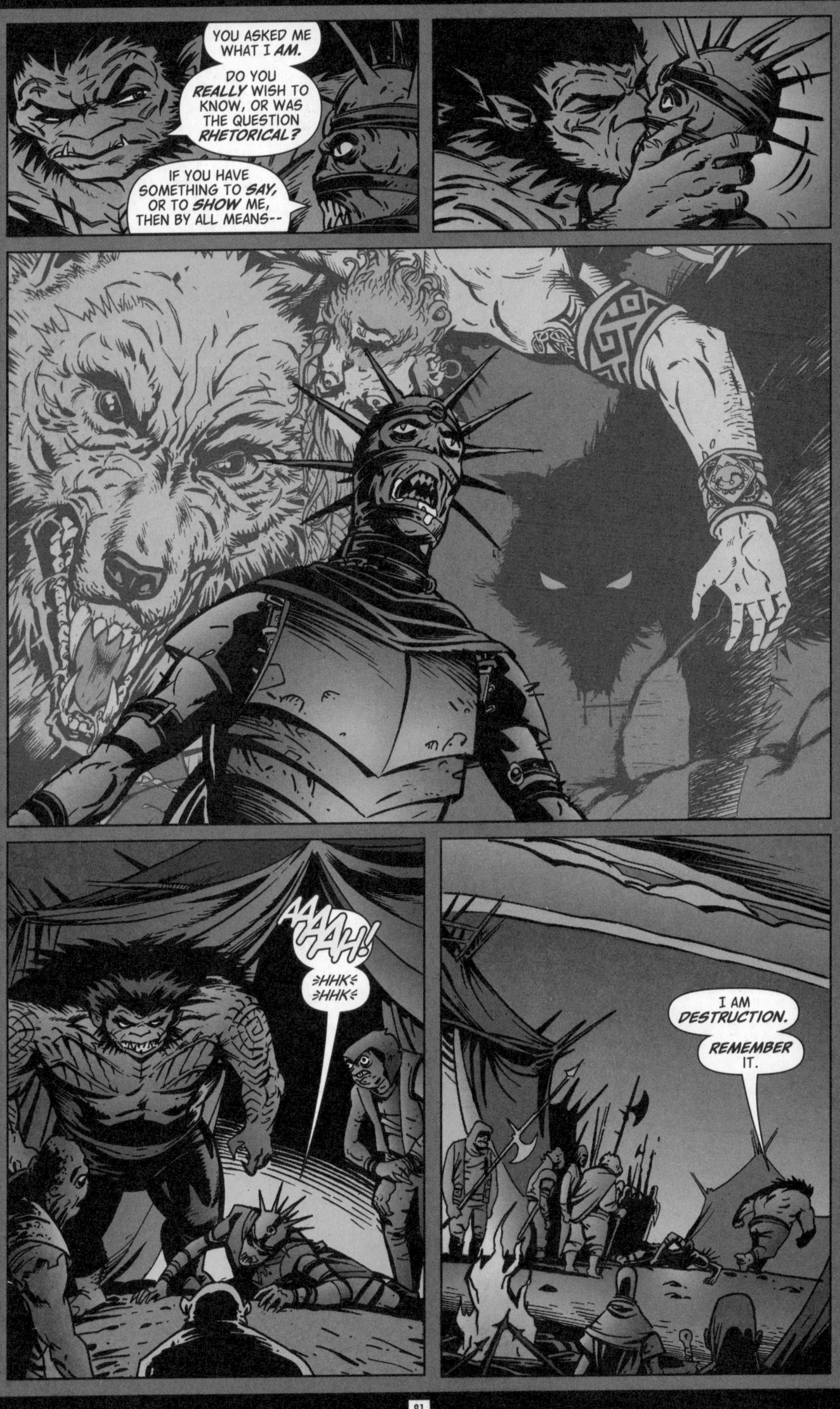
YOU ASKED ME WHAT I AM.
DO YOU REALLY WISH TO KNOW, OR WAS THE QUESTION RHETORICAL?
IF YOU HAVE SOMETHING TO SAY, OR TO SHOW ME, THEN BY ALL MEANS--
AAAAAAH!
HHK HHK
I AM DESTRUCTION.
REMEMBER IT.

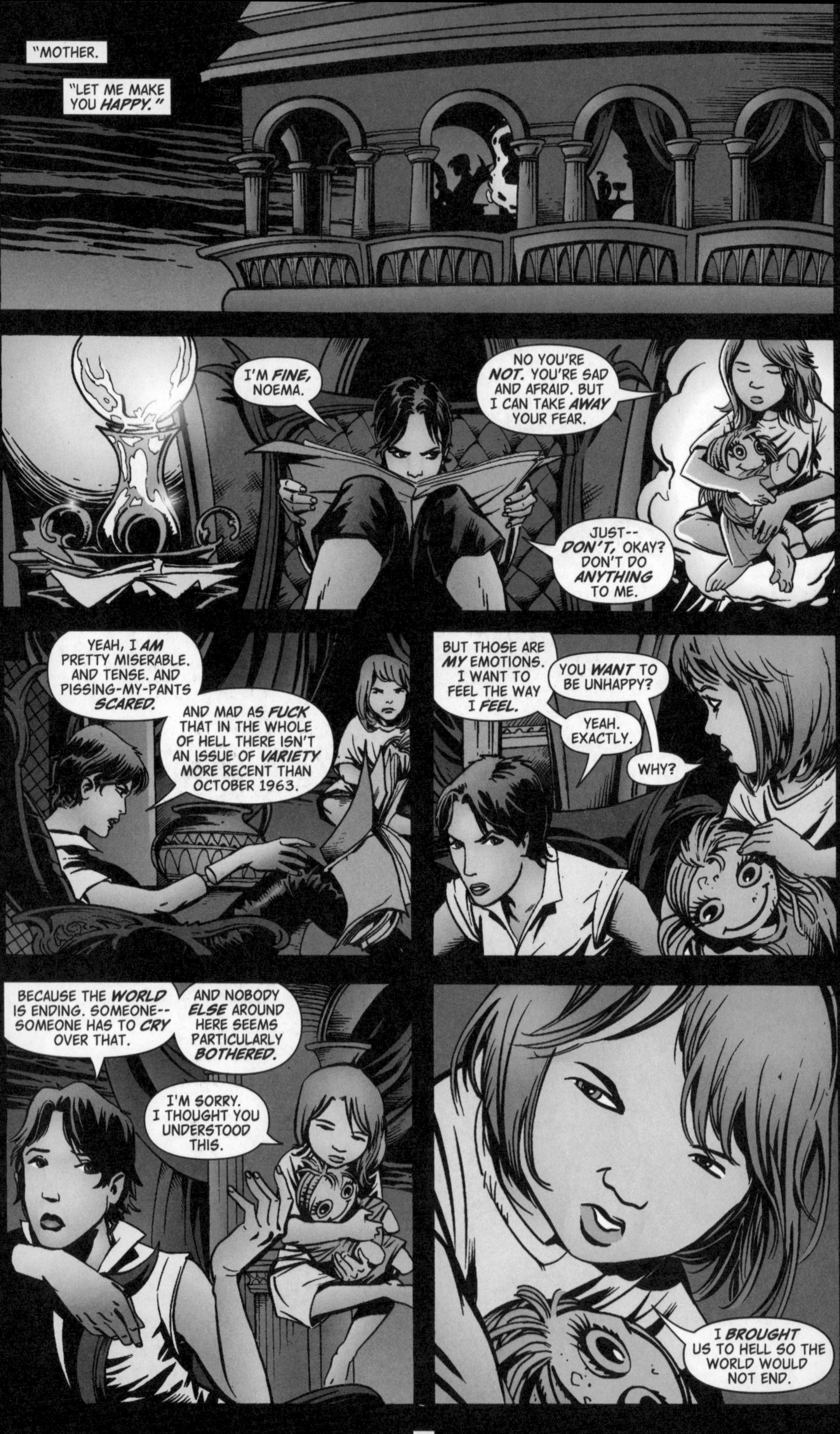
"MOTHER.
"LET ME MAKE YOU HAPPY."
I'M FINE, NOEMA.
NO YOU'RE NOT. YOU'RE SAD AND AFRAID. BUT I CAN TAKE AWAY YOUR FEAR.
JUST-- DON'T, OKAY? DON'T DO ANYTHING TO ME.
YEAH, I AM PRETTY MISERABLE. AND TENSE. AND PISSING-MY-PANTS SCARED.
AND MAD AS FUCK THAT IN THE WHOLE OF HELL THERE ISN'T AN ISSUE OF VARIETY MORE RECENT THAN OCTOBER 1963.
BUT THOSE ARE MY EMOTIONS. I WANT TO FEEL THE WAY I FEEL.
YOU WANT TO BE UNHAPPY?
YEAH. EXACTLY.
WHY?
BECAUSE THE WORLD IS ENDING. SOMEONE-- SOMEONE HAS TO CRY OVER THAT.
AND NOBODY ELSE AROUND HERE SEEMS PARTICULARLY BOTHERED.
I'M SORRY. I THOUGHT YOU UNDERSTOOD THIS.
I BROUGHT US TO HELL SO THE WORLD WOULD NOT END.

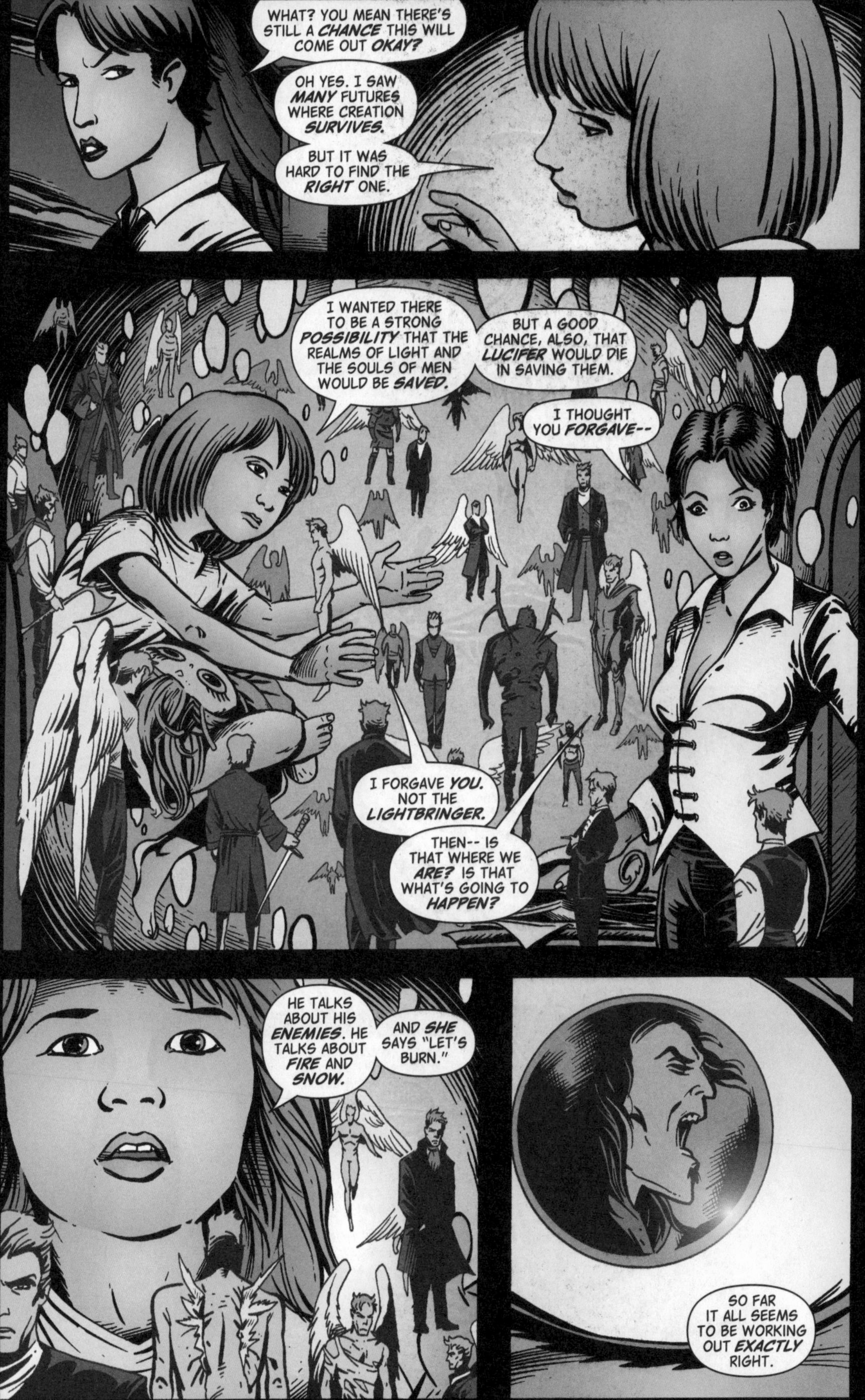
WHAT? YOU MEAN THERE'S STILL A CHANCE THIS WILL COME OUT OKAY?
OH YES. I SAW MANY FUTURES WHERE CREATION SURVIVES.
BUT IT WAS HARD TO FIND THE RIGHT ONE.
I WANTED THERE TO BE A STRONG POSSIBILITY THAT THE REALMS OF LIGHT AND THE SOULS OF MEN WOULD BE SAVED.
BUT A GOOD CHANCE, ALSO, THAT LUCIFER WOULD DIE IN SAVING THEM.
I THOUGHT YOU FORGAVE--
I FORGAVE YOU. NOT THE LIGHTBRINGER.
THEN-- IS THAT WHERE WE ARE? IS THAT WHAT'S GOING TO HAPPEN?
HE TALKS ABOUT HIS ENEMIES. HE TALKS ABOUT FIRE AND SNOW.
AND SHE SAYS "LET'S BURN."
SO FAR IT ALL SEEMS TO BE WORKING OUT EXACTLY RIGHT.

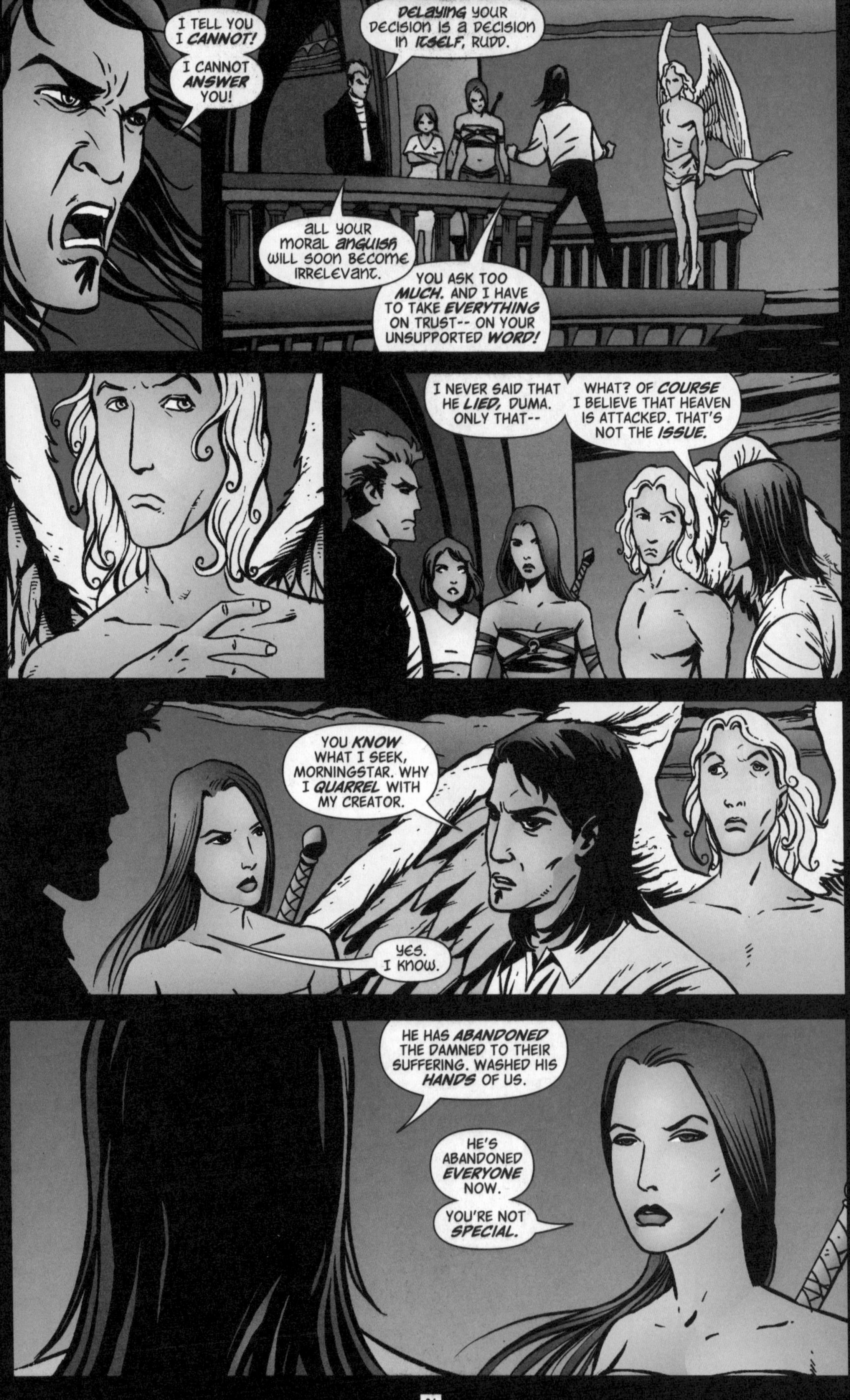
I TELL YOU I CANNOT!
I CANNOT ANSWER YOU!
DELAYING YOUR DECISION IS A DECISION IN ITSELF, RUDD.
ALL YOUR MORAL ANGUISH WILL SOON BECOME IRRELEVANT.
YOU ASK TOO MUCH. AND I HAVE TO TAKE EVERYTHING ON TRUST-- ON YOUR UNSUPPORTED WORD!
I NEVER SAID THAT HE LIED, DUMA. ONLY THAT--
WHAT? OF COURSE I BELIEVE THAT HEAVEN IS ATTACKED. THAT'S NOT THE ISSUE.
YOU KNOW WHAT I SEEK, MORNINGSTAR. WHY I QUARREL WITH MY CREATOR.
YES. I KNOW.
HE HAS ABANDONED THE DAMNED TO THEIR SUFFERING. WASHED HIS HANDS OF US.
HE'S ABANDONED EVERYONE NOW.
YOU'RE NOT SPECIAL.

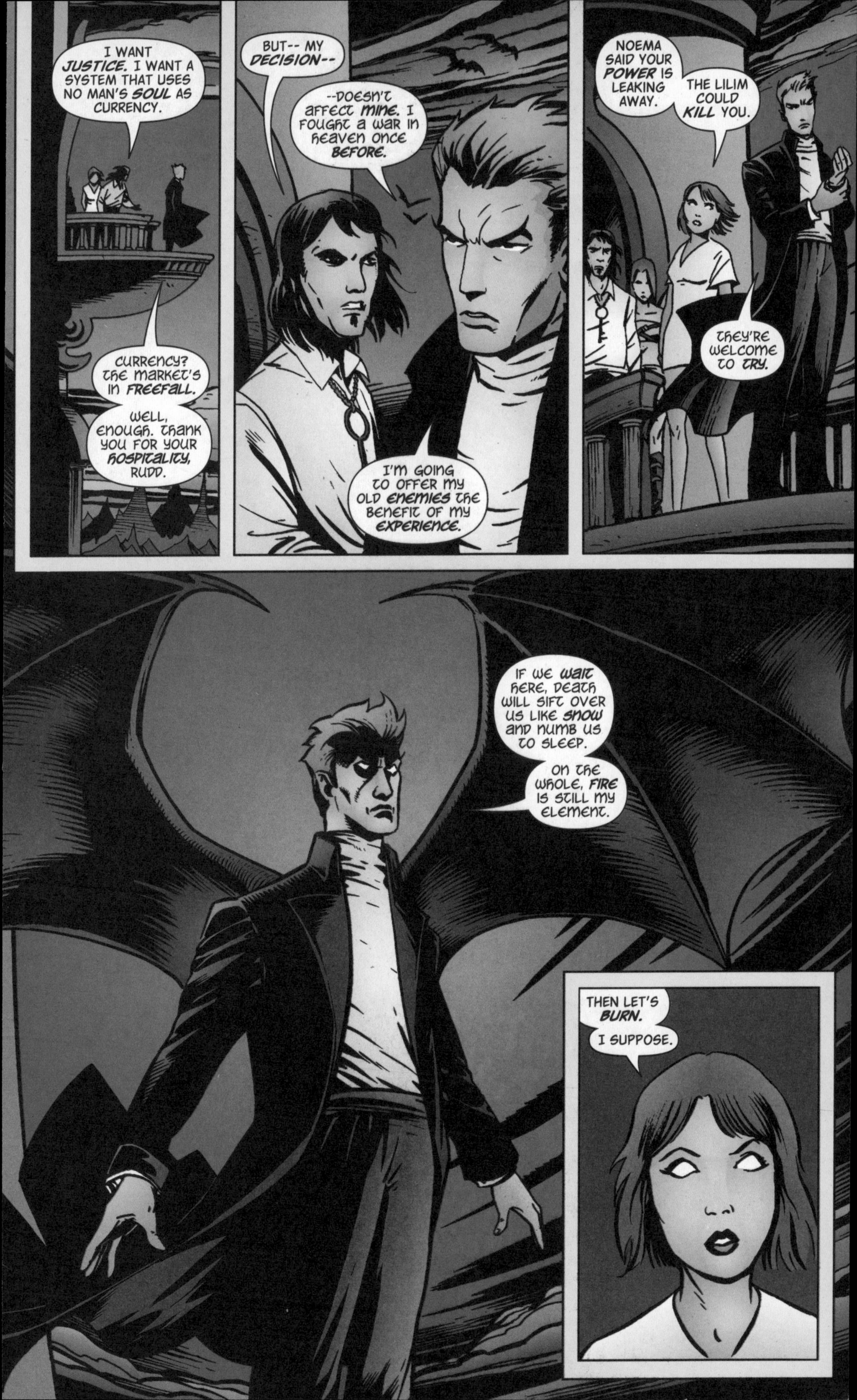

I WANT JUSTICE. I WANT A SYSTEM THAT USES NO MAN'S SOUL AS CURRENCY.
CURRENCY? THE MARKET'S IN FREEFALL.
WELL, ENOUGH. THANK YOU FOR YOUR HOSPITALITY, RUDD.
BUT-- MY DECISION--
--DOESN'T AFFECT MINE. I FOUGHT A WAR IN HEAVEN ONCE BEFORE.
I'M GOING TO OFFER MY OLD ENEMIES THE BENEFIT OF MY EXPERIENCE.
NOEMA SAID YOUR POWER IS LEAKING AWAY.
THE LILIM COULD KILL YOU.
THEY'RE WELCOME TO TRY.
IF WE WAIT HERE, DEATH WILL SIFT OVER US LIKE SNOW AND NUMB US TO SLEEP.
ON THE WHOLE, FIRE IS STILL MY ELEMENT.
THEN LET'S BURN.
I SUPPOSE.

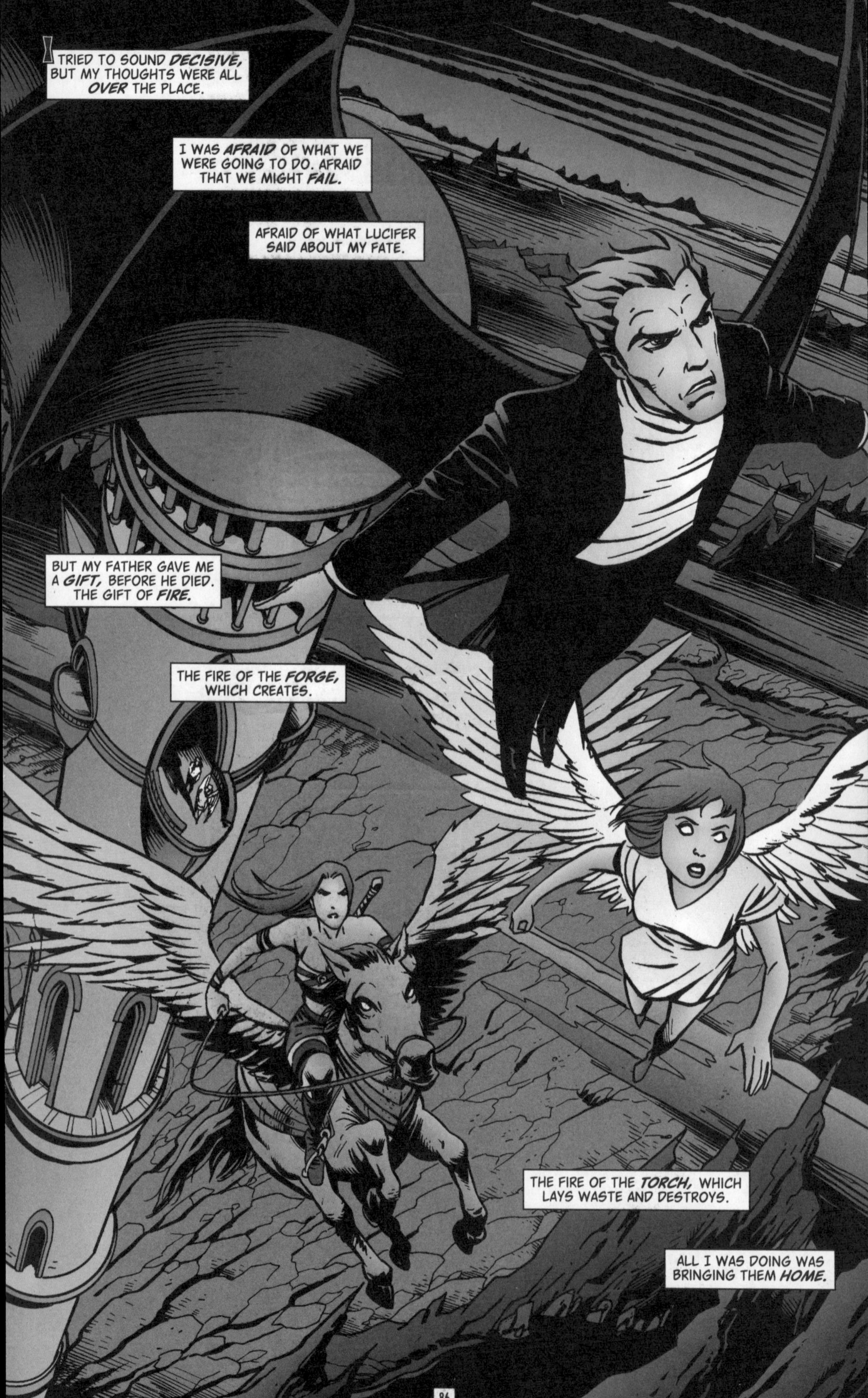
I TRIED TO SOUND DECISIVE, BUT MY THOUGHTS WERE ALL OVER THE PLACE.
I WAS AFRAID OF WHAT WE WERE GOING TO DO. AFRAID THAT WE MIGHT FAIL.
AFRAID OF WHAT LUCIFER SAID ABOUT MY FATE.
BUT MY FATHER GAVE ME A GIFT, BEFORE HE DIED. THE GIFT OF FIRE.
THE FIRE OF THE FORGE, WHICH CREATES.
THE FIRE OF THE TORCH, WHICH LAYS WASTE AND DESTROYS.
ALL I WAS DOING WAS BRINGING THEM HOME.

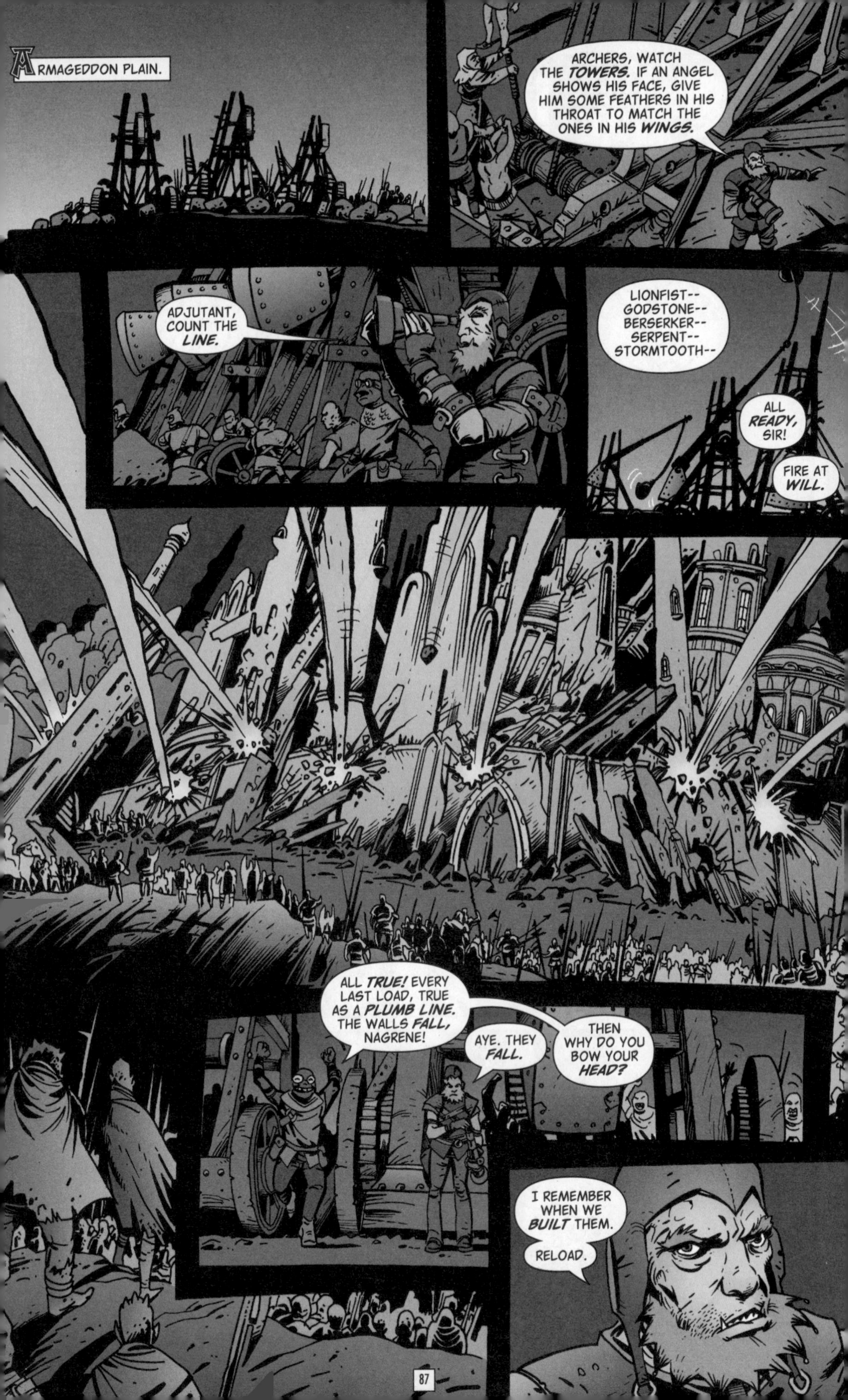

ARMAGEDDON PLAIN.
ARCHERS, WATCH THE TOWERS. IF AN ANGEL SHOWS HIS FACE, GIVE HIM SOME FEATHERS IN HIS THROAT TO MATCH THE ONES IN HIS WINGS.
ADJUTANT, COUNT THE LINE.
LIONFIST-- GODSTONE-- BERSERKER-- SERPENT-- STORMTOOTH--
ALL READY, SIR!
FIRE AT WILL.
ALL TRUE! EVERY LAST LOAD, TRUE AS A PLUMB LINE. THE WALLS FALL, NAGRENE!
AYE. THEY FALL.
THEN WHY DO YOU BOW YOUR HEAD?
I REMEMBER WHEN WE BUILT THEM.
RELOAD.

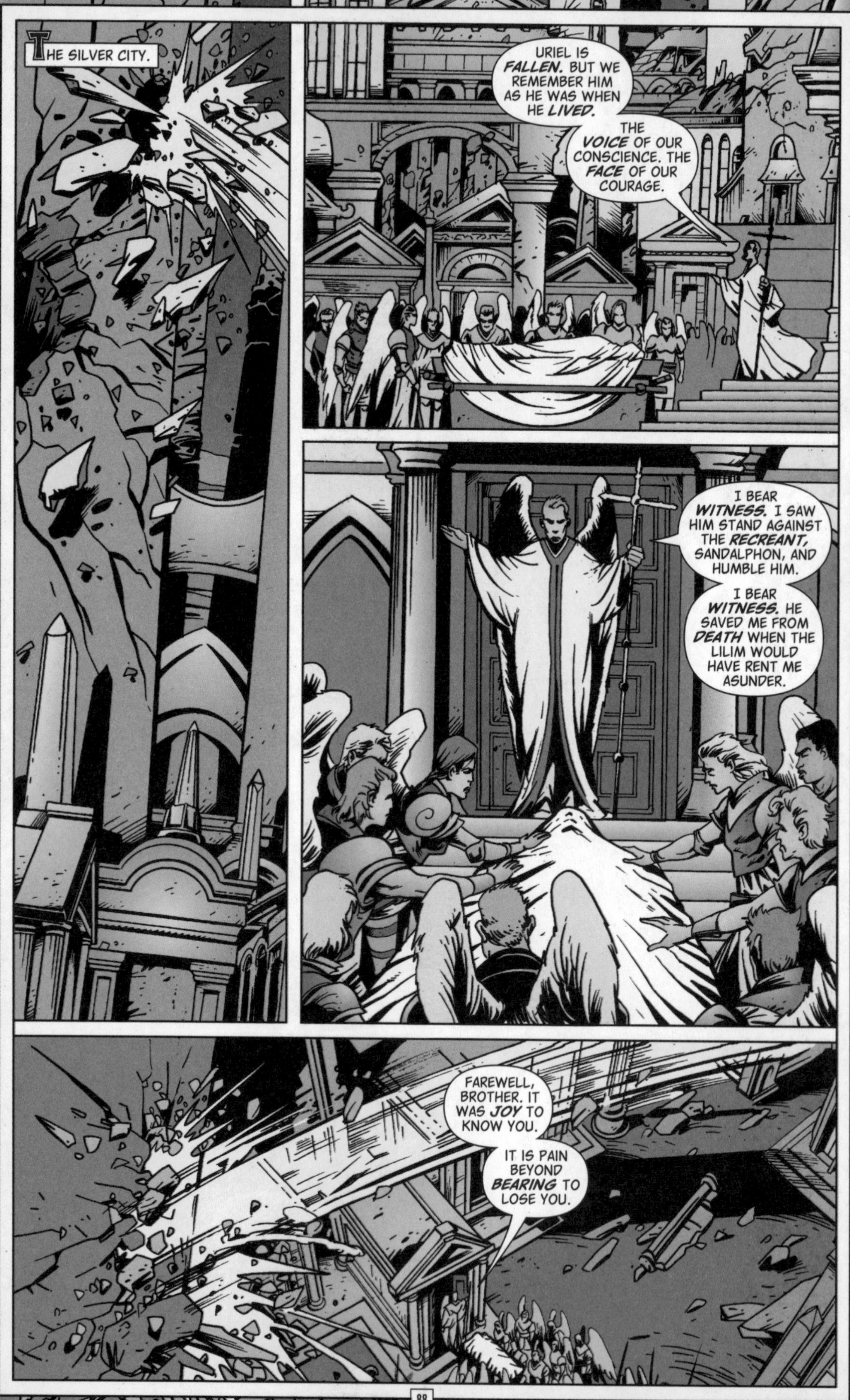
THE SILVER CITY.
URIEL IS FALLEN. BUT WE REMEMBER HIM AS HE WAS WHEN HE LIVED.
THE VOICE OF OUR CONSCIENCE. THE FACE OF OUR COURAGE.
I BEAR WITNESS. I SAW HIM STAND AGAINST THE RECREANT, SANDALPHON, AND HUMBLE HIM.
I BEAR WITNESS. HE SAVED ME FROM DEATH WHEN THE LILIM WOULD HAVE RENT ME ASUNDER.
FAREWELL, BROTHER. IT WAS JOY TO KNOW YOU.
IT IS PAIN BEYOND BEARING TO LOSE YOU.

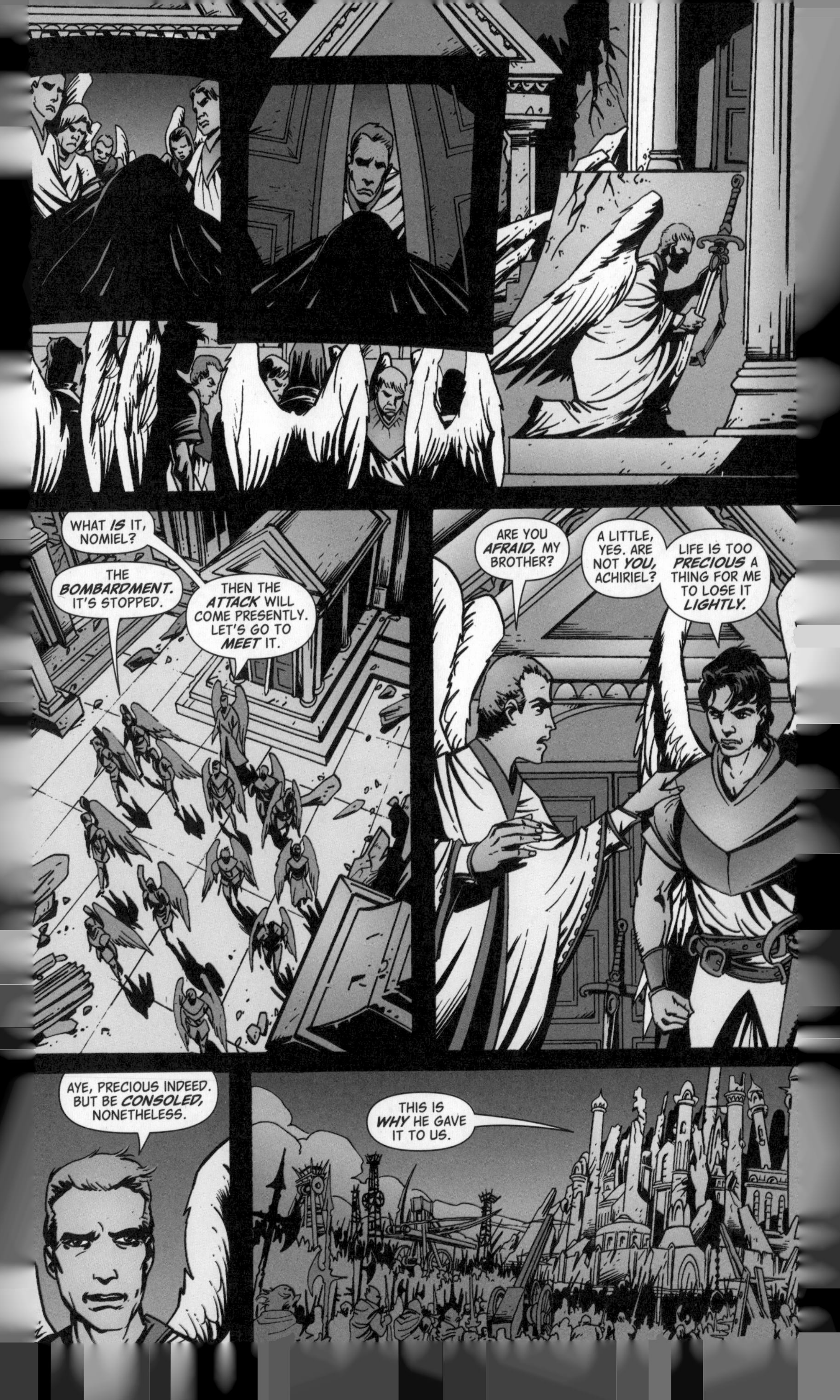
WHAT IS IT, NOMIEL?
THE BOMBARDMENT. IT'S STOPPED.
THEN THE ATTACK WILL COME PRESENTLY. LET'S GO TO MEET IT.
ARE YOU AFRAID, MY BROTHER?
A LITTLE, YES. ARE NOT YOU, ACHIRIEL?
LIFE IS TOO PRECIOUS A THING FOR ME TO LOSE IT LIGHTLY.
AYE, PRECIOUS INDEED. BUT BE CONSOLED, NONETHELESS.
THIS IS WHY HE GAVE IT TO US.

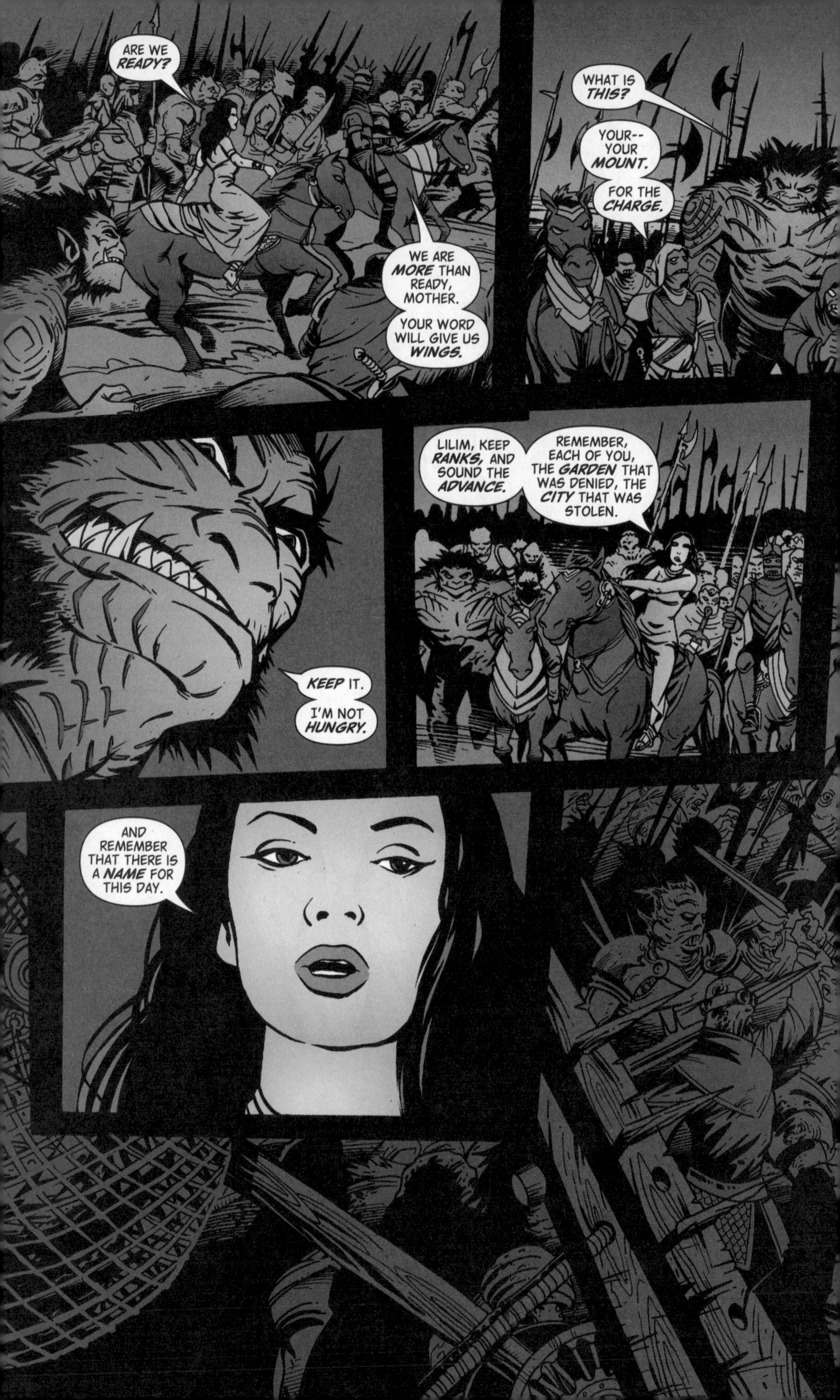

ARE WE READY?
WE ARE MORE THAN READY, MOTHER.
YOUR WORD WILL GIVE US WINGS.
WHAT IS THIS?
YOUR-- YOUR MOUNT.
FOR THE CHARGE.
KEEP IT.
I'M NOT HUNGRY.
LILIM, KEEP RANKS, AND SOUND THE ADVANCE.
REMEMBER, EACH OF YOU, THE GARDEN THAT WAS DENIED, THE CITY THAT WAS STOLEN.
AND REMEMBER THAT THERE IS A NAME FOR THIS DAY.

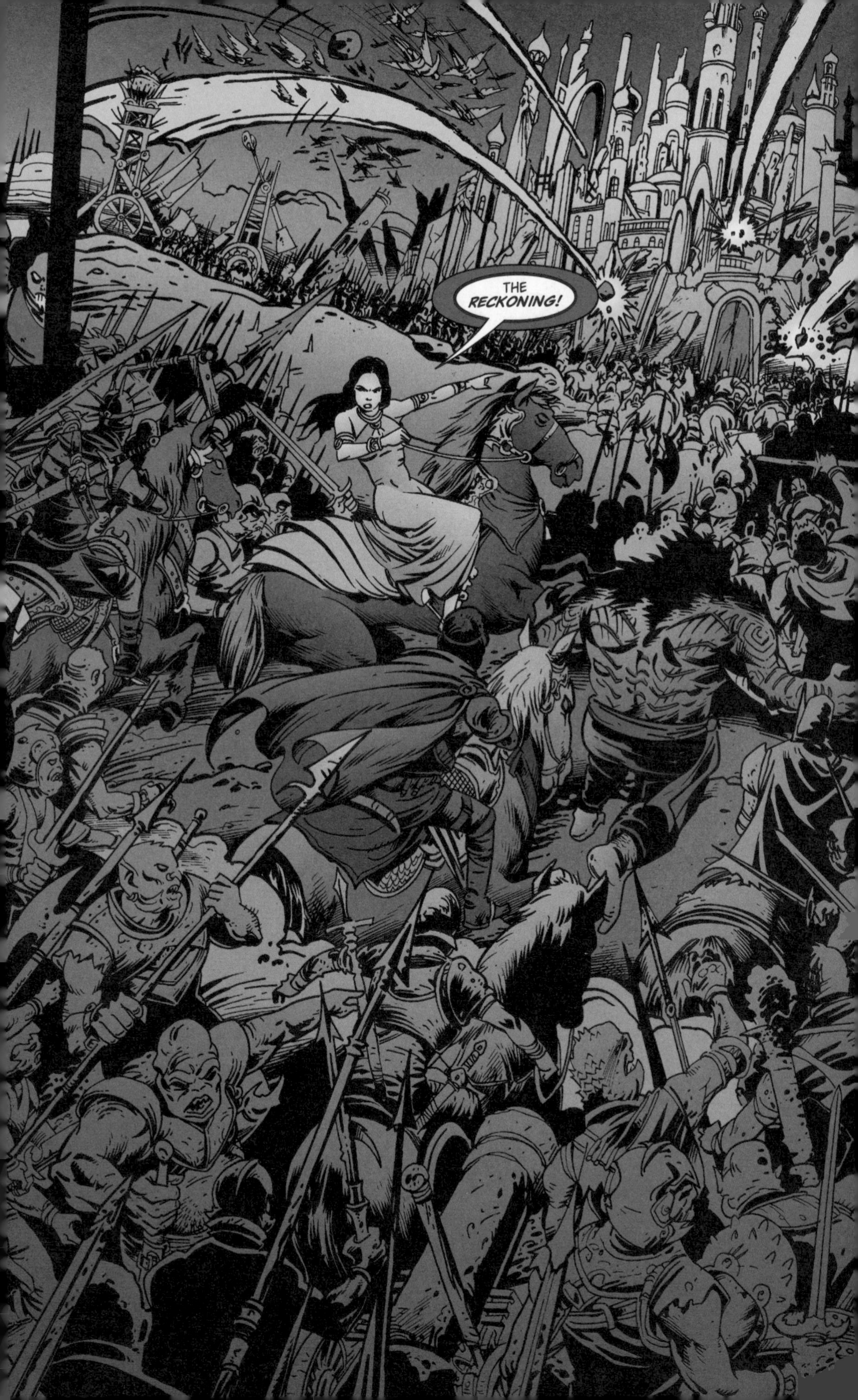
THE *RECKONING!*

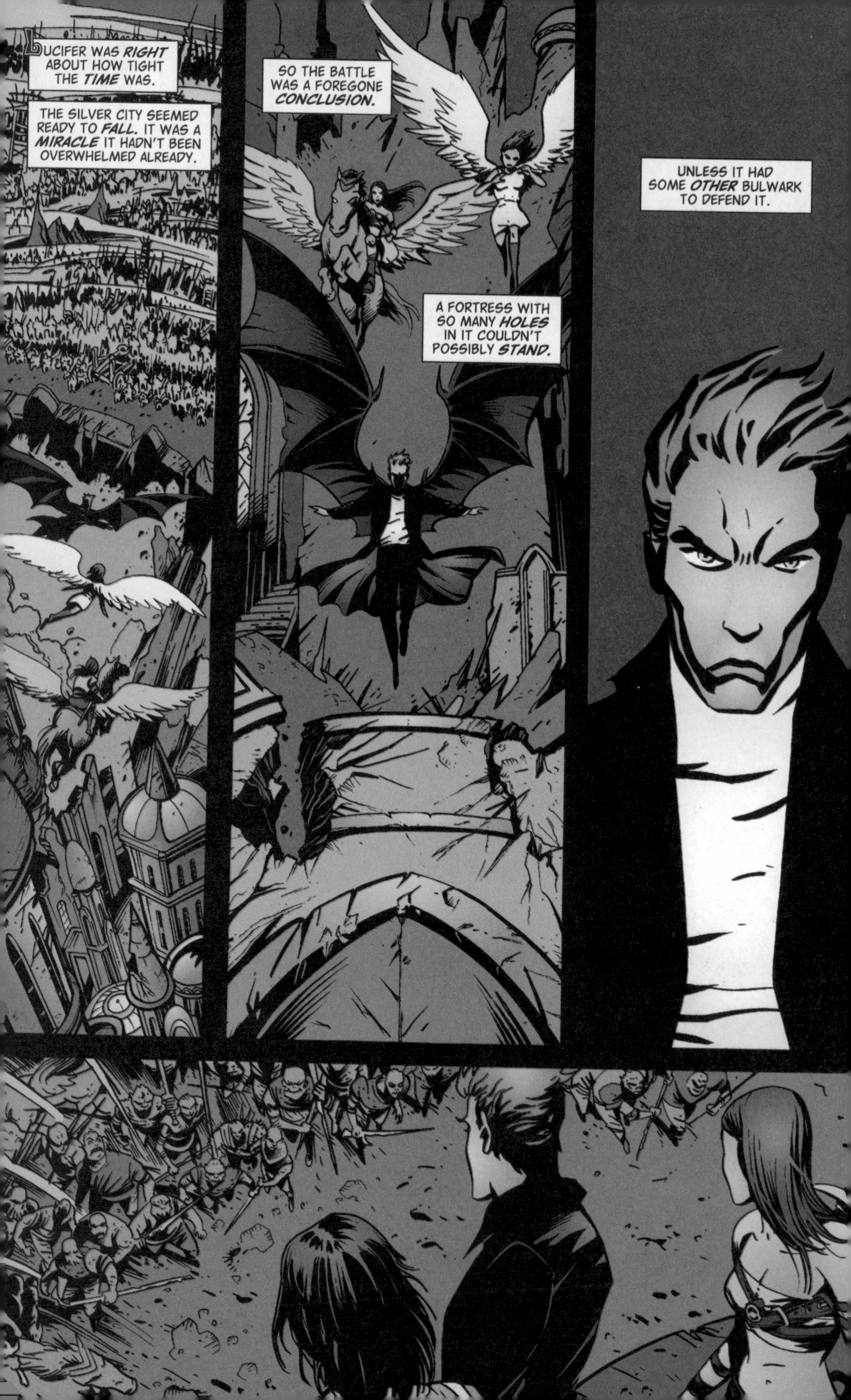
LUCIFER WAS RIGHT ABOUT HOW TIGHT THE TIME WAS.
THE SILVER CITY SEEMED READY TO FALL. IT WAS A MIRACLE IT HADN'T BEEN OVERWHELMED ALREADY.
SO THE BATTLE WAS A FOREGONE CONCLUSION.
A FORTRESS WITH SO MANY HOLES IN IT COULDN'T POSSIBLY STAND.
UNLESS IT HAD SOME OTHER BULWARK TO DEFEND IT.

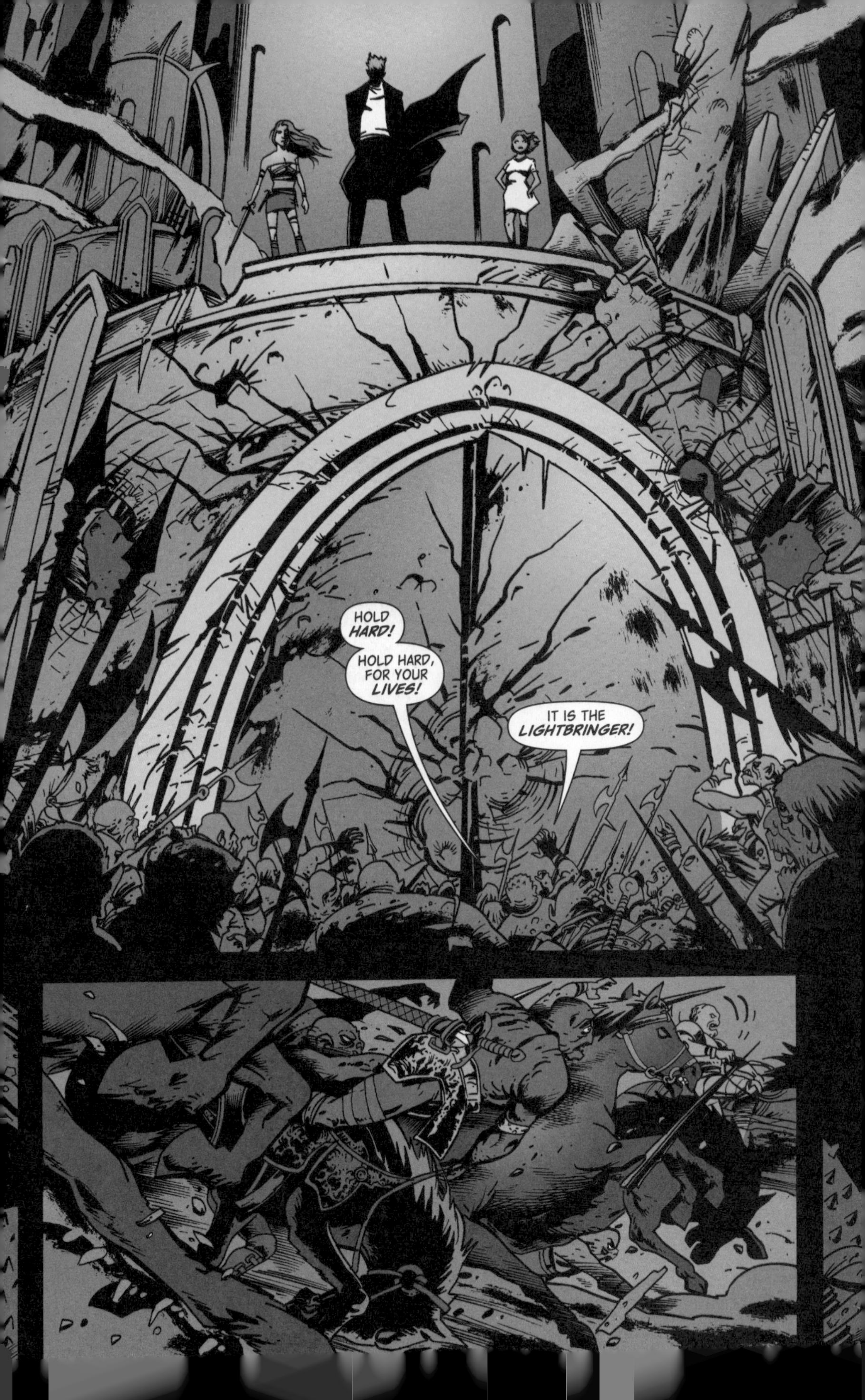
HOLD HARD!
HOLD HARD, FOR YOUR LIVES!
IT IS THE LIGHTBRINGER!

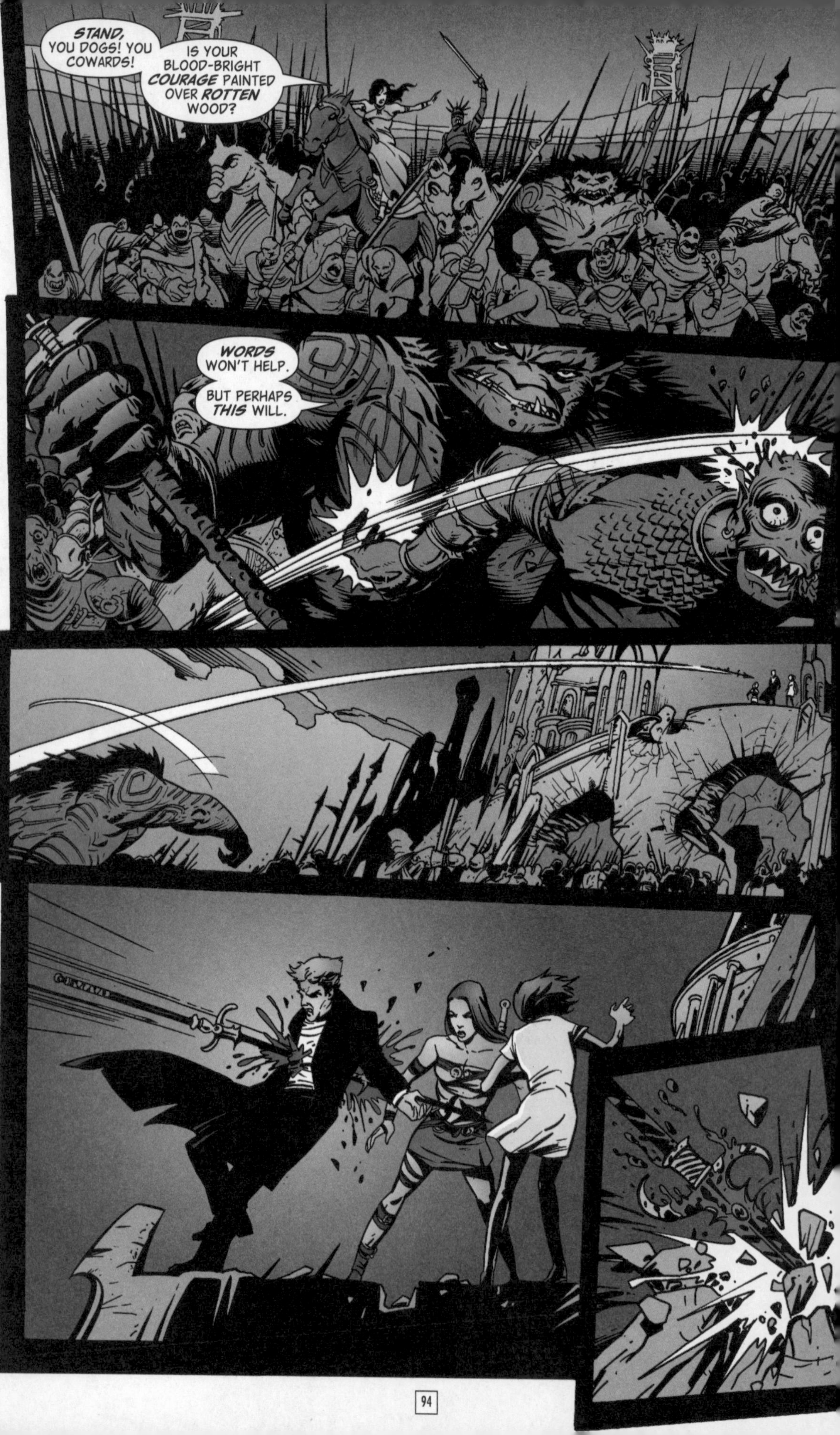
STAND, YOU DOGS! YOU COWARDS!
IS YOUR BLOOD-BRIGHT COURAGE PAINTED OVER ROTTEN WOOD?
WORDS WON'T HELP.
BUT PERHAPS THIS WILL.

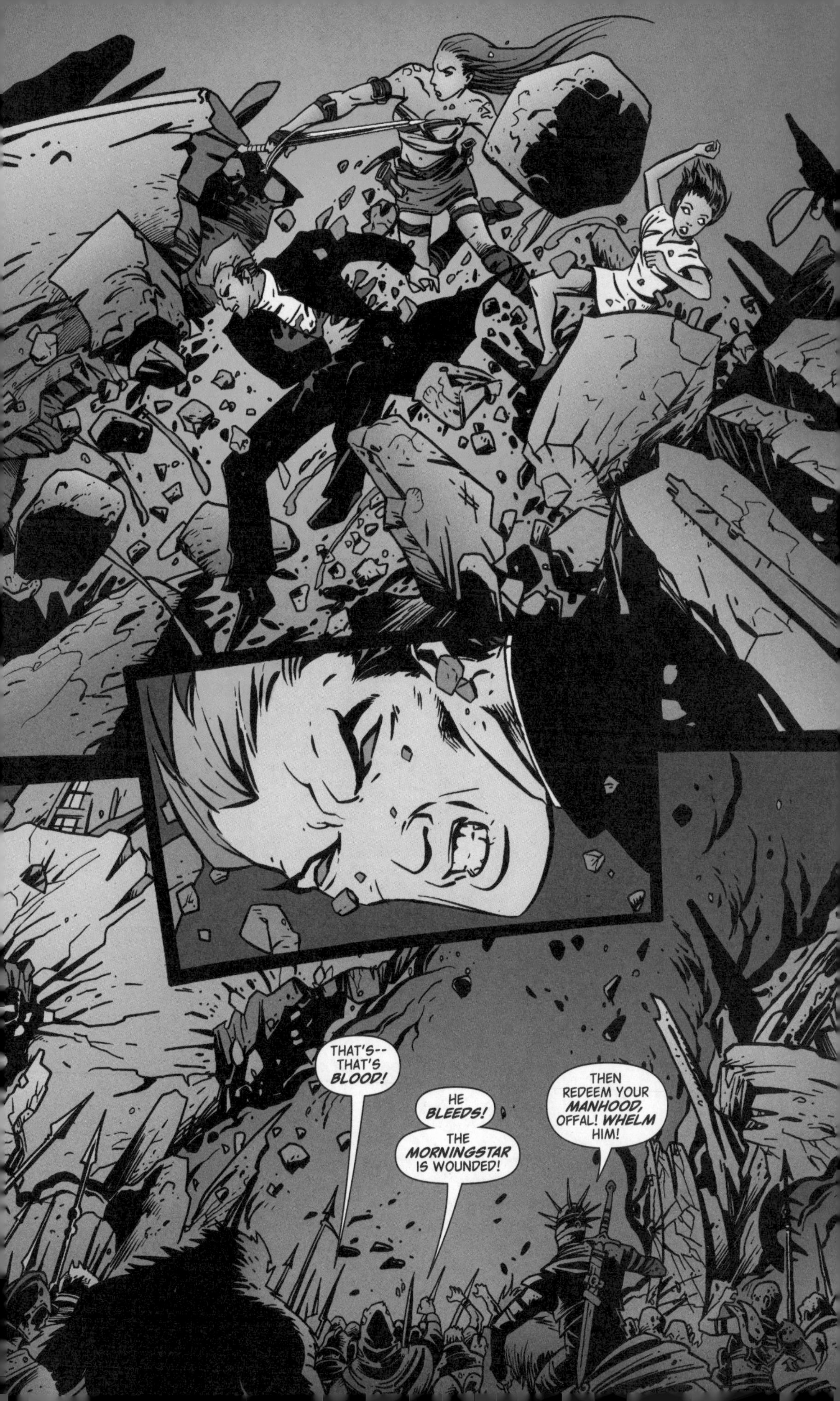
THAT'S--
THAT'S
BLOOD!
HE
BLEEDS!
THE
MORNINGSTAR
IS WOUNDED!
THEN
REDEEM YOUR
MANHOOD,
OFFAL! WHELM
HIM!

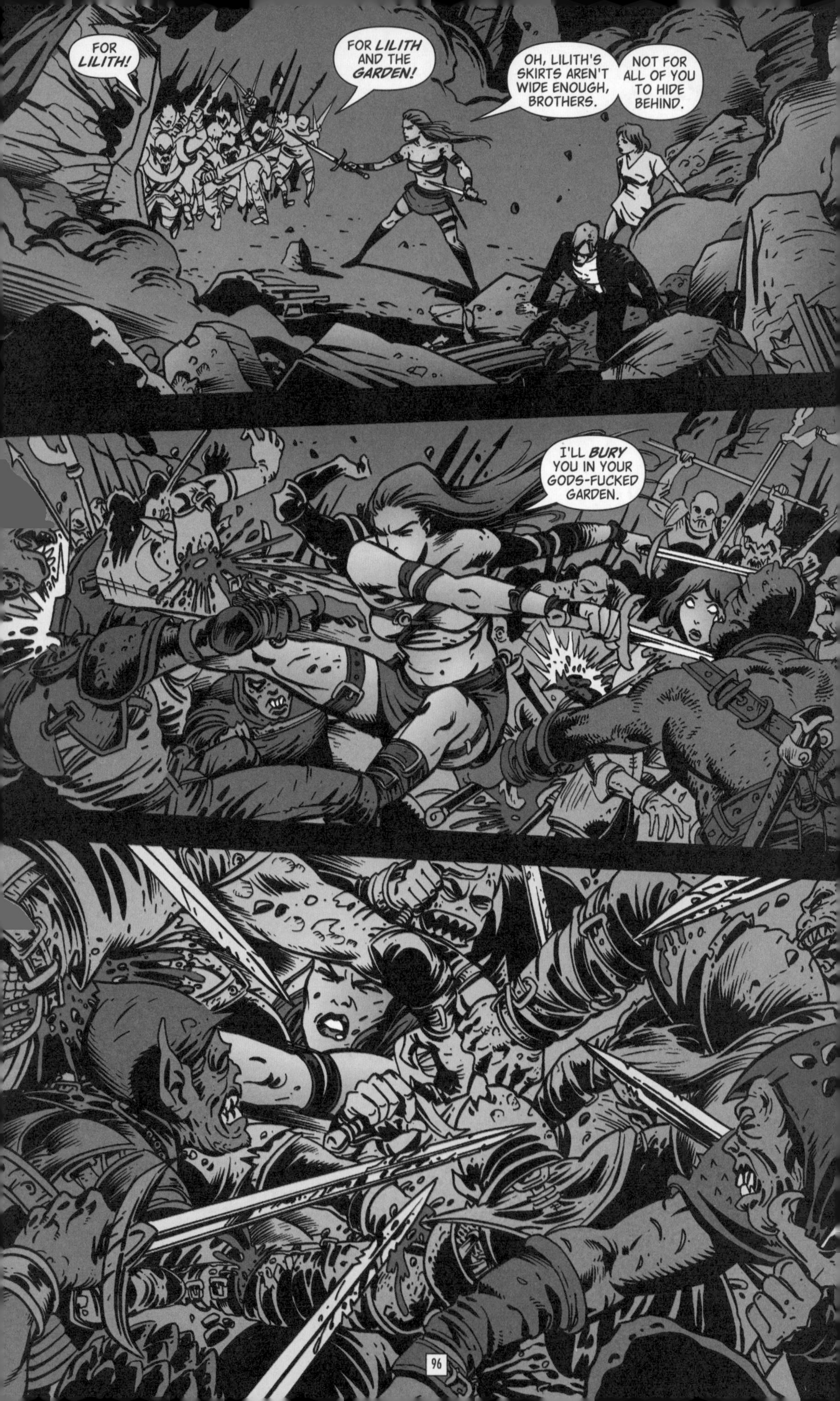

FOR LILITH!
FOR LILITH AND THE GARDEN!
OH, LILITH'S SKIRTS AREN'T WIDE ENOUGH, BROTHERS.
NOT FOR ALL OF YOU TO HIDE BEHIND.
I'LL BURY YOU IN YOUR GODS-FUCKED GARDEN.

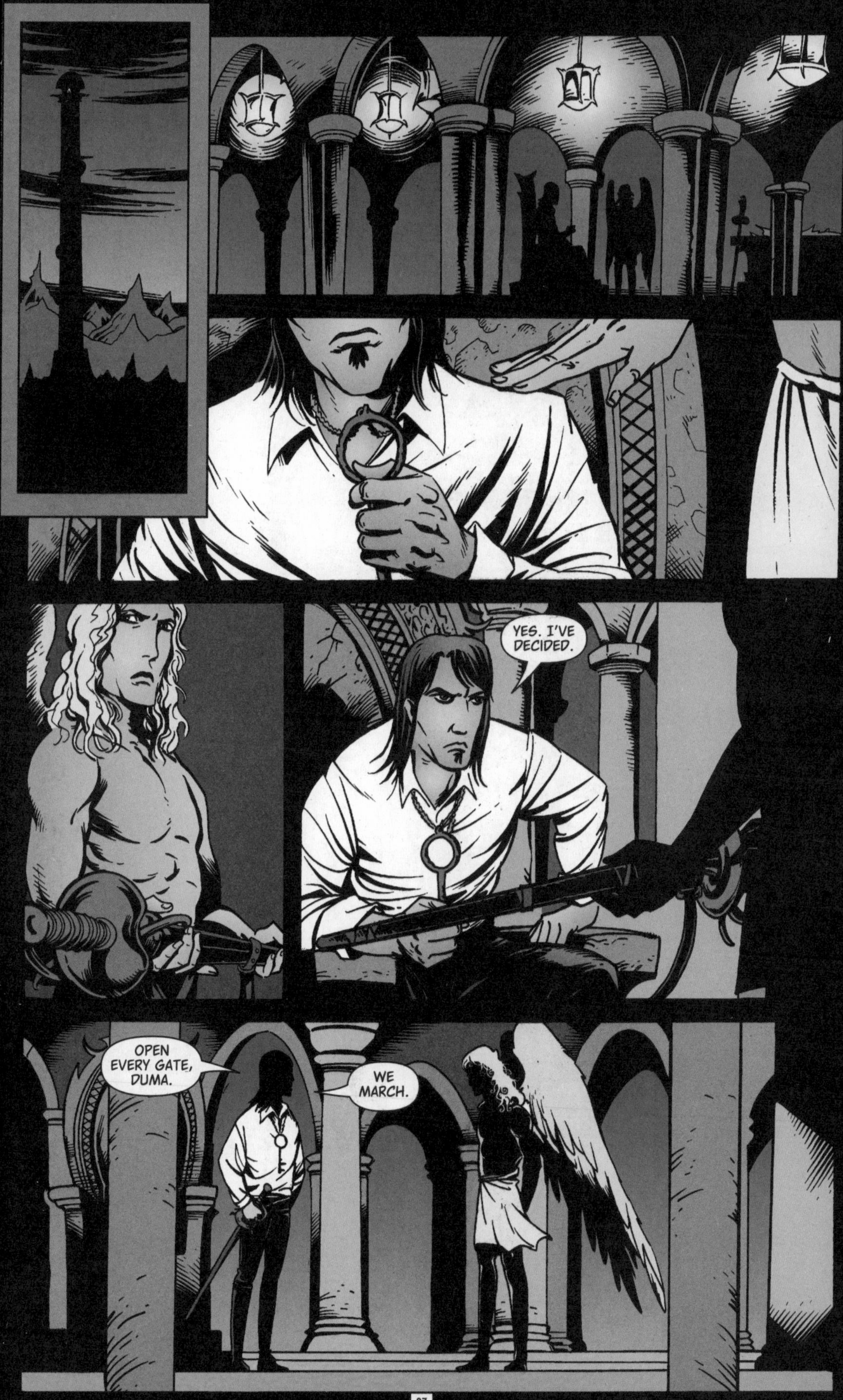
YES. I'VE DECIDED.
OPEN EVERY GATE, DUMA.
WE MARCH.

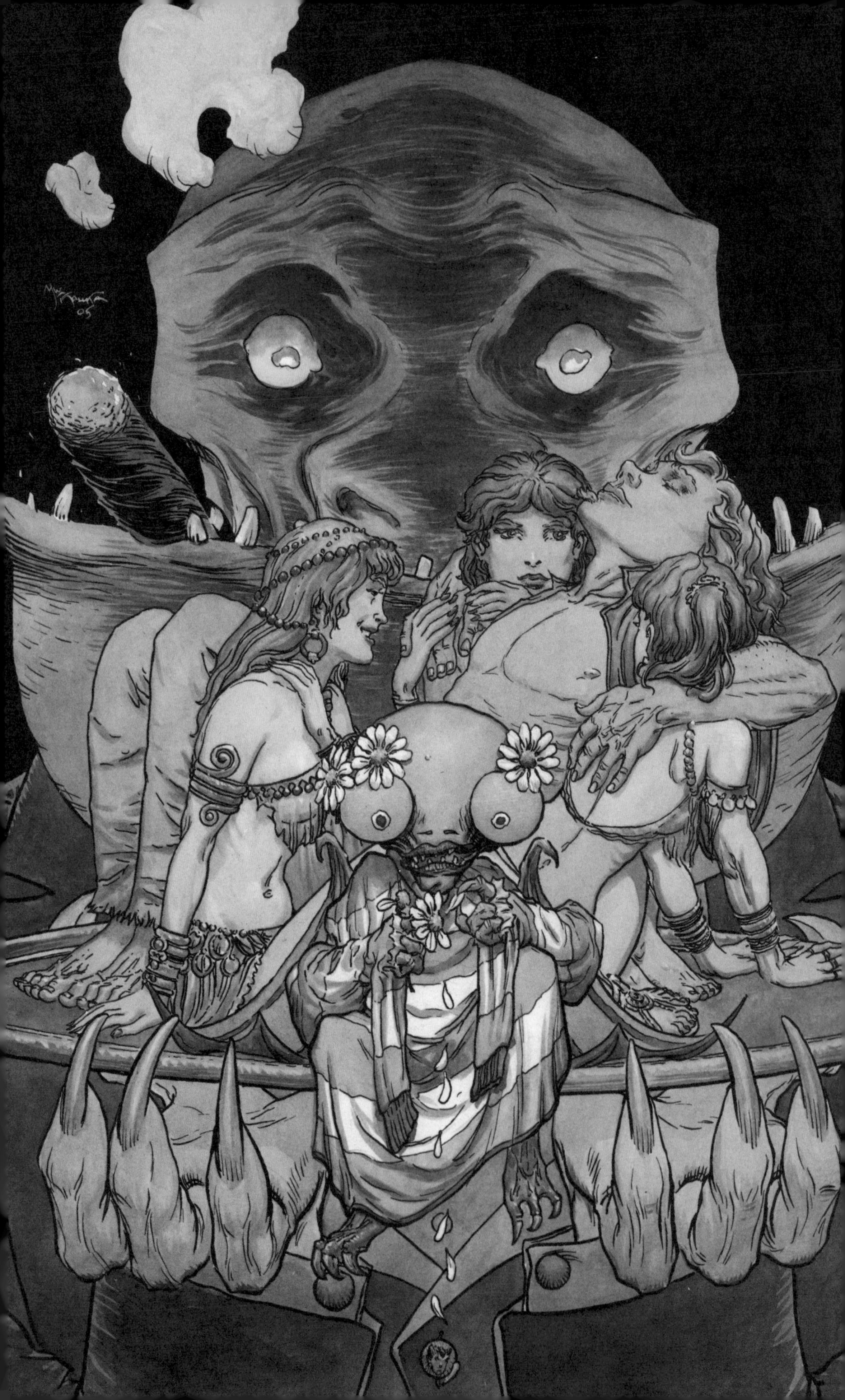

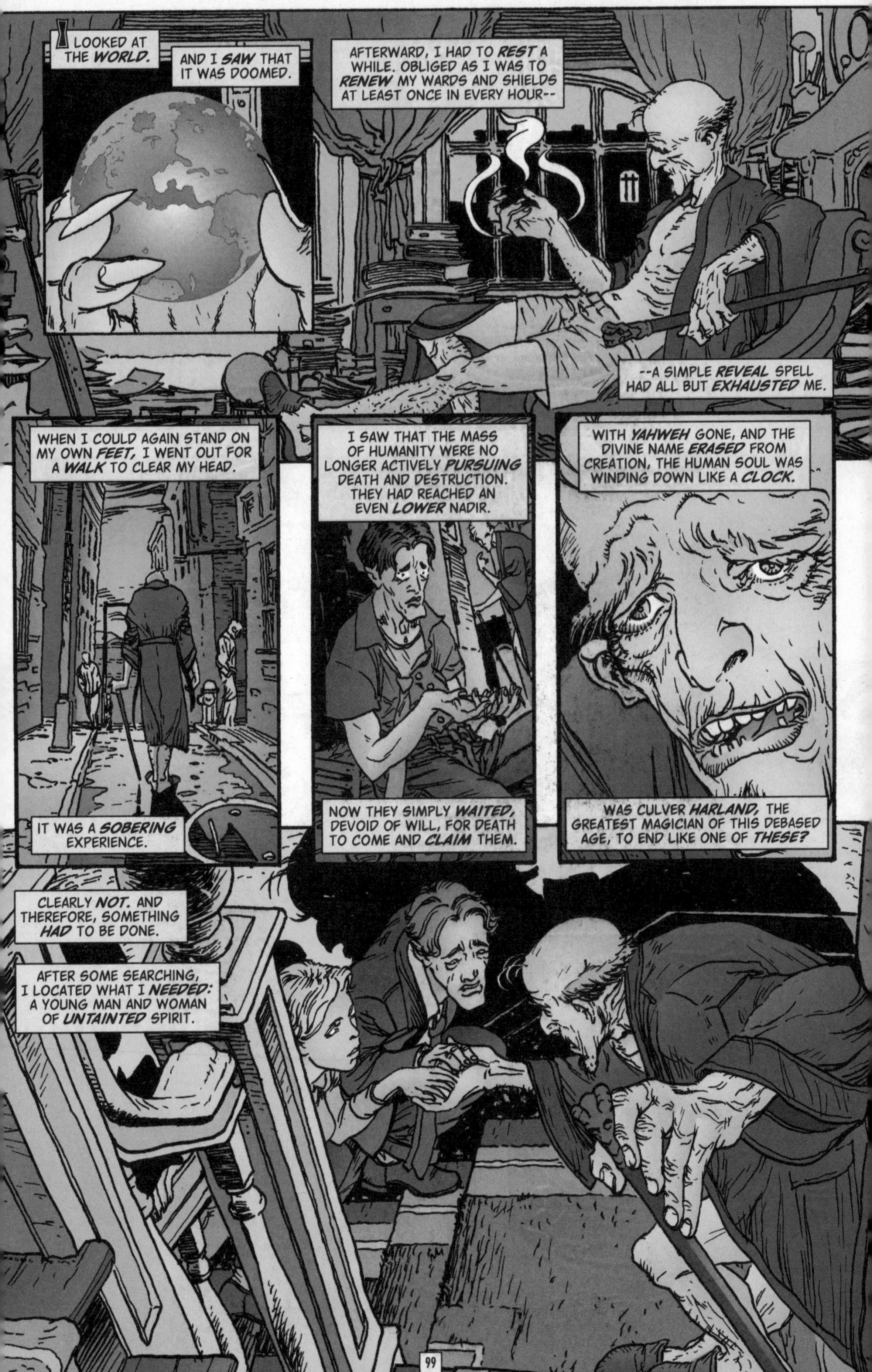
I LOOKED AT THE WORLD.
AND I SAW THAT IT WAS DOOMED.
AFTERWARD, I HAD TO REST A WHILE. OBLIGED AS I WAS TO RENEW MY WARDS AND SHIELDS AT LEAST ONCE IN EVERY HOUR--
--A SIMPLE REVEAL SPELL HAD ALL BUT EXHAUSTED ME.
WHEN I COULD AGAIN STAND ON MY OWN FEET, I WENT OUT FOR A WALK TO CLEAR MY HEAD.
IT WAS A SOBERING EXPERIENCE.
I SAW THAT THE MASS OF HUMANITY WERE NO LONGER ACTIVELY PURSUING DEATH AND DESTRUCTION. THEY HAD REACHED AN EVEN LOWER NADIR.
NOW THEY SIMPLY WAITED, DEVOID OF WILL, FOR DEATH TO COME AND CLAIM THEM.
WITH YAHWEH GONE, AND THE DIVINE NAME ERASED FROM CREATION, THE HUMAN SOUL WAS WINDING DOWN LIKE A CLOCK.
WAS CULVER HARLAND, THE GREATEST MAGICIAN OF THIS DEBASED AGE, TO END LIKE ONE OF THESE?
CLEARLY NOT. AND THEREFORE, SOMETHING HAD TO BE DONE.
AFTER SOME SEARCHING, I LOCATED WHAT I NEEDED: A YOUNG MAN AND WOMAN OF UNTAINTED SPIRIT.

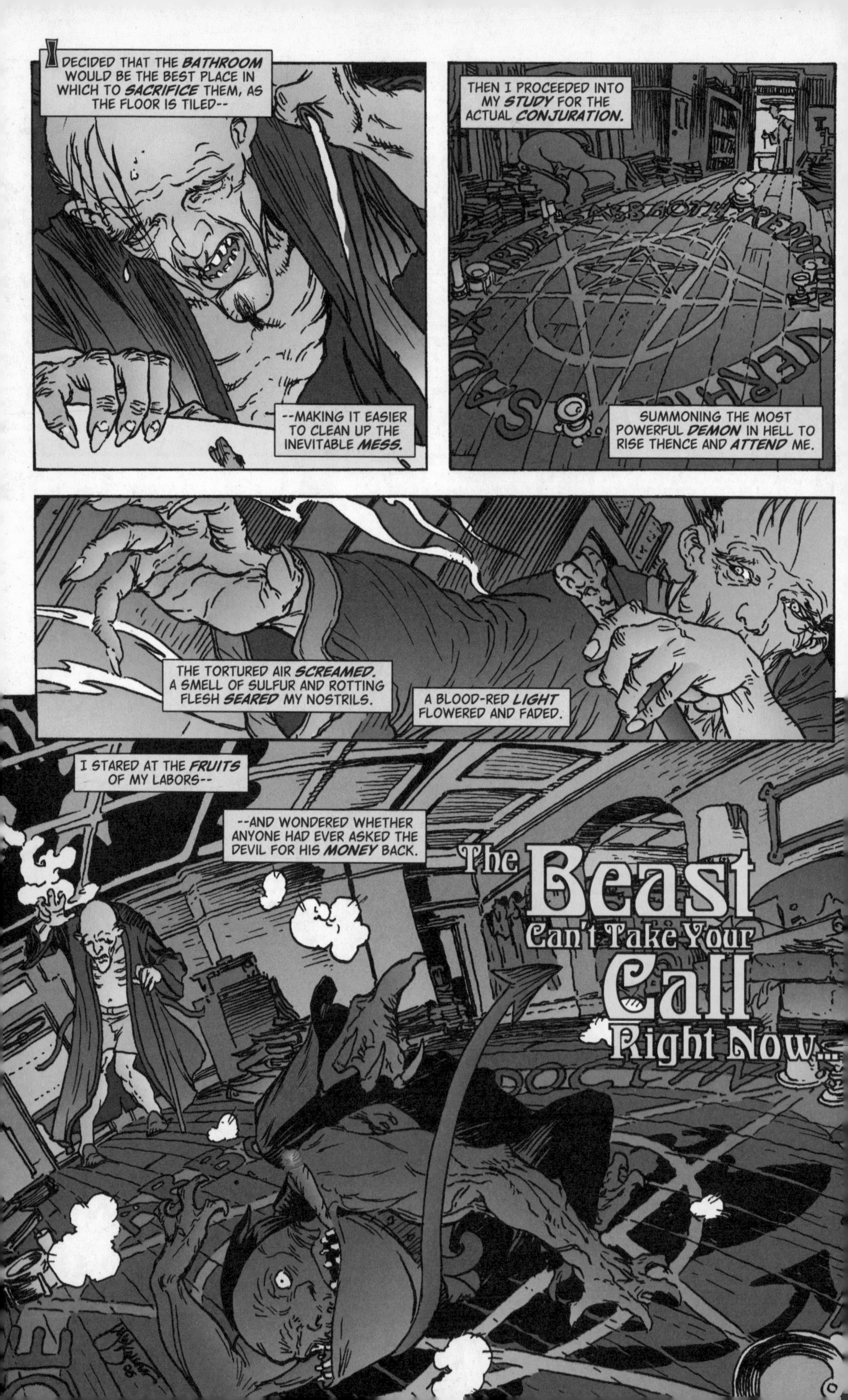
I DECIDED THAT THE BATHROOM WOULD BE THE BEST PLACE IN WHICH TO SACRIFICE THEM, AS THE FLOOR IS TILED--
--MAKING IT EASIER TO CLEAN UP THE INEVITABLE MESS.
THEN I PROCEEDED INTO MY STUDY FOR THE ACTUAL CONJURATION.
SUMMONING THE MOST POWERFUL DEMON IN HELL TO RISE THENCE AND ATTEND ME.
THE TORTURED AIR SCREAMED. A SMELL OF SULFUR AND ROTTING FLESH SEARED MY NOSTRILS.
A BLOOD-RED LIGHT FLOWERED AND FADED.
I STARED AT THE FRUITS OF MY LABORS--
--AND WONDERED WHETHER ANYONE HAD EVER ASKED THE DEVIL FOR HIS MONEY BACK.
The Beast Can't Take Your Call Right Now...

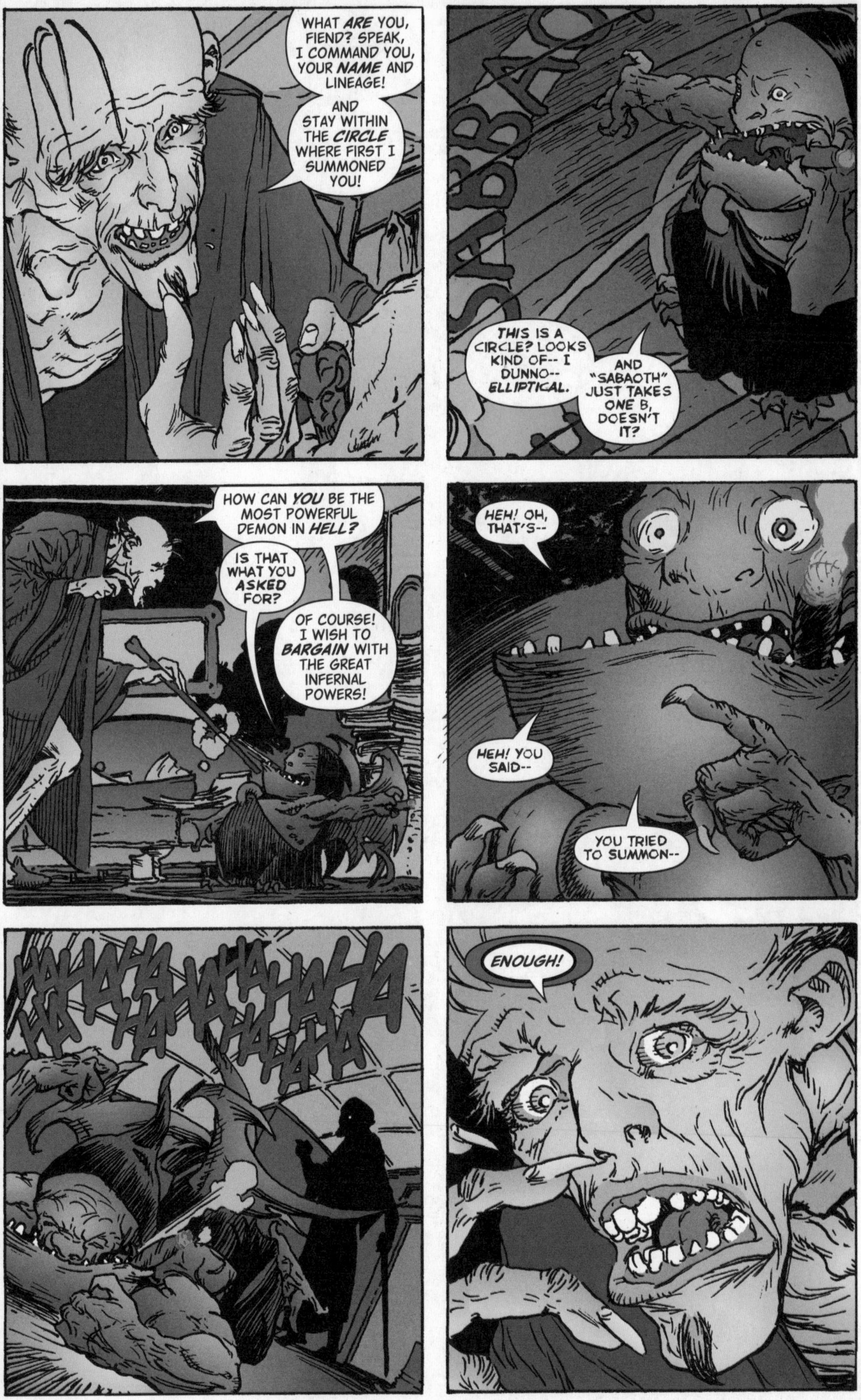
WHAT *ARE* YOU, FIEND? SPEAK, I COMMAND YOU, YOUR *NAME* AND LINEAGE!
AND STAY WITHIN THE *CIRCLE* WHERE FIRST I SUMMONED YOU!
THIS IS A CIRCLE? LOOKS KIND OF-- I DUNNO-- *ELLIPTICAL.*
AND "SABAOTH" JUST TAKES *ONE* B, DOESN'T IT?
HOW CAN *YOU* BE THE MOST POWERFUL DEMON IN *HELL?*
IS THAT WHAT YOU *ASKED* FOR?
OF COURSE! I WISH TO *BARGAIN* WITH THE GREAT INFERNAL POWERS!
HEH! OH, THAT'S--
HEH! YOU SAID--
YOU TRIED TO SUMMON--
HAHAHAHAHAHAHA
HAHAHAHAHAHA
HAHAHA
ENOUGH!

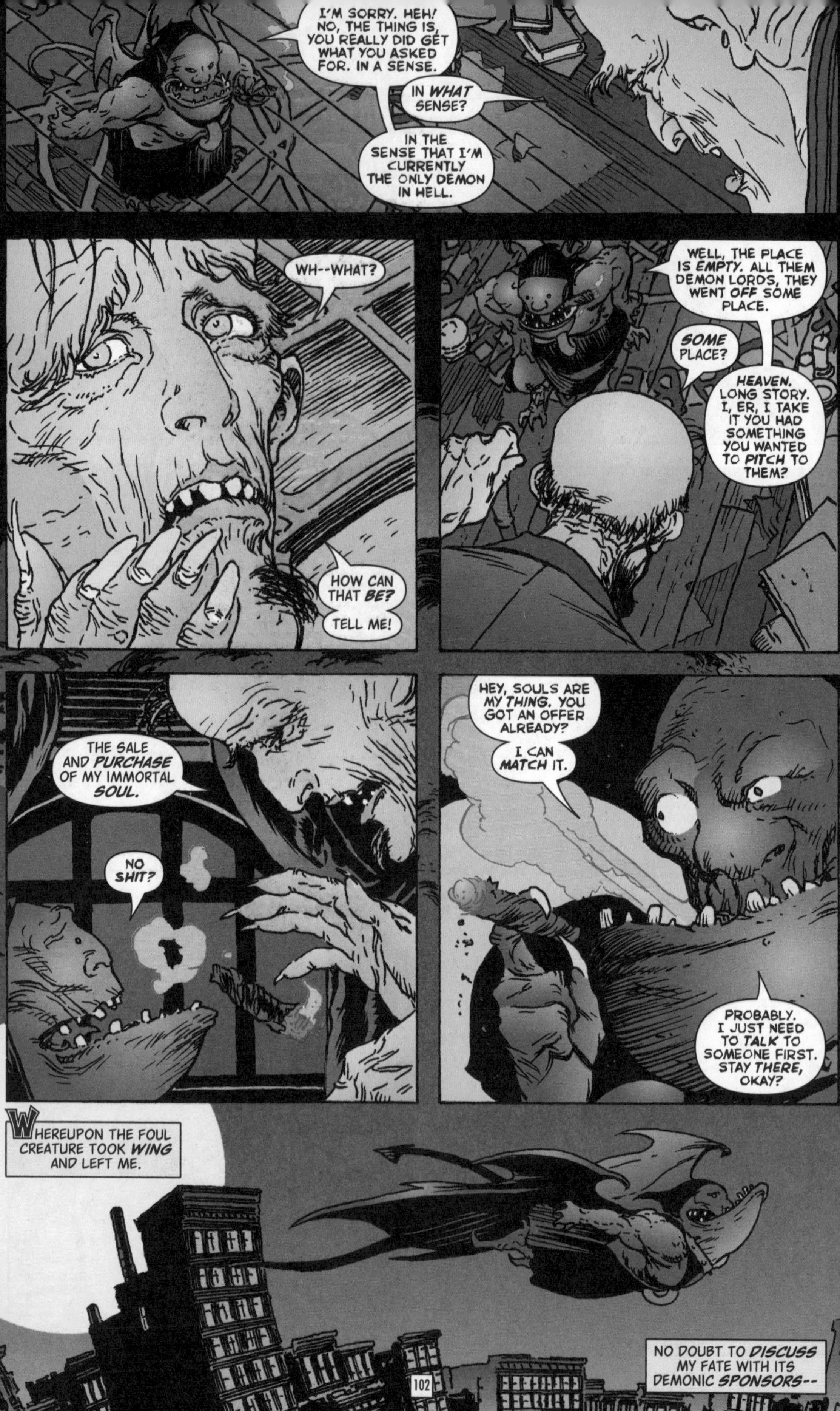

I'M SORRY. HEH! NO, THE THING IS, YOU REALLY DID GET WHAT YOU ASKED FOR. IN A SENSE.
IN WHAT SENSE?
IN THE SENSE THAT I'M CURRENTLY THE ONLY DEMON IN HELL.
WH--WHAT?
HOW CAN THAT BE?
TELL ME!
WELL, THE PLACE IS EMPTY. ALL THEM DEMON LORDS, THEY WENT OFF SOME PLACE.
SOME PLACE?
HEAVEN. LONG STORY. I, ER, I TAKE IT YOU HAD SOMETHING YOU WANTED TO PITCH TO THEM?
THE SALE AND PURCHASE OF MY IMMORTAL SOUL.
NO SHIT?
HEY, SOULS ARE MY THING. YOU GOT AN OFFER ALREADY?
I CAN MATCH IT.
PROBABLY. I JUST NEED TO TALK TO SOMEONE FIRST. STAY THERE, OKAY?
WHEREUPON THE FOUL CREATURE TOOK WING AND LEFT ME.
NO DOUBT TO DISCUSS MY FATE WITH ITS DEMONIC SPONSORS--

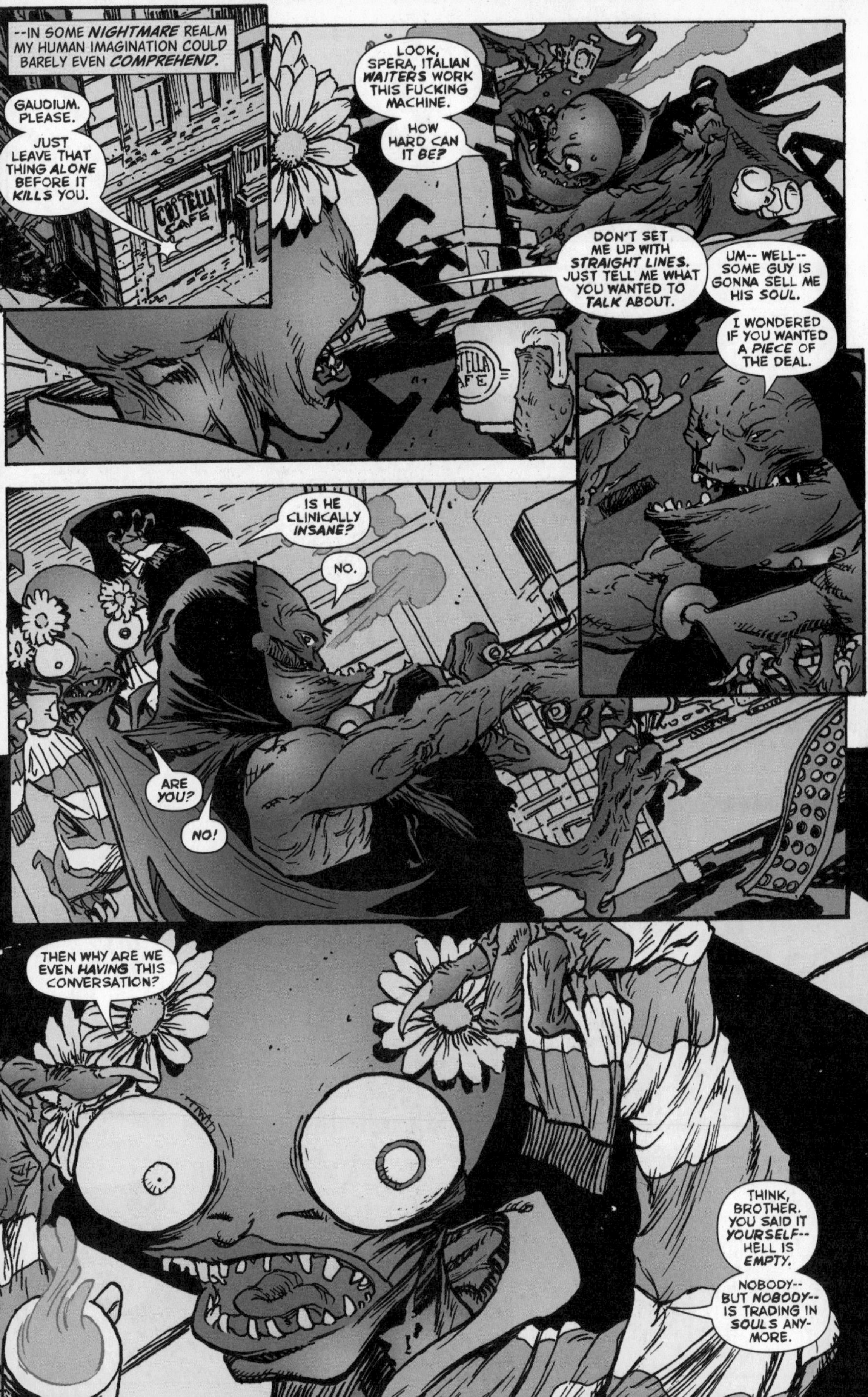
--IN SOME NIGHTMARE REALM MY HUMAN IMAGINATION COULD BARELY EVEN COMPREHEND.
GAUDIUM. PLEASE.
JUST LEAVE THAT THING ALONE BEFORE IT KILLS YOU.
COSTELLA CAFE
LOOK, SPERA, ITALIAN WAITERS WORK THIS FUCKING MACHINE.
HOW HARD CAN IT BE?
DON'T SET ME UP WITH STRAIGHT LINES. JUST TELL ME WHAT YOU WANTED TO TALK ABOUT.
UM-- WELL-- SOME GUY IS GONNA SELL ME HIS SOUL.
I WONDERED IF YOU WANTED A PIECE OF THE DEAL.
IS HE CLINICALLY INSANE?
NO.
ARE YOU?
NO!
THEN WHY ARE WE EVEN HAVING THIS CONVERSATION?
THINK, BROTHER. YOU SAID IT YOURSELF-- HELL IS EMPTY.
NOBODY-- BUT NOBODY-- IS TRADING IN SOULS ANY-MORE.

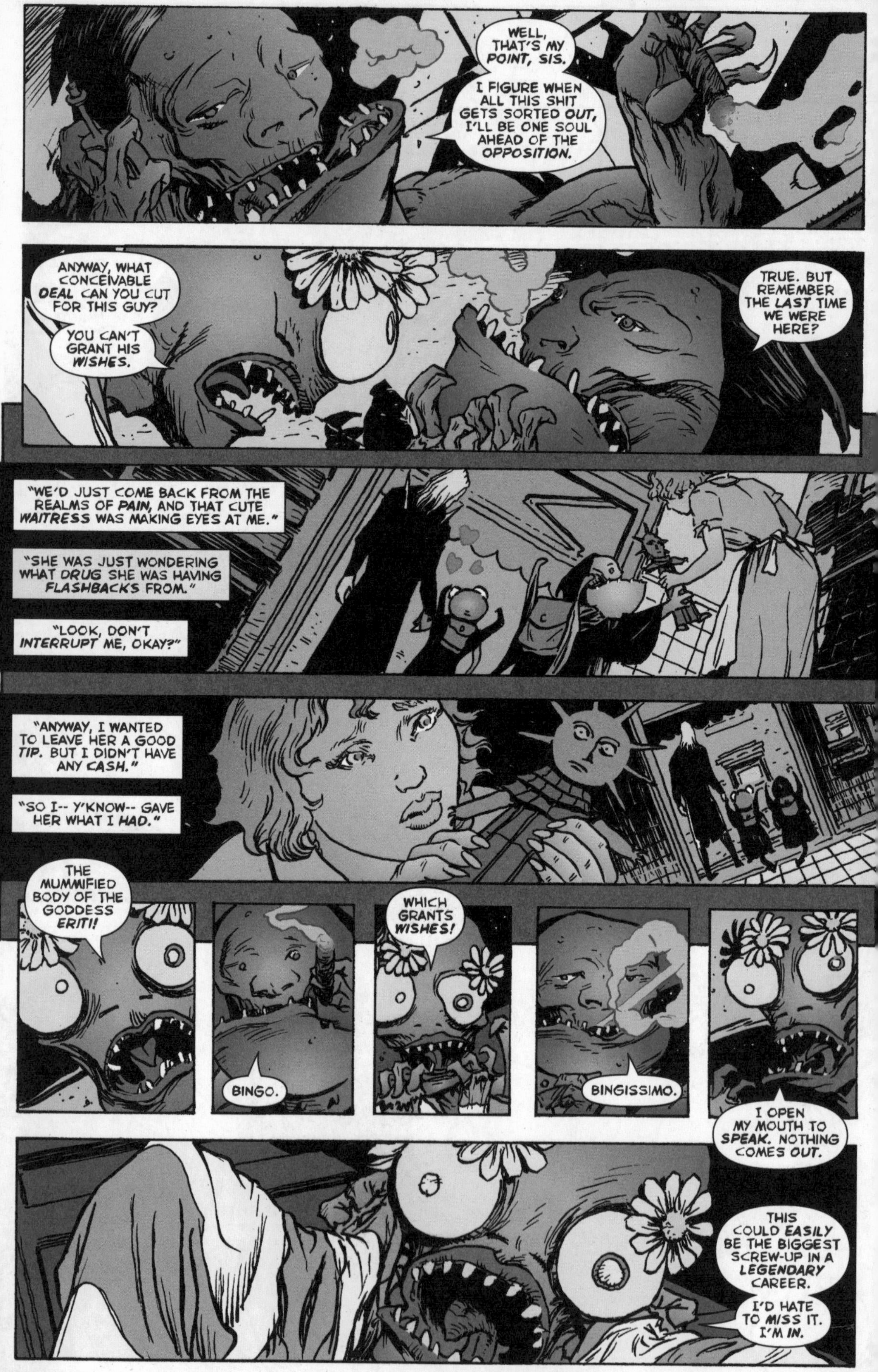
WELL, THAT'S MY POINT, SIS.
I FIGURE WHEN ALL THIS SHIT GETS SORTED OUT, I'LL BE ONE SOUL AHEAD OF THE OPPOSITION.
ANYWAY, WHAT CONCEIVABLE DEAL CAN YOU CUT FOR THIS GUY?
YOU CAN'T GRANT HIS WISHES.
TRUE. BUT REMEMBER THE LAST TIME WE WERE HERE?
"WE'D JUST COME BACK FROM THE REALMS OF PAIN, AND THAT CUTE WAITRESS WAS MAKING EYES AT ME."
"SHE WAS JUST WONDERING WHAT DRUG SHE WAS HAVING FLASHBACKS FROM."
"LOOK, DON'T INTERRUPT ME, OKAY?"
"ANYWAY, I WANTED TO LEAVE HER A GOOD TIP. BUT I DIDN'T HAVE ANY CASH."
"SO I-- Y'KNOW-- GAVE HER WHAT I HAD."
THE MUMMIFIED BODY OF THE GODDESS ERITI!
BINGO.
WHICH GRANTS WISHES!
BINGISSIMO.
I OPEN MY MOUTH TO SPEAK. NOTHING COMES OUT.
THIS COULD EASILY BE THE BIGGEST SCREW-UP IN A LEGENDARY CAREER.
I'D HATE TO MISS IT. I'M IN.

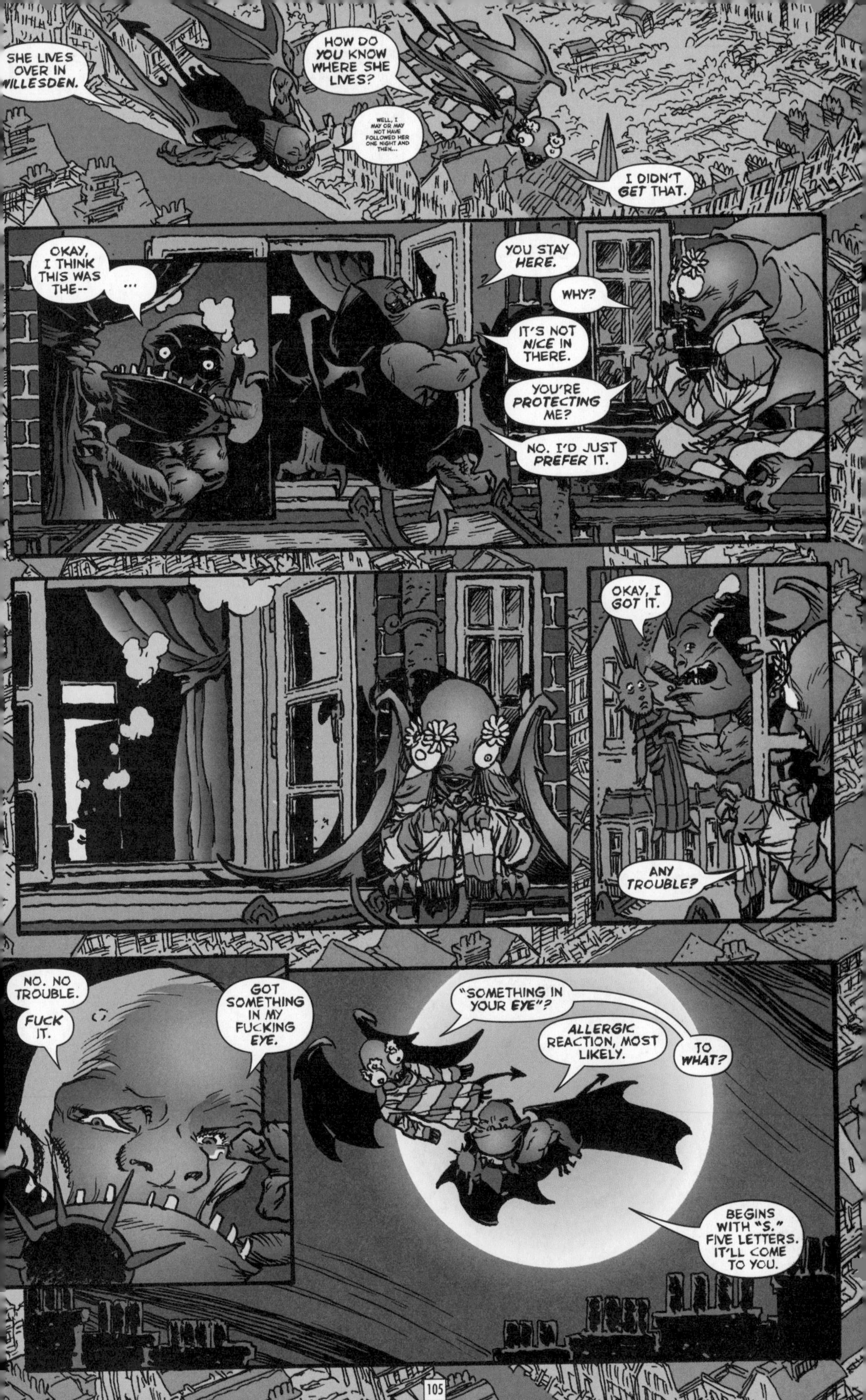
SHE LIVES OVER IN WILLESDEN.
HOW DO YOU KNOW WHERE SHE LIVES?
WELL, I MAY OR MAY NOT HAVE FOLLOWED HER ONE NIGHT AND THEN...
I DIDN'T GET THAT.
OKAY, I THINK THIS WAS THE--
...
YOU STAY HERE.
WHY?
IT'S NOT NICE IN THERE.
YOU'RE PROTECTING ME?
NO. I'D JUST PREFER IT.
OKAY, I GOT IT.
ANY TROUBLE?
NO. NO TROUBLE.
FUCK IT.
GOT SOMETHING IN MY FUCKING EYE.
"SOMETHING IN YOUR EYE"?
ALLERGIC REACTION, MOST LIKELY.
TO WHAT?
BEGINS WITH "S." FIVE LETTERS. IT'LL COME TO YOU.

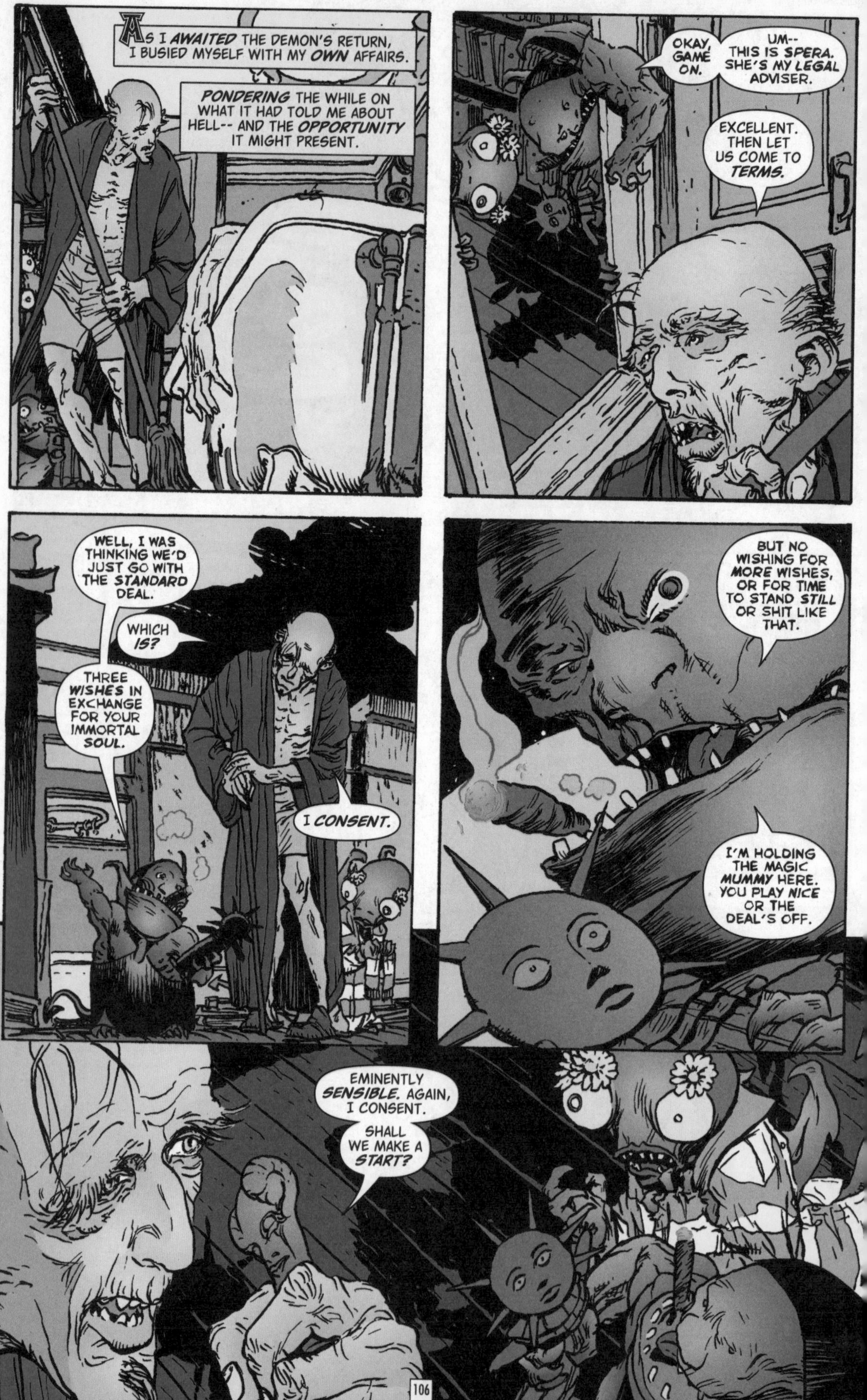
AS I AWAITED THE DEMON'S RETURN, I BUSIED MYSELF WITH MY OWN AFFAIRS.
PONDERING THE WHILE ON WHAT IT HAD TOLD ME ABOUT HELL-- AND THE OPPORTUNITY IT MIGHT PRESENT.
OKAY, GAME ON.
UM-- THIS IS SPERA. SHE'S MY LEGAL ADVISER.
EXCELLENT. THEN LET US COME TO TERMS.
WELL, I WAS THINKING WE'D JUST GO WITH THE STANDARD DEAL.
WHICH IS?
THREE WISHES IN EXCHANGE FOR YOUR IMMORTAL SOUL.
I CONSENT.
BUT NO WISHING FOR MORE WISHES, OR FOR TIME TO STAND STILL OR SHIT LIKE THAT.
I'M HOLDING THE MAGIC MUMMY HERE. YOU PLAY NICE OR THE DEAL'S OFF.
EMINENTLY SENSIBLE. AGAIN, I CONSENT.
SHALL WE MAKE A START?

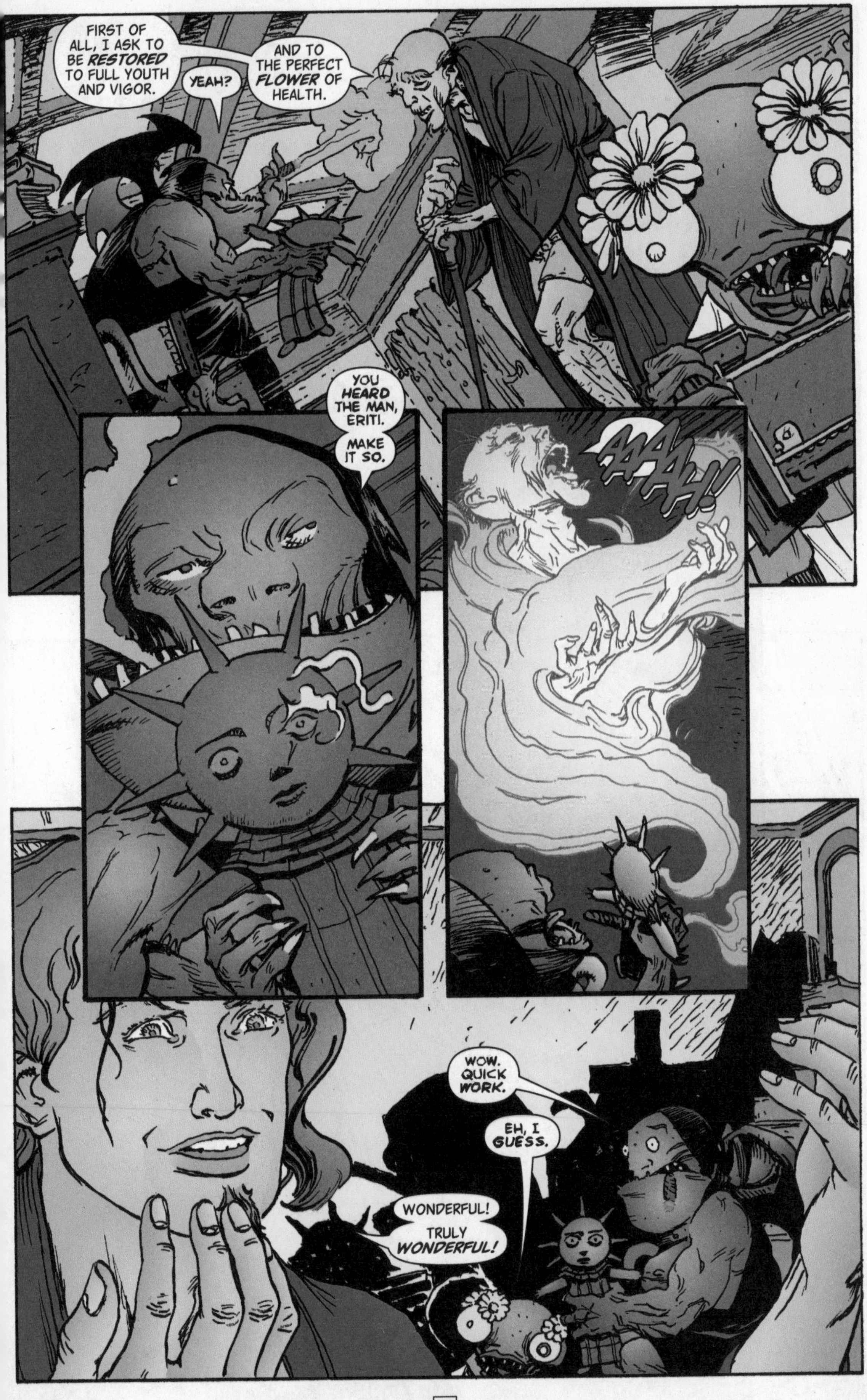
FIRST OF ALL, I ASK TO BE RESTORED TO FULL YOUTH AND VIGOR.
YEAH?
AND TO THE PERFECT FLOWER OF HEALTH.
YOU HEARD THE MAN, ERITI.
MAKE IT SO.
AAAAAH!!
WOW. QUICK WORK.
EH, I GUESS.
WONDERFUL!
TRULY WONDERFUL!

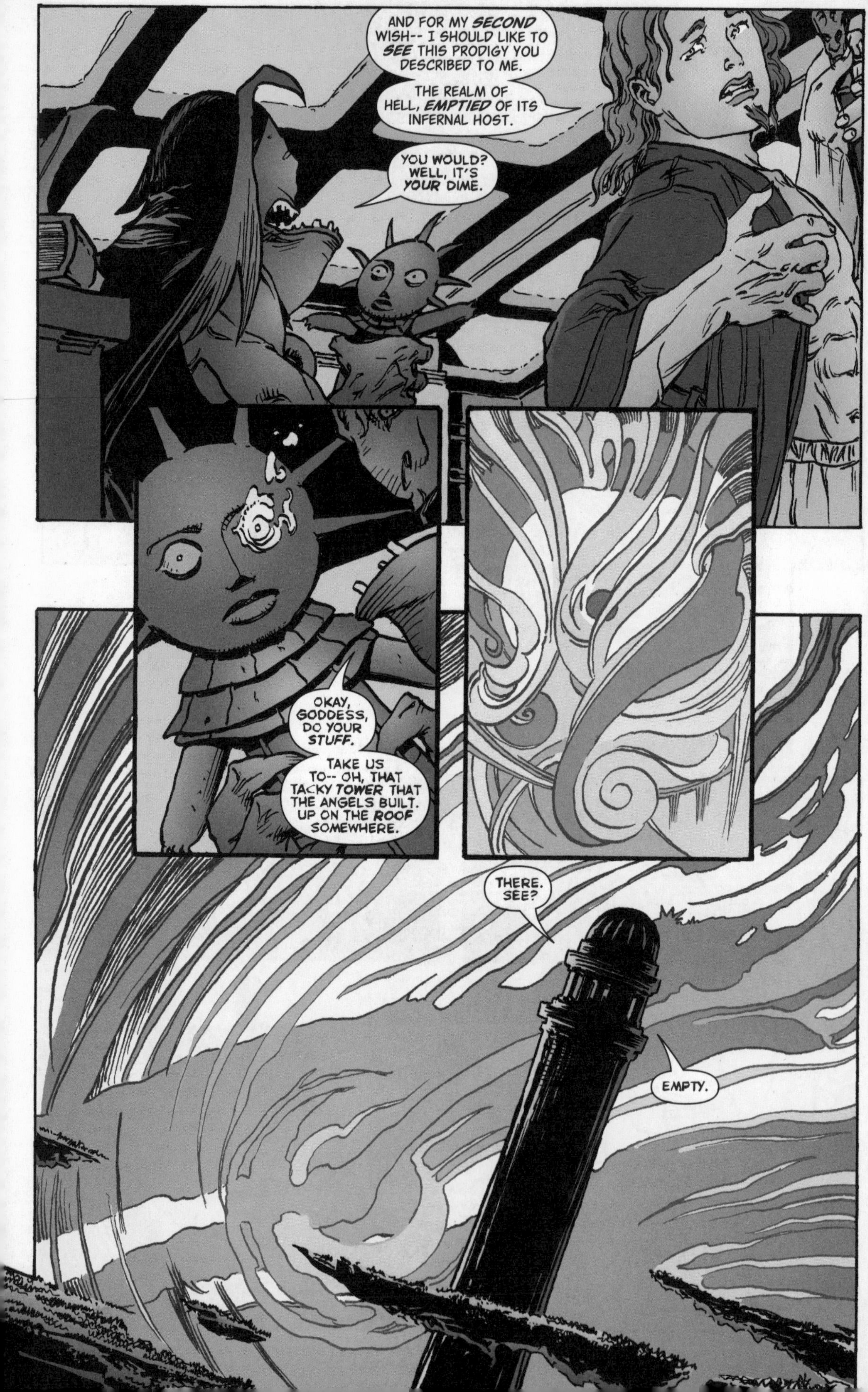
AND FOR MY SECOND WISH-- I SHOULD LIKE TO SEE THIS PRODIGY YOU DESCRIBED TO ME.
THE REALM OF HELL, EMPTIED OF ITS INFERNAL HOST.
YOU WOULD? WELL, IT'S YOUR DIME.
OKAY, GODDESS, DO YOUR STUFF.
TAKE US TO-- OH, THAT TACKY TOWER THAT THE ANGELS BUILT. UP ON THE ROOF SOMEWHERE.
THERE. SEE?
EMPTY.

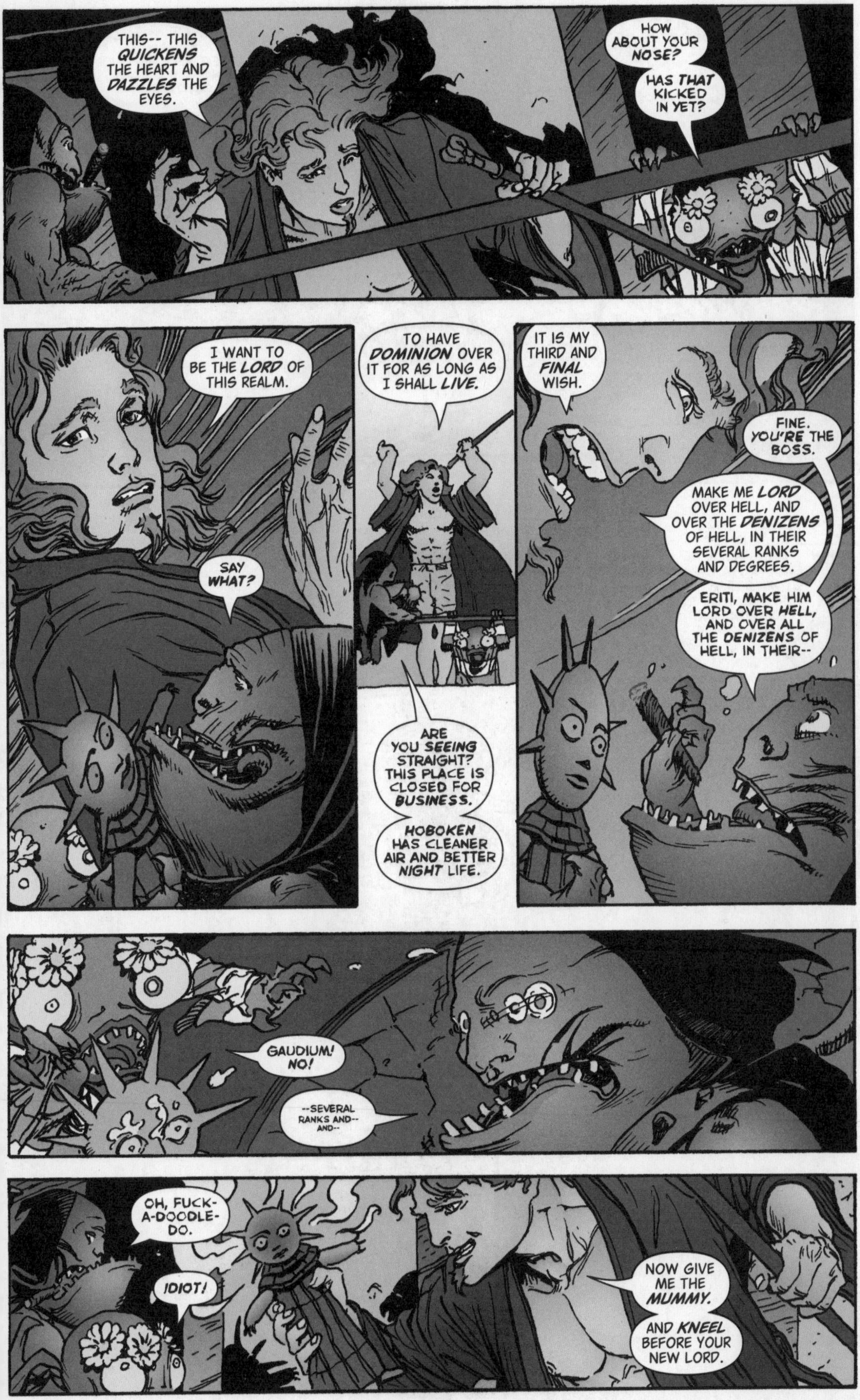
THIS-- THIS QUICKENS THE HEART AND DAZZLES THE EYES.
HOW ABOUT YOUR NOSE?
HAS THAT KICKED IN YET?
I WANT TO BE THE LORD OF THIS REALM.
SAY WHAT?
TO HAVE DOMINION OVER IT FOR AS LONG AS I SHALL LIVE.
ARE YOU SEEING STRAIGHT? THIS PLACE IS CLOSED FOR BUSINESS.
HOBOKEN HAS CLEANER AIR AND BETTER NIGHT LIFE.
IT IS MY THIRD AND FINAL WISH.
FINE. YOU'RE THE BOSS.
MAKE ME LORD OVER HELL, AND OVER THE DENIZENS OF HELL, IN THEIR SEVERAL RANKS AND DEGREES.
ERITI, MAKE HIM LORD OVER HELL, AND OVER ALL THE DENIZENS OF HELL, IN THEIR--
GAUDIUM! NO!
--SEVERAL RANKS AND-- AND--
OH, FUCK-A-DOODLE-DO.
IDIOT!
NOW GIVE ME THE MUMMY.
AND KNEEL BEFORE YOUR NEW LORD.

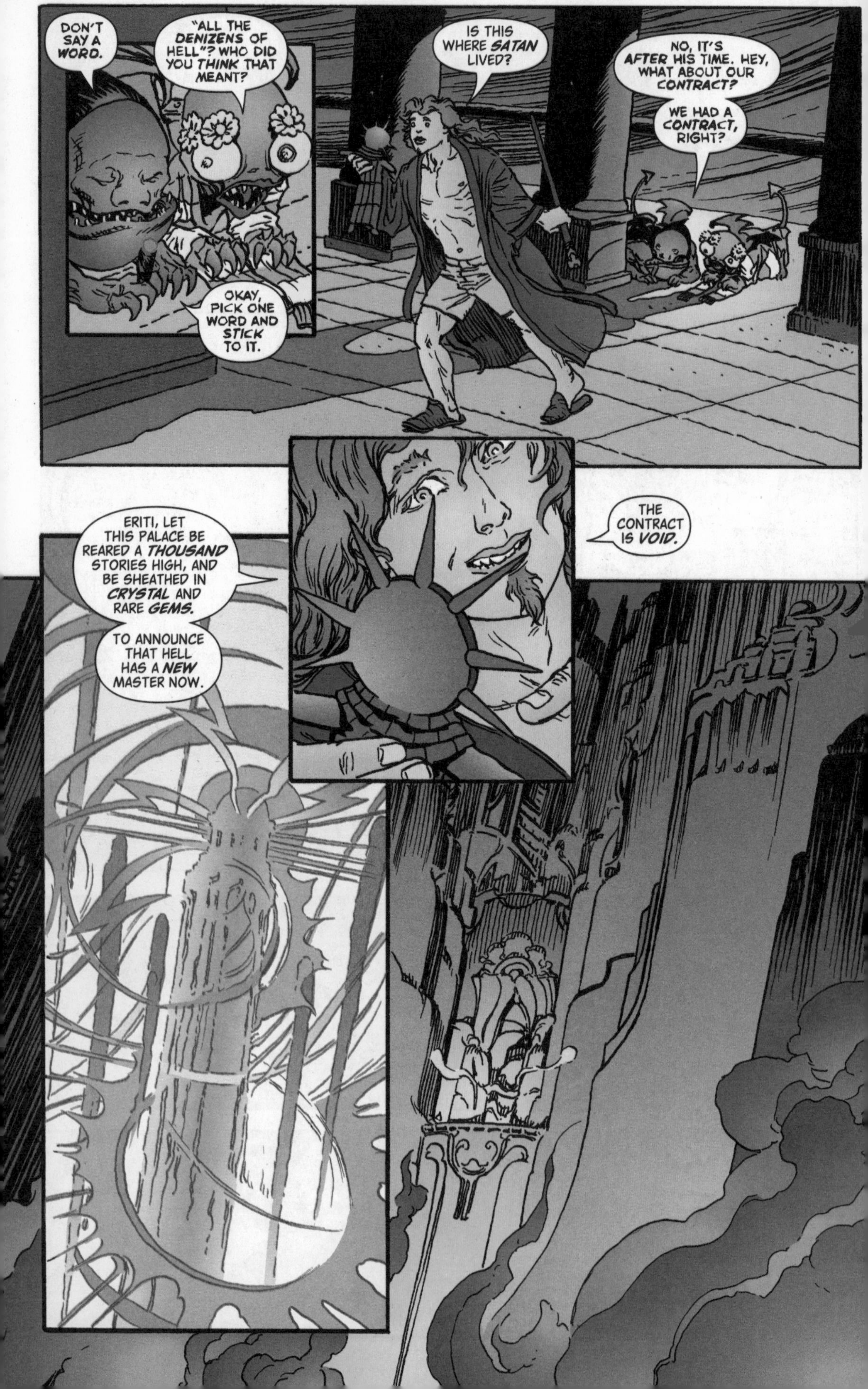

DON'T SAY A WORD.
"ALL THE DENIZENS OF HELL"? WHO DID YOU THINK THAT MEANT?
OKAY, PICK ONE WORD AND STICK TO IT.
IS THIS WHERE SATAN LIVED?
NO, IT'S AFTER HIS TIME. HEY, WHAT ABOUT OUR CONTRACT?
WE HAD A CONTRACT, RIGHT?
THE CONTRACT IS VOID.
ERITI, LET THIS PALACE BE REARED A THOUSAND STORIES HIGH, AND BE SHEATHED IN CRYSTAL AND RARE GEMS.
TO ANNOUNCE THAT HELL HAS A NEW MASTER NOW.

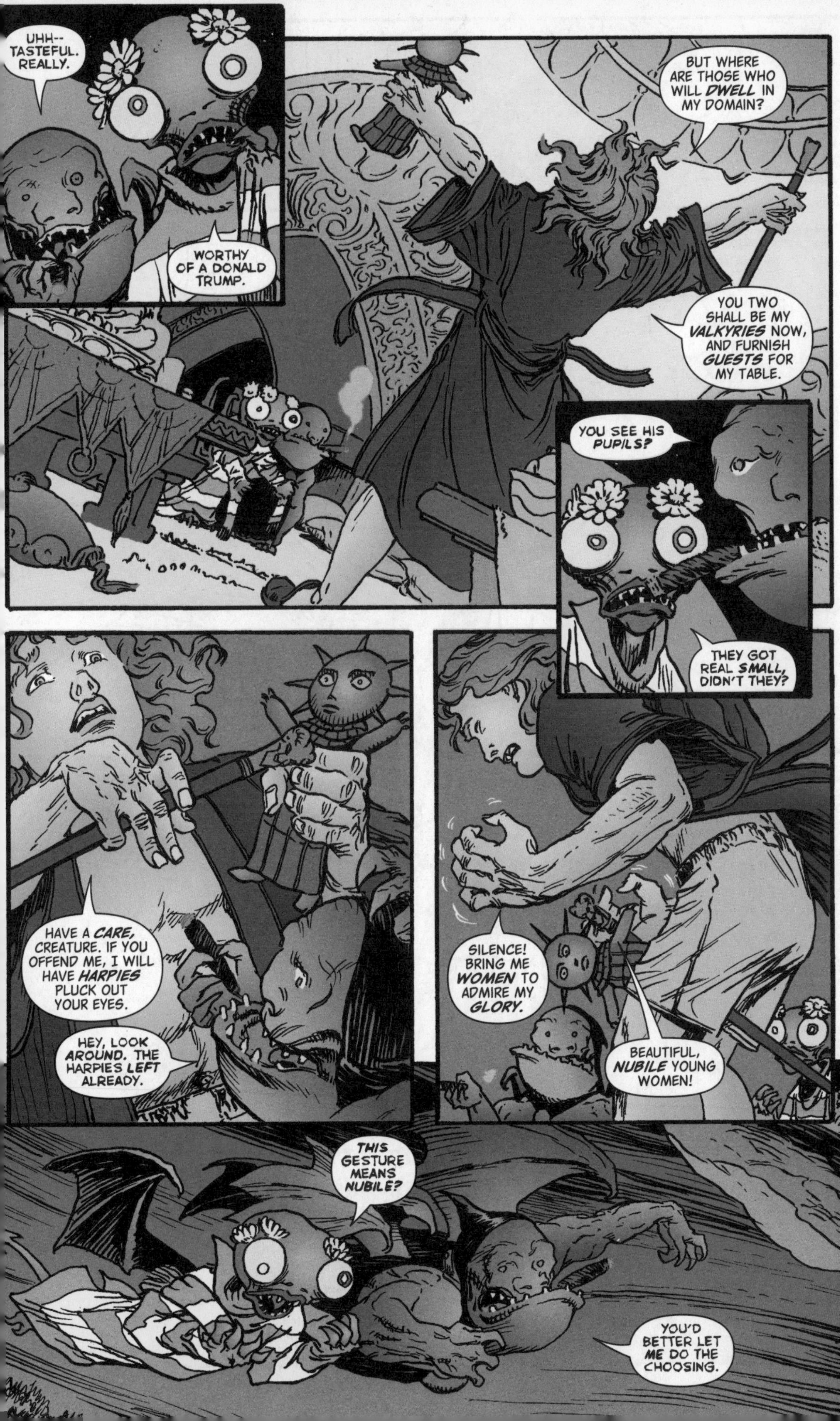
UHH-- TASTEFUL. REALLY.
WORTHY OF A DONALD TRUMP.
BUT WHERE ARE THOSE WHO WILL DWELL IN MY DOMAIN?
YOU TWO SHALL BE MY VALKYRIES NOW, AND FURNISH GUESTS FOR MY TABLE.
YOU SEE HIS PUPILS?
THEY GOT REAL SMALL, DIDN'T THEY?
HAVE A CARE, CREATURE. IF YOU OFFEND ME, I WILL HAVE HARPIES PLUCK OUT YOUR EYES.
HEY, LOOK AROUND. THE HARPIES LEFT ALREADY.
SILENCE! BRING ME WOMEN TO ADMIRE MY GLORY.
BEAUTIFUL, NUBILE YOUNG WOMEN!
THIS GESTURE MEANS NUBILE?
YOU'D BETTER LET ME DO THE CHOOSING.

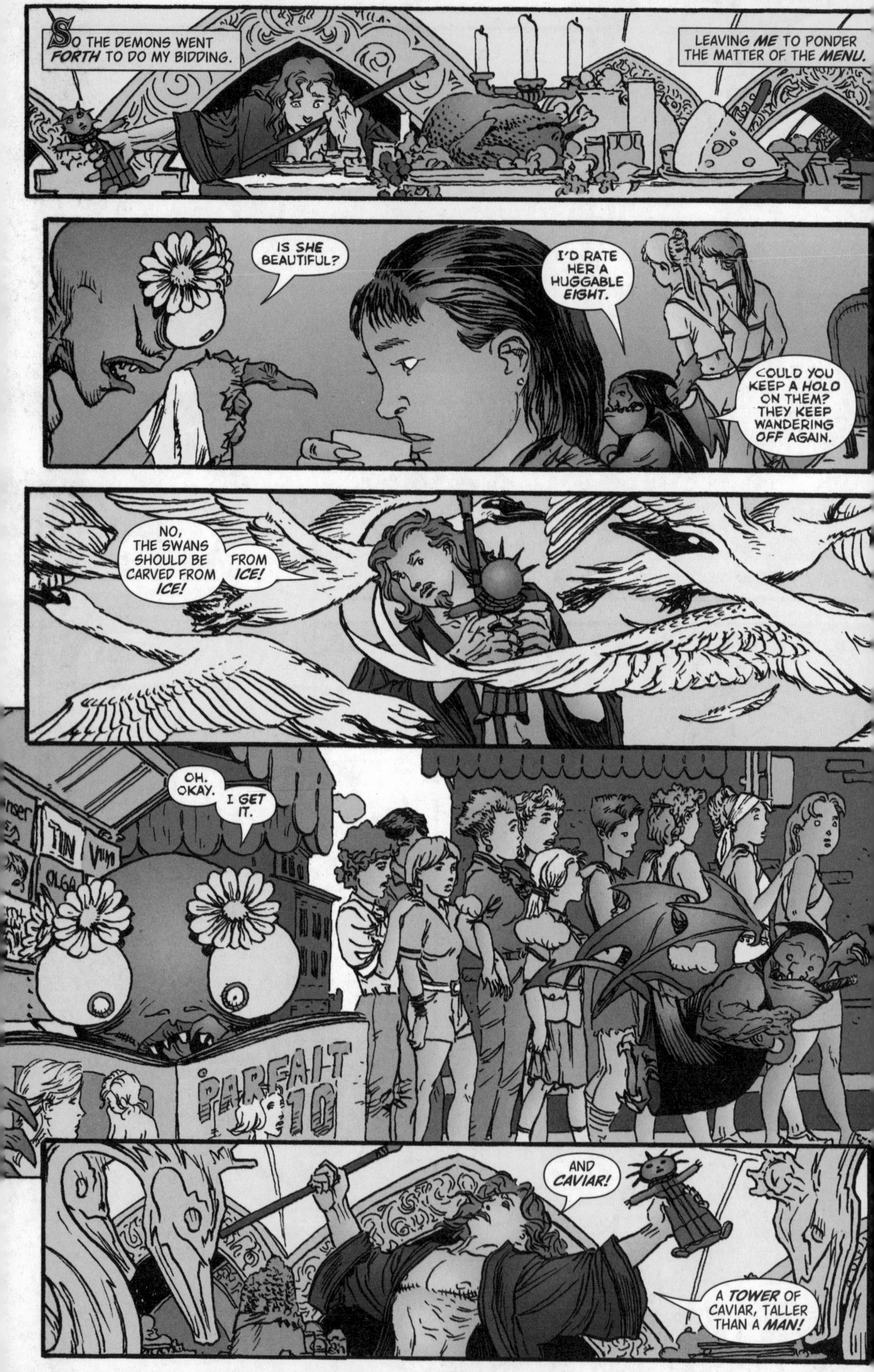

SO THE DEMONS WENT FORTH TO DO MY BIDDING.
LEAVING ME TO PONDER THE MATTER OF THE MENU.
IS SHE BEAUTIFUL?
I'D RATE HER A HUGGABLE EIGHT.
COULD YOU KEEP A HOLD ON THEM? THEY KEEP WANDERING OFF AGAIN.
NO, THE SWANS SHOULD BE CARVED FROM ICE!
FROM ICE!
OH. OKAY.
I GET IT.
PARFAIT 10
AND CAVIAR!
A TOWER OF CAVIAR, TALLER THAN A MAN!

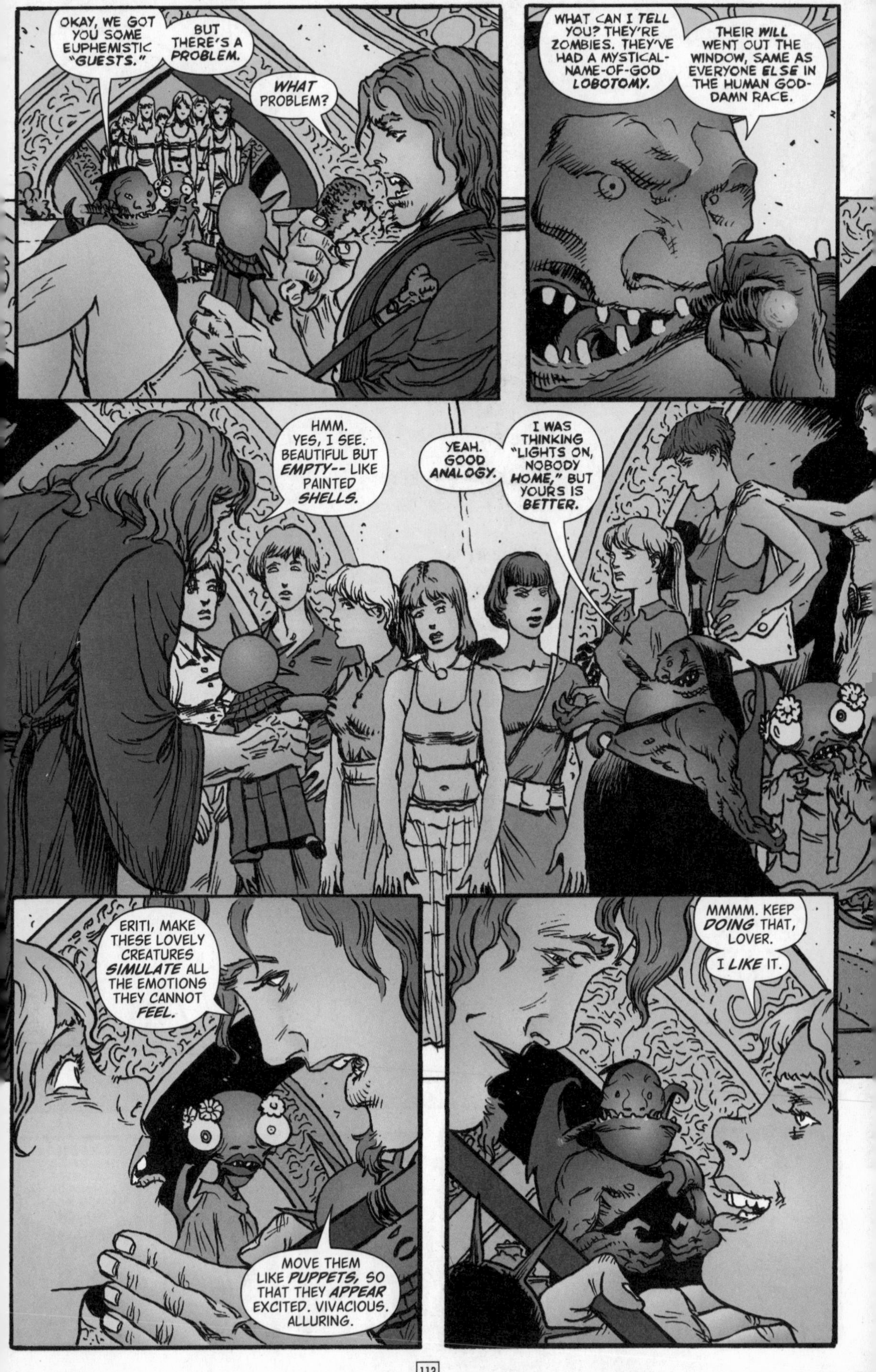

OKAY, WE GOT YOU SOME EUPHEMISTIC "GUESTS."
BUT THERE'S A PROBLEM.
WHAT PROBLEM?
WHAT CAN I TELL YOU? THEY'RE ZOMBIES. THEY'VE HAD A MYSTICAL-NAME-OF-GOD LOBOTOMY.
THEIR WILL WENT OUT THE WINDOW, SAME AS EVERYONE ELSE IN THE HUMAN GOD-DAMN RACE.
HMM. YES, I SEE. BEAUTIFUL BUT EMPTY-- LIKE PAINTED SHELLS.
YEAH. GOOD ANALOGY.
I WAS THINKING "LIGHTS ON, NOBODY HOME," BUT YOURS IS BETTER.
ERITI, MAKE THESE LOVELY CREATURES SIMULATE ALL THE EMOTIONS THEY CANNOT FEEL.
MOVE THEM LIKE PUPPETS, SO THAT THEY APPEAR EXCITED. VIVACIOUS. ALLURING.
MMMM. KEEP DOING THAT, LOVER.
I LIKE IT.

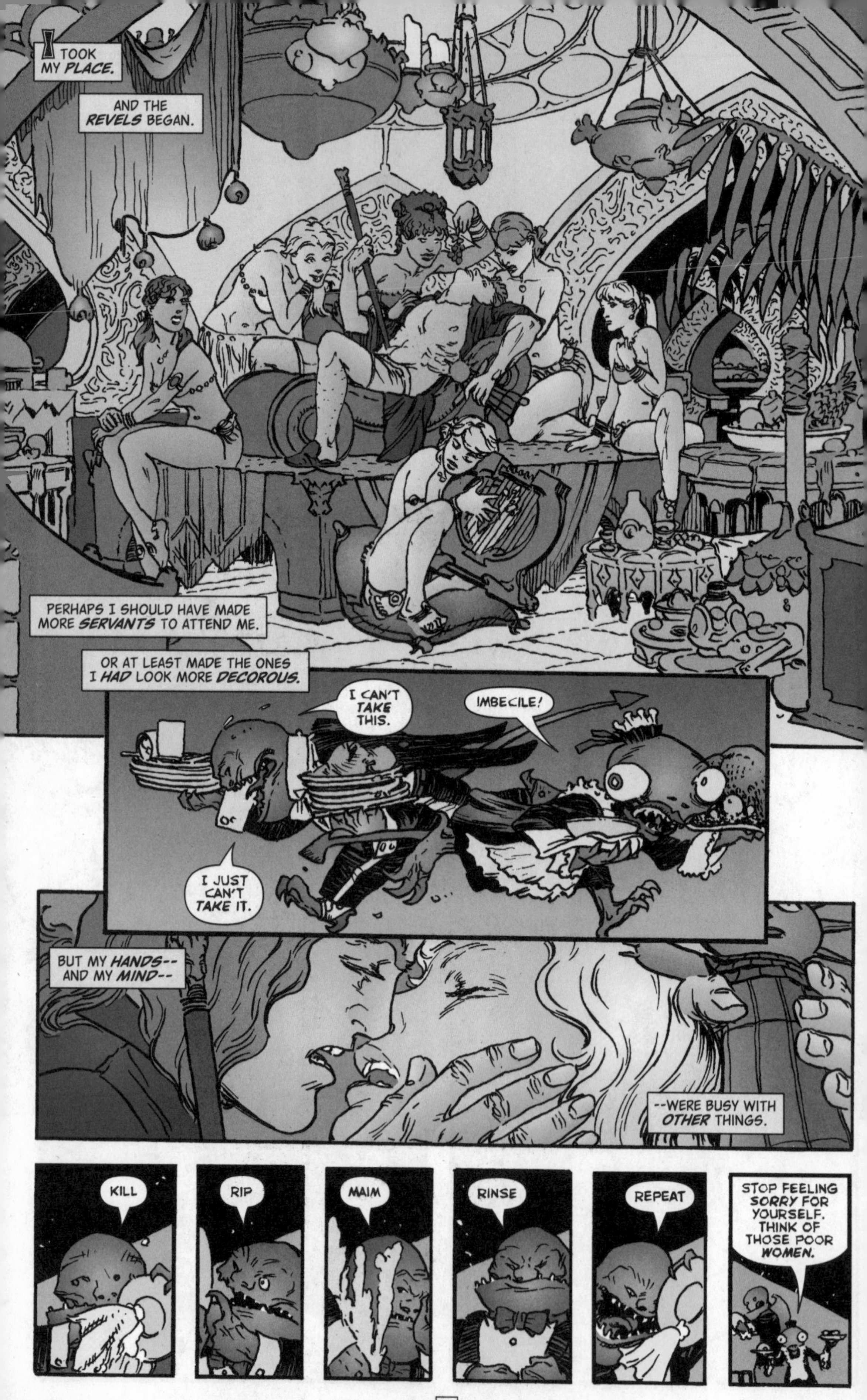
I TOOK MY PLACE.
AND THE REVELS BEGAN.
PERHAPS I SHOULD HAVE MADE MORE SERVANTS TO ATTEND ME.
OR AT LEAST MADE THE ONES I HAD LOOK MORE DECOROUS.
I CAN'T TAKE THIS.
IMBECILE!
I JUST CAN'T TAKE IT.
BUT MY HANDS-- AND MY MIND--
--WERE BUSY WITH OTHER THINGS.
KILL
RIP
MAIM
RINSE
REPEAT
STOP FEELING SORRY FOR YOURSELF. THINK OF THOSE POOR WOMEN.

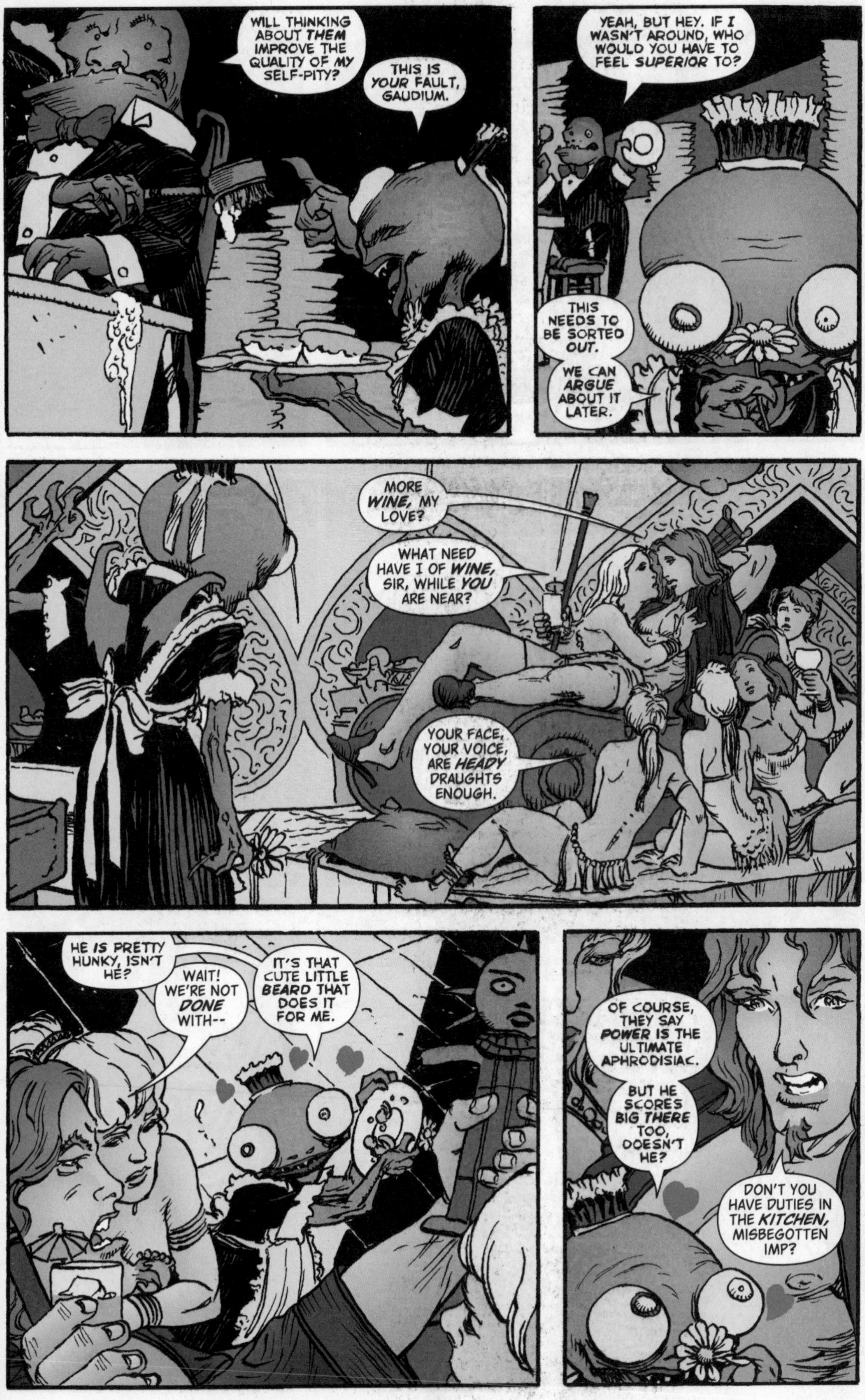
WILL THINKING ABOUT THEM IMPROVE THE QUALITY OF MY SELF-PITY?
THIS IS YOUR FAULT, GAUDIUM.
YEAH, BUT HEY. IF I WASN'T AROUND, WHO WOULD YOU HAVE TO FEEL SUPERIOR TO?
THIS NEEDS TO BE SORTED OUT.
WE CAN ARGUE ABOUT IT LATER.
MORE WINE, MY LOVE?
WHAT NEED HAVE I OF WINE, SIR, WHILE YOU ARE NEAR?
YOUR FACE, YOUR VOICE, ARE HEADY DRAUGHTS ENOUGH.
HE IS PRETTY HUNKY, ISN'T HE?
WAIT! WE'RE NOT DONE WITH--
IT'S THAT CUTE LITTLE BEARD THAT DOES IT FOR ME.
OF COURSE, THEY SAY POWER IS THE ULTIMATE APHRODISIAC.
BUT HE SCORES BIG THERE TOO, DOESN'T HE?
DON'T YOU HAVE DUTIES IN THE KITCHEN, MISBEGOTTEN IMP?

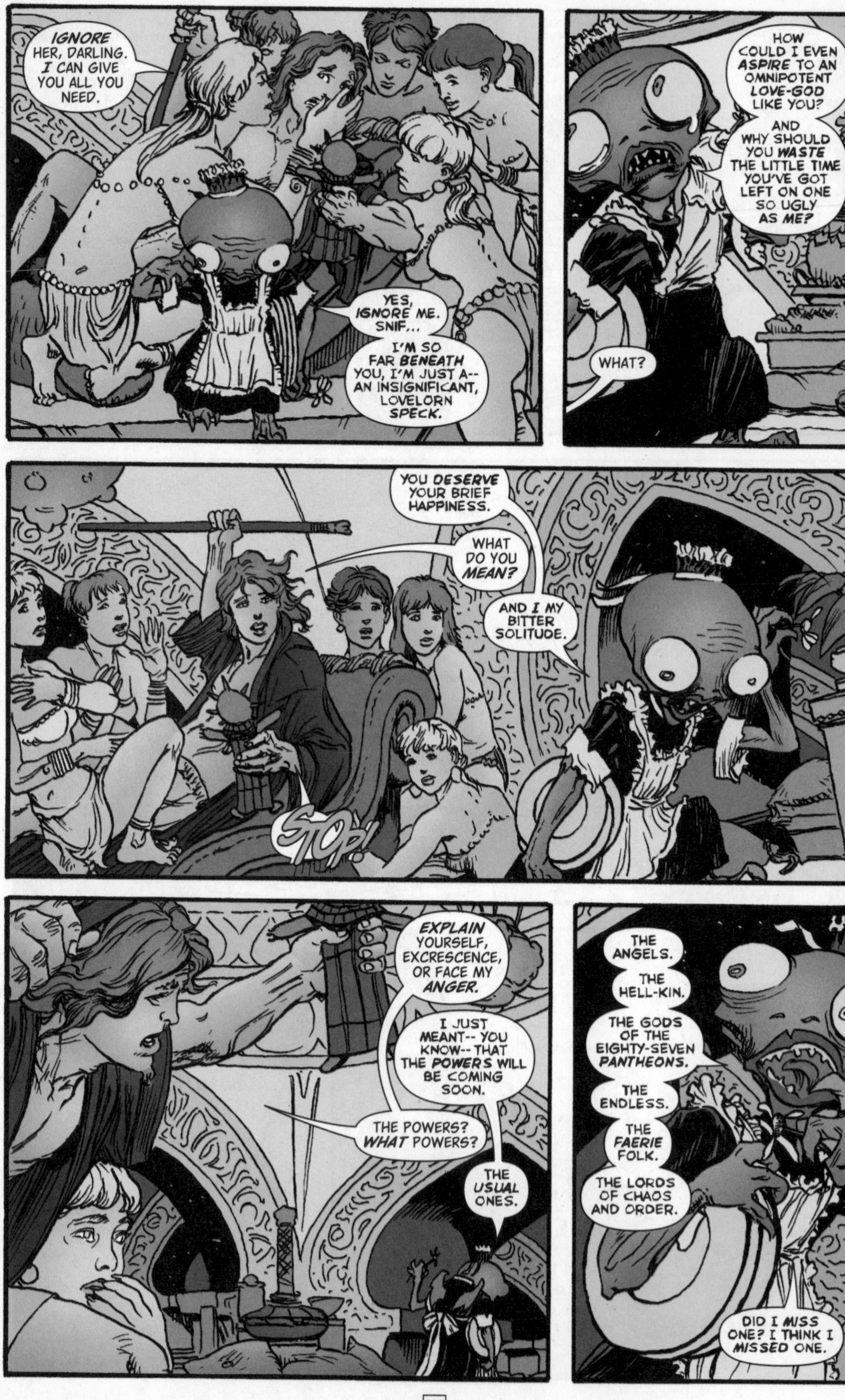
IGNORE HER, DARLING. I CAN GIVE YOU ALL YOU NEED.
YES, IGNORE ME. SNIF...
I'M SO FAR BENEATH YOU, I'M JUST A-- AN INSIGNIFICANT, LOVELORN SPECK.
HOW COULD I EVEN ASPIRE TO AN OMNIPOTENT LOVE-GOD LIKE YOU?
AND WHY SHOULD YOU WASTE THE LITTLE TIME YOU'VE GOT LEFT ON ONE SO UGLY AS ME?
WHAT?
YOU DESERVE YOUR BRIEF HAPPINESS.
WHAT DO YOU MEAN?
AND I MY BITTER SOLITUDE.
STOP!
EXPLAIN YOURSELF, EXCRESCENCE, OR FACE MY ANGER.
I JUST MEANT-- YOU KNOW-- THAT THE POWERS WILL BE COMING SOON.
THE POWERS? WHAT POWERS?
THE USUAL ONES.
THE ANGELS.
THE HELL-KIN.
THE GODS OF THE EIGHTY-SEVEN PANTHEONS.
THE ENDLESS.
THE FAERIE FOLK.
THE LORDS OF CHAOS AND ORDER.
DID I MISS ONE? I THINK I MISSED ONE.

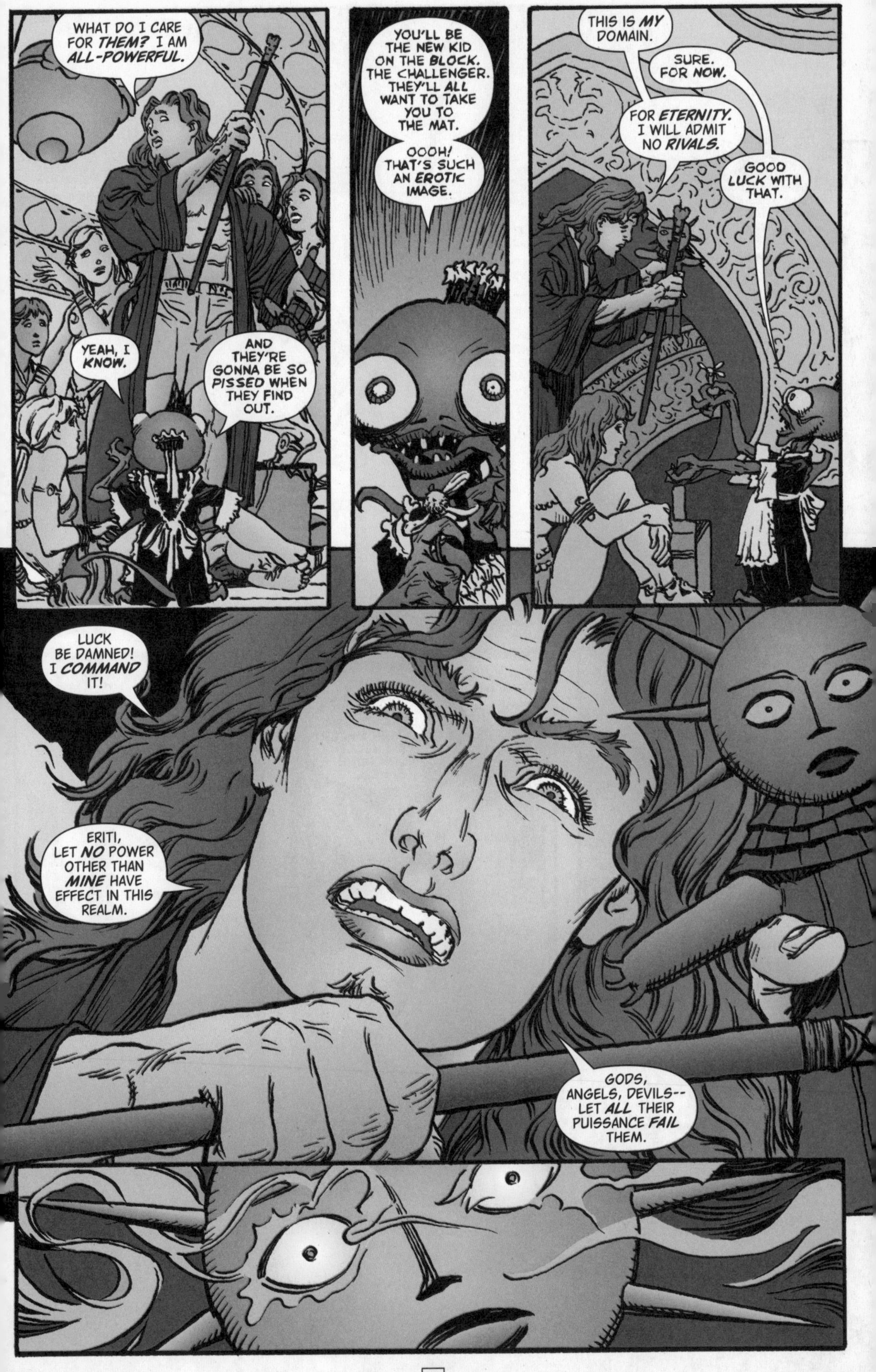
WHAT DO I CARE FOR THEM? I AM ALL-POWERFUL.
YEAH, I KNOW.
AND THEY'RE GONNA BE SO PISSED WHEN THEY FIND OUT.
YOU'LL BE THE NEW KID ON THE BLOCK. THE CHALLENGER. THEY'LL ALL WANT TO TAKE YOU TO THE MAT.
OOOH! THAT'S SUCH AN EROTIC IMAGE.
THIS IS MY DOMAIN.
SURE. FOR NOW.
FOR ETERNITY. I WILL ADMIT NO RIVALS.
GOOD LUCK WITH THAT.
LUCK BE DAMNED! I COMMAND IT!
ERITI, LET NO POWER OTHER THAN MINE HAVE EFFECT IN THIS REALM.
GODS, ANGELS, DEVILS-- LET ALL THEIR PUISSANCE FAIL THEM.

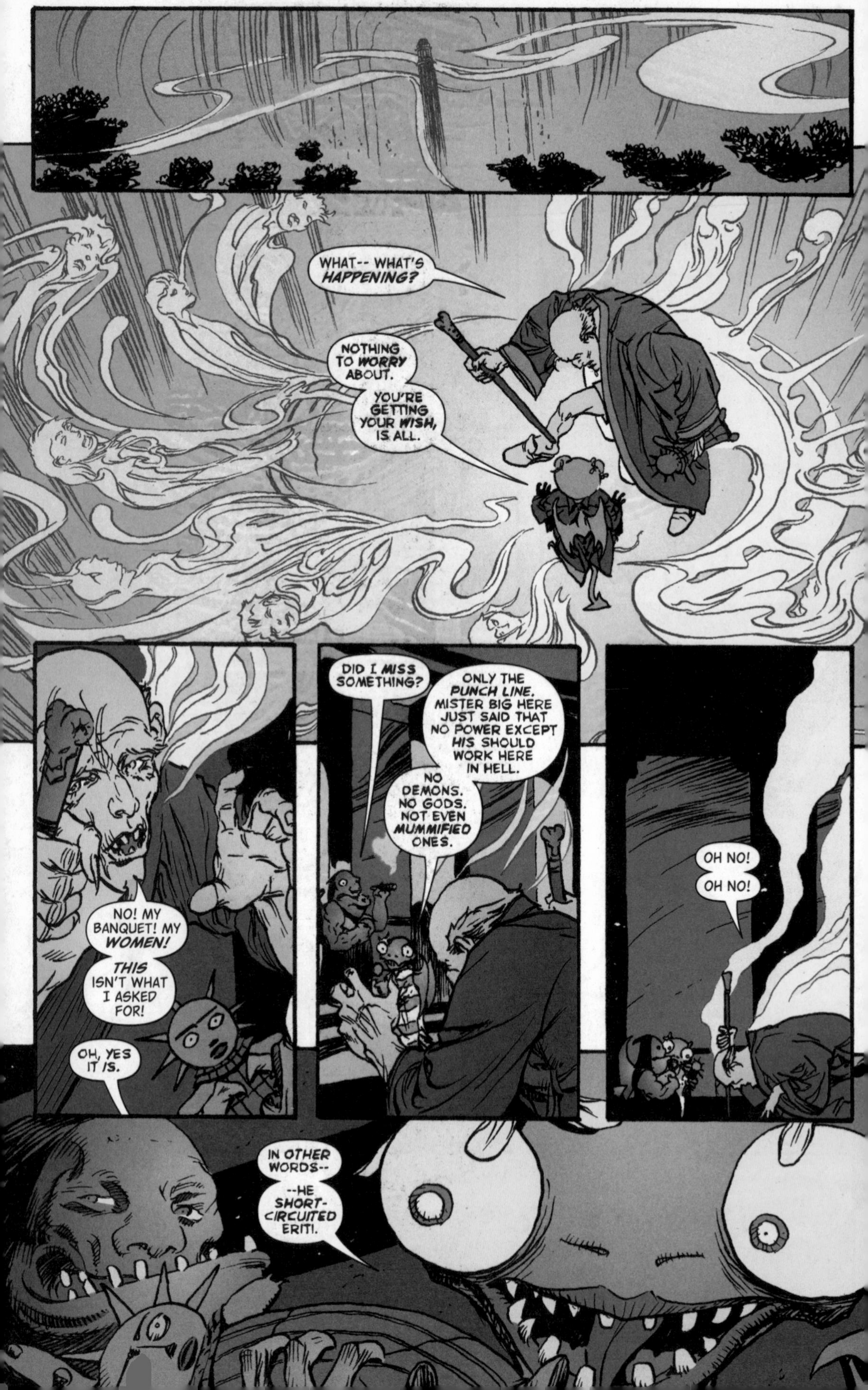
WHAT-- WHAT'S HAPPENING?
NOTHING TO WORRY ABOUT.
YOU'RE GETTING YOUR WISH, IS ALL.
NO! MY BANQUET! MY WOMEN!
THIS ISN'T WHAT I ASKED FOR!
OH, YES IT IS.
DID I MISS SOMETHING?
ONLY THE PUNCH LINE. MISTER BIG HERE JUST SAID THAT NO POWER EXCEPT HIS SHOULD WORK HERE IN HELL.
NO DEMONS. NO GODS. NOT EVEN MUMMIFIED ONES.
OH NO!
OH NO!
IN OTHER WORDS--
--HE SHORT-CIRCUITED ERITI.

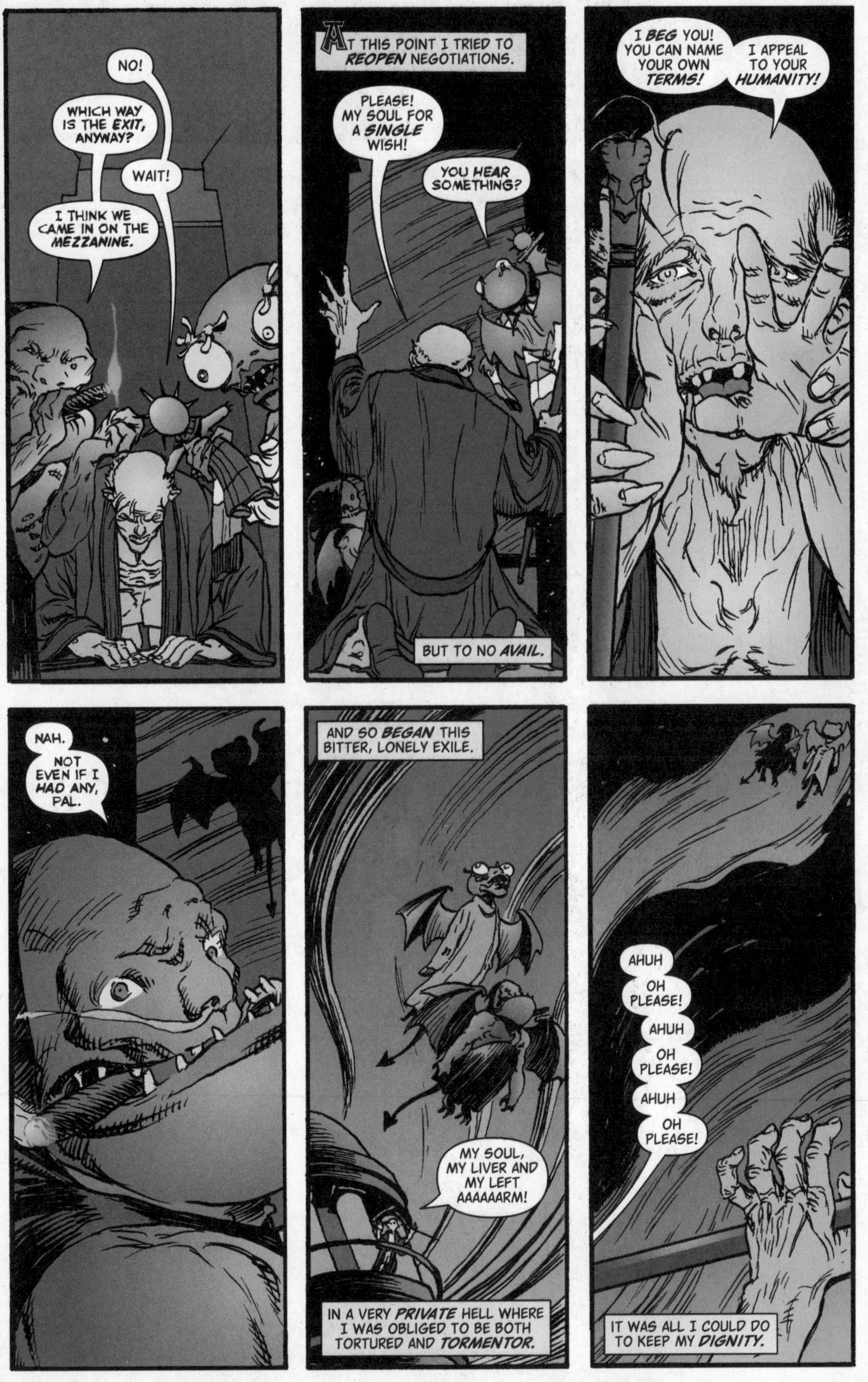
NO!
WHICH WAY IS THE EXIT, ANYWAY?
WAIT!
I THINK WE CAME IN ON THE MEZZANINE.
AT THIS POINT I TRIED TO REOPEN NEGOTIATIONS.
PLEASE! MY SOUL FOR A SINGLE WISH!
YOU HEAR SOMETHING?
BUT TO NO AVAIL.
I BEG YOU! YOU CAN NAME YOUR OWN TERMS!
I APPEAL TO YOUR HUMANITY!
NAH.
NOT EVEN IF I HAD ANY, PAL.
AND SO BEGAN THIS BITTER, LONELY EXILE.
MY SOUL, MY LIVER AND MY LEFT AAAAAARM!
IN A VERY PRIVATE HELL WHERE I WAS OBLIGED TO BE BOTH TORTURED AND TORMENTOR.
AHUH
OH PLEASE!
AHUH
OH PLEASE!
AHUH
OH PLEASE!
IT WAS ALL I COULD DO TO KEEP MY DIGNITY.

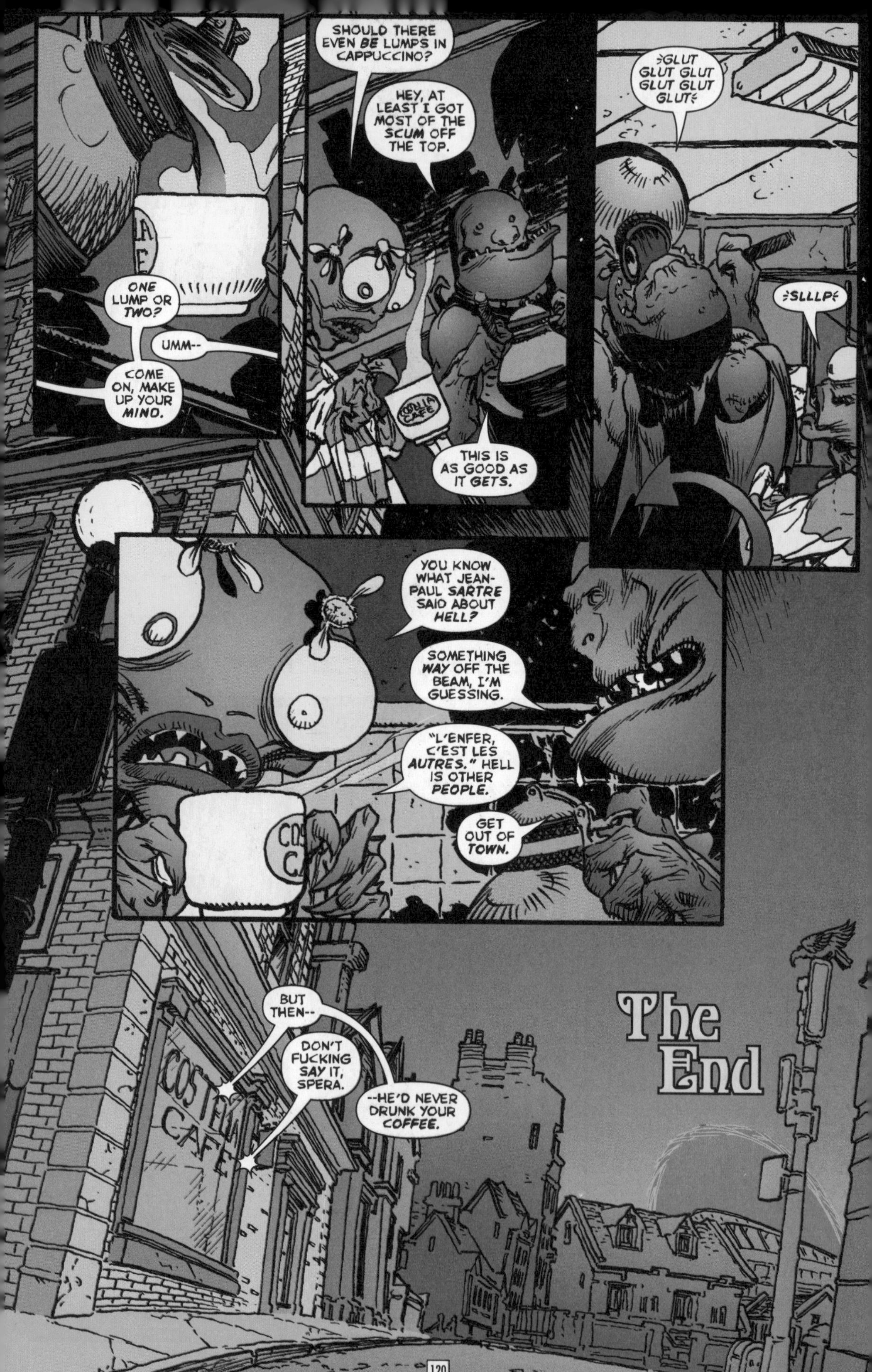
ONE LUMP OR TWO?
UMM--
COME ON, MAKE UP YOUR MIND.
SHOULD THERE EVEN BE LUMPS IN CAPPUCCINO?
HEY, AT LEAST I GOT MOST OF THE SCUM OFF THE TOP.
THIS IS AS GOOD AS IT GETS.
GLUT GLUT GLUT GLUT GLUT GLUT
SLLLP
YOU KNOW WHAT JEAN-PAUL SARTRE SAID ABOUT HELL?
SOMETHING WAY OFF THE BEAM, I'M GUESSING.
"L'ENFER, C'EST LES AUTRES." HELL IS OTHER PEOPLE.
GET OUT OF TOWN.
BUT THEN--
DON'T FUCKING SAY IT, SPERA.
--HE'D NEVER DRUNK YOUR COFFEE.
The End

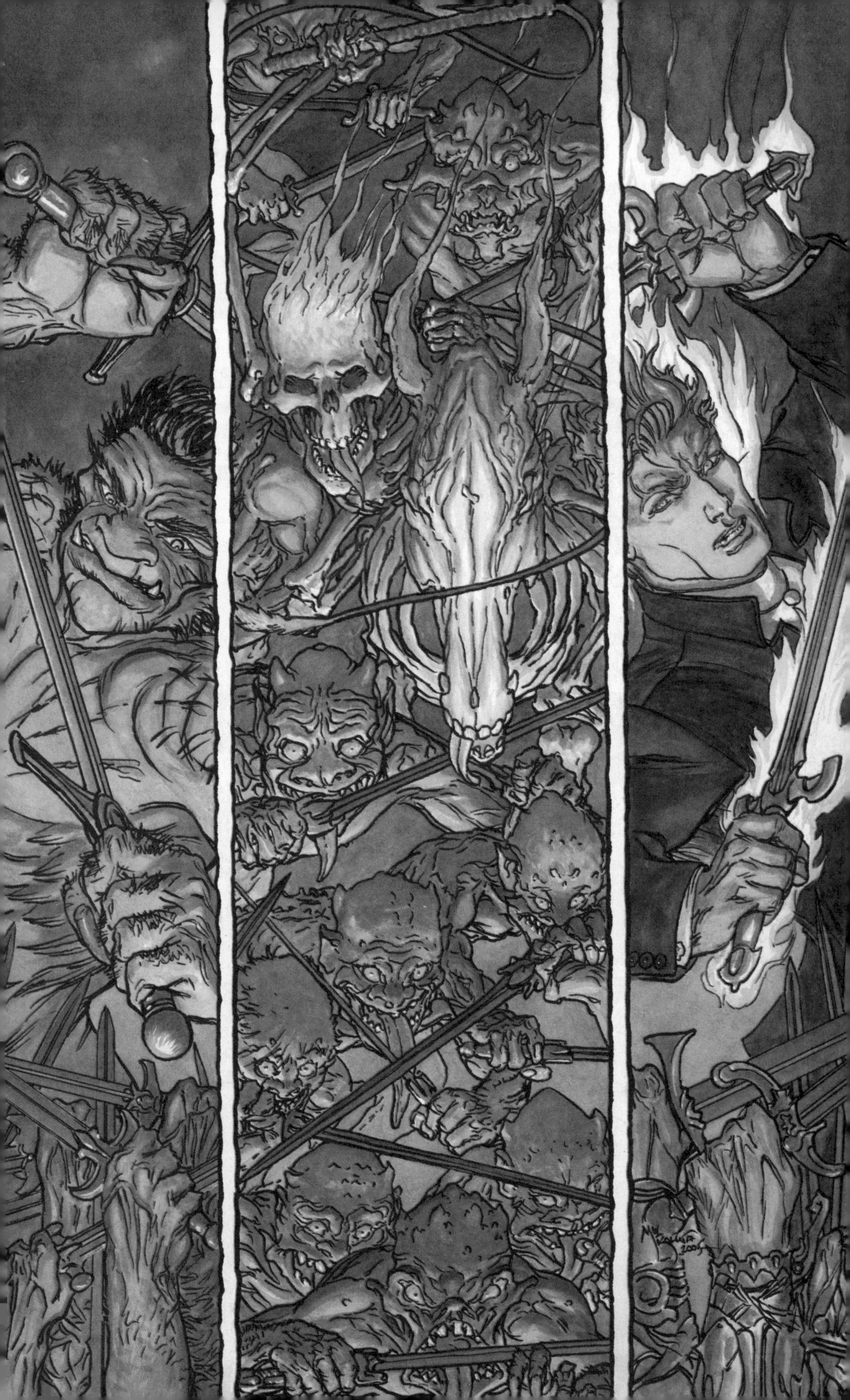

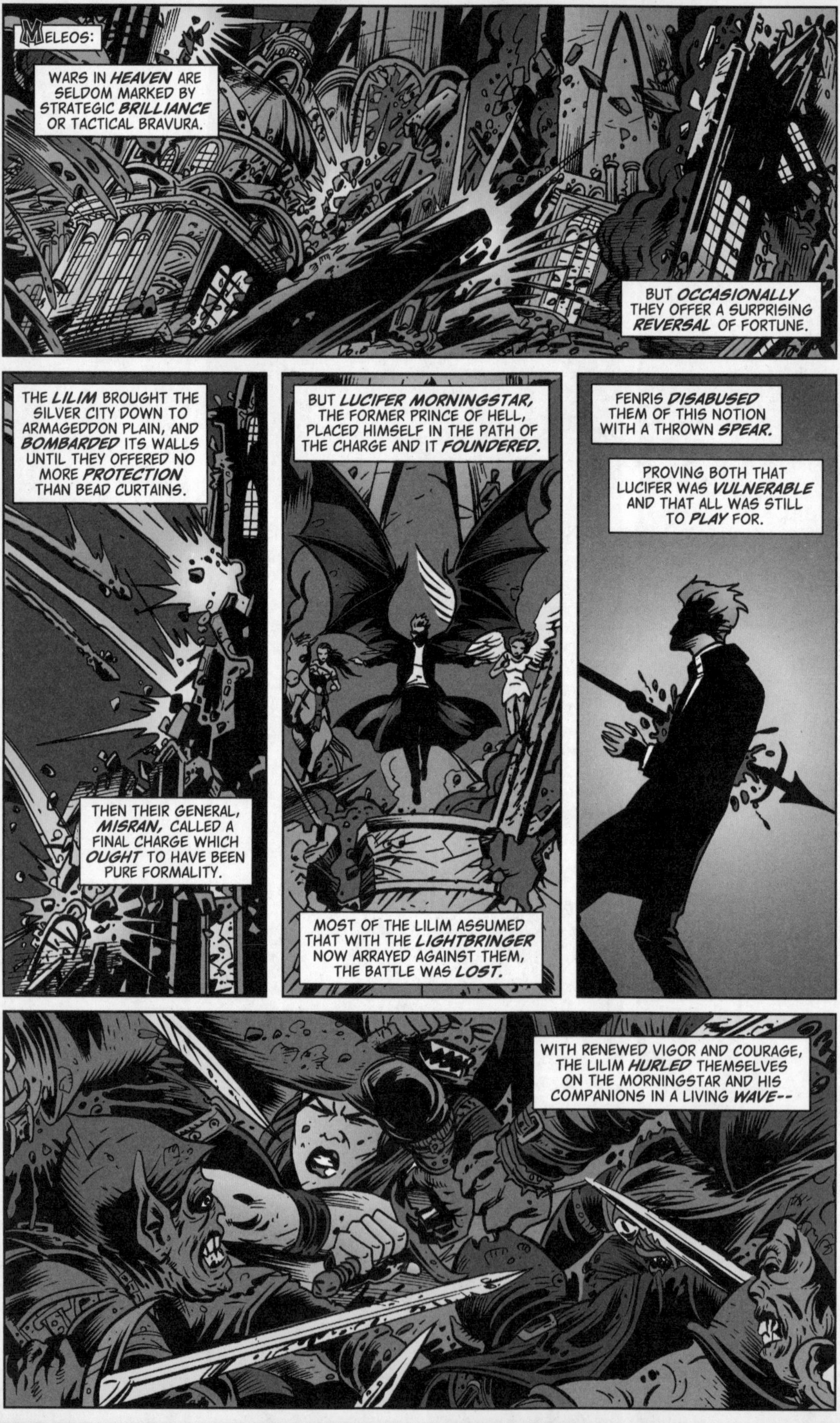
MELEOS:
WARS IN HEAVEN ARE SELDOM MARKED BY STRATEGIC BRILLIANCE OR TACTICAL BRAVURA.
BUT OCCASIONALLY THEY OFFER A SURPRISING REVERSAL OF FORTUNE.
THE LILIM BROUGHT THE SILVER CITY DOWN TO ARMAGEDDON PLAIN, AND BOMBARDED ITS WALLS UNTIL THEY OFFERED NO MORE PROTECTION THAN BEAD CURTAINS.
THEN THEIR GENERAL, MISRAN, CALLED A FINAL CHARGE WHICH OUGHT TO HAVE BEEN PURE FORMALITY.
BUT LUCIFER MORNINGSTAR, THE FORMER PRINCE OF HELL, PLACED HIMSELF IN THE PATH OF THE CHARGE AND IT FOUNDERED.
MOST OF THE LILIM ASSUMED THAT WITH THE LIGHTBRINGER NOW ARRAYED AGAINST THEM, THE BATTLE WAS LOST.
FENRIS DISABUSED THEM OF THIS NOTION WITH A THROWN SPEAR.
PROVING BOTH THAT LUCIFER WAS VULNERABLE AND THAT ALL WAS STILL TO PLAY FOR.
WITH RENEWED VIGOR AND COURAGE, THE LILIM HURLED THEMSELVES ON THE MORNINGSTAR AND HIS COMPANIONS IN A LIVING WAVE--

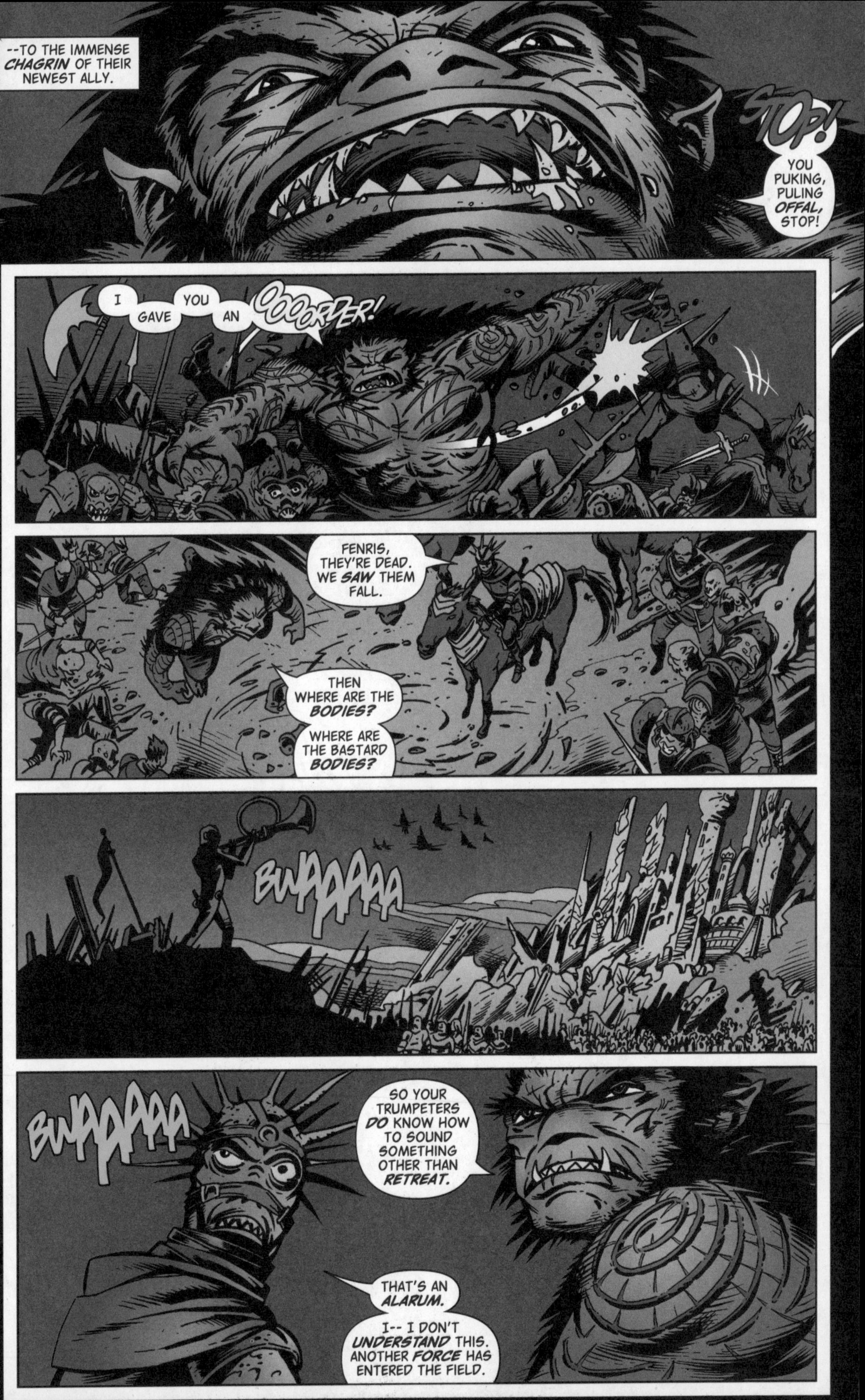
--TO THE IMMENSE CHAGRIN OF THEIR NEWEST ALLY.
STOP!
YOU PUKING, PULING OFFAL, STOP!
I GAVE YOU AN OOOORDER!
FENRIS, THEY'RE DEAD. WE SAW THEM FALL.
THEN WHERE ARE THE BODIES?
WHERE ARE THE BASTARD BODIES?
BWAAAAA
BWAAAAA
SO YOUR TRUMPETERS DO KNOW HOW TO SOUND SOMETHING OTHER THAN RETREAT.
THAT'S AN ALARUM.
I-- I DON'T UNDERSTAND THIS. ANOTHER FORCE HAS ENTERED THE FIELD.

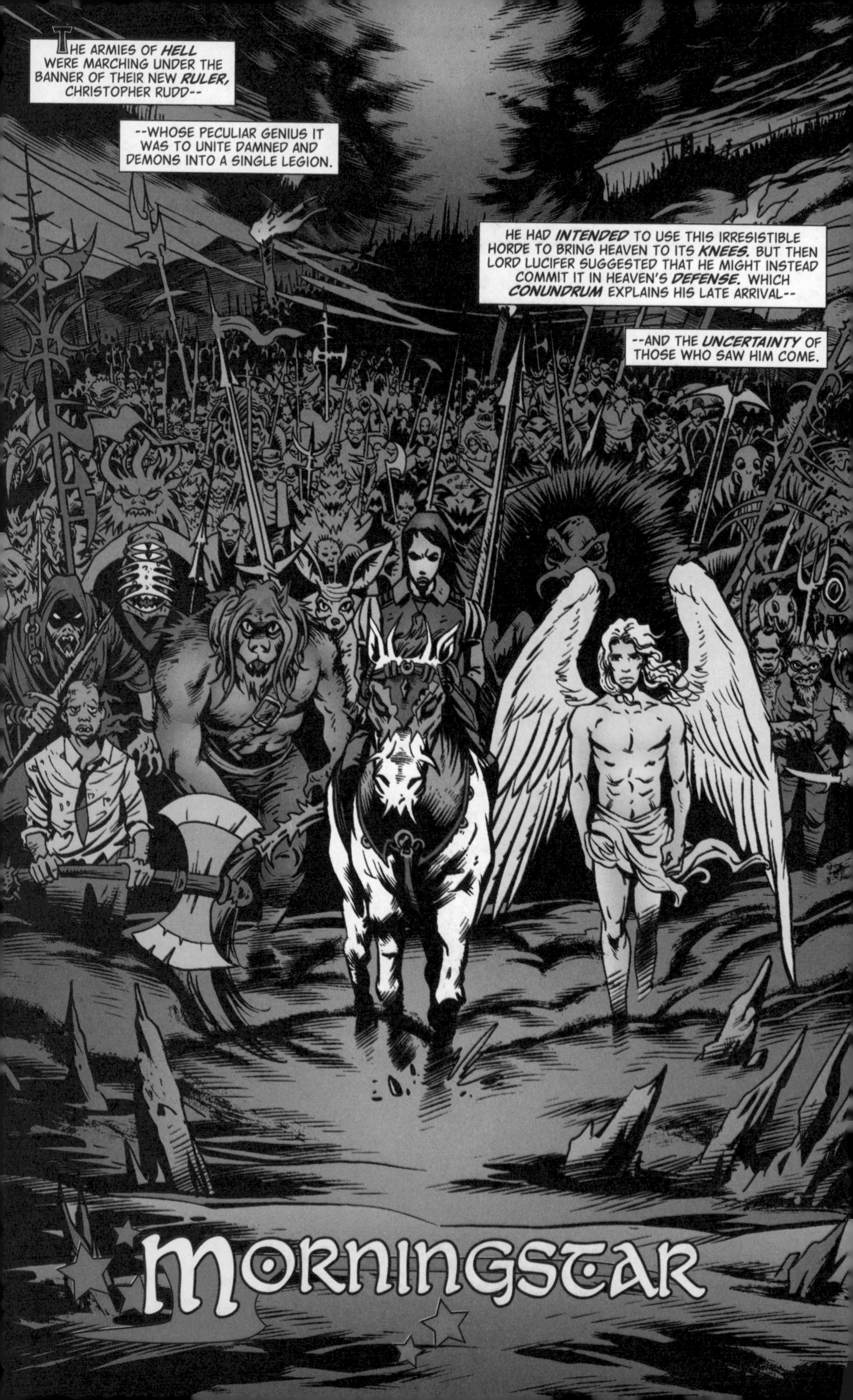
THE ARMIES OF HELL WERE MARCHING UNDER THE BANNER OF THEIR NEW RULER, CHRISTOPHER RUDD--
--WHOSE PECULIAR GENIUS IT WAS TO UNITE DAMNED AND DEMONS INTO A SINGLE LEGION.
HE HAD INTENDED TO USE THIS IRRESISTIBLE HORDE TO BRING HEAVEN TO ITS KNEES. BUT THEN LORD LUCIFER SUGGESTED THAT HE MIGHT INSTEAD COMMIT IT IN HEAVEN'S DEFENSE. WHICH CONUNDRUM EXPLAINS HIS LATE ARRIVAL--
--AND THE UNCERTAINTY OF THOSE WHO SAW HIM COME.
MORNINGSTAR

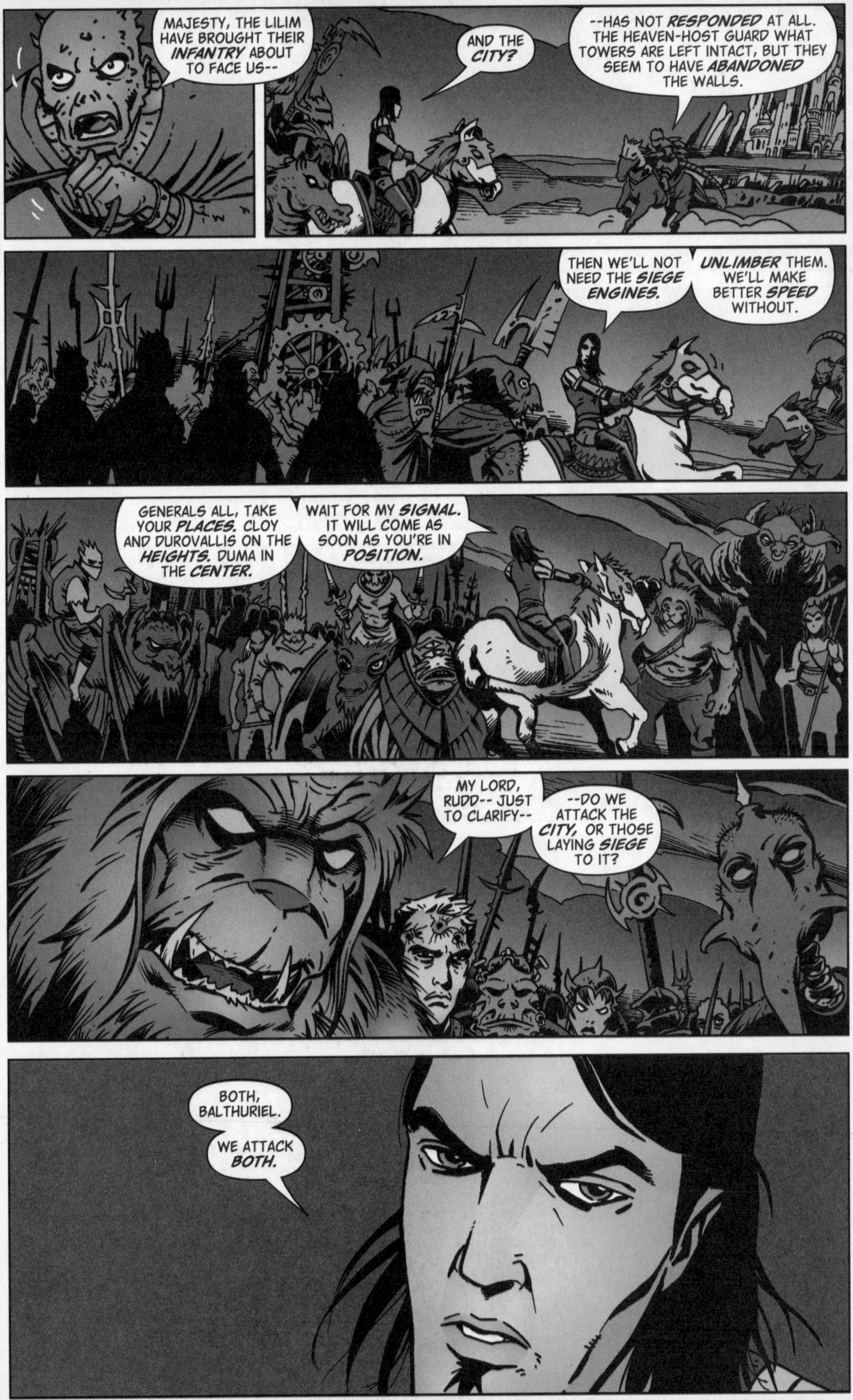
MAJESTY, THE LILIM HAVE BROUGHT THEIR INFANTRY ABOUT TO FACE US--
AND THE CITY?
--HAS NOT RESPONDED AT ALL. THE HEAVEN-HOST GUARD WHAT TOWERS ARE LEFT INTACT, BUT THEY SEEM TO HAVE ABANDONED THE WALLS.
THEN WE'LL NOT NEED THE SIEGE ENGINES.
UNLIMBER THEM. WE'LL MAKE BETTER SPEED WITHOUT.
GENERALS ALL, TAKE YOUR PLACES. CLOY AND DUROVALLIS ON THE HEIGHTS. DUMA IN THE CENTER.
WAIT FOR MY SIGNAL. IT WILL COME AS SOON AS YOU'RE IN POSITION.
MY LORD, RUDD-- JUST TO CLARIFY--
--DO WE ATTACK THE CITY, OR THOSE LAYING SIEGE TO IT?
BOTH, BALTHURIEL.
WE ATTACK BOTH.

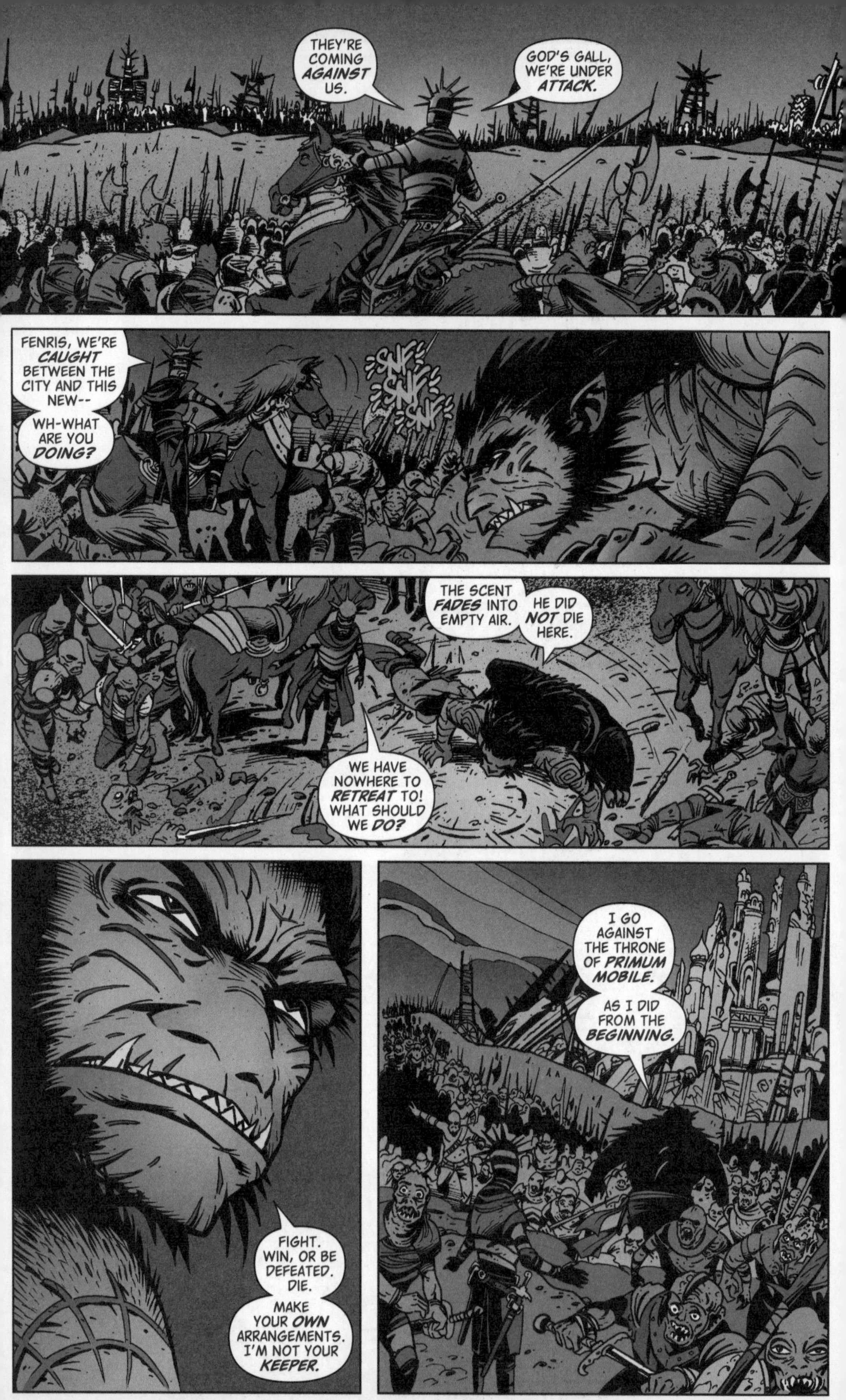
THEY'RE COMING *AGAINST* US.
GOD'S GALL, WE'RE UNDER *ATTACK.*
FENRIS, WE'RE *CAUGHT* BETWEEN THE CITY AND THIS NEW--
WH-WHAT ARE YOU *DOING?*
SNF SNF SNF
THE SCENT *FADES* INTO EMPTY AIR.
HE DID *NOT* DIE HERE.
WE HAVE NOWHERE TO *RETREAT* TO! WHAT SHOULD WE *DO?*
FIGHT. WIN, OR BE DEFEATED. DIE.
MAKE YOUR *OWN* ARRANGEMENTS. I'M NOT YOUR *KEEPER.*
I GO AGAINST THE THRONE OF *PRIMUM MOBILE.*
AS I DID FROM THE *BEGINNING.*

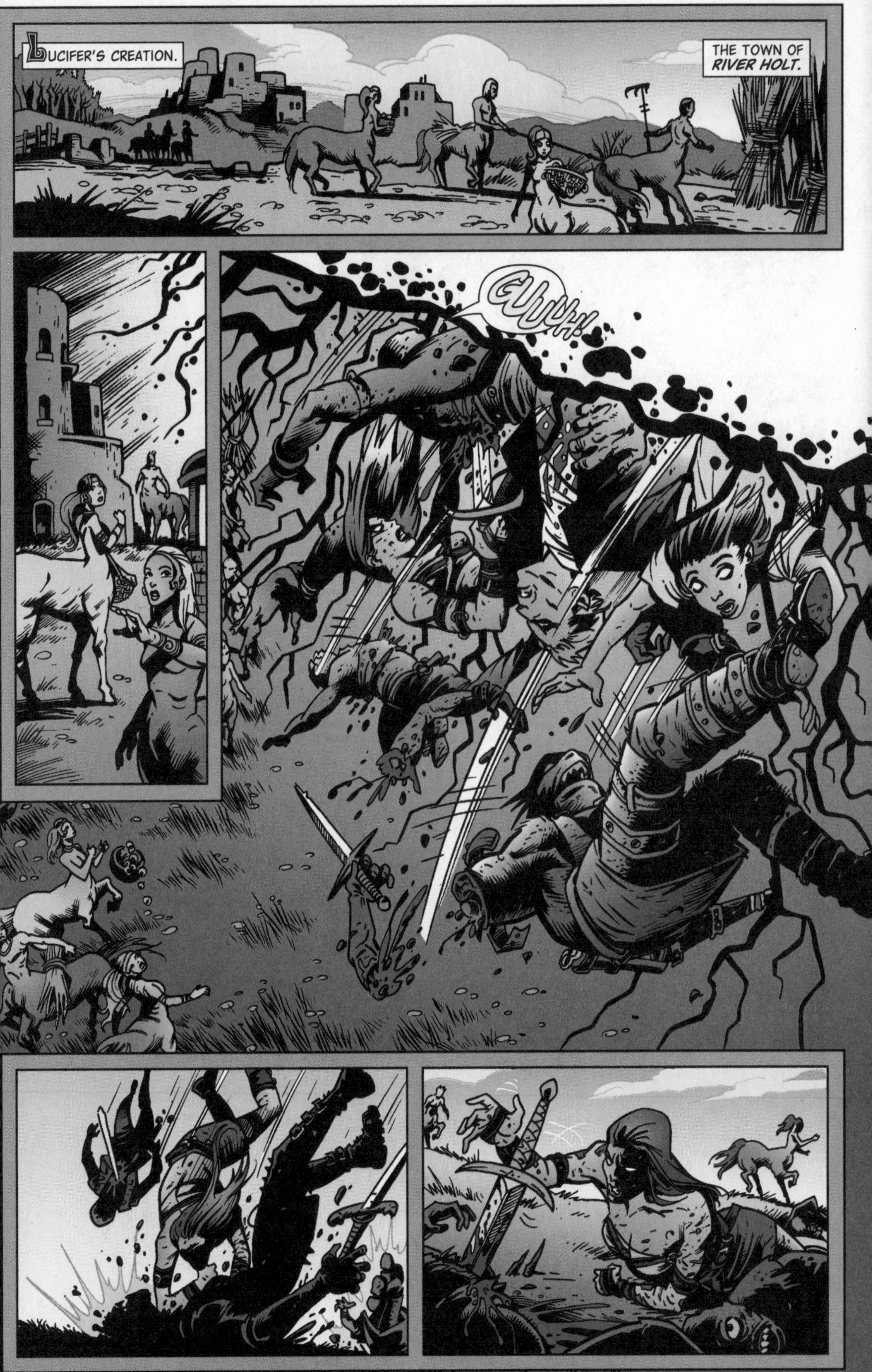
LUCIFER'S CREATION.
THE TOWN OF RIVER HOLT.
GUUUH!

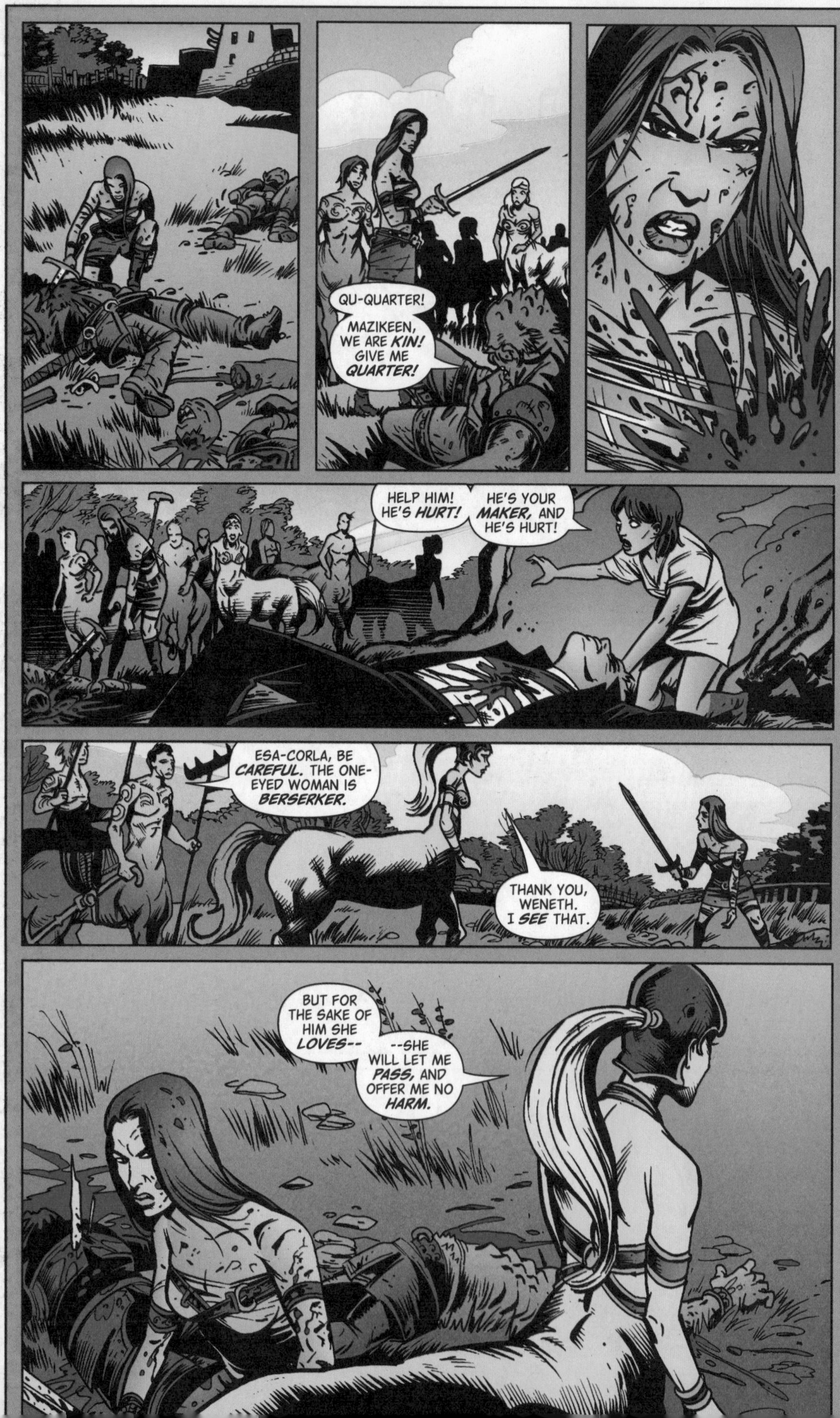
QU-QUARTER!
MAZIKEEN, WE ARE *KIN!* GIVE ME *QUARTER!*
HELP HIM! HE'S *HURT!*
HE'S YOUR *MAKER,* AND HE'S HURT!
ESA-CORLA, BE *CAREFUL.* THE ONE-EYED WOMAN IS *BERSERKER.*
THANK YOU, WENETH. I *SEE* THAT.
BUT FOR THE SAKE OF HIM SHE *LOVES--*
--SHE WILL LET ME *PASS,* AND OFFER ME NO *HARM.*

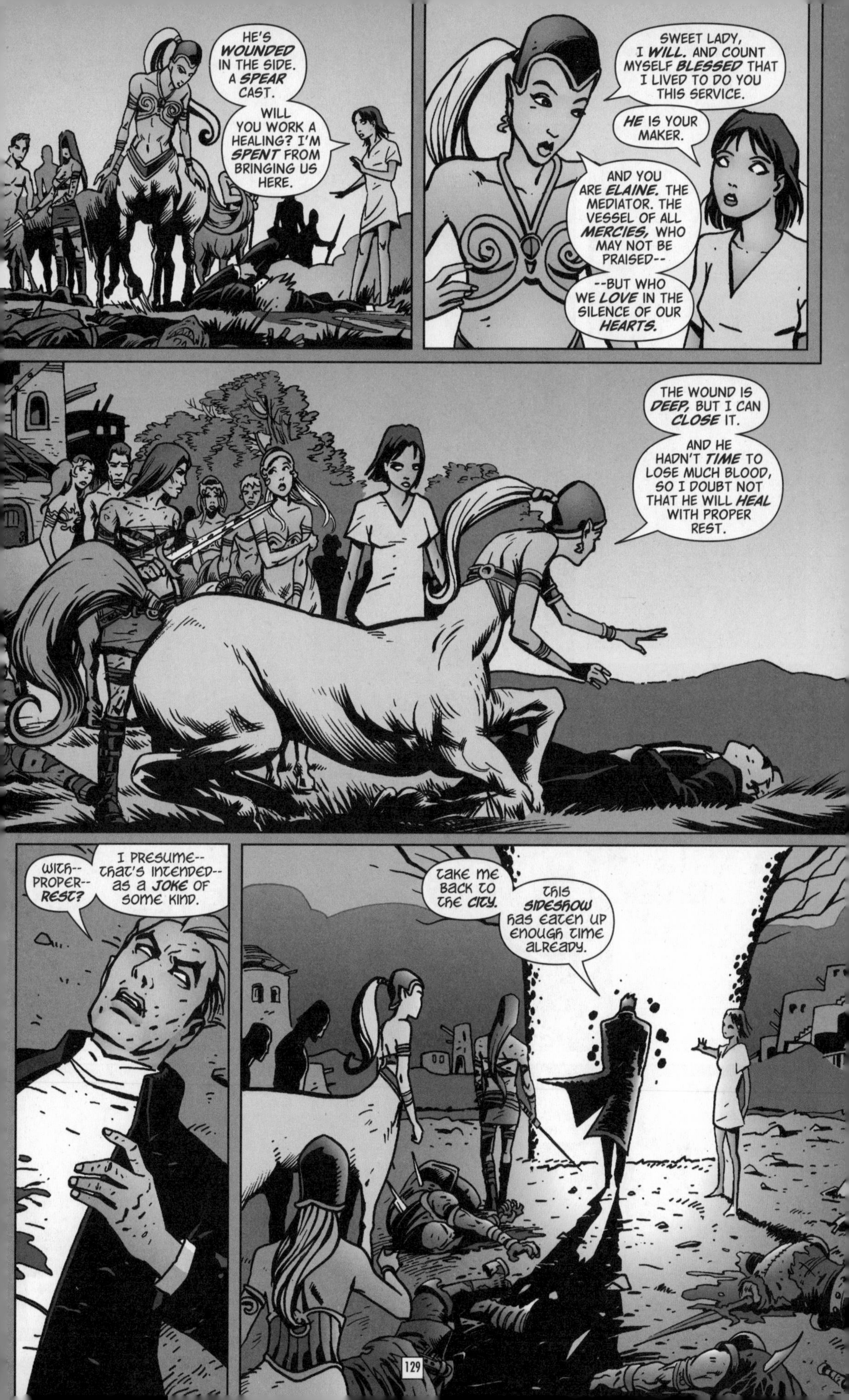
HE'S WOUNDED IN THE SIDE. A SPEAR CAST.
WILL YOU WORK A HEALING? I'M SPENT FROM BRINGING US HERE.
SWEET LADY, I WILL. AND COUNT MYSELF BLESSED THAT I LIVED TO DO YOU THIS SERVICE.
HE IS YOUR MAKER.
AND YOU ARE ELAINE. THE MEDIATOR. THE VESSEL OF ALL MERCIES, WHO MAY NOT BE PRAISED--
--BUT WHO WE LOVE IN THE SILENCE OF OUR HEARTS.
THE WOUND IS DEEP, BUT I CAN CLOSE IT.
AND HE HADN'T TIME TO LOSE MUCH BLOOD, SO I DOUBT NOT THAT HE WILL HEAL WITH PROPER REST.
WITH-- PROPER-- REST?
I PRESUME-- THAT'S INTENDED-- AS A JOKE OF SOME KIND.
TAKE ME BACK TO THE CITY.
THIS SIDESHOW HAS EATEN UP ENOUGH TIME ALREADY.

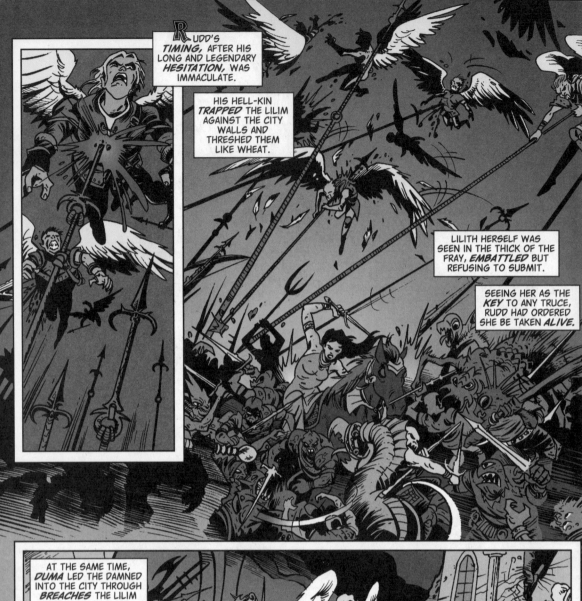

RUDD'S *TIMING,* AFTER HIS LONG AND LEGENDARY *HESITATION,* WAS IMMACULATE.

HIS HELL-KIN *TRAPPED* THE LILIM AGAINST THE CITY WALLS AND THRESHED THEM LIKE WHEAT.

LILITH HERSELF WAS SEEN IN THE THICK OF THE FRAY, *EMBATTLED* BUT REFUSING TO SUBMIT.

SEEING HER AS THE *KEY* TO ANY TRUCE, RUDD HAD ORDERED SHE BE TAKEN *ALIVE.*

AT THE SAME TIME, *DUMA* LED THE DAMNED INTO THE CITY THROUGH *BREACHES* THE LILIM HAD ALREADY MADE.

AND THE *HEAVEN-HOST,* ABASHED, SURRENDERED WITHOUT A *FIGHT.* FOR THE DISPOSITION OF THESE DAMNED SOULS WAS ALREADY *ORDAINED,* AND THEREFORE TO END THEM WAS TO GO AGAINST *YAHWEH'S* DECREE.

WITHIN THE CITY, THEN, VICTORY WAS *BLOODLESS.*

THE ANGELS *SUBMITTING* TO THEIR FATE WITH BEMUSED AWE, AS IF THEY COULD NOT QUITE *BELIEVE* THIS DAY HAD COME.

WHILE ON *ARMAGEDDON* PLAIN BLOOD RAN IN *RIVERS.*

AS HAD INDEED BEEN *PROPHESIED,* A GREAT WHILE BEFORE.

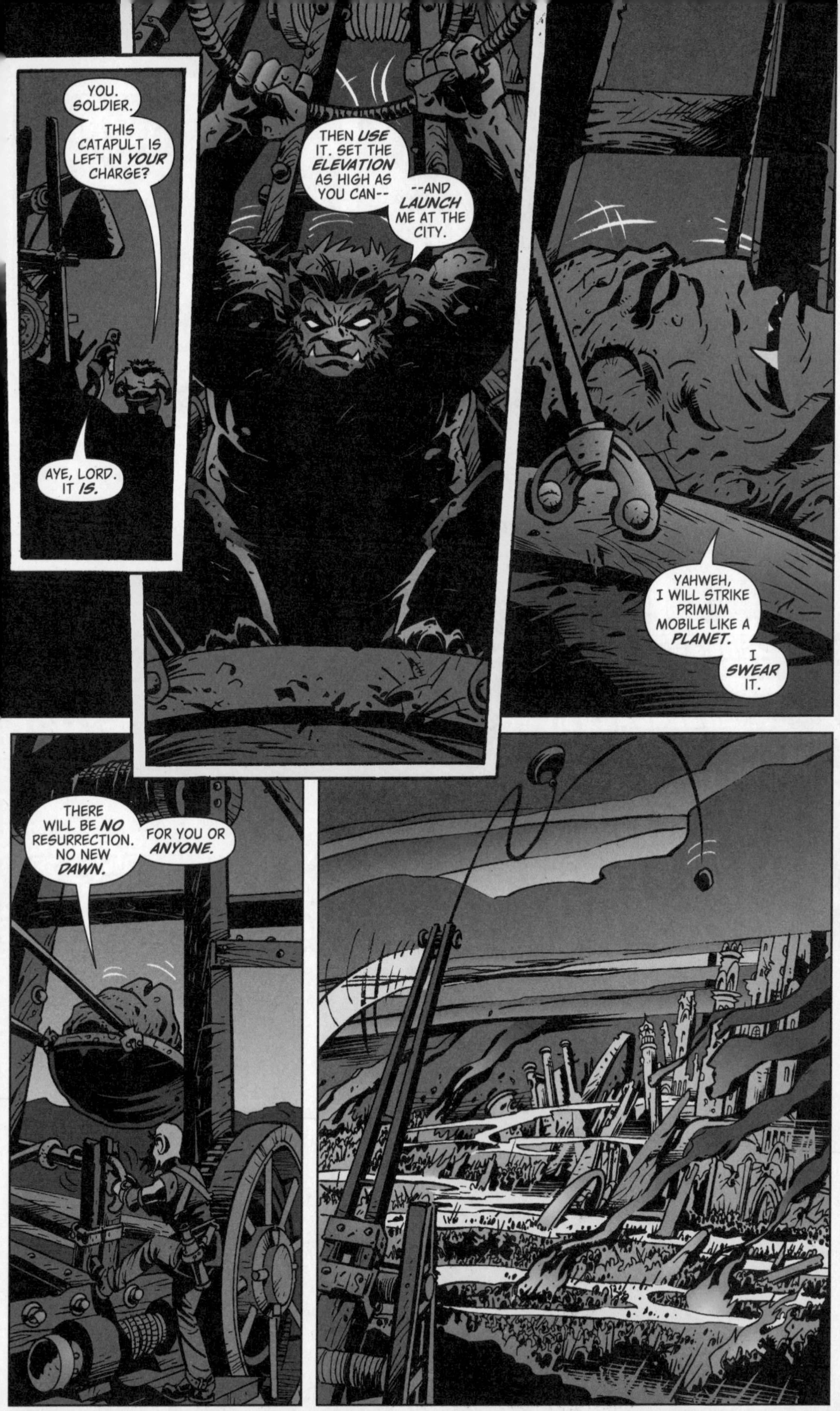

YOU. SOLDIER.
THIS CATAPULT IS LEFT IN YOUR CHARGE?
AYE, LORD. IT IS.
THEN USE IT. SET THE ELEVATION AS HIGH AS YOU CAN--
--AND LAUNCH ME AT THE CITY.
YAHWEH, I WILL STRIKE PRIMUM MOBILE LIKE A PLANET.
I SWEAR IT.
THERE WILL BE NO RESURRECTION. NO NEW DAWN.
FOR YOU OR ANYONE.

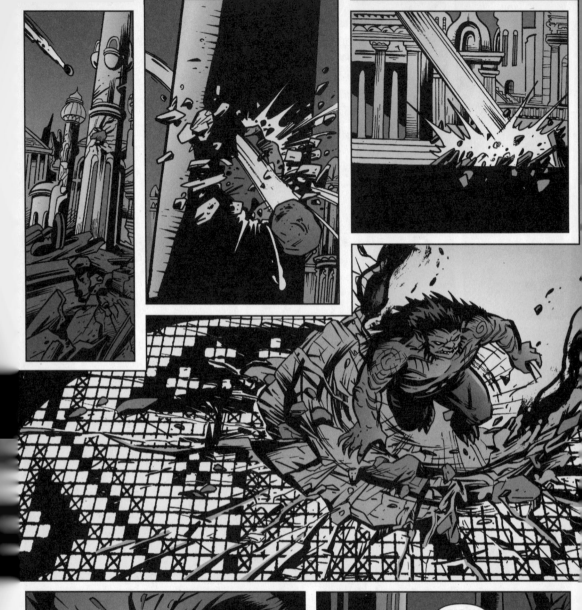

SNK
SCHT
SCHT

AAAAAH!
NOW THERE--
THERE IT *IS*
AGAIN.

LEAD ME THE
REST OF THE *WAY,*
MORNINGSTAR.

LEAD ME
TO THE
THRONE.

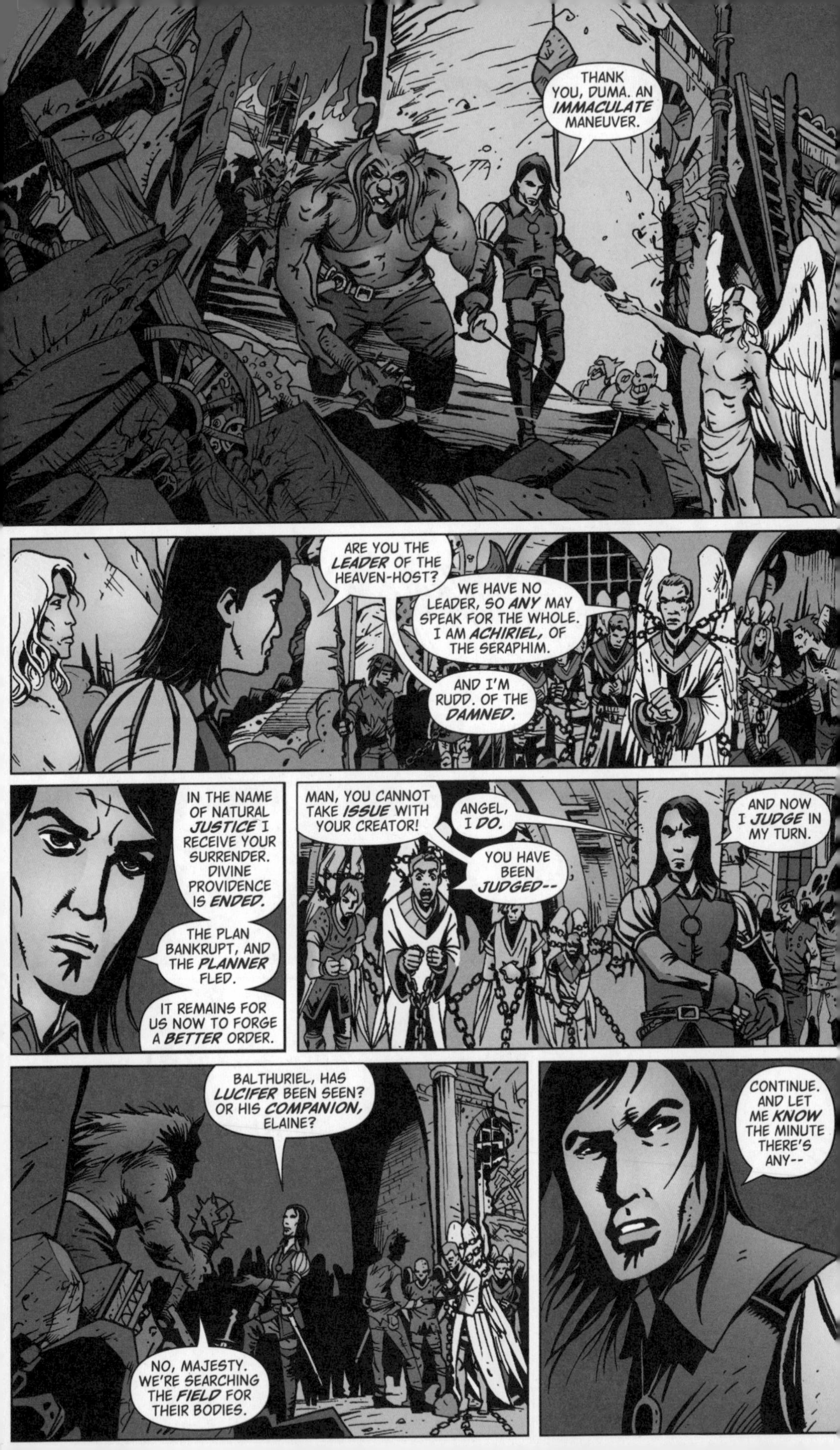
THANK YOU, DUMA. AN IMMACULATE MANEUVER.
ARE YOU THE LEADER OF THE HEAVEN-HOST?
WE HAVE NO LEADER, SO ANY MAY SPEAK FOR THE WHOLE. I AM ACHIRIEL, OF THE SERAPHIM.
AND I'M RUDD. OF THE DAMNED.
IN THE NAME OF NATURAL JUSTICE I RECEIVE YOUR SURRENDER. DIVINE PROVIDENCE IS ENDED.
THE PLAN BANKRUPT, AND THE PLANNER FLED.
IT REMAINS FOR US NOW TO FORGE A BETTER ORDER.
MAN, YOU CANNOT TAKE ISSUE WITH YOUR CREATOR!
ANGEL, I DO.
YOU HAVE BEEN JUDGED--
AND NOW I JUDGE IN MY TURN.
BALTHURIEL, HAS LUCIFER BEEN SEEN? OR HIS COMPANION, ELAINE?
NO, MAJESTY. WE'RE SEARCHING THE FIELD FOR THEIR BODIES.
CONTINUE. AND LET ME KNOW THE MINUTE THERE'S ANY--

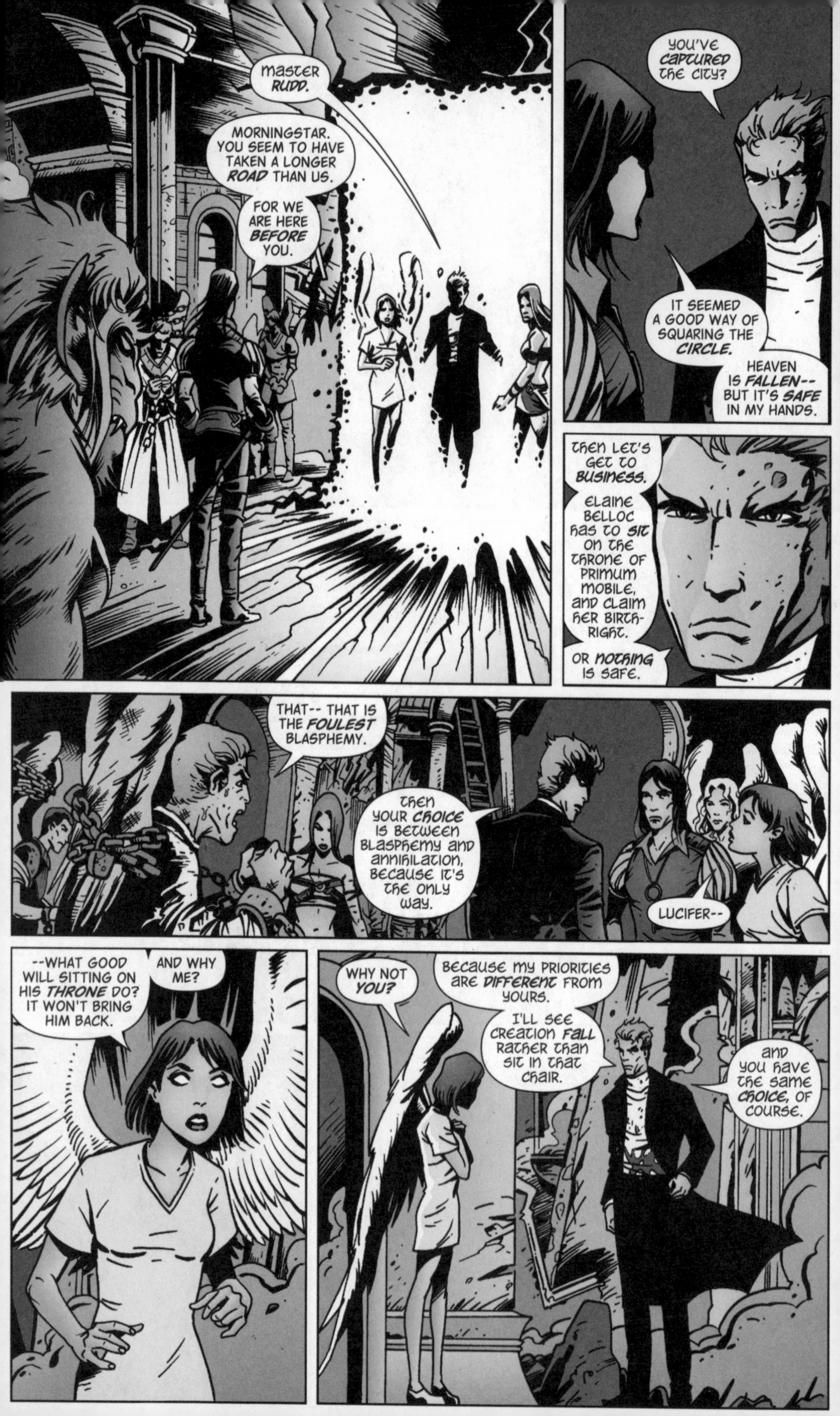
MASTER RUDD.
MORNINGSTAR. YOU SEEM TO HAVE TAKEN A LONGER ROAD THAN US.
FOR WE ARE HERE BEFORE YOU.
YOU'VE CAPTURED THE CITY?
IT SEEMED A GOOD WAY OF SQUARING THE CIRCLE.
HEAVEN IS FALLEN-- BUT IT'S SAFE IN MY HANDS.
THEN LET'S GET TO BUSINESS.
ELAINE BELLOC HAS TO SIT ON THE THRONE OF PRIMUM MOBILE, AND CLAIM HER BIRTH-RIGHT.
OR NOTHING IS SAFE.
THAT-- THAT IS THE FOULEST BLASPHEMY.
THEN YOUR CHOICE IS BETWEEN BLASPHEMY AND ANNIHILATION, BECAUSE IT'S THE ONLY WAY.
LUCIFER--
--WHAT GOOD WILL SITTING ON HIS THRONE DO? IT WON'T BRING HIM BACK.
AND WHY ME?
WHY NOT YOU?
BECAUSE MY PRIORITIES ARE DIFFERENT FROM YOURS.
I'LL SEE CREATION FALL RATHER THAN SIT IN THAT CHAIR.
AND YOU HAVE THE SAME CHOICE, OF COURSE.

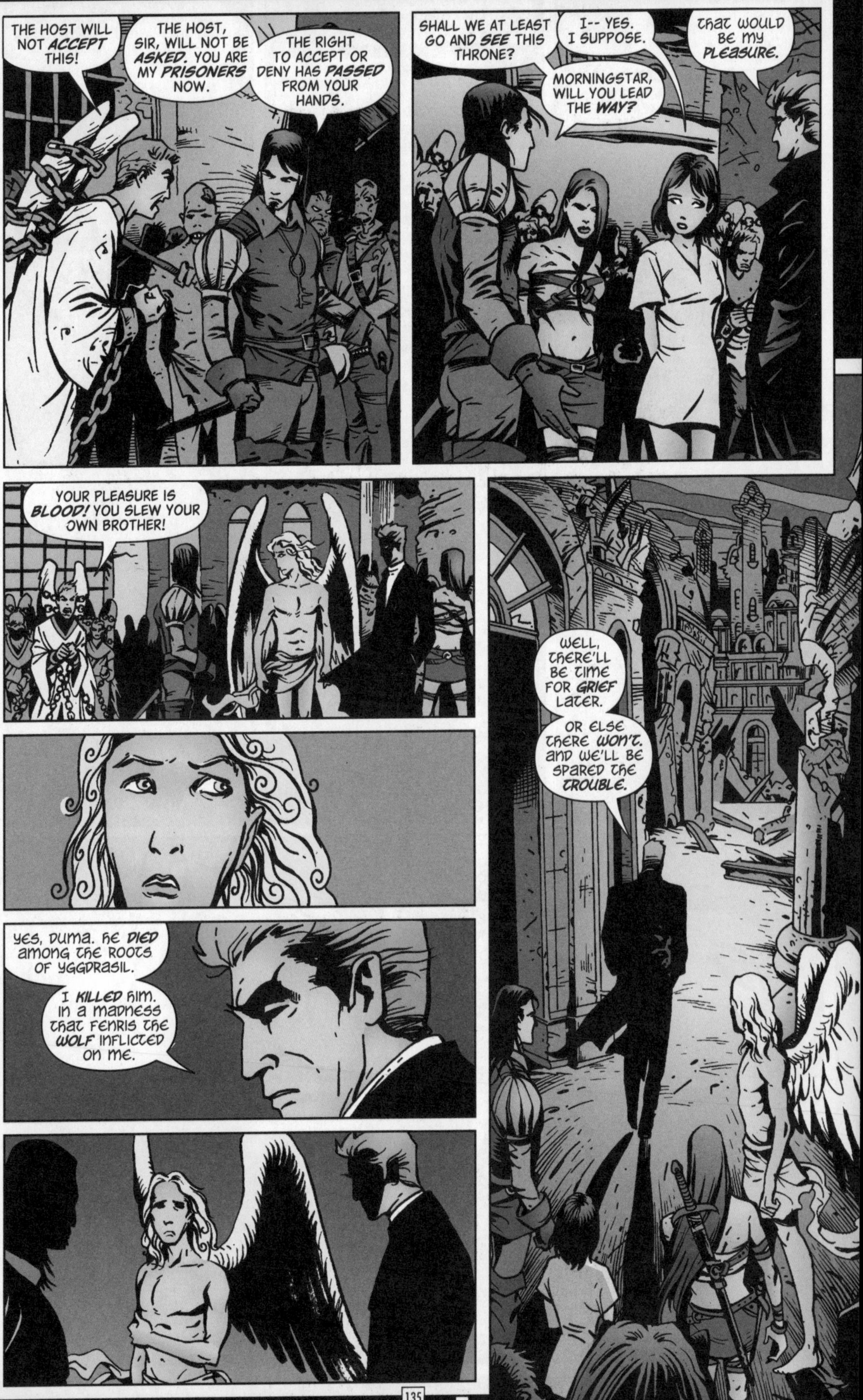

THE HOST WILL NOT ACCEPT THIS!
THE HOST, SIR, WILL NOT BE ASKED. YOU ARE MY PRISONERS NOW.
THE RIGHT TO ACCEPT OR DENY HAS PASSED FROM YOUR HANDS.
SHALL WE AT LEAST GO AND SEE THIS THRONE?
I-- YES. I SUPPOSE.
MORNINGSTAR, WILL YOU LEAD THE WAY?
THAT WOULD BE MY PLEASURE.
YOUR PLEASURE IS BLOOD! YOU SLEW YOUR OWN BROTHER!
YES, DUMA. HE DIED AMONG THE ROOTS OF YGGDRASIL.
I KILLED HIM. IN A MADNESS THAT FENRIS THE WOLF INFLICTED ON ME.
WELL, THERE'LL BE TIME FOR GRIEF LATER.
OR ELSE THERE WON'T. AND WE'LL BE SPARED THE TROUBLE.

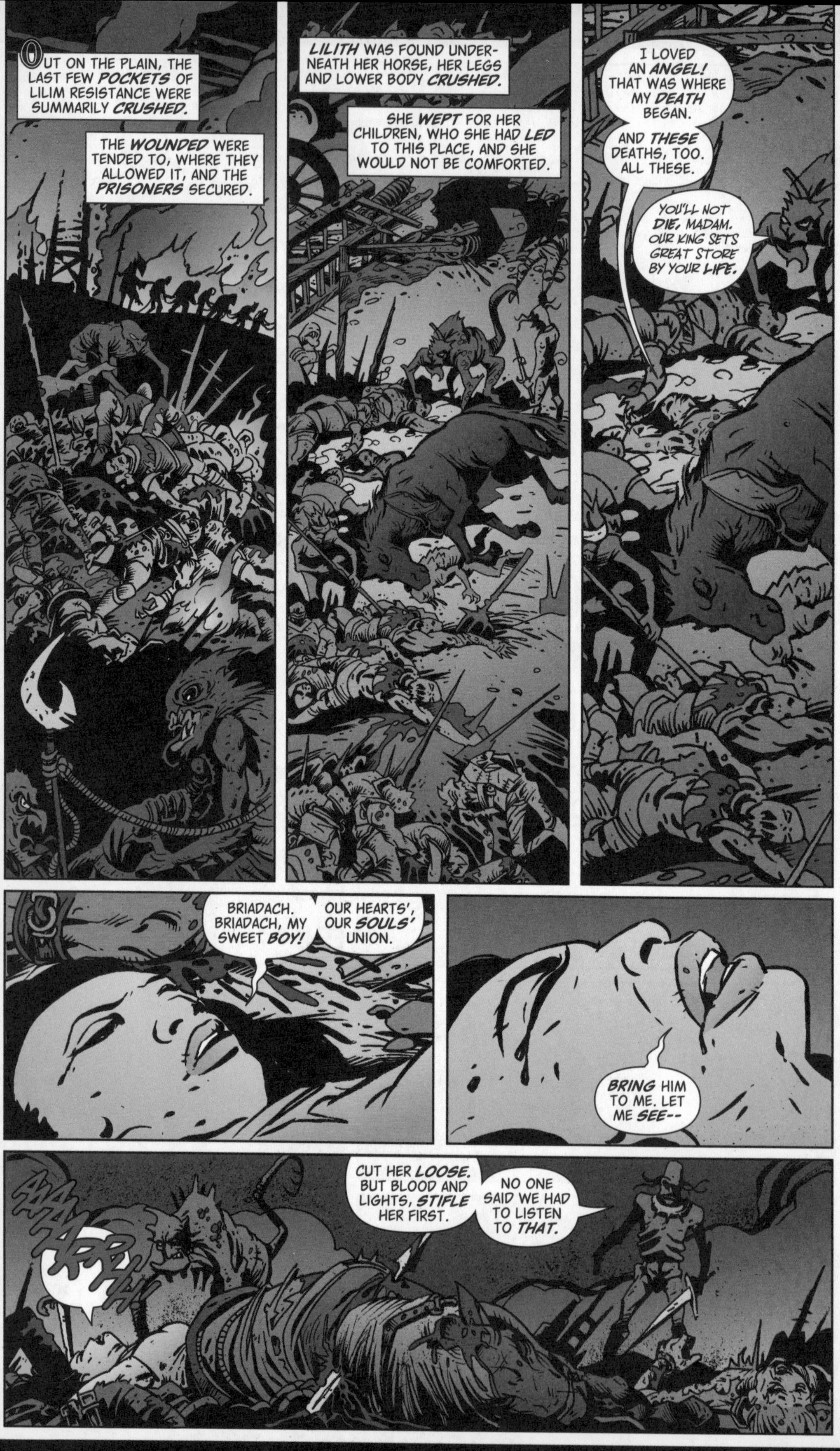

OUT ON THE PLAIN, THE LAST FEW POCKETS OF LILIM RESISTANCE WERE SUMMARILY CRUSHED.
THE WOUNDED WERE TENDED TO, WHERE THEY ALLOWED IT, AND THE PRISONERS SECURED.
LILITH WAS FOUND UNDERNEATH HER HORSE, HER LEGS AND LOWER BODY CRUSHED.
SHE WEPT FOR HER CHILDREN, WHO SHE HAD LED TO THIS PLACE, AND SHE WOULD NOT BE COMFORTED.
I LOVED AN ANGEL! THAT WAS WHERE MY DEATH BEGAN.
AND THESE DEATHS, TOO. ALL THESE.
YOU'LL NOT DIE, MADAM. OUR KING SETS GREAT STORE BY YOUR LIFE.
BRIADACH. BRIADACH, MY SWEET BOY!
OUR HEARTS', OUR SOULS' UNION.
BRING HIM TO ME. LET ME SEE--
AAAARRH
CUT HER LOOSE. BUT BLOOD AND LIGHTS, STIFLE HER FIRST.
NO ONE SAID WE HAD TO LISTEN TO THAT.

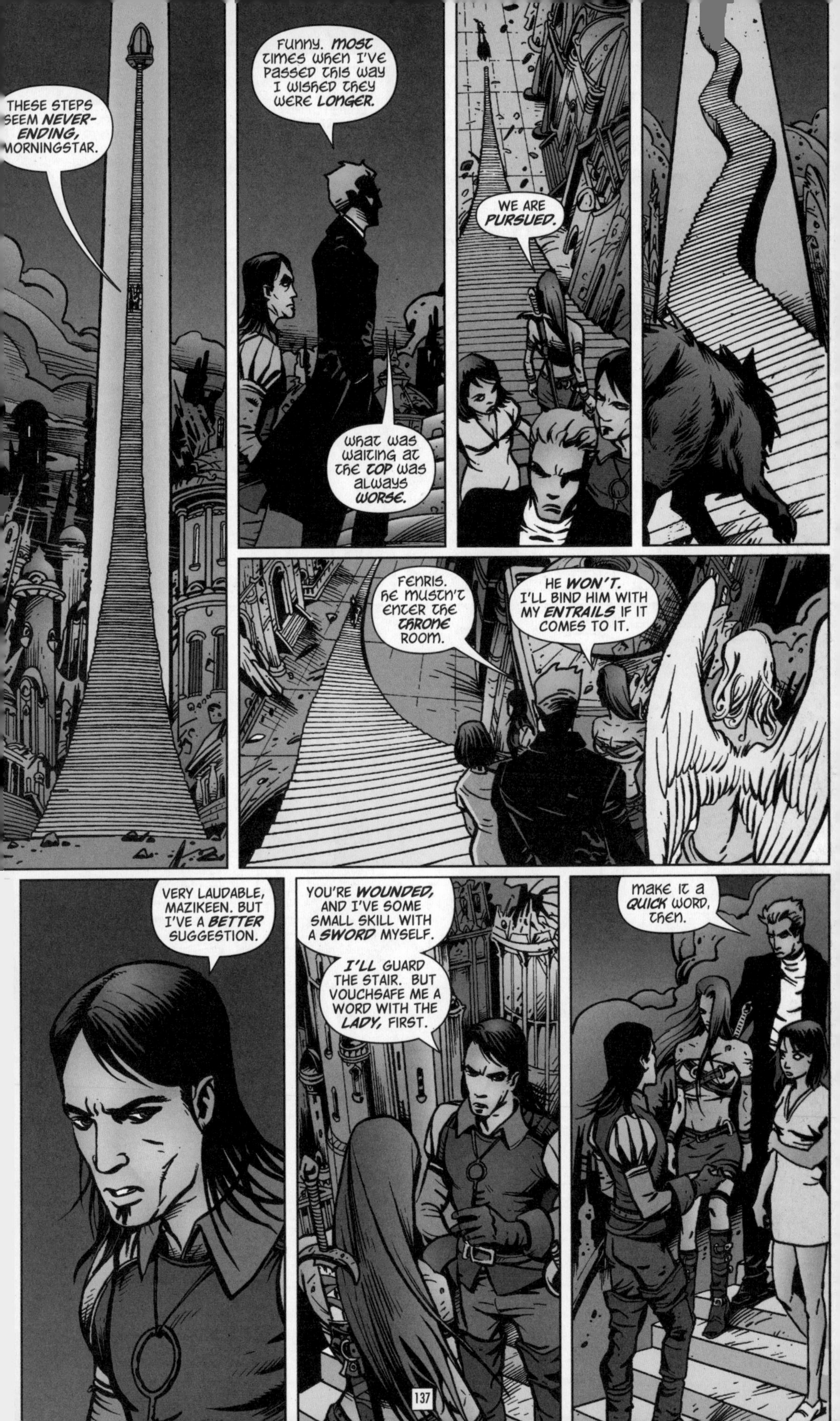
THESE STEPS SEEM NEVER-ENDING, MORNINGSTAR.
FUNNY. MOST TIMES WHEN I'VE PASSED THIS WAY I WISHED THEY WERE LONGER.
WHAT WAS WAITING AT THE TOP WAS ALWAYS WORSE.
WE ARE PURSUED.
FENRIS. HE MUSTN'T ENTER THE THRONE ROOM.
HE WON'T. I'LL BIND HIM WITH MY ENTRAILS IF IT COMES TO IT.
VERY LAUDABLE, MAZIKEEN. BUT I'VE A BETTER SUGGESTION.
YOU'RE WOUNDED, AND I'VE SOME SMALL SKILL WITH A SWORD MYSELF.
I'LL GUARD THE STAIR. BUT VOUCHSAFE ME A WORD WITH THE LADY, FIRST.
MAKE IT A QUICK WORD, THEN.

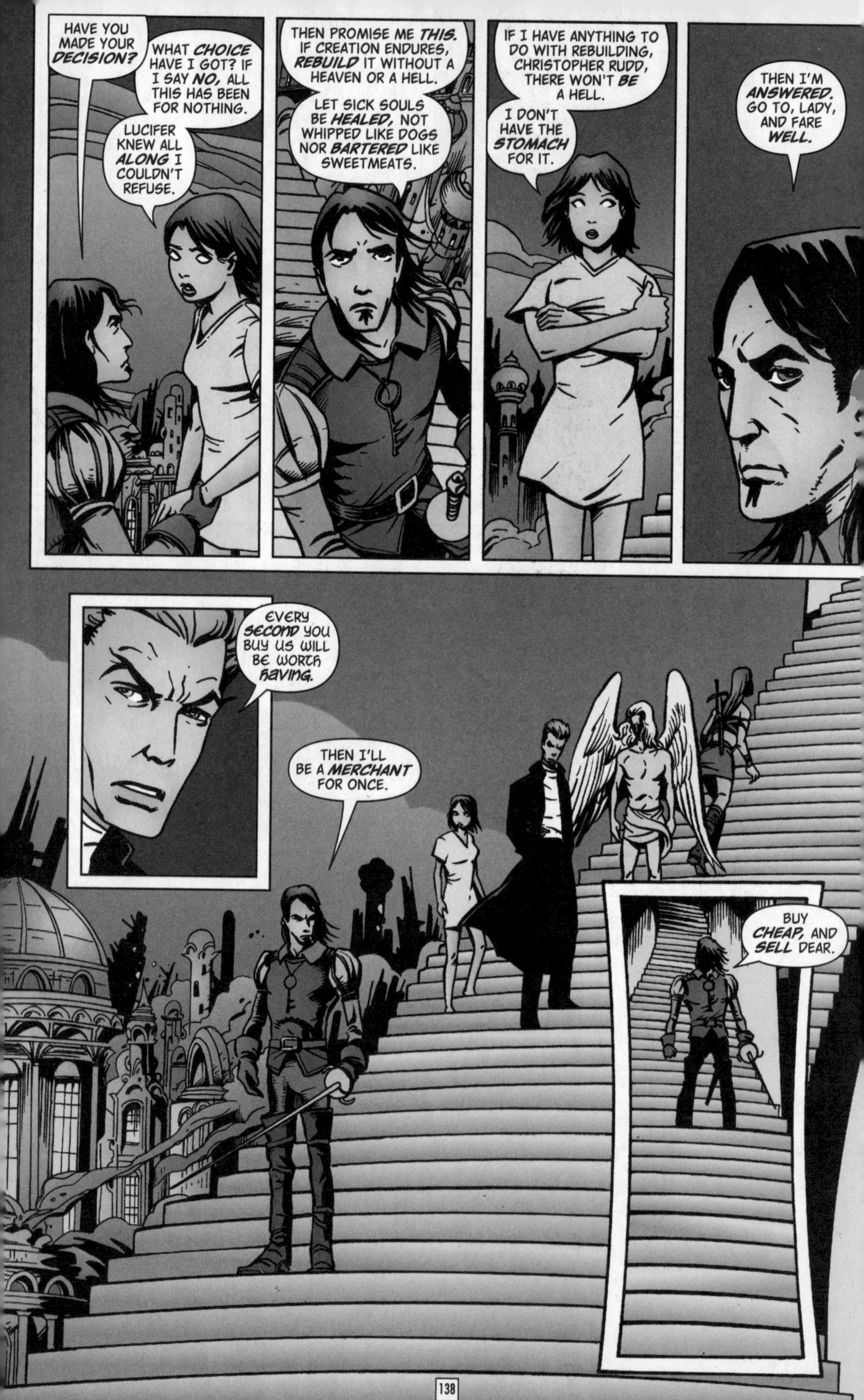
HAVE YOU MADE YOUR DECISION?
WHAT CHOICE HAVE I GOT? IF I SAY NO, ALL THIS HAS BEEN FOR NOTHING.
LUCIFER KNEW ALL ALONG I COULDN'T REFUSE.
THEN PROMISE ME THIS. IF CREATION ENDURES, REBUILD IT WITHOUT A HEAVEN OR A HELL.
LET SICK SOULS BE HEALED, NOT WHIPPED LIKE DOGS NOR BARTERED LIKE SWEETMEATS.
IF I HAVE ANYTHING TO DO WITH REBUILDING, CHRISTOPHER RUDD, THERE WON'T BE A HELL.
I DON'T HAVE THE STOMACH FOR IT.
THEN I'M ANSWERED. GO TO, LADY, AND FARE WELL.
EVERY SECOND YOU BUY US WILL BE WORTH HAVING.
THEN I'LL BE A MERCHANT FOR ONCE.
BUY CHEAP, AND SELL DEAR.

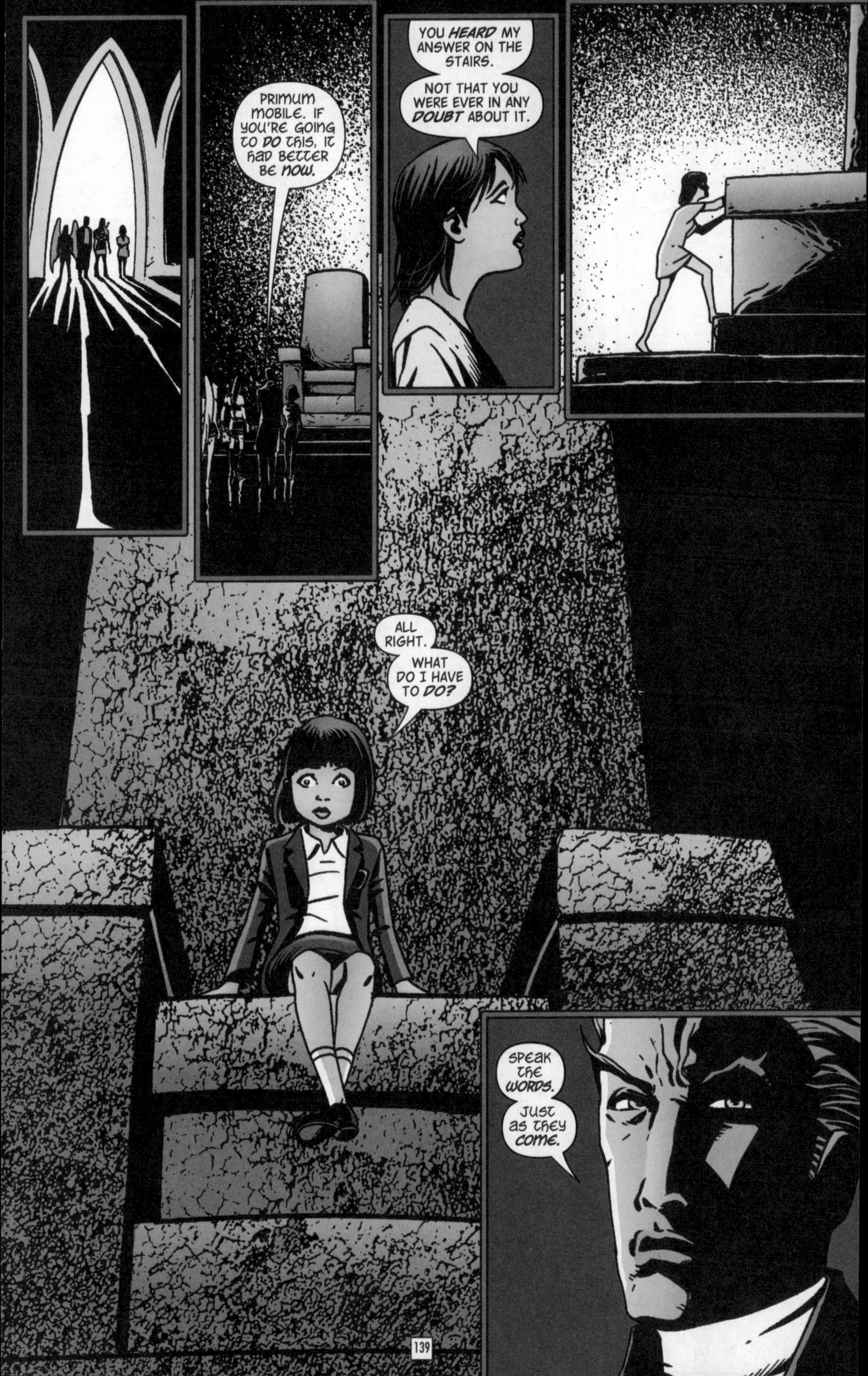
PRIMUM MOBILE. IF YOU'RE GOING TO DO THIS, IT HAD BETTER BE NOW.
YOU HEARD MY ANSWER ON THE STAIRS.
NOT THAT YOU WERE EVER IN ANY DOUBT ABOUT IT.
ALL RIGHT.
WHAT DO I HAVE TO DO?
SPEAK THE WORDS.
JUST AS THEY COME.

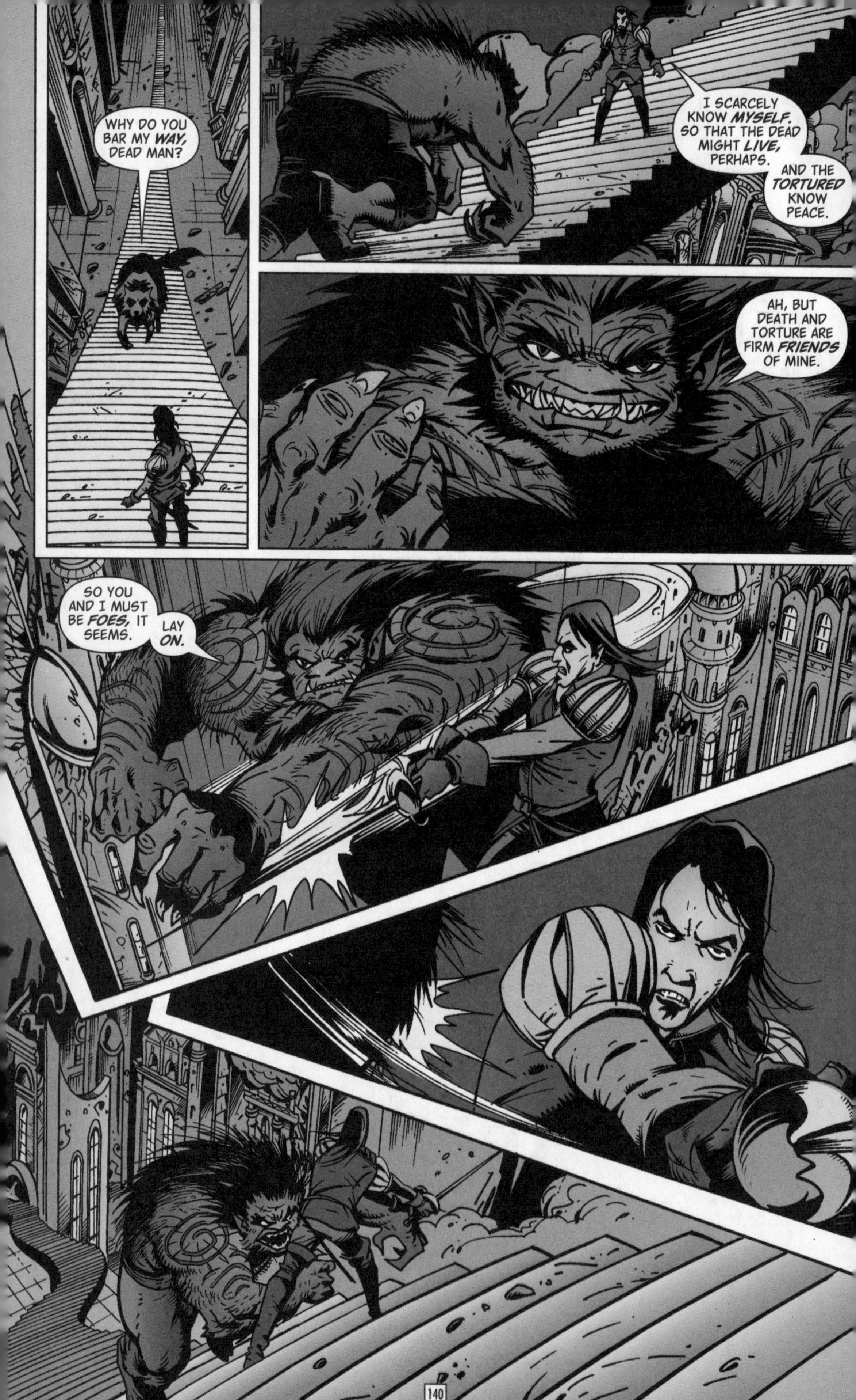
WHY DO YOU BAR MY *WAY,* DEAD MAN?
I SCARCELY KNOW *MYSELF.* SO THAT THE DEAD MIGHT *LIVE,* PERHAPS.
AND THE *TORTURED* KNOW PEACE.
AH, BUT DEATH AND TORTURE ARE FIRM *FRIENDS* OF MINE.
SO YOU AND I MUST BE *FOES,* IT SEEMS.
LAY *ON.*

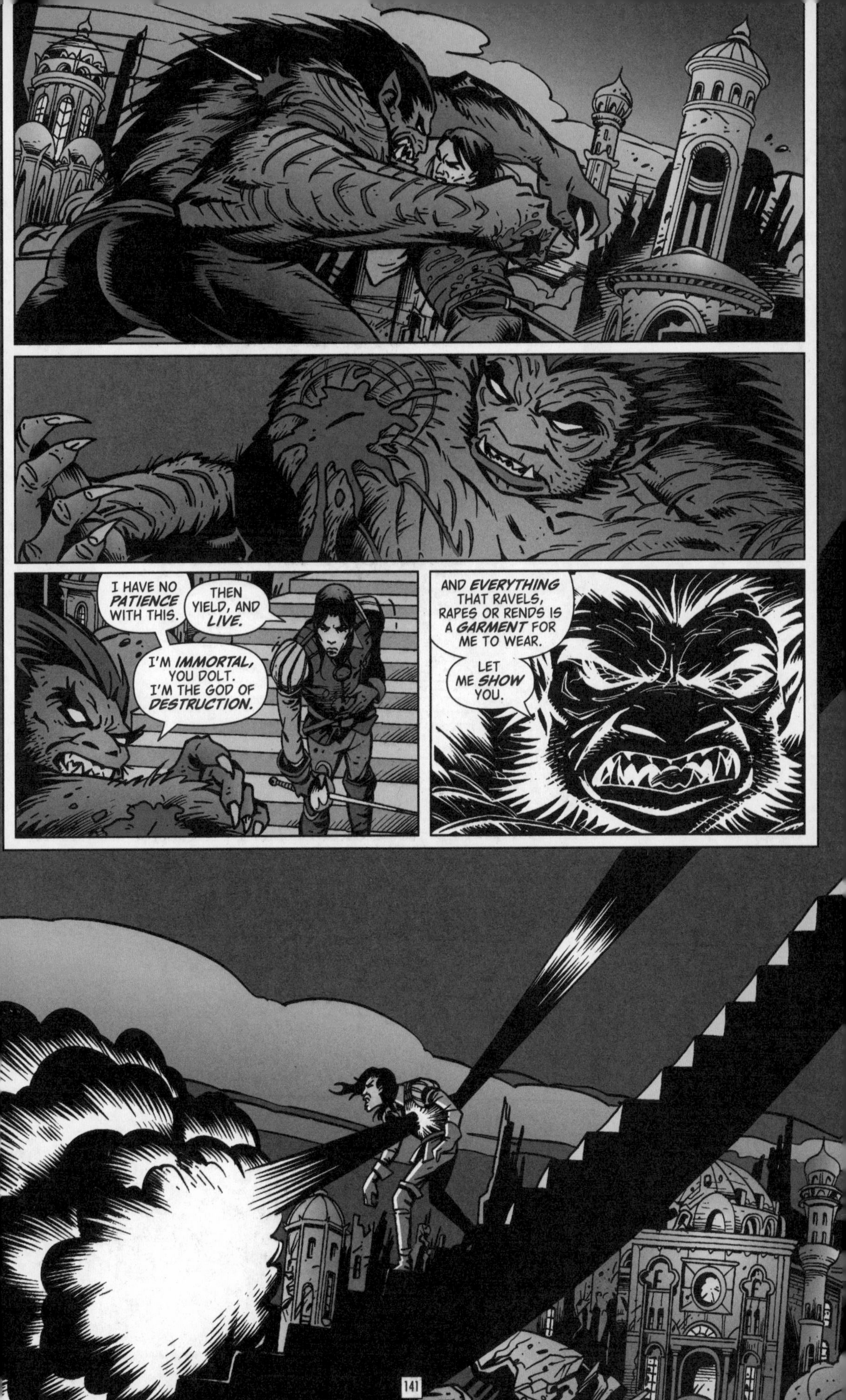

I HAVE NO PATIENCE WITH THIS.
THEN YIELD, AND LIVE.
I'M IMMORTAL, YOU DOLT. I'M THE GOD OF DESTRUCTION.
AND EVERYTHING THAT RAVELS, RAPES OR RENDS IS A GARMENT FOR ME TO WEAR.
LET ME SHOW YOU.

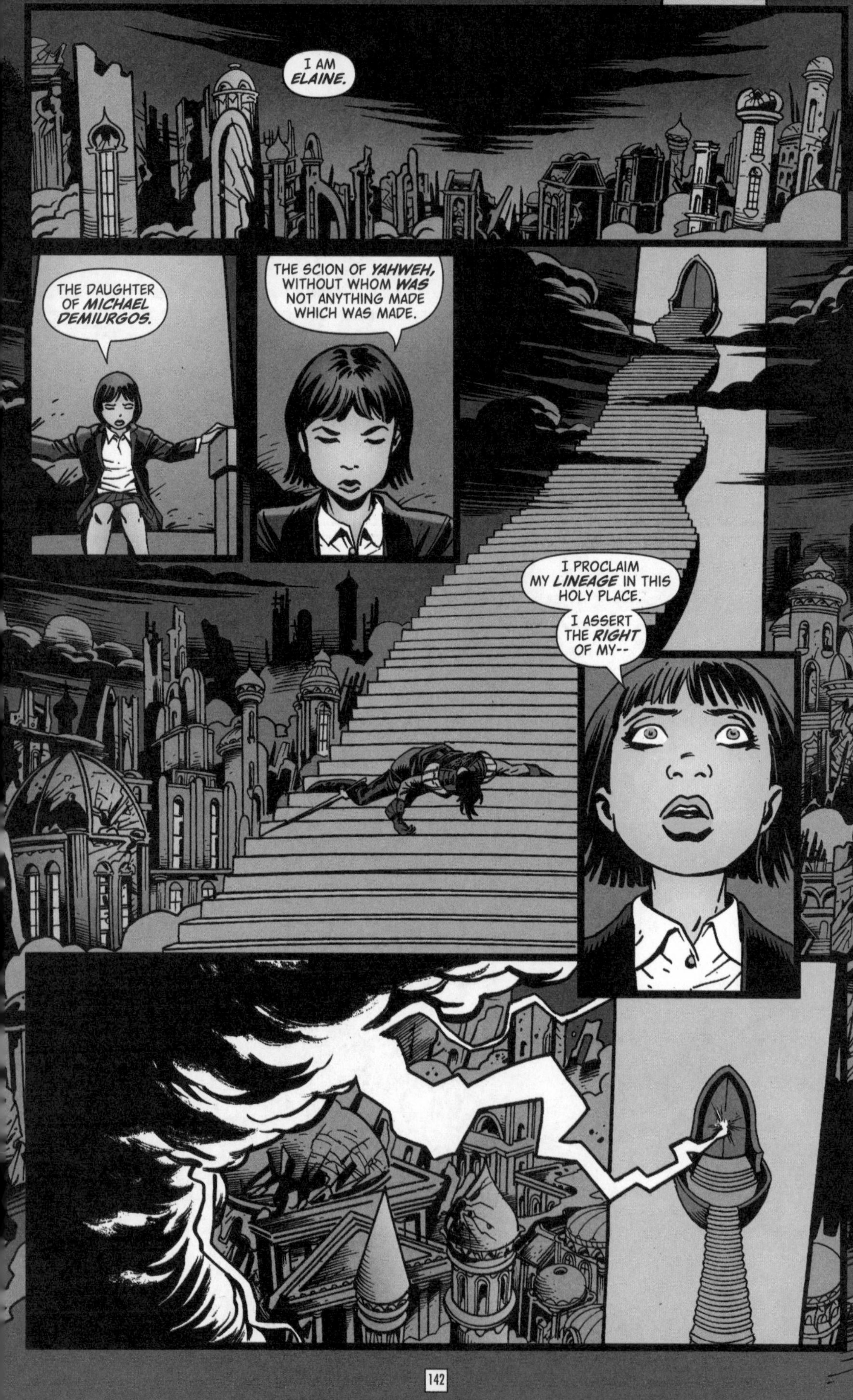
I AM ELAINE.
THE DAUGHTER OF MICHAEL DEMIURGOS.
THE SCION OF YAHWEH, WITHOUT WHOM WAS NOT ANYTHING MADE WHICH WAS MADE.
I PROCLAIM MY LINEAGE IN THIS HOLY PLACE.
I ASSERT THE RIGHT OF MY--

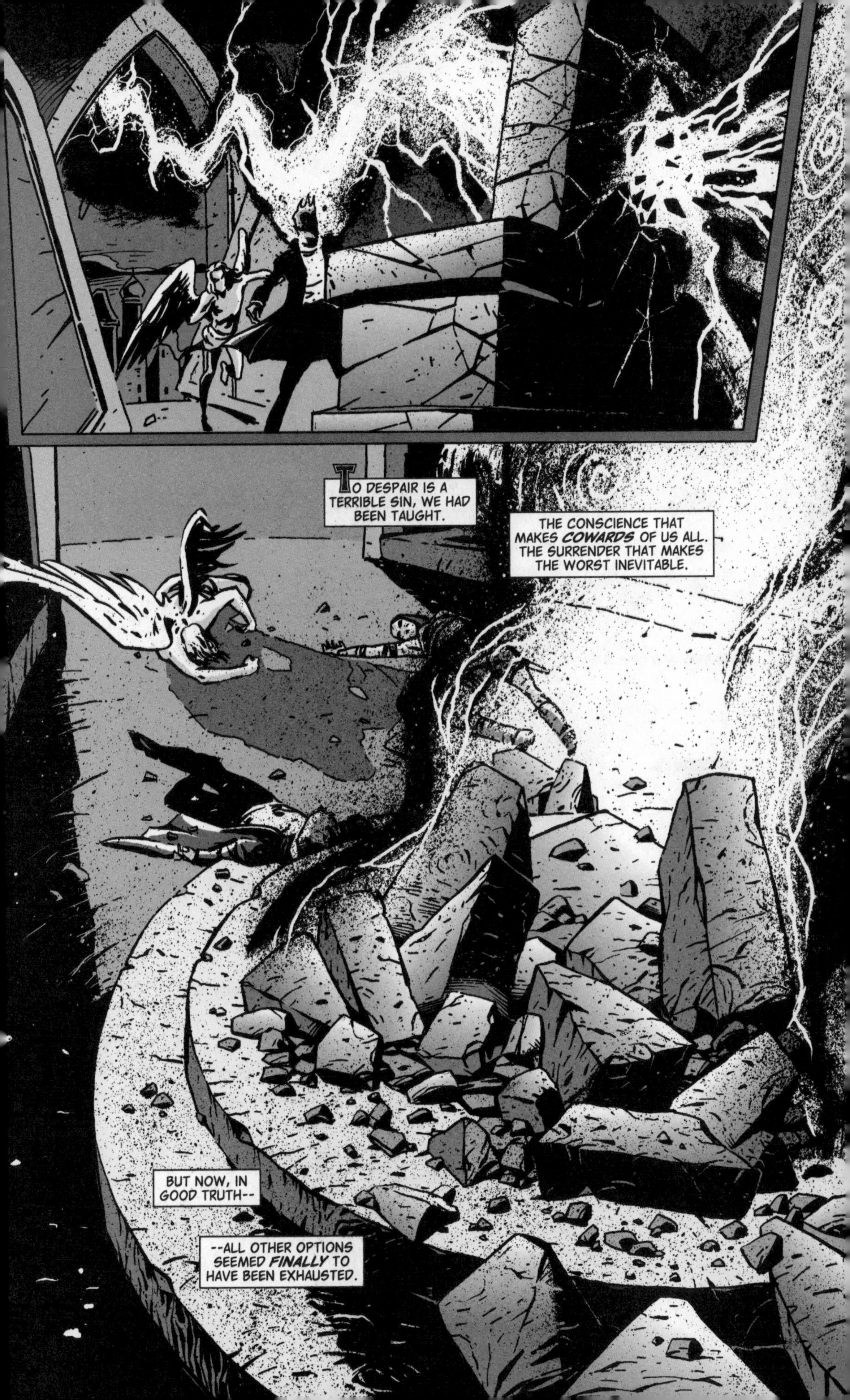
TO DESPAIR IS A TERRIBLE SIN, WE HAD BEEN TAUGHT.
THE CONSCIENCE THAT MAKES COWARDS OF US ALL. THE SURRENDER THAT MAKES THE WORST INEVITABLE.
BUT NOW, IN GOOD TRUTH--
--ALL OTHER OPTIONS SEEMED FINALLY TO HAVE BEEN EXHAUSTED.

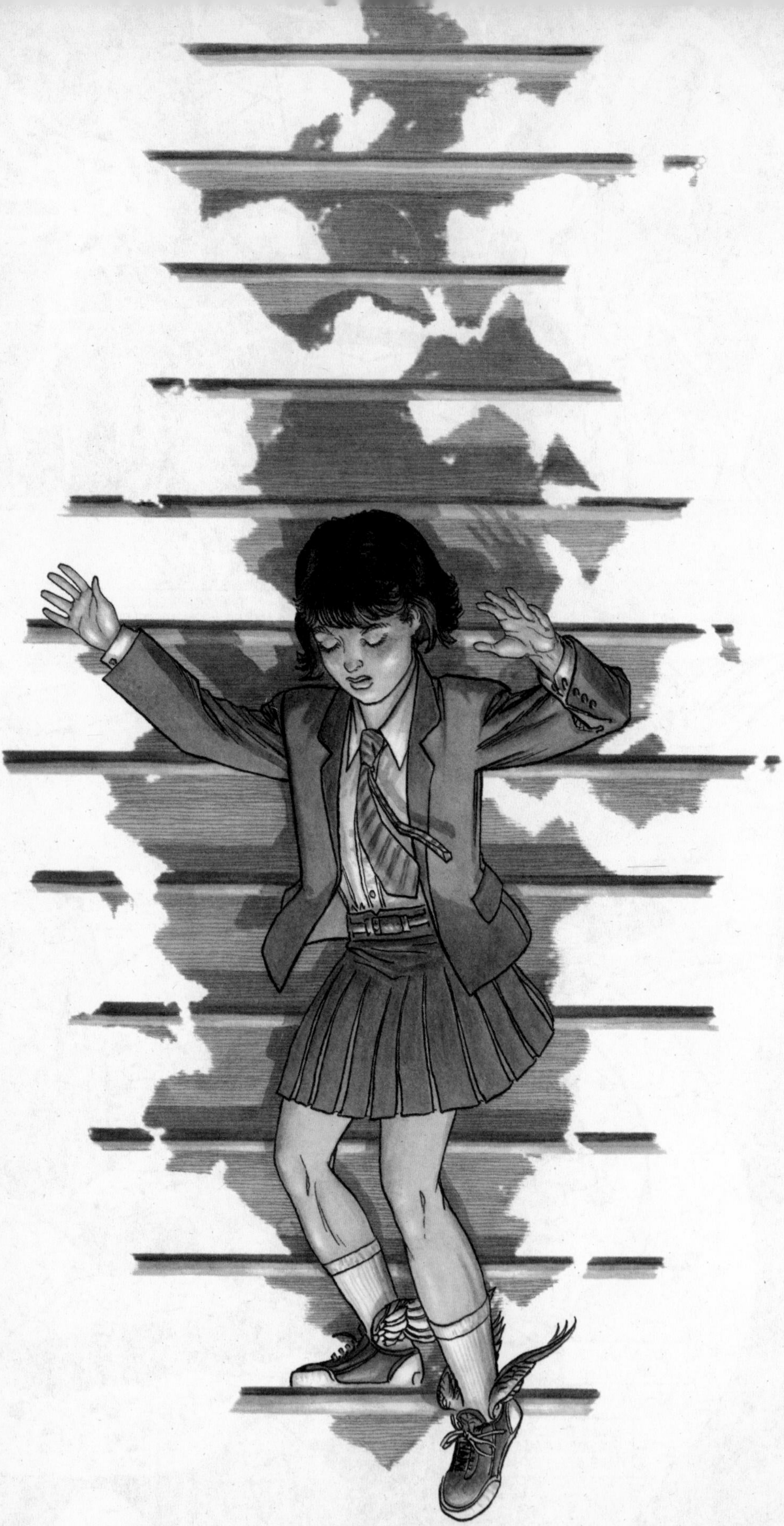

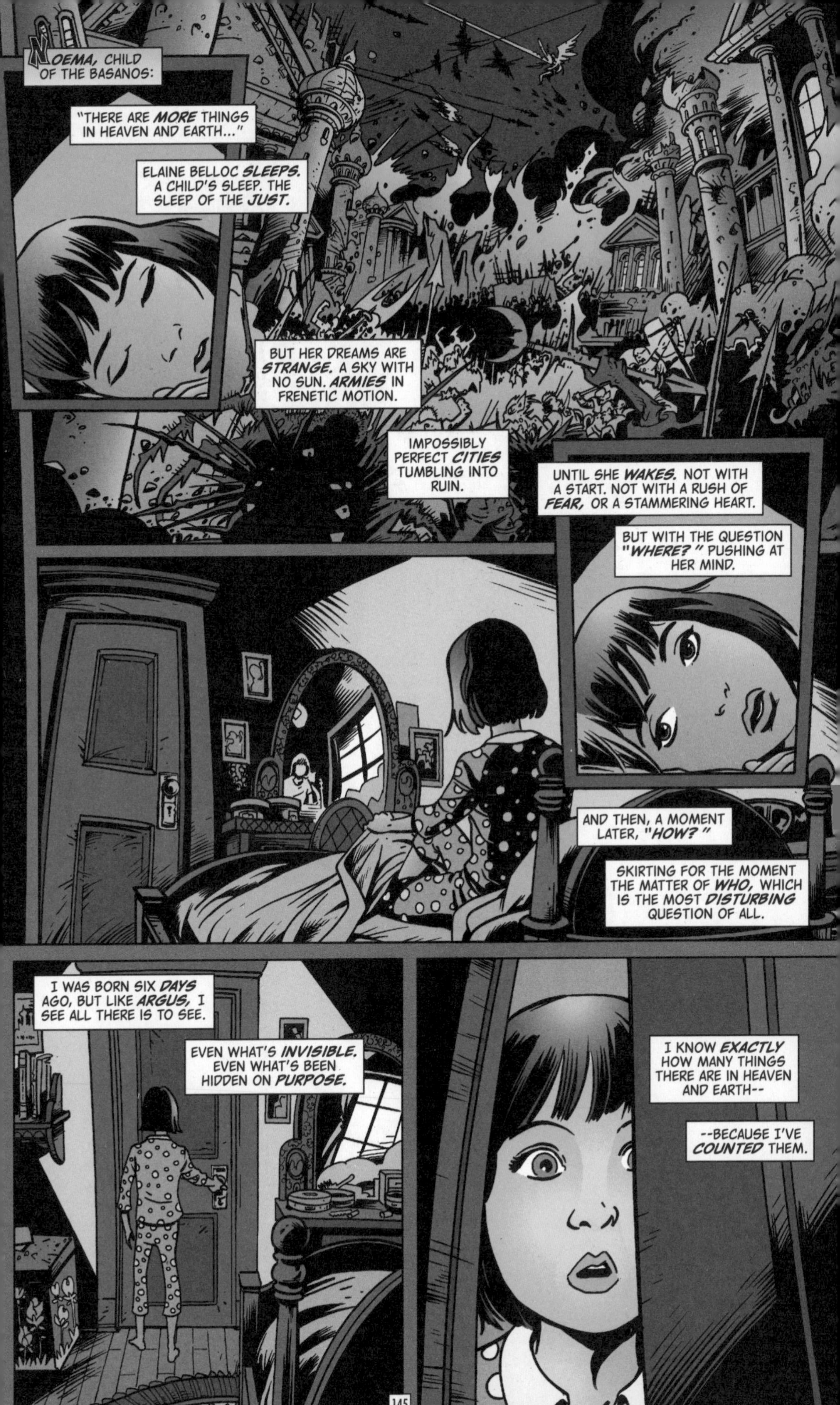
NOEMA, CHILD OF THE BASANOS:
"THERE ARE MORE THINGS IN HEAVEN AND EARTH..."
ELAINE BELLOC SLEEPS. A CHILD'S SLEEP. THE SLEEP OF THE JUST.
BUT HER DREAMS ARE STRANGE. A SKY WITH NO SUN. ARMIES IN FRENETIC MOTION.
IMPOSSIBLY PERFECT CITIES TUMBLING INTO RUIN.
UNTIL SHE WAKES. NOT WITH A START. NOT WITH A RUSH OF FEAR, OR A STAMMERING HEART.
BUT WITH THE QUESTION "WHERE?" PUSHING AT HER MIND.
AND THEN, A MOMENT LATER, "HOW?"
SKIRTING FOR THE MOMENT THE MATTER OF WHO, WHICH IS THE MOST DISTURBING QUESTION OF ALL.
I WAS BORN SIX DAYS AGO, BUT LIKE ARGUS, I SEE ALL THERE IS TO SEE.
EVEN WHAT'S INVISIBLE. EVEN WHAT'S BEEN HIDDEN ON PURPOSE.
I KNOW EXACTLY HOW MANY THINGS THERE ARE IN HEAVEN AND EARTH--
--BECAUSE I'VE COUNTED THEM.

THIS ONE IS *NEW.*

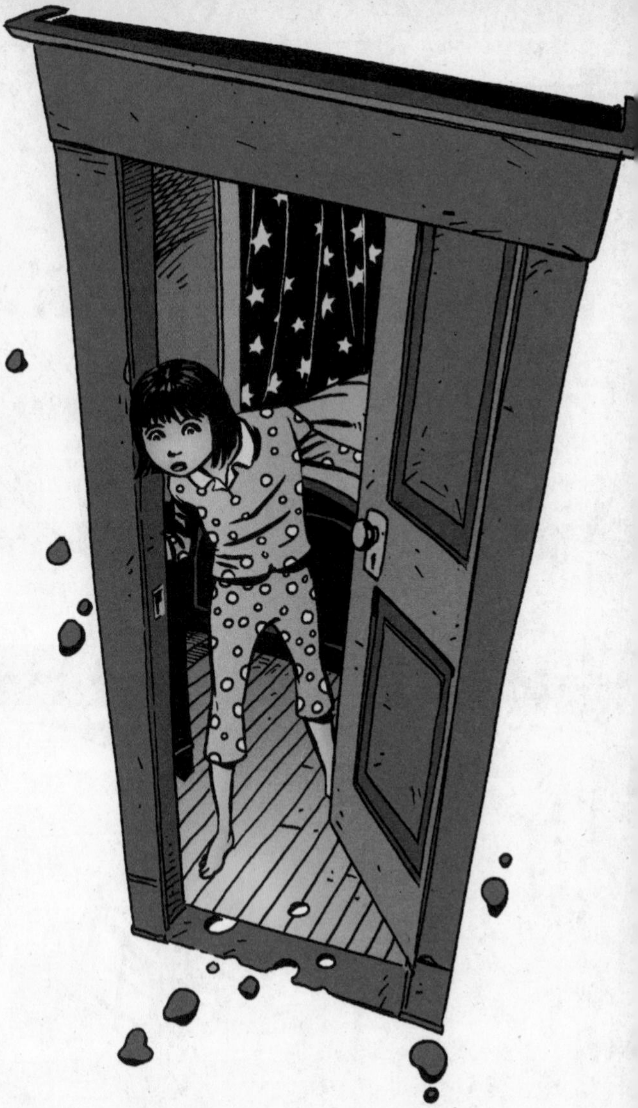

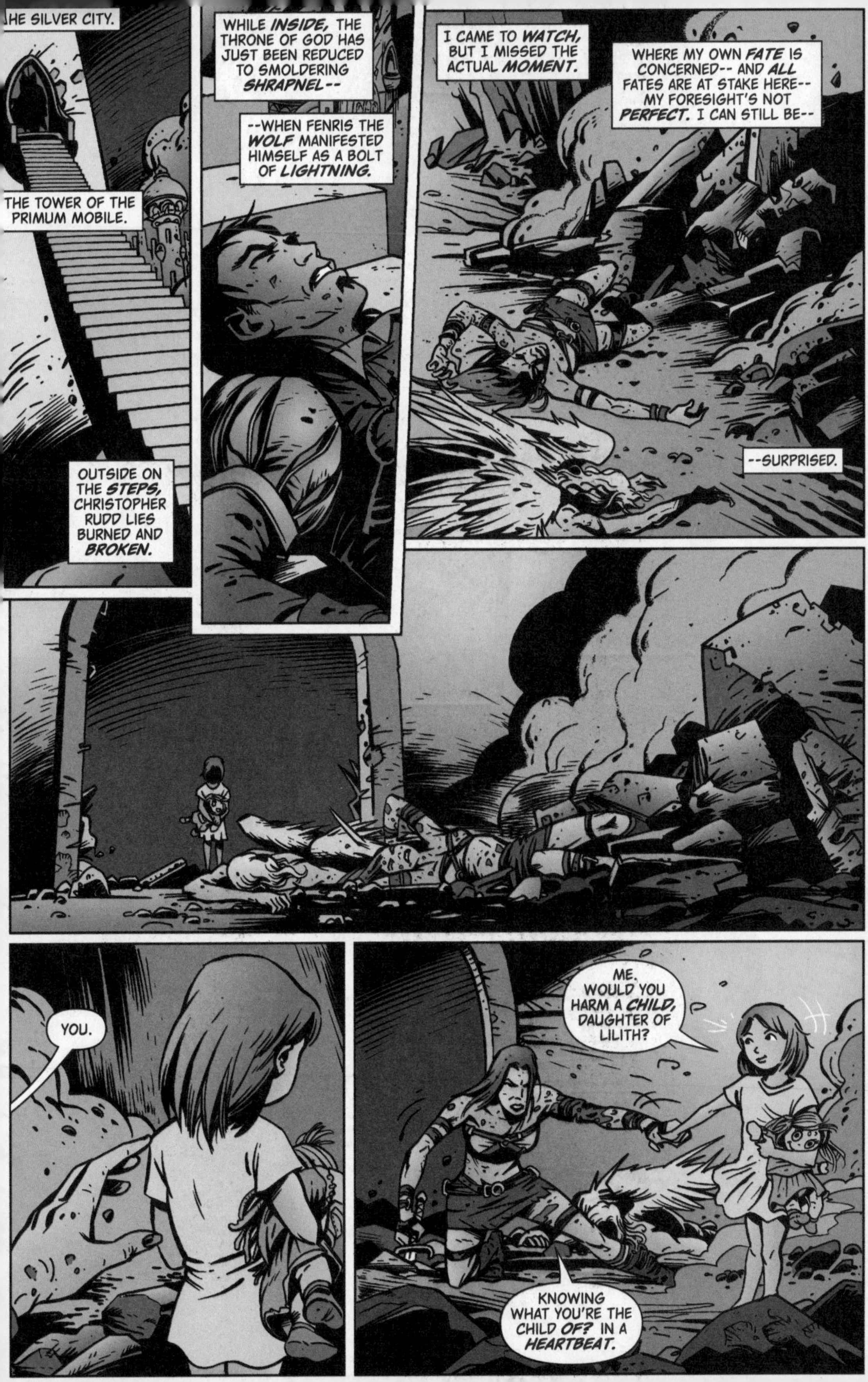

AHE SILVER CITY.
THE TOWER OF THE PRIMUM MOBILE.
OUTSIDE ON THE STEPS, CHRISTOPHER RUDD LIES BURNED AND BROKEN.
WHILE INSIDE, THE THRONE OF GOD HAS JUST BEEN REDUCED TO SMOLDERING SHRAPNEL--
--WHEN FENRIS THE WOLF MANIFESTED HIMSELF AS A BOLT OF LIGHTNING.
I CAME TO WATCH, BUT I MISSED THE ACTUAL MOMENT.
WHERE MY OWN FATE IS CONCERNED-- AND ALL FATES ARE AT STAKE HERE-- MY FORESIGHT'S NOT PERFECT. I CAN STILL BE--
--SURPRISED.
YOU.
ME. WOULD YOU HARM A CHILD, DAUGHTER OF LILITH?
KNOWING WHAT YOU'RE THE CHILD OF? IN A HEARTBEAT.

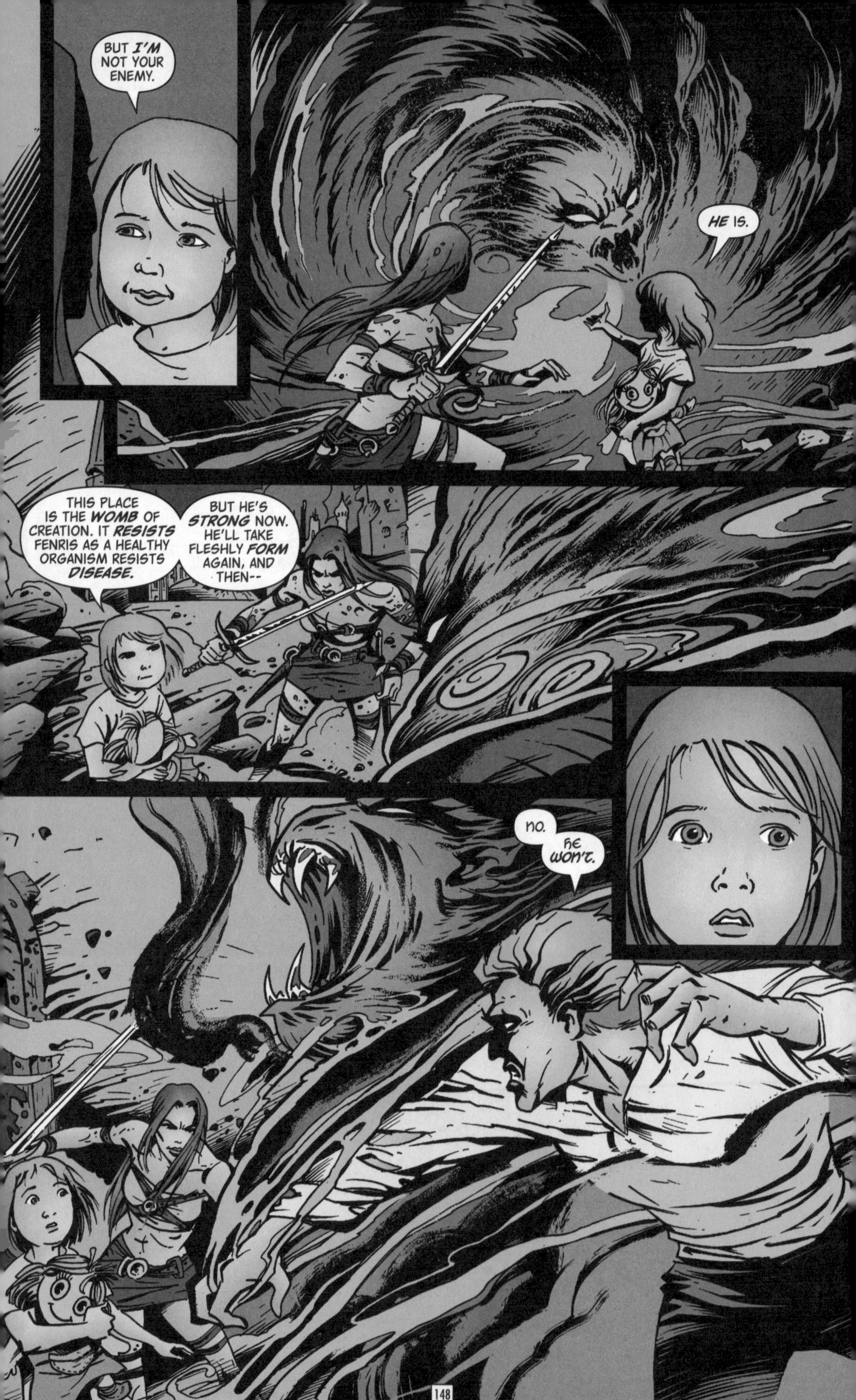
BUT I'M NOT YOUR ENEMY.
HE IS.
THIS PLACE IS THE WOMB OF CREATION. IT RESISTS FENRIS AS A HEALTHY ORGANISM RESISTS DISEASE.
BUT HE'S STRONG NOW. HE'LL TAKE FLESHLY FORM AGAIN, AND THEN--
no.
he won't.

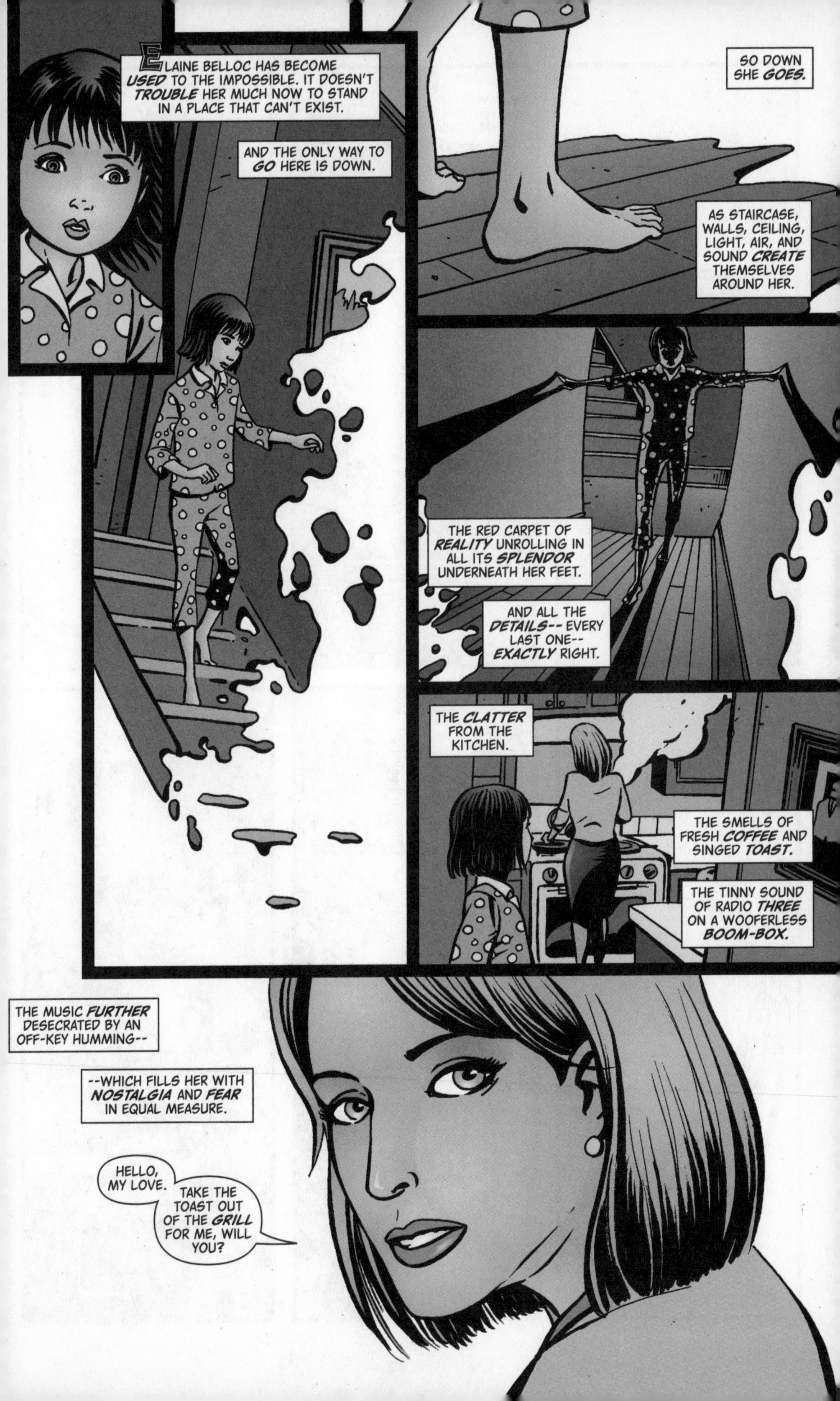
ELAINE BELLOC HAS BECOME USED TO THE IMPOSSIBLE. IT DOESN'T TROUBLE HER MUCH NOW TO STAND IN A PLACE THAT CAN'T EXIST.
AND THE ONLY WAY TO GO HERE IS DOWN.
SO DOWN SHE GOES.
AS STAIRCASE, WALLS, CEILING, LIGHT, AIR, AND SOUND CREATE THEMSELVES AROUND HER.
THE RED CARPET OF REALITY UNROLLING IN ALL ITS SPLENDOR UNDERNEATH HER FEET.
AND ALL THE DETAILS-- EVERY LAST ONE-- EXACTLY RIGHT.
THE CLATTER FROM THE KITCHEN.
THE SMELLS OF FRESH COFFEE AND SINGED TOAST.
THE TINNY SOUND OF RADIO THREE ON A WOOFERLESS BOOM-BOX.
THE MUSIC FURTHER DESECRATED BY AN OFF-KEY HUMMING--
--WHICH FILLS HER WITH NOSTALGIA AND FEAR IN EQUAL MEASURE.
HELLO, MY LOVE.
TAKE THE TOAST OUT OF THE GRILL FOR ME, WILL YOU?

DON'T **DO** THAT. IT'S NOT **FAIR**.

WHAT DO YOU **MEAN?**

YOU'RE **NOT** MY REAL MOM. WHY DO YOU WANT TO **LOOK** LIKE HER?

I HAVE TO LOOK LIKE **SOMETHING** THAT YOU KNOW. TO ATTACH MYSELF TO A CONCEPT YOUR MIND CAN **GRASP.**

YOUR MOTHER SEEMED LIKE AN APPROPRIATE **METAPHOR,** BECAUSE IN A **SENSE**-- IN **SEVERAL** SENSES--

--YOUR **BLOOD** IS MY **BLOOD.**

YAHWEH.

ELAINE.

IT'S **STILL** NOT FAIR.

THEN LET IT **PASS.**

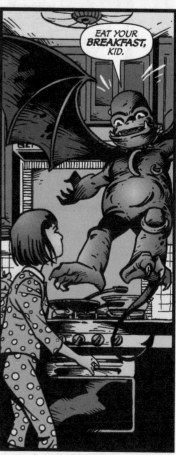

EAT YOUR **BREAKFAST,** KID.

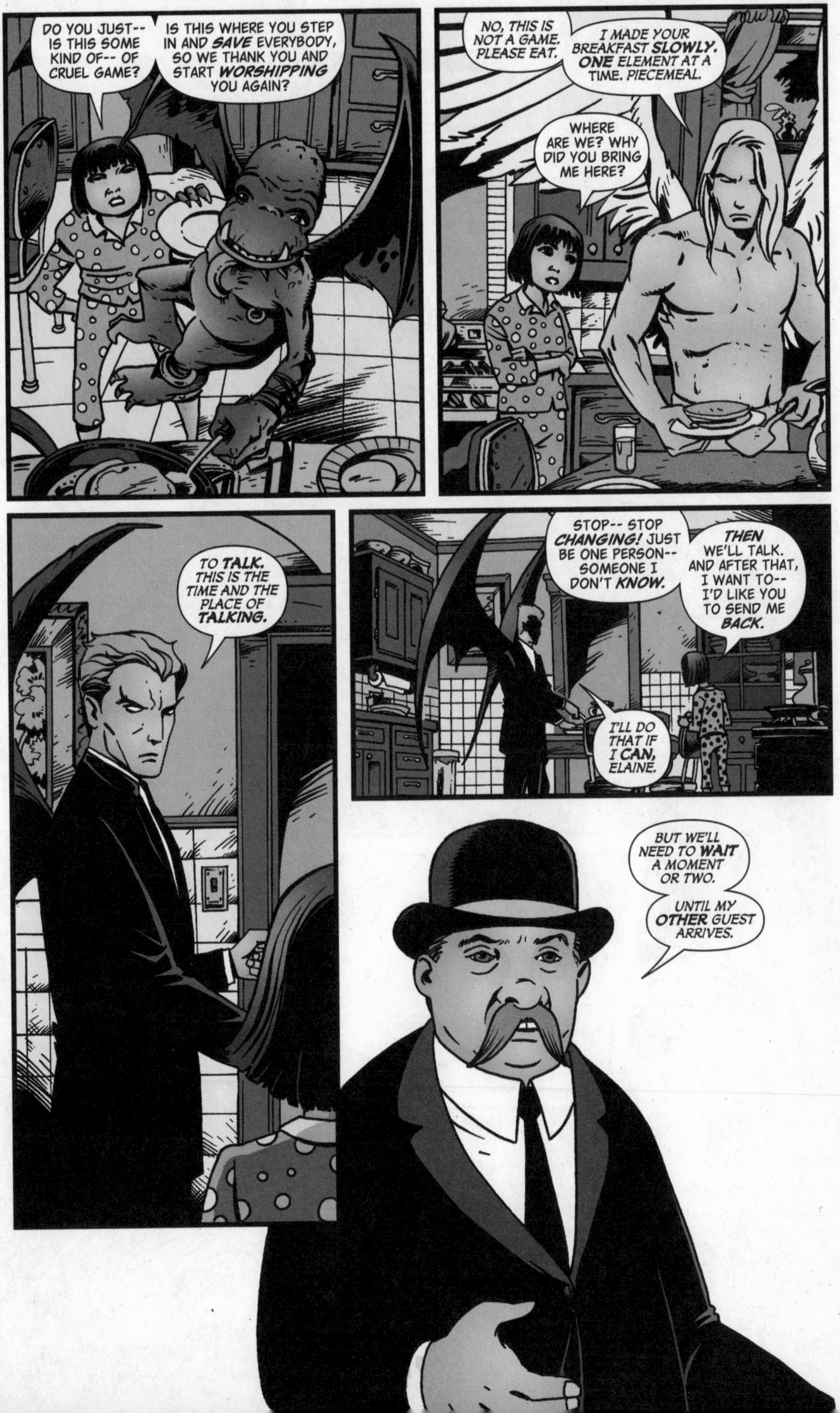
DO YOU JUST-- IS THIS SOME KIND OF-- OF CRUEL GAME?
IS THIS WHERE YOU STEP IN AND SAVE EVERYBODY, SO WE THANK YOU AND START WORSHIPPING YOU AGAIN?
NO, THIS IS NOT A GAME. PLEASE EAT.
I MADE YOUR BREAKFAST SLOWLY. ONE ELEMENT AT A TIME. PIECEMEAL.
WHERE ARE WE? WHY DID YOU BRING ME HERE?
TO TALK. THIS IS THE TIME AND THE PLACE OF TALKING.
STOP-- STOP CHANGING! JUST BE ONE PERSON-- SOMEONE I DON'T KNOW.
THEN WE'LL TALK. AND AFTER THAT, I WANT TO-- I'D LIKE YOU TO SEND ME BACK.
I'LL DO THAT IF I CAN, ELAINE.
BUT WE'LL NEED TO WAIT A MOMENT OR TWO.
UNTIL MY OTHER GUEST ARRIVES.

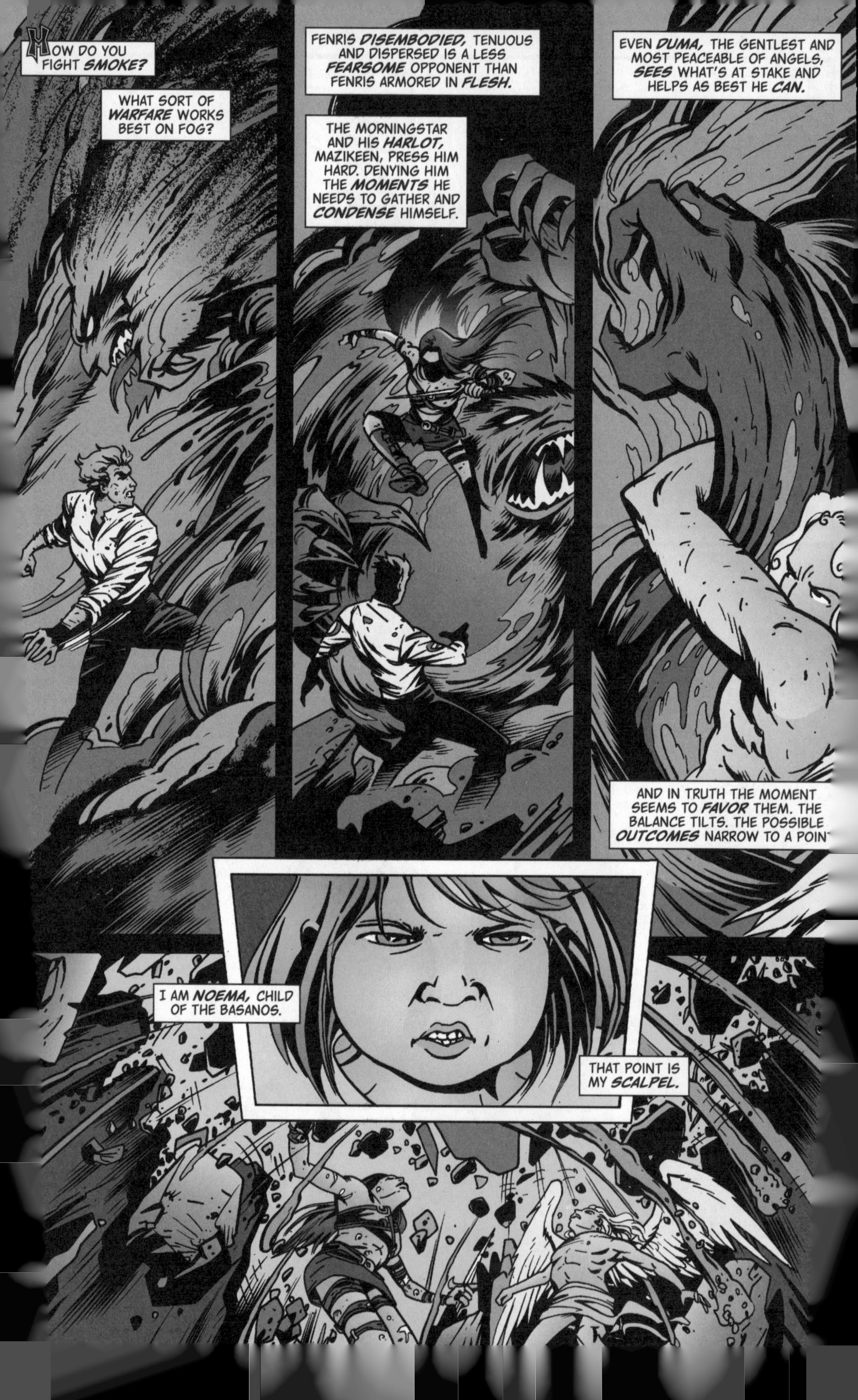
HOW DO YOU FIGHT SMOKE?
WHAT SORT OF WARFARE WORKS BEST ON FOG?
FENRIS DISEMBODIED, TENUOUS AND DISPERSED IS A LESS FEARSOME OPPONENT THAN FENRIS ARMORED IN FLESH.
THE MORNINGSTAR AND HIS HARLOT, MAZIKEEN, PRESS HIM HARD. DENYING HIM THE MOMENTS HE NEEDS TO GATHER AND CONDENSE HIMSELF.
EVEN DUMA, THE GENTLEST AND MOST PEACEABLE OF ANGELS, SEES WHAT'S AT STAKE AND HELPS AS BEST HE CAN.
AND IN TRUTH THE MOMENT SEEMS TO FAVOR THEM. THE BALANCE TILTS. THE POSSIBLE OUTCOMES NARROW TO A POINT
I AM NOEMA, CHILD OF THE BASANOS.
THAT POINT IS MY SCALPEL.

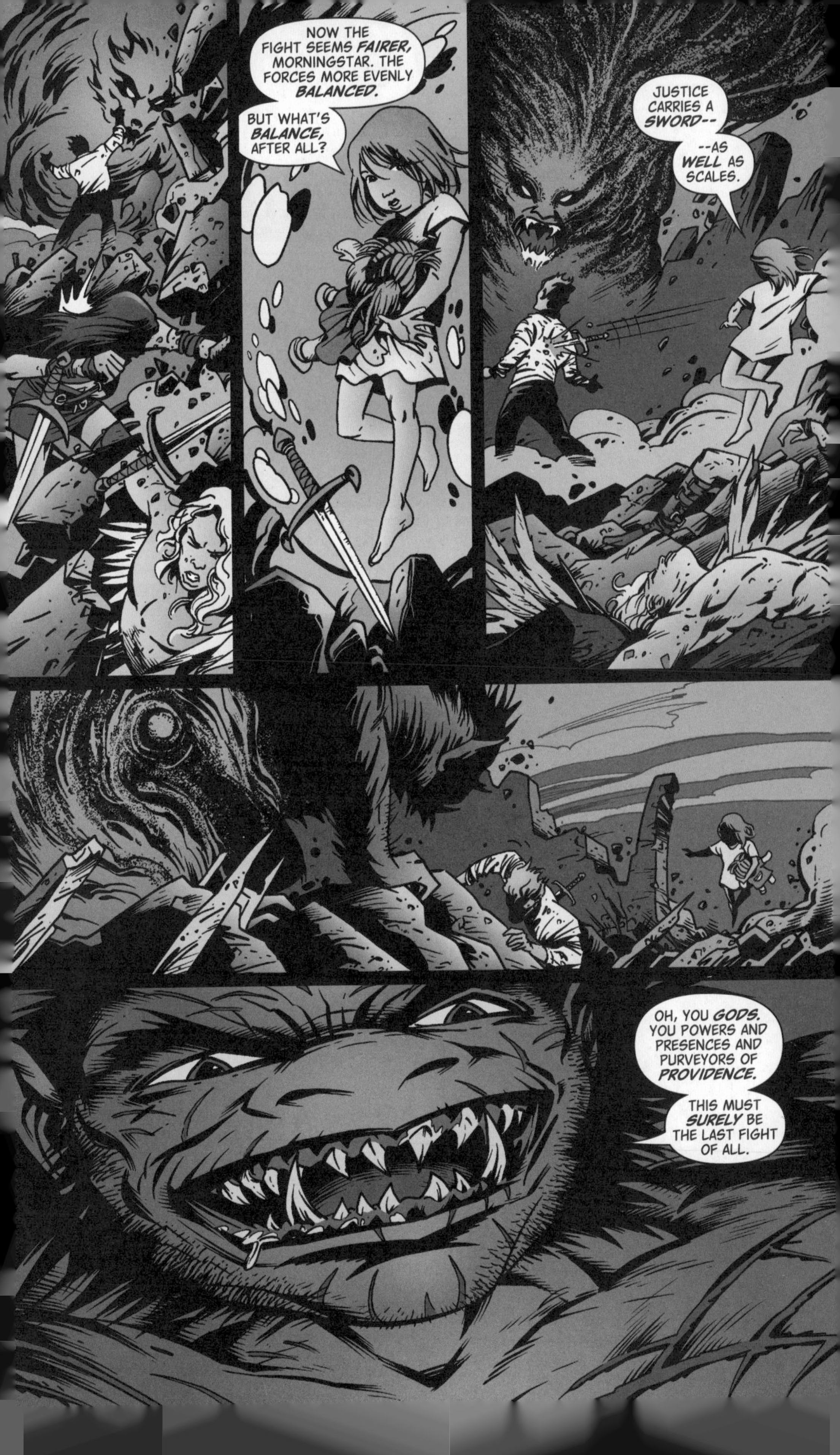
NOW THE FIGHT SEEMS FAIRER, MORNINGSTAR. THE FORCES MORE EVENLY BALANCED.
BUT WHAT'S BALANCE, AFTER ALL?
JUSTICE CARRIES A SWORD--
--AS WELL AS SCALES.
OH, YOU GODS. YOU POWERS AND PRESENCES AND PURVEYORS OF PROVIDENCE.
THIS MUST SURELY BE THE LAST FIGHT OF ALL.

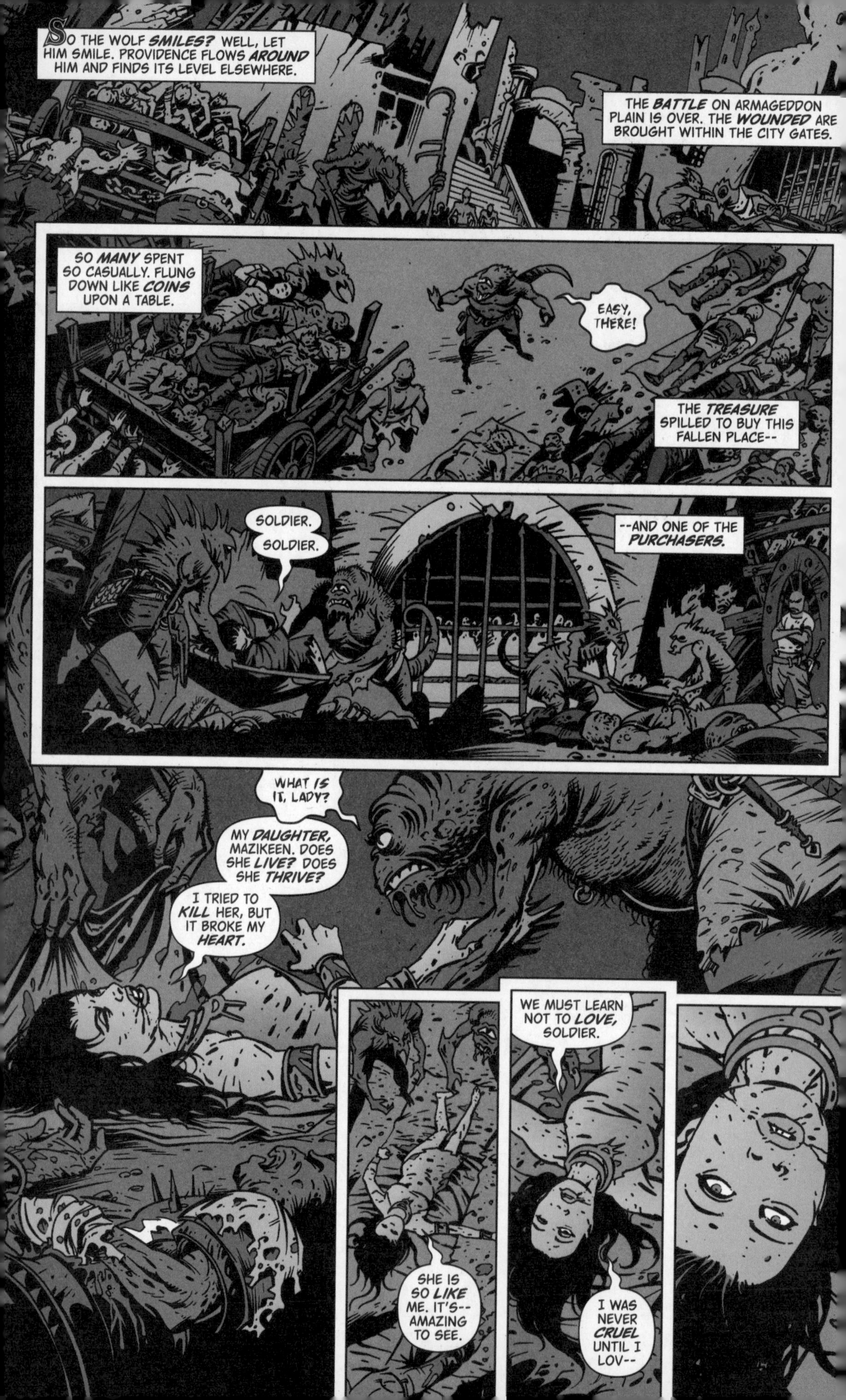
SO THE WOLF SMILES? WELL, LET HIM SMILE. PROVIDENCE FLOWS AROUND HIM AND FINDS ITS LEVEL ELSEWHERE.
THE BATTLE ON ARMAGEDDON PLAIN IS OVER. THE WOUNDED ARE BROUGHT WITHIN THE CITY GATES.
SO MANY SPENT SO CASUALLY. FLUNG DOWN LIKE COINS UPON A TABLE.
EASY, THERE!
THE TREASURE SPILLED TO BUY THIS FALLEN PLACE--
--AND ONE OF THE PURCHASERS.
SOLDIER.
SOLDIER.
WHAT IS IT, LADY?
MY DAUGHTER, MAZIKEEN. DOES SHE LIVE? DOES SHE THRIVE?
I TRIED TO KILL HER, BUT IT BROKE MY HEART.
SHE IS SO LIKE ME. IT'S-- AMAZING TO SEE.
WE MUST LEARN NOT TO LOVE, SOLDIER.
I WAS NEVER CRUEL UNTIL I LOV--

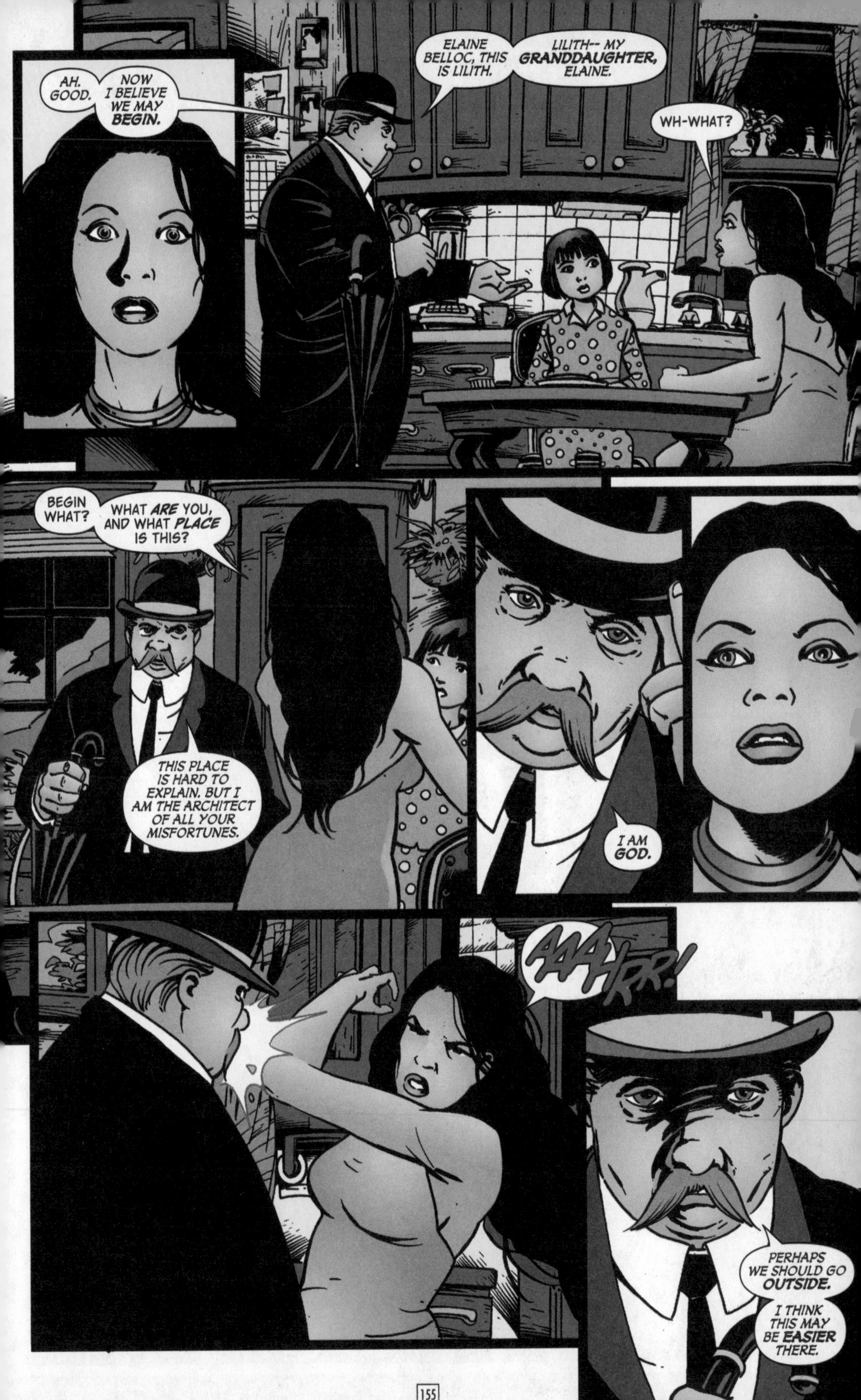
AH. GOOD.
NOW I BELIEVE WE MAY BEGIN.
ELAINE BELLOC, THIS IS LILITH.
LILITH-- MY GRANDDAUGHTER, ELAINE.
WH-WHAT?
BEGIN WHAT?
WHAT ARE YOU, AND WHAT PLACE IS THIS?
THIS PLACE IS HARD TO EXPLAIN. BUT I AM THE ARCHITECT OF ALL YOUR MISFORTUNES.
I AM GOD.
AAAHRR!
PERHAPS WE SHOULD GO OUTSIDE.
I THINK THIS MAY BE EASIER THERE.

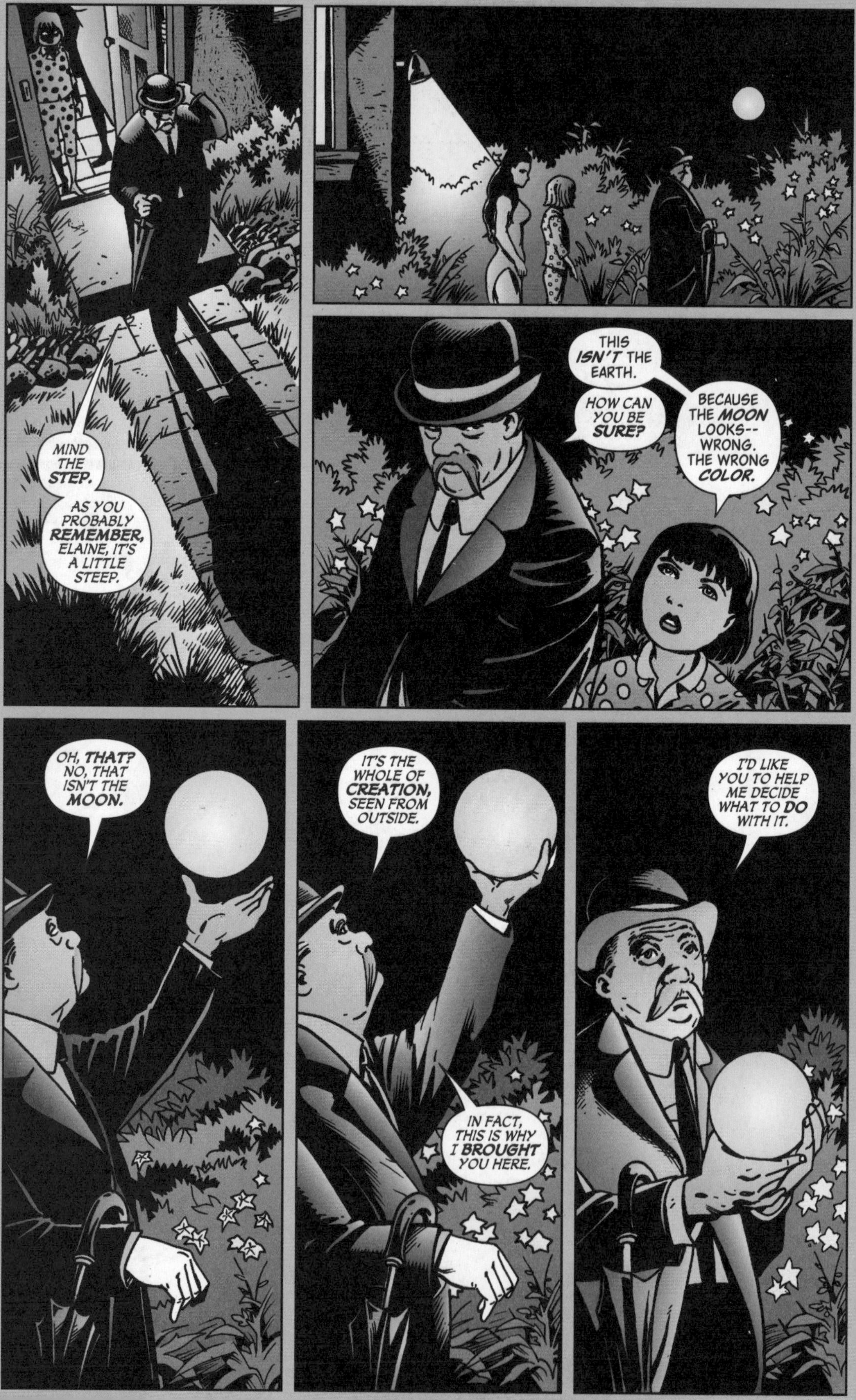
MIND THE STEP.
AS YOU PROBABLY REMEMBER, ELAINE, IT'S A LITTLE STEEP.
THIS ISN'T THE EARTH.
HOW CAN YOU BE SURE?
BECAUSE THE MOON LOOKS--WRONG. THE WRONG COLOR.
OH, THAT? NO, THAT ISN'T THE MOON.
IT'S THE WHOLE OF CREATION, SEEN FROM OUTSIDE.
IN FACT, THIS IS WHY I BROUGHT YOU HERE.
I'D LIKE YOU TO HELP ME DECIDE WHAT TO DO WITH IT.

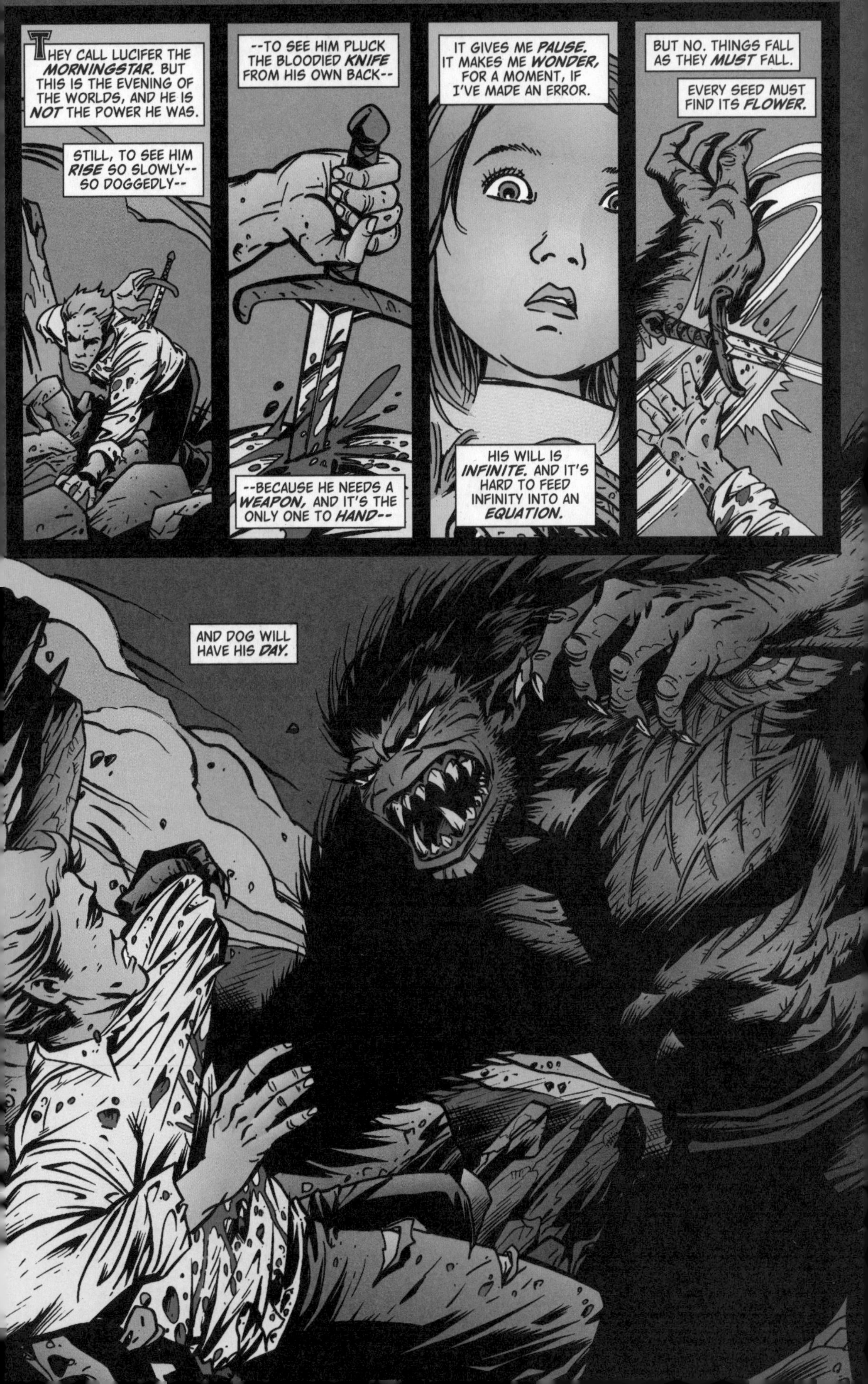
THEY CALL LUCIFER THE MORNINGSTAR. BUT THIS IS THE EVENING OF THE WORLDS, AND HE IS NOT THE POWER HE WAS.
STILL, TO SEE HIM RISE SO SLOWLY-- SO DOGGEDLY--
--TO SEE HIM PLUCK THE BLOODIED KNIFE FROM HIS OWN BACK--
--BECAUSE HE NEEDS A WEAPON, AND IT'S THE ONLY ONE TO HAND--
IT GIVES ME PAUSE. IT MAKES ME WONDER, FOR A MOMENT, IF I'VE MADE AN ERROR.
HIS WILL IS INFINITE. AND IT'S HARD TO FEED INFINITY INTO AN EQUATION.
BUT NO. THINGS FALL AS THEY MUST FALL.
EVERY SEED MUST FIND ITS FLOWER.
AND DOG WILL HAVE HIS DAY.

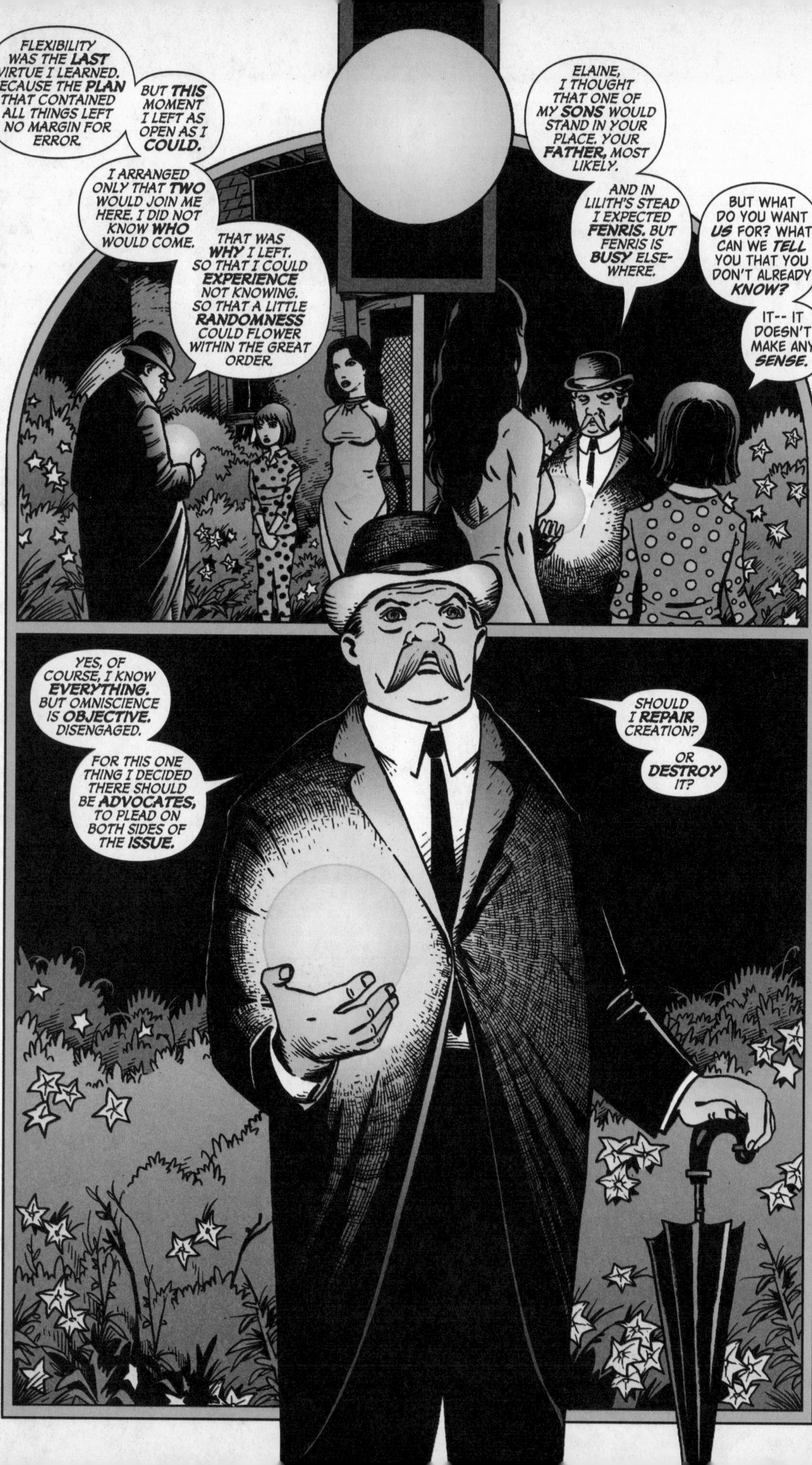
FLEXIBILITY WAS THE LAST VIRTUE I LEARNED. BECAUSE THE PLAN THAT CONTAINED ALL THINGS LEFT NO MARGIN FOR ERROR.
BUT THIS MOMENT I LEFT AS OPEN AS I COULD.
I ARRANGED ONLY THAT TWO WOULD JOIN ME HERE. I DID NOT KNOW WHO WOULD COME.
THAT WAS WHY I LEFT. SO THAT I COULD EXPERIENCE NOT KNOWING. SO THAT A LITTLE RANDOMNESS COULD FLOWER WITHIN THE GREAT ORDER.
ELAINE, I THOUGHT THAT ONE OF MY SONS WOULD STAND IN YOUR PLACE. YOUR FATHER, MOST LIKELY.
AND IN LILITH'S STEAD I EXPECTED FENRIS. BUT FENRIS IS BUSY ELSE-WHERE.
BUT WHAT DO YOU WANT US FOR? WHAT CAN WE TELL YOU THAT YOU DON'T ALREADY KNOW?
IT-- IT DOESN'T MAKE ANY SENSE.
YES, OF COURSE, I KNOW EVERYTHING. BUT OMNISCIENCE IS OBJECTIVE. DISENGAGED.
FOR THIS ONE THING I DECIDED THERE SHOULD BE ADVOCATES, TO PLEAD ON BOTH SIDES OF THE ISSUE.
SHOULD I REPAIR CREATION?
OR DESTROY IT?

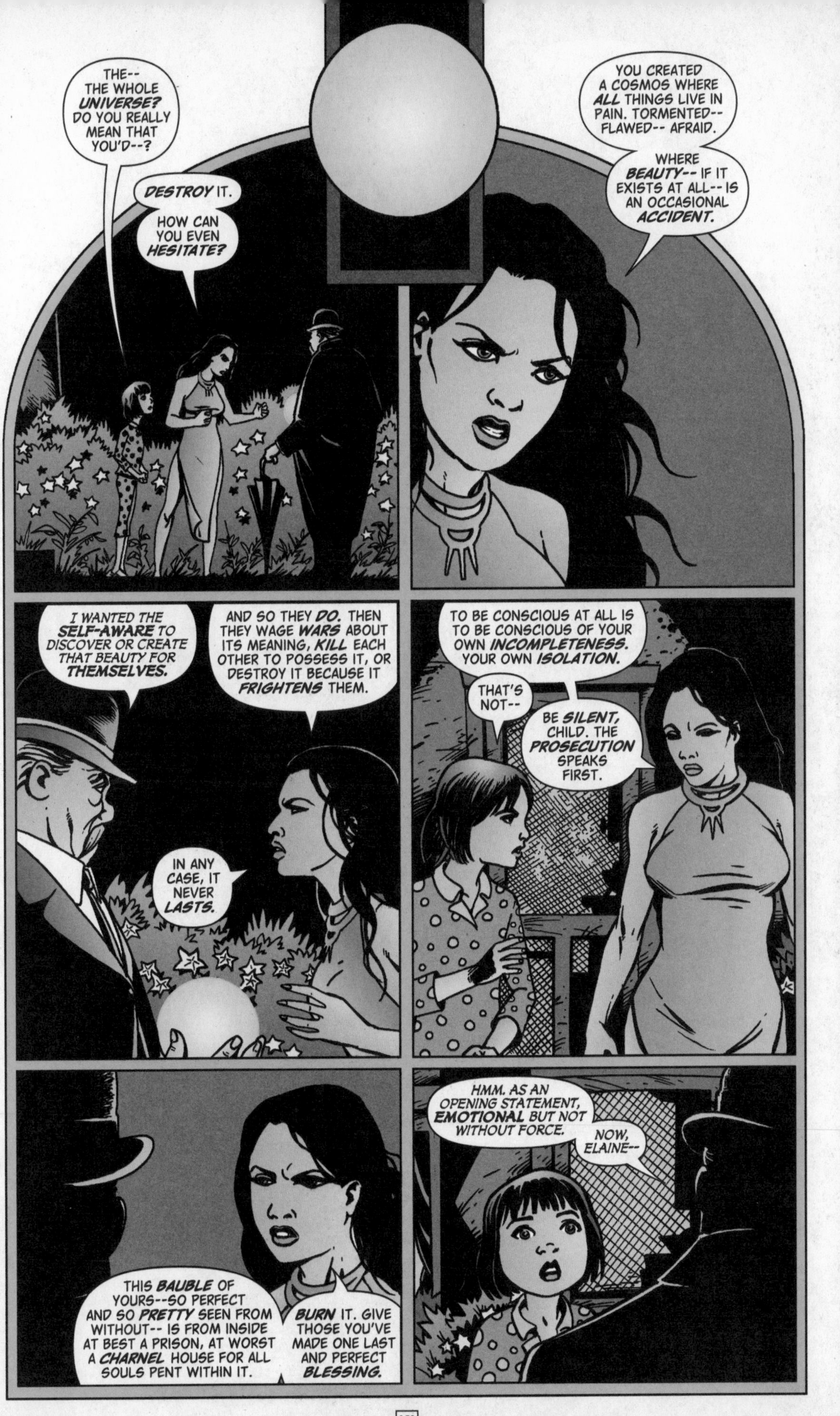
THE-- THE WHOLE UNIVERSE? DO YOU REALLY MEAN THAT YOU'D--?
DESTROY IT.
HOW CAN YOU EVEN HESITATE?
YOU CREATED A COSMOS WHERE ALL THINGS LIVE IN PAIN. TORMENTED-- FLAWED-- AFRAID.
WHERE BEAUTY-- IF IT EXISTS AT ALL-- IS AN OCCASIONAL ACCIDENT.
I WANTED THE SELF-AWARE TO DISCOVER OR CREATE THAT BEAUTY FOR THEMSELVES.
AND SO THEY DO. THEN THEY WAGE WARS ABOUT ITS MEANING, KILL EACH OTHER TO POSSESS IT, OR DESTROY IT BECAUSE IT FRIGHTENS THEM.
IN ANY CASE, IT NEVER LASTS.
TO BE CONSCIOUS AT ALL IS TO BE CONSCIOUS OF YOUR OWN INCOMPLETENESS. YOUR OWN ISOLATION.
THAT'S NOT--
BE SILENT, CHILD. THE PROSECUTION SPEAKS FIRST.
THIS BAUBLE OF YOURS--SO PERFECT AND SO PRETTY SEEN FROM WITHOUT-- IS FROM INSIDE AT BEST A PRISON, AT WORST A CHARNEL HOUSE FOR ALL SOULS PENT WITHIN IT.
BURN IT. GIVE THOSE YOU'VE MADE ONE LAST AND PERFECT BLESSING.
HMM. AS AN OPENING STATEMENT, EMOTIONAL BUT NOT WITHOUT FORCE.
NOW, ELAINE--

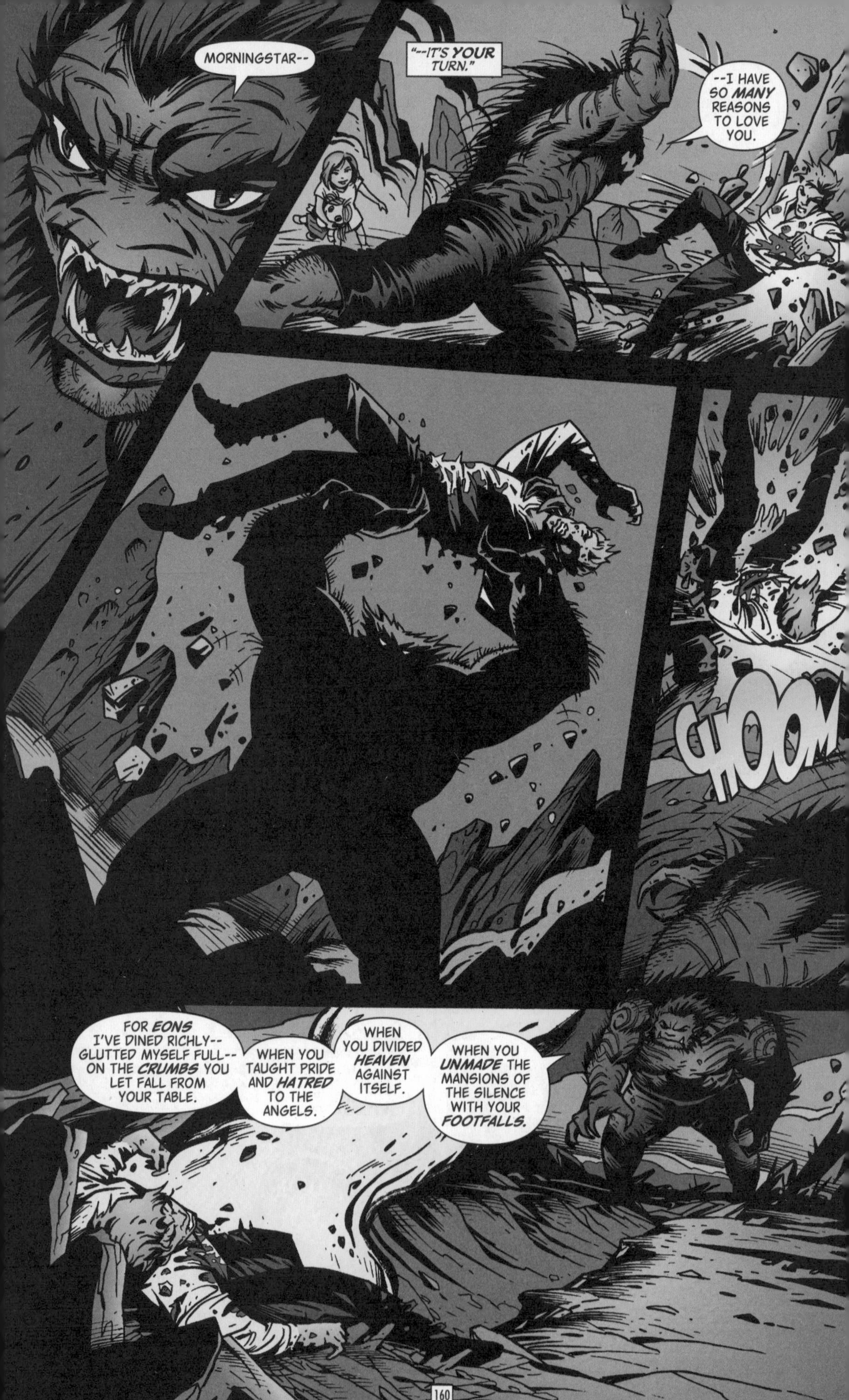
MORNINGSTAR--
"--IT'S YOUR TURN."
--I HAVE SO MANY REASONS TO LOVE YOU.
CHOOM
FOR EONS I'VE DINED RICHLY-- GLUTTED MYSELF FULL-- ON THE CRUMBS YOU LET FALL FROM YOUR TABLE.
WHEN YOU TAUGHT PRIDE AND HATRED TO THE ANGELS.
WHEN YOU DIVIDED HEAVEN AGAINST ITSELF.
WHEN YOU UNMADE THE MANSIONS OF THE SILENCE WITH YOUR FOOTFALLS.

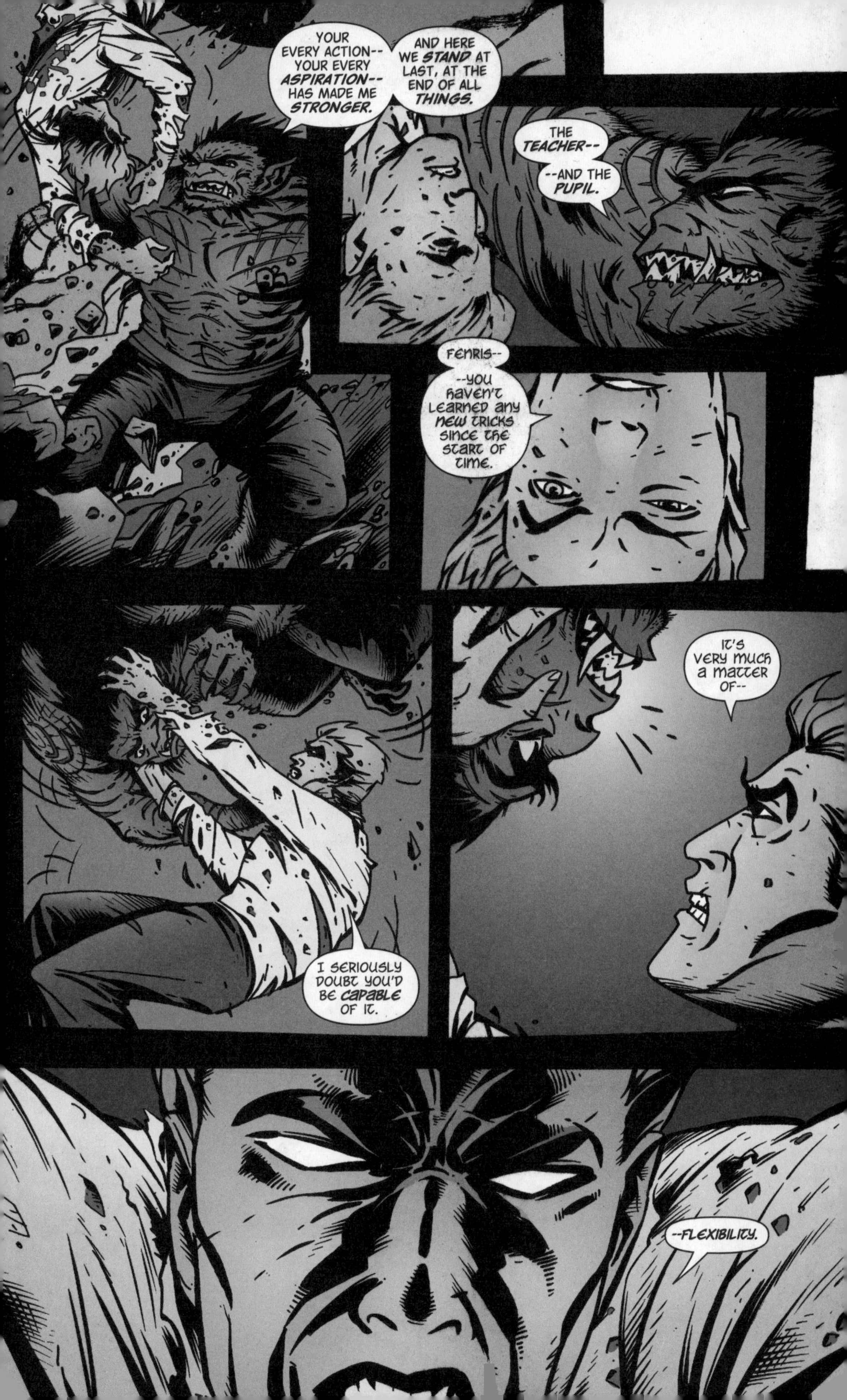
YOUR EVERY ACTION-- YOUR EVERY ASPIRATION-- HAS MADE ME STRONGER.
AND HERE WE STAND AT LAST, AT THE END OF ALL THINGS.
THE TEACHER--
--AND THE PUPIL.
FENRIS--
--YOU HAVEN'T LEARNED ANY NEW TRICKS SINCE THE START OF TIME.
I SERIOUSLY DOUBT YOU'D BE CAPABLE OF IT.
IT'S VERY MUCH A MATTER OF--
--FLEXIBILITY.

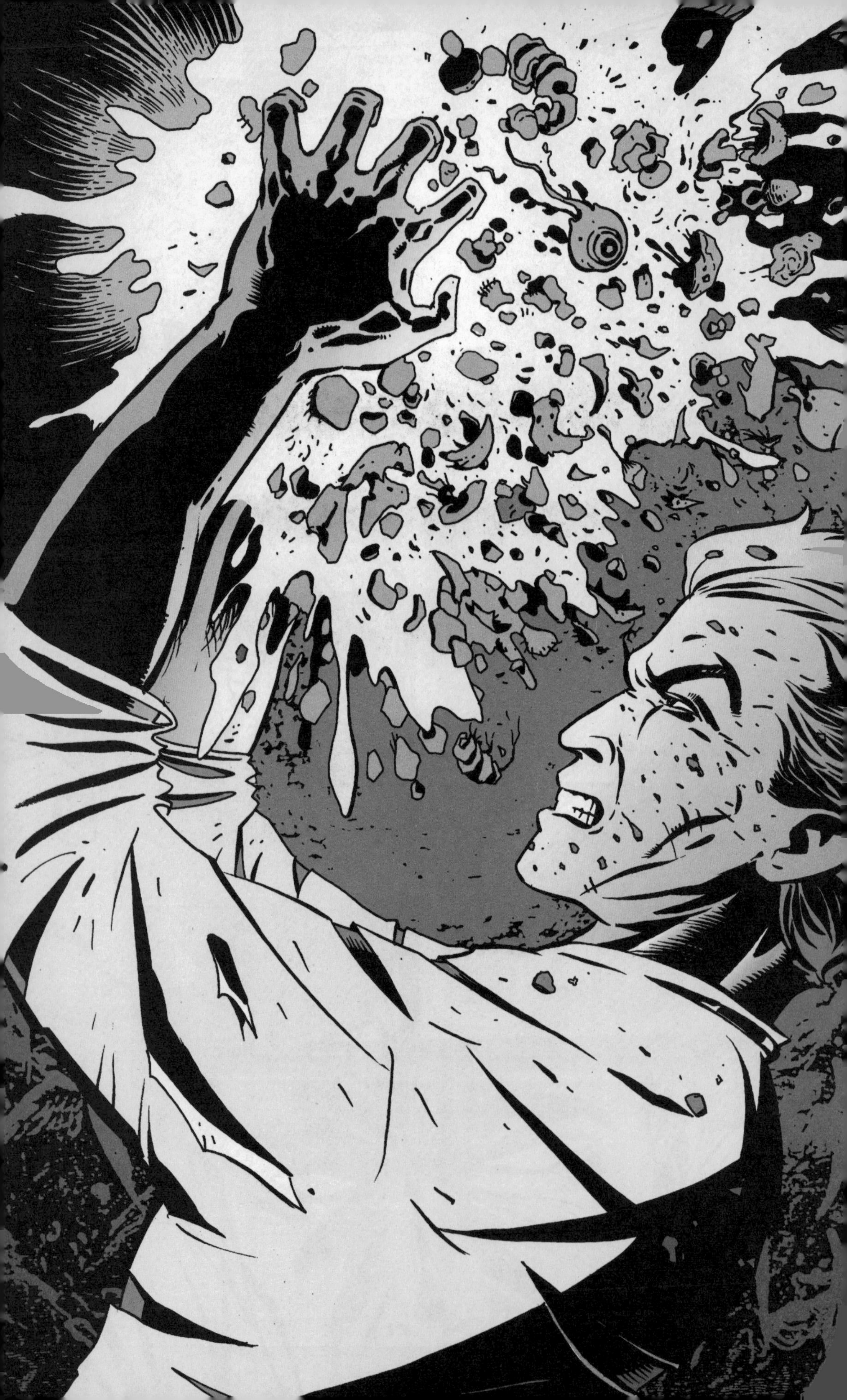

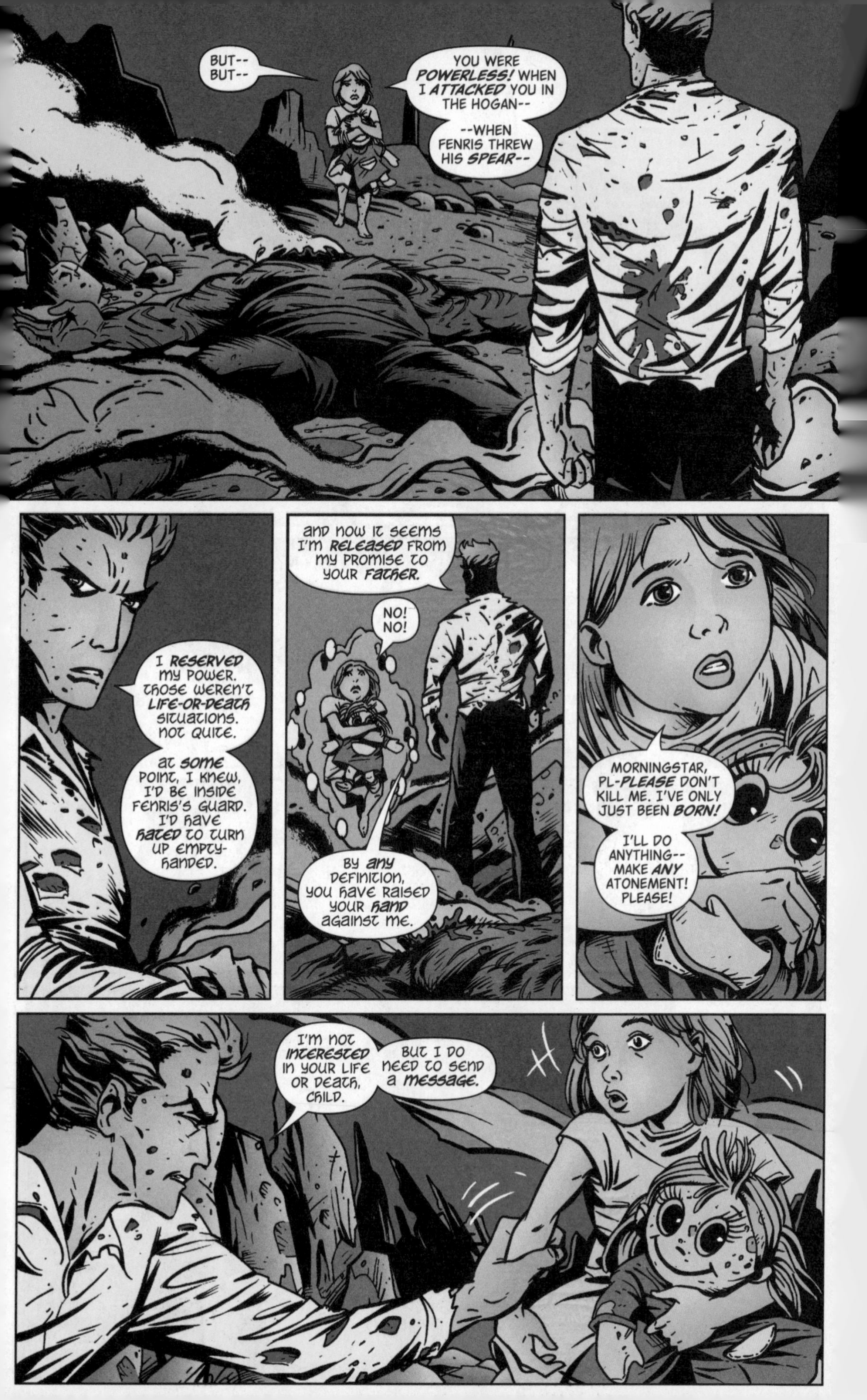
BUT--
BUT--
YOU WERE POWERLESS! WHEN I ATTACKED YOU IN THE HOGAN--
--WHEN FENRIS THREW HIS SPEAR--
I RESERVED MY POWER. THOSE WEREN'T LIFE-OR-DEATH SITUATIONS. NOT QUITE.
AT SOME POINT, I KNEW, I'D BE INSIDE FENRIS'S GUARD. I'D HAVE HATED TO TURN UP EMPTY-HANDED.
AND NOW IT SEEMS I'M RELEASED FROM MY PROMISE TO YOUR FATHER.
NO! NO!
BY ANY DEFINITION, YOU HAVE RAISED YOUR HAND AGAINST ME.
MORNINGSTAR, PL-PLEASE DON'T KILL ME. I'VE ONLY JUST BEEN BORN!
I'LL DO ANYTHING-- MAKE ANY ATONEMENT! PLEASE!
I'M NOT INTERESTED IN YOUR LIFE OR DEATH, CHILD.
BUT I DO NEED TO SEND A MESSAGE.

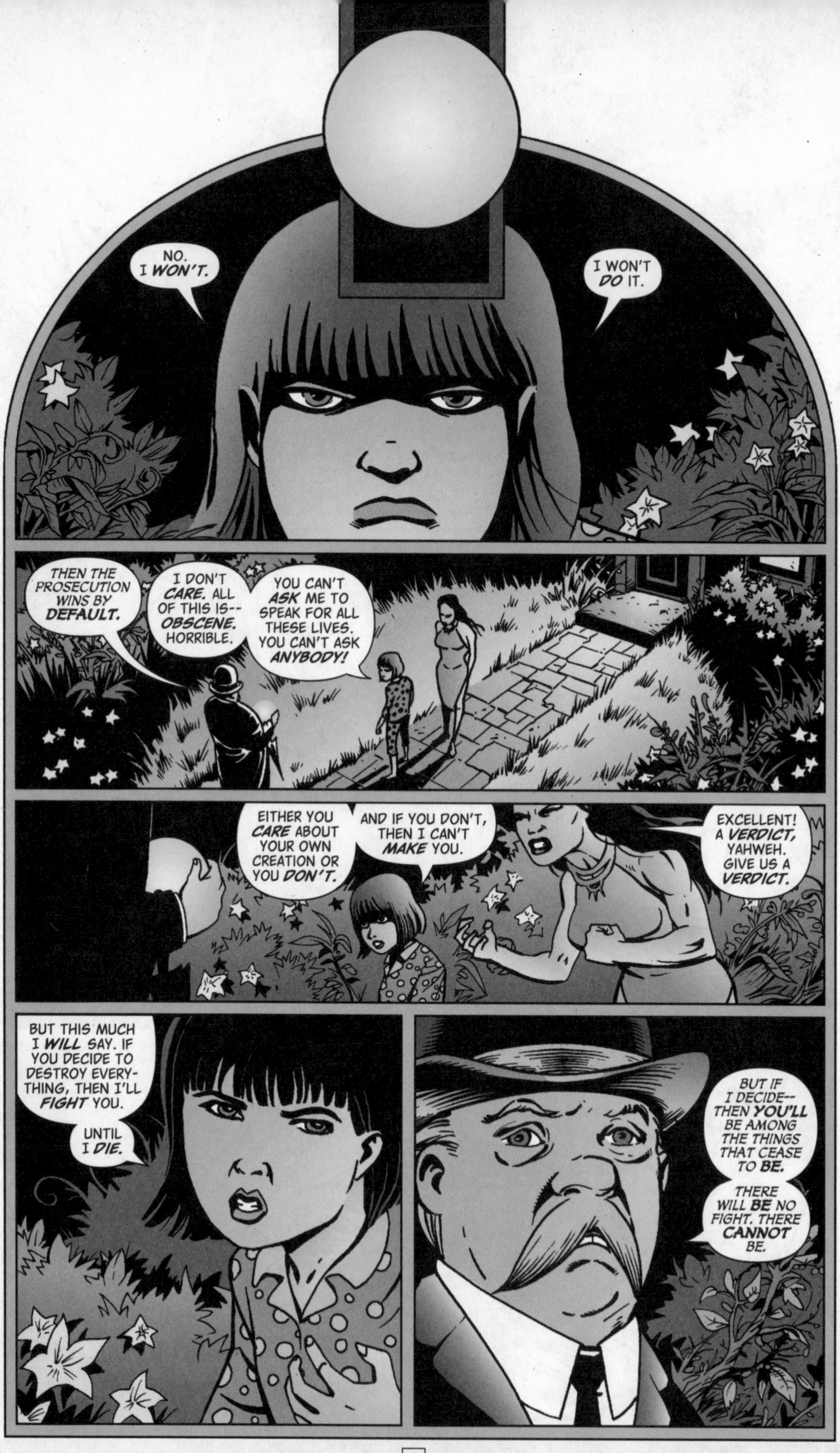
NO. I WON'T.
I WON'T DO IT.
THEN THE PROSECUTION WINS BY DEFAULT.
I DON'T CARE. ALL OF THIS IS-- OBSCENE. HORRIBLE.
YOU CAN'T ASK ME TO SPEAK FOR ALL THESE LIVES. YOU CAN'T ASK ANYBODY!
EITHER YOU CARE ABOUT YOUR OWN CREATION OR YOU DON'T.
AND IF YOU DON'T, THEN I CAN'T MAKE YOU.
EXCELLENT! A VERDICT, YAHWEH. GIVE US A VERDICT.
BUT THIS MUCH I WILL SAY. IF YOU DECIDE TO DESTROY EVERY-THING, THEN I'LL FIGHT YOU.
UNTIL I DIE.
BUT IF I DECIDE-- THEN YOU'LL BE AMONG THE THINGS THAT CEASE TO BE.
THERE WILL BE NO FIGHT. THERE CANNOT BE.

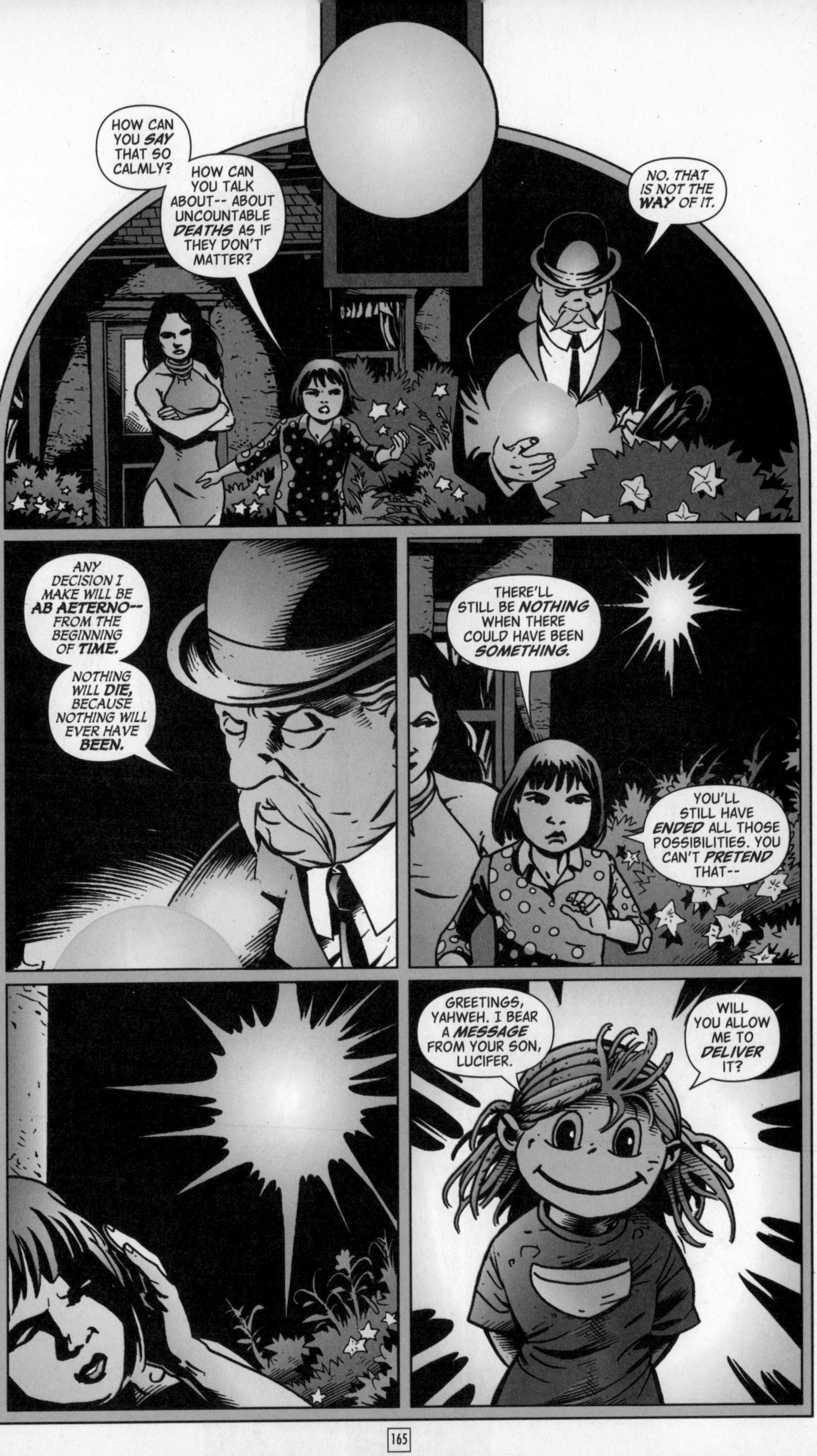

HOW CAN YOU SAY THAT SO CALMLY?
HOW CAN YOU TALK ABOUT-- ABOUT UNCOUNTABLE DEATHS AS IF THEY DON'T MATTER?
NO. THAT IS NOT THE WAY OF IT.
ANY DECISION I MAKE WILL BE AB AETERNO-- FROM THE BEGINNING OF TIME.
NOTHING WILL DIE, BECAUSE NOTHING WILL EVER HAVE BEEN.
THERE'LL STILL BE NOTHING WHEN THERE COULD HAVE BEEN SOMETHING.
YOU'LL STILL HAVE ENDED ALL THOSE POSSIBILITIES. YOU CAN'T PRETEND THAT--
GREETINGS, YAHWEH. I BEAR A MESSAGE FROM YOUR SON, LUCIFER.
WILL YOU ALLOW ME TO DELIVER IT?

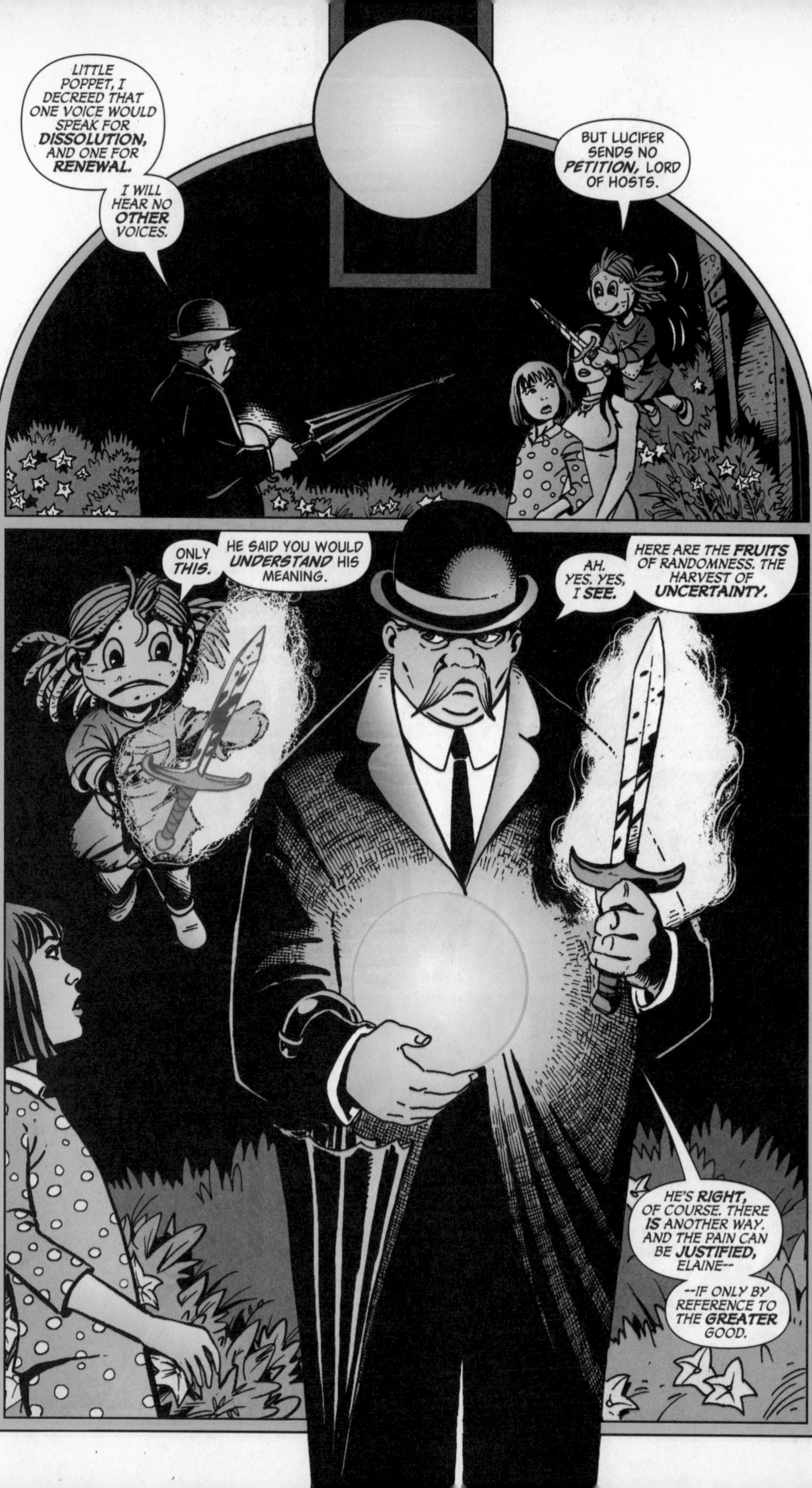
LITTLE POPPET, I DECREED THAT ONE VOICE WOULD SPEAK FOR DISSOLUTION, AND ONE FOR RENEWAL.
I WILL HEAR NO OTHER VOICES.
BUT LUCIFER SENDS NO PETITION, LORD OF HOSTS.
ONLY THIS.
HE SAID YOU WOULD UNDERSTAND HIS MEANING.
AH. YES. YES, I SEE.
HERE ARE THE FRUITS OF RANDOMNESS. THE HARVEST OF UNCERTAINTY.
HE'S RIGHT, OF COURSE. THERE IS ANOTHER WAY. AND THE PAIN CAN BE JUSTIFIED, ELAINE--
--IF ONLY BY REFERENCE TO THE GREATER GOOD.

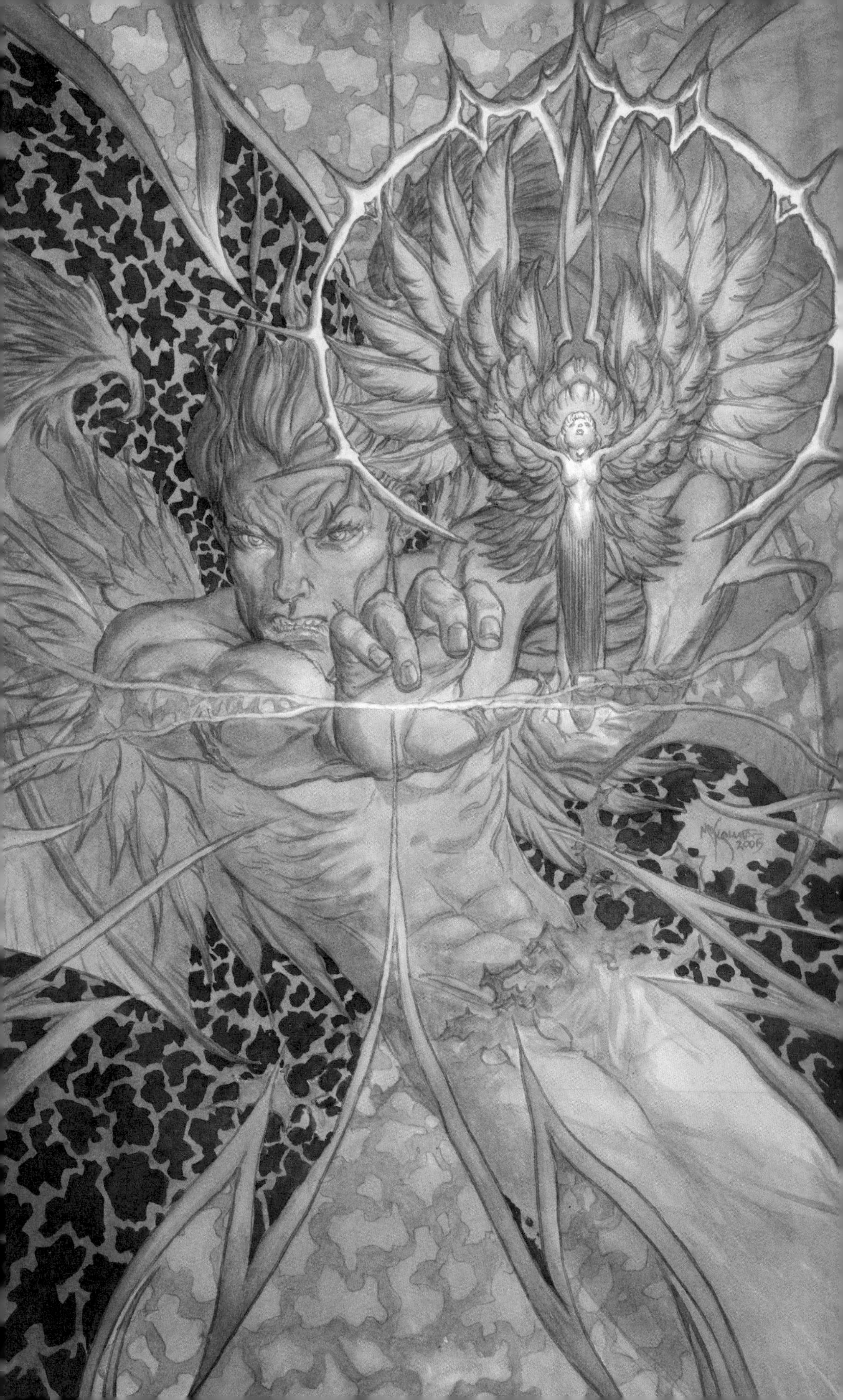

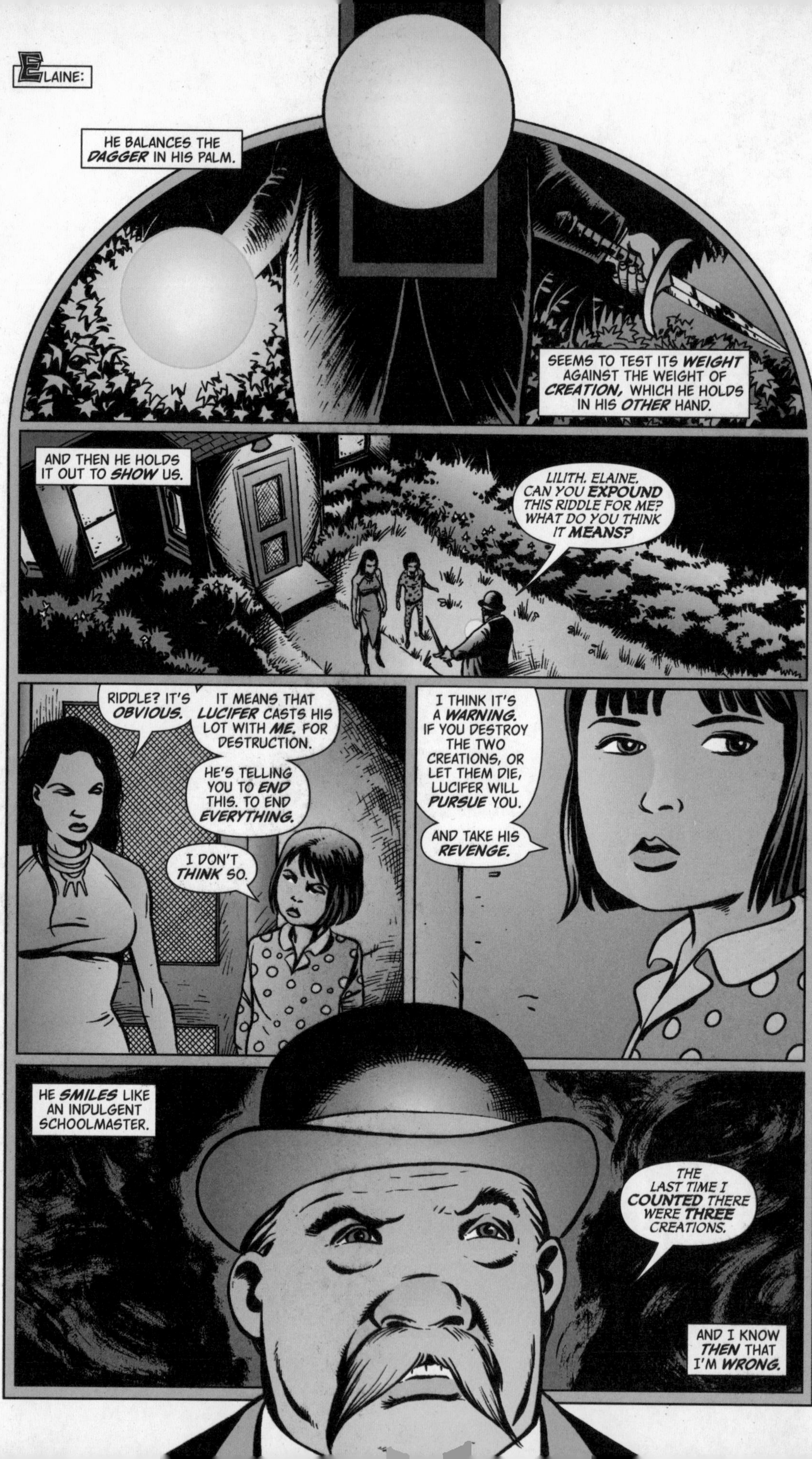
ELAINE:
HE BALANCES THE DAGGER IN HIS PALM.
SEEMS TO TEST ITS WEIGHT AGAINST THE WEIGHT OF CREATION, WHICH HE HOLDS IN HIS OTHER HAND.
AND THEN HE HOLDS IT OUT TO SHOW US.
LILITH. ELAINE. CAN YOU EXPOUND THIS RIDDLE FOR ME? WHAT DO YOU THINK IT MEANS?
RIDDLE? IT'S OBVIOUS.
IT MEANS THAT LUCIFER CASTS HIS LOT WITH ME. FOR DESTRUCTION.
HE'S TELLING YOU TO END THIS. TO END EVERYTHING.
I DON'T THINK SO.
I THINK IT'S A WARNING. IF YOU DESTROY THE TWO CREATIONS, OR LET THEM DIE, LUCIFER WILL PURSUE YOU.
AND TAKE HIS REVENGE.
HE SMILES LIKE AN INDULGENT SCHOOLMASTER.
THE LAST TIME I COUNTED THERE WERE THREE CREATIONS.
AND I KNOW THEN THAT I'M WRONG.

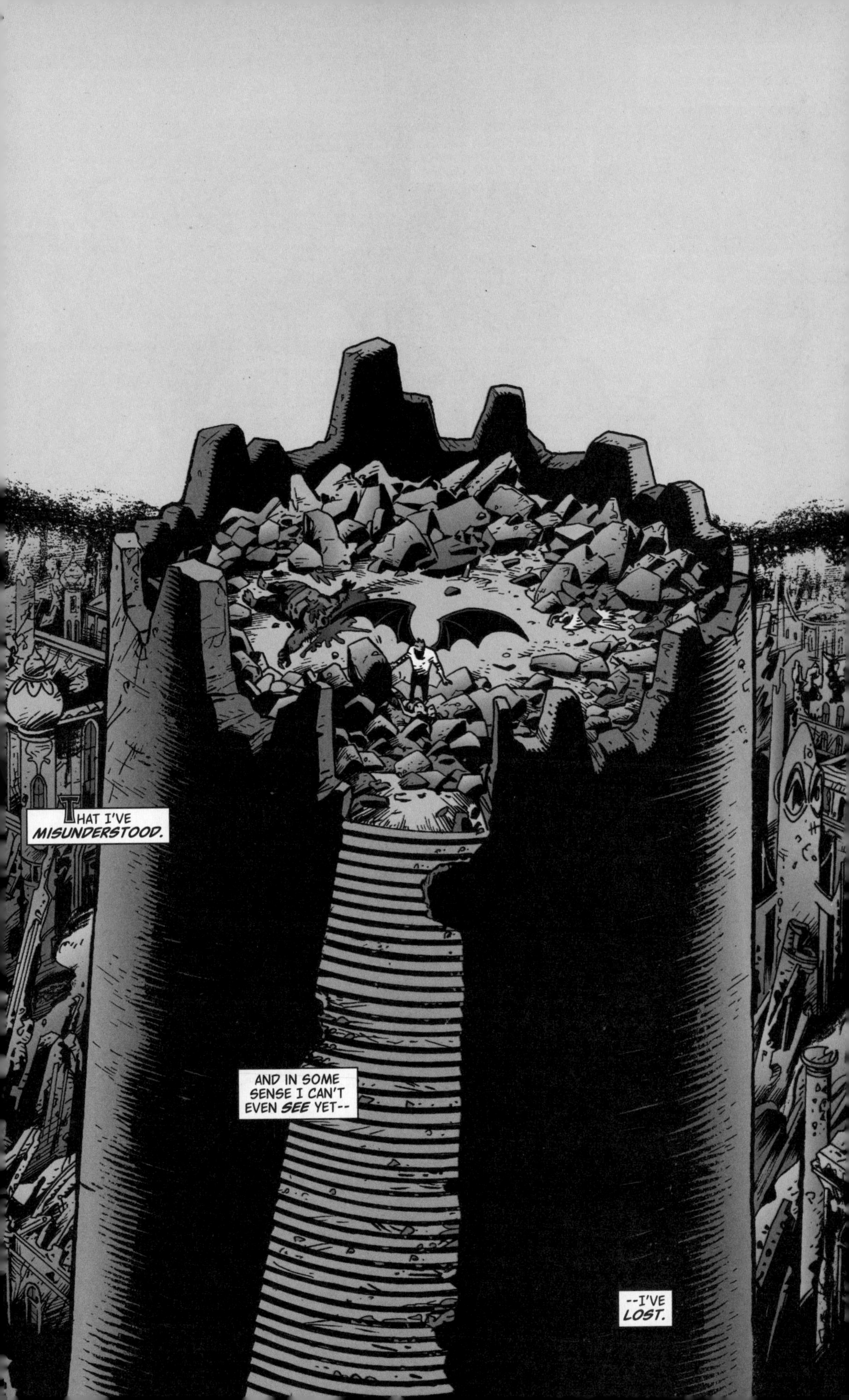
THAT I'VE MISUNDERSTOOD.
AND IN SOME SENSE I CAN'T EVEN SEE YET--
--I'VE LOST.

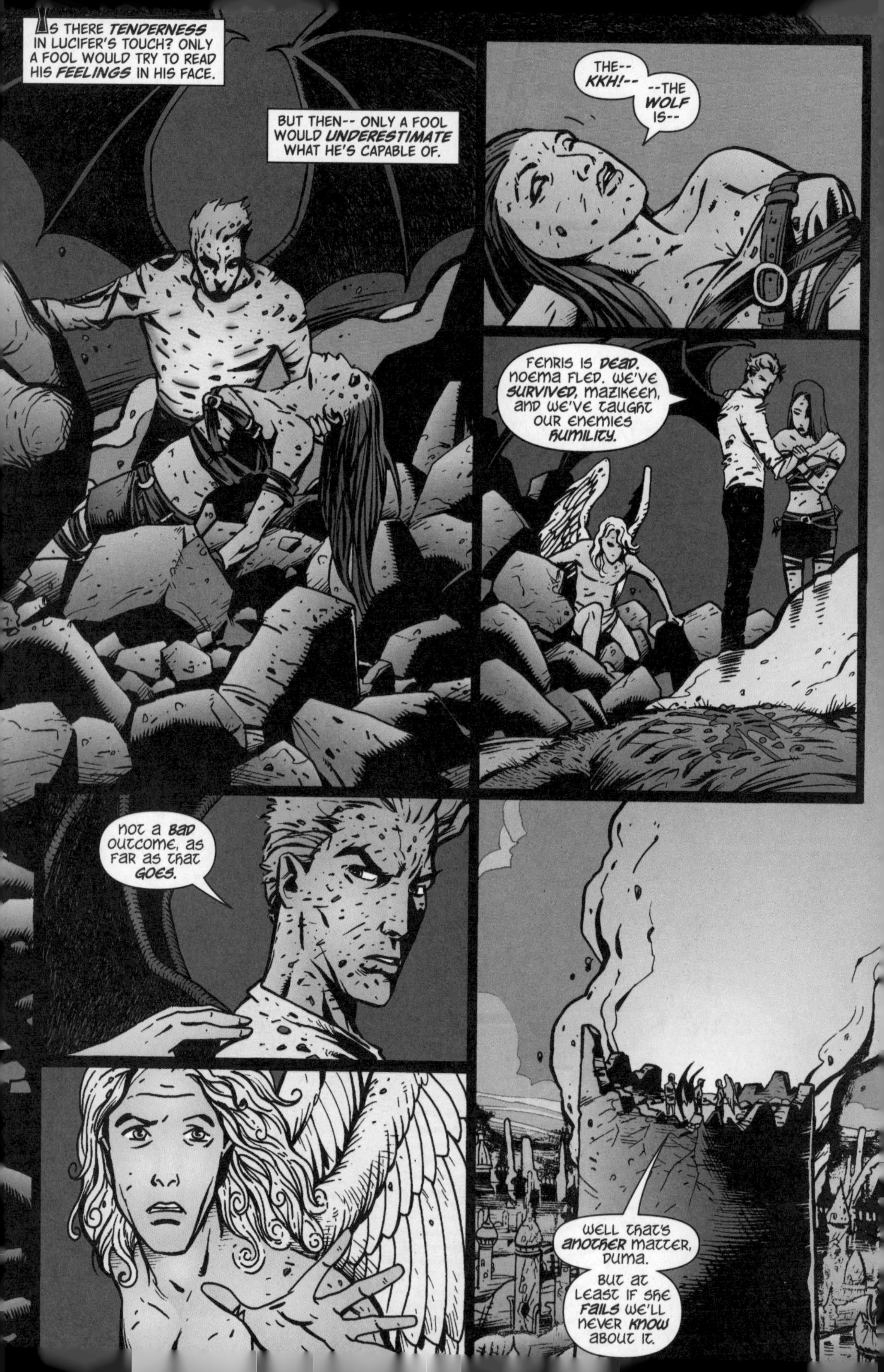
IS THERE TENDERNESS IN LUCIFER'S TOUCH? ONLY A FOOL WOULD TRY TO READ HIS FEELINGS IN HIS FACE.
BUT THEN-- ONLY A FOOL WOULD UNDERESTIMATE WHAT HE'S CAPABLE OF.
THE-- KKH!-- --THE WOLF IS--
FENRIS IS DEAD. NOEMA FLED. WE'VE SURVIVED, MAZIKEEN, AND WE'VE TAUGHT OUR ENEMIES HUMILITY.
NOT A BAD OUTCOME, AS FAR AS THAT GOES.
WELL THAT'S ANOTHER MATTER, DUMA.
BUT AT LEAST IF SHE FAILS WE'LL NEVER KNOW ABOUT IT.

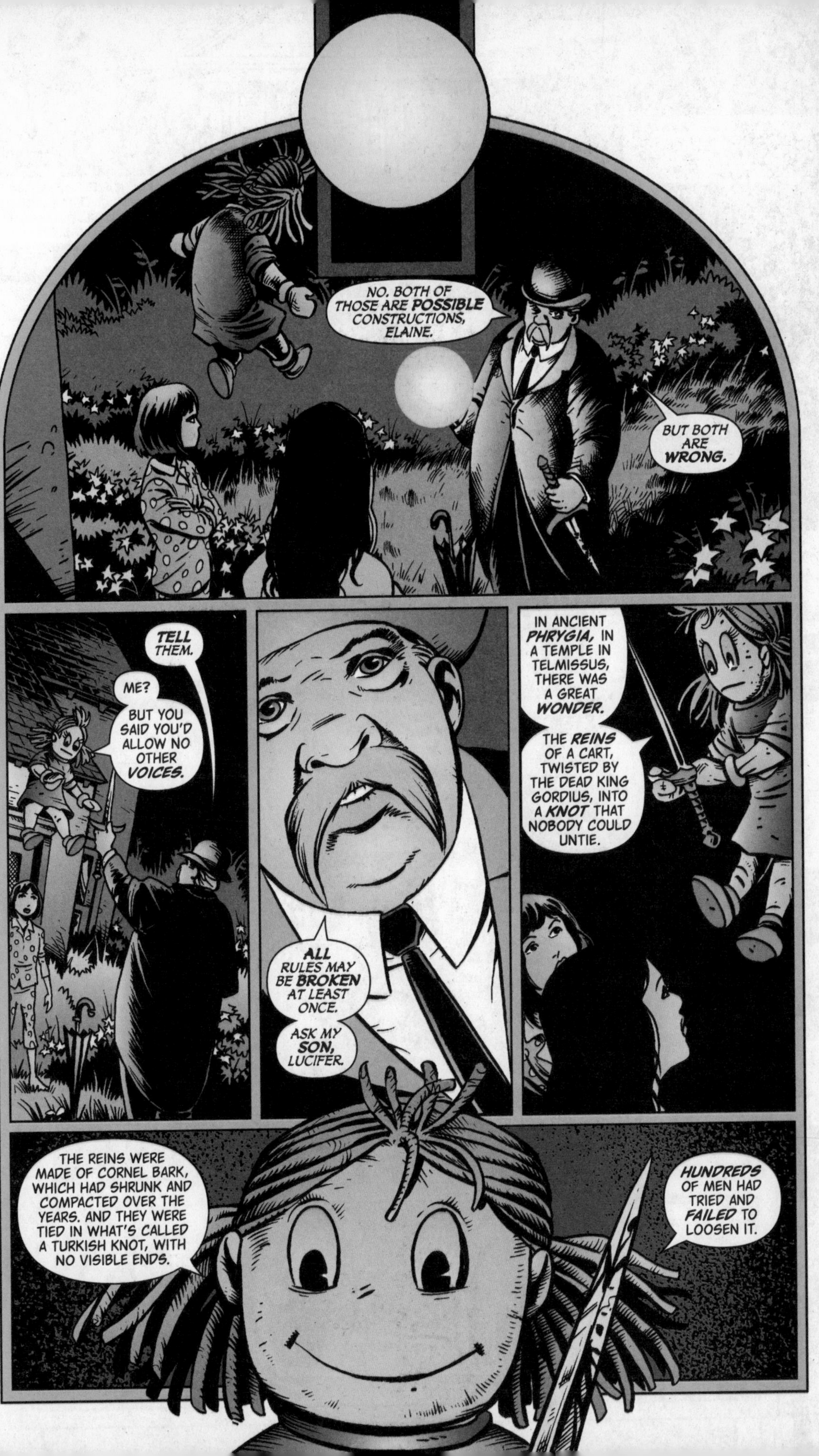

NO. BOTH OF THOSE ARE **POSSIBLE** CONSTRUCTIONS, ELAINE.
BUT BOTH ARE **WRONG.**
TELL THEM.
ME?
BUT YOU SAID YOU'D ALLOW NO OTHER ***VOICES.***
ALL RULES MAY BE **BROKEN** AT LEAST ONCE.
ASK MY **SON,** LUCIFER.
IN ANCIENT ***PHRYGIA,*** IN A TEMPLE IN TELMISSUS, THERE WAS A GREAT ***WONDER.***
THE ***REINS*** OF A CART, TWISTED BY THE DEAD KING GORDIUS, INTO A ***KNOT*** THAT NOBODY COULD UNTIE.
THE REINS WERE MADE OF CORNEL BARK, WHICH HAD SHRUNK AND COMPACTED OVER THE YEARS. AND THEY WERE TIED IN WHAT'S CALLED A TURKISH KNOT, WITH NO VISIBLE ENDS.
HUNDREDS OF MEN HAD TRIED AND ***FAILED*** TO LOOSEN IT.

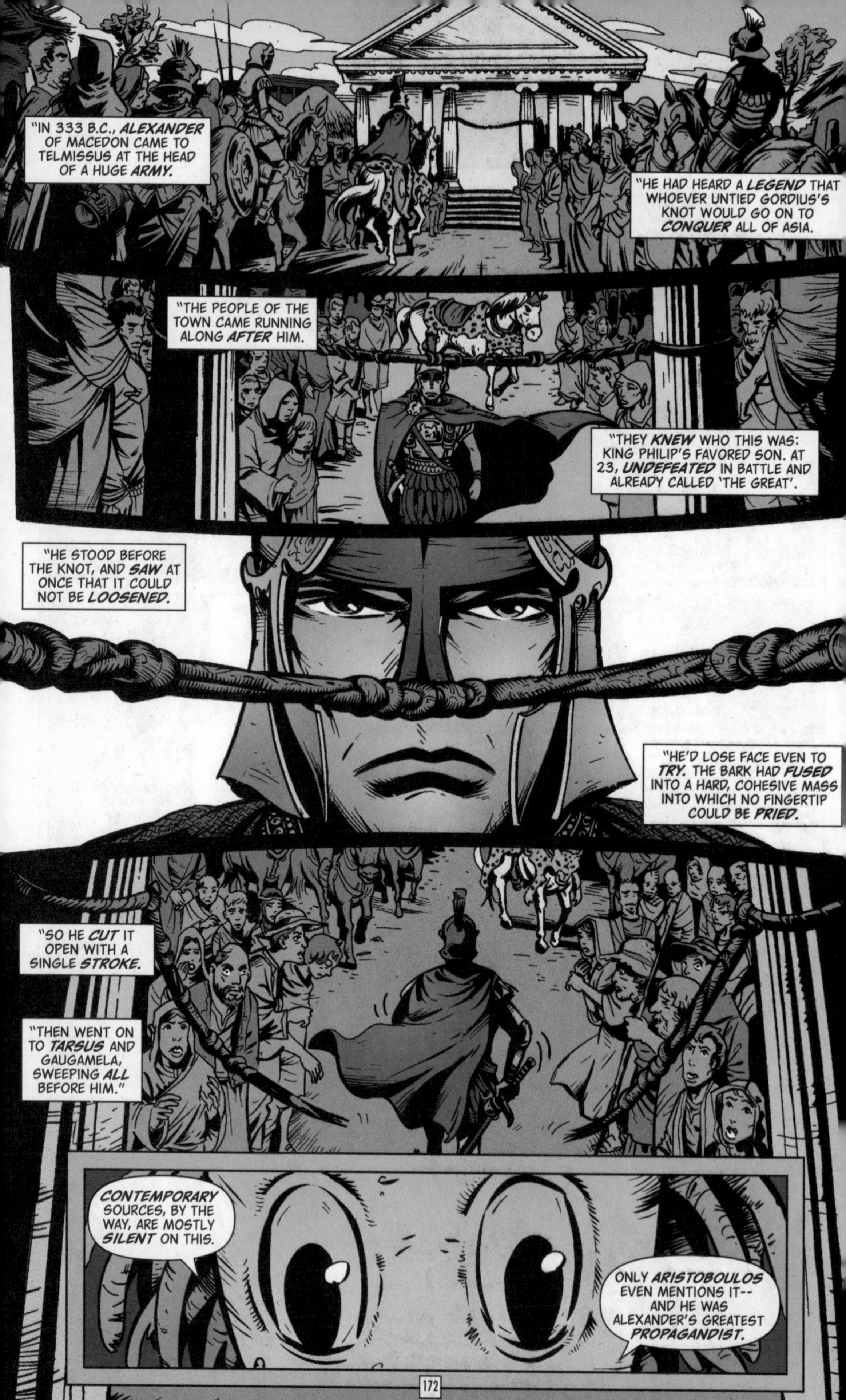
"IN 333 B.C., ALEXANDER OF MACEDON CAME TO TELMISSUS AT THE HEAD OF A HUGE ARMY.
"HE HAD HEARD A LEGEND THAT WHOEVER UNTIED GORDIUS'S KNOT WOULD GO ON TO CONQUER ALL OF ASIA.
"THE PEOPLE OF THE TOWN CAME RUNNING ALONG AFTER HIM.
"THEY KNEW WHO THIS WAS: KING PHILIP'S FAVORED SON. AT 23, UNDEFEATED IN BATTLE AND ALREADY CALLED 'THE GREAT'.
"HE STOOD BEFORE THE KNOT, AND SAW AT ONCE THAT IT COULD NOT BE LOOSENED.
"HE'D LOSE FACE EVEN TO TRY. THE BARK HAD FUSED INTO A HARD, COHESIVE MASS INTO WHICH NO FINGERTIP COULD BE PRIED.
"SO HE CUT IT OPEN WITH A SINGLE STROKE.
"THEN WENT ON TO TARSUS AND GAUGAMELA, SWEEPING ALL BEFORE HIM."
CONTEMPORARY SOURCES, BY THE WAY, ARE MOSTLY SILENT ON THIS.
ONLY ARISTOBOULOS EVEN MENTIONS IT-- AND HE WAS ALEXANDER'S GREATEST PROPAGANDIST.

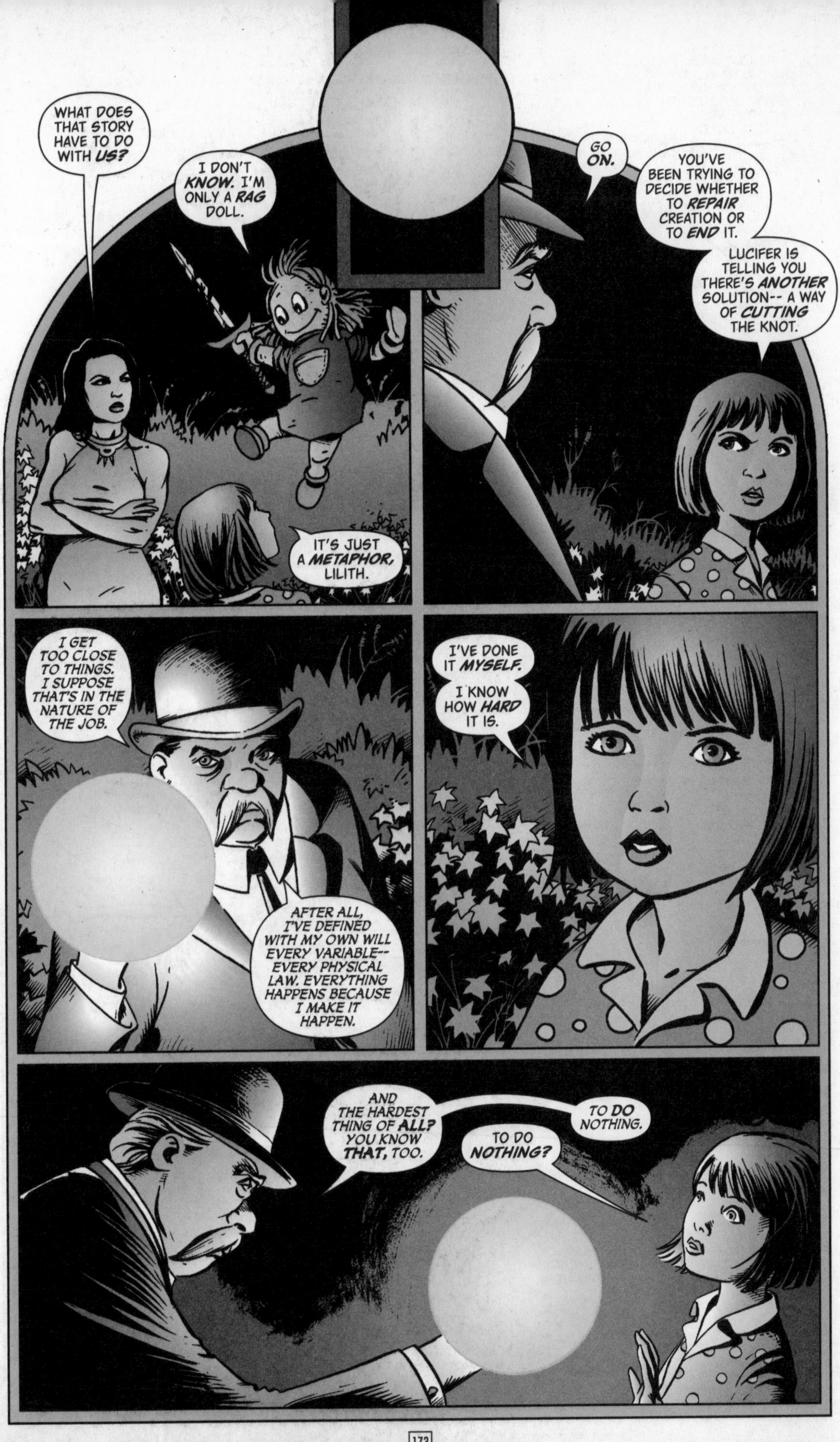
WHAT DOES THAT STORY HAVE TO DO WITH US?
I DON'T KNOW. I'M ONLY A RAG DOLL.
IT'S JUST A METAPHOR, LILITH.
GO ON.
YOU'VE BEEN TRYING TO DECIDE WHETHER TO REPAIR CREATION OR TO END IT.
LUCIFER IS TELLING YOU THERE'S ANOTHER SOLUTION-- A WAY OF CUTTING THE KNOT.
I GET TOO CLOSE TO THINGS. I SUPPOSE THAT'S IN THE NATURE OF THE JOB.
AFTER ALL, I'VE DEFINED WITH MY OWN WILL EVERY VARIABLE-- EVERY PHYSICAL LAW. EVERYTHING HAPPENS BECAUSE I MAKE IT HAPPEN.
I'VE DONE IT MYSELF.
I KNOW HOW HARD IT IS.
AND THE HARDEST THING OF ALL? YOU KNOW THAT, TOO.
TO DO NOTHING.
TO DO NOTHING?

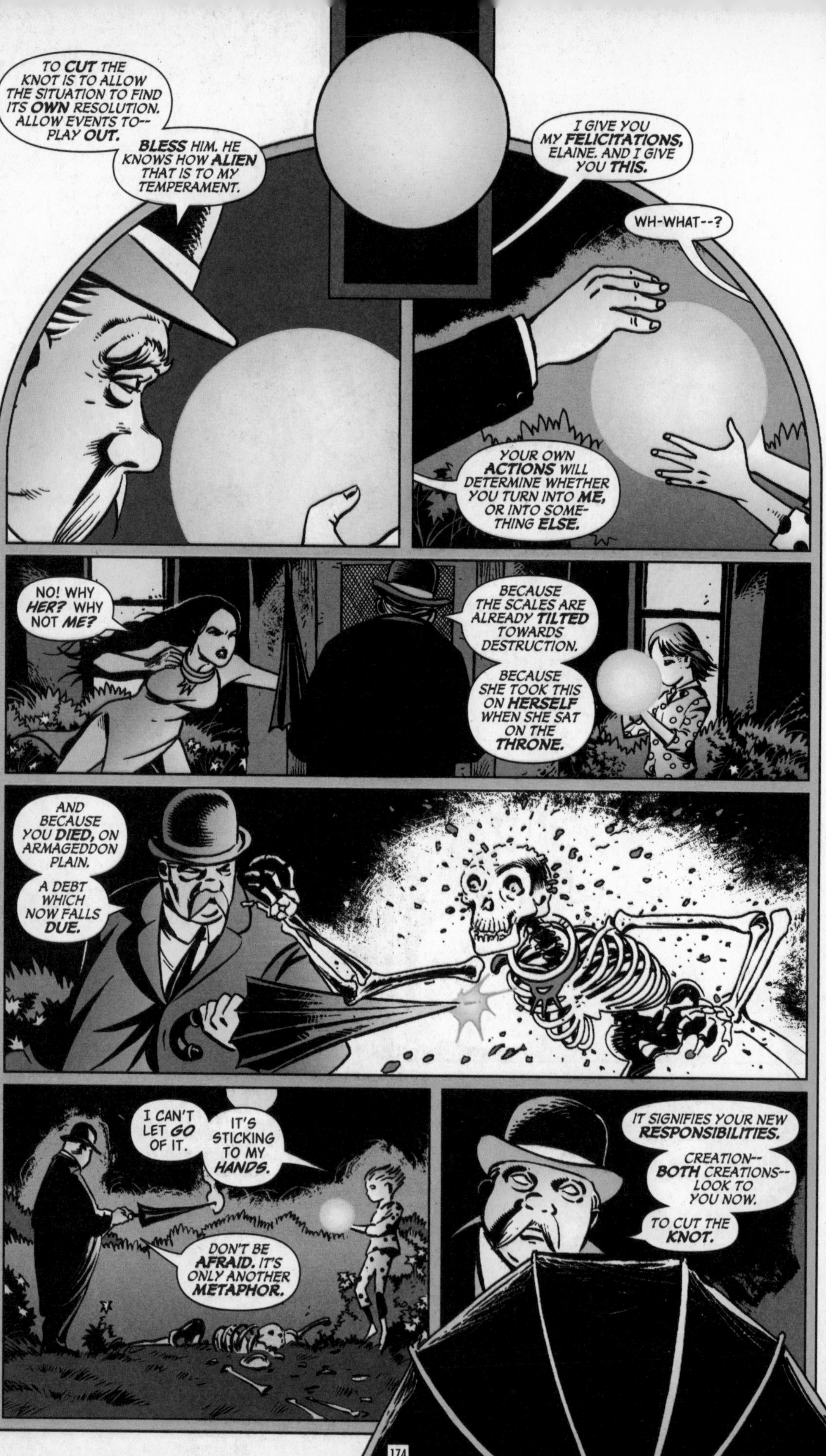

TO CUT THE KNOT IS TO ALLOW THE SITUATION TO FIND ITS OWN RESOLUTION. ALLOW EVENTS TO-- PLAY OUT.
BLESS HIM. HE KNOWS HOW ALIEN THAT IS TO MY TEMPERAMENT.
I GIVE YOU MY FELICITATIONS, ELAINE. AND I GIVE YOU THIS.
WH-WHAT--?
YOUR OWN ACTIONS WILL DETERMINE WHETHER YOU TURN INTO ME, OR INTO SOMETHING ELSE.
NO! WHY HER? WHY NOT ME?
BECAUSE THE SCALES ARE ALREADY TILTED TOWARDS DESTRUCTION.
BECAUSE SHE TOOK THIS ON HERSELF WHEN SHE SAT ON THE THRONE.
AND BECAUSE YOU DIED, ON ARMAGEDDON PLAIN.
A DEBT WHICH NOW FALLS DUE.
I CAN'T LET GO OF IT.
IT'S STICKING TO MY HANDS.
DON'T BE AFRAID. IT'S ONLY ANOTHER METAPHOR.
IT SIGNIFIES YOUR NEW RESPONSIBILITIES.
CREATION-- BOTH CREATIONS-- LOOK TO YOU NOW.
TO CUT THE KNOT.

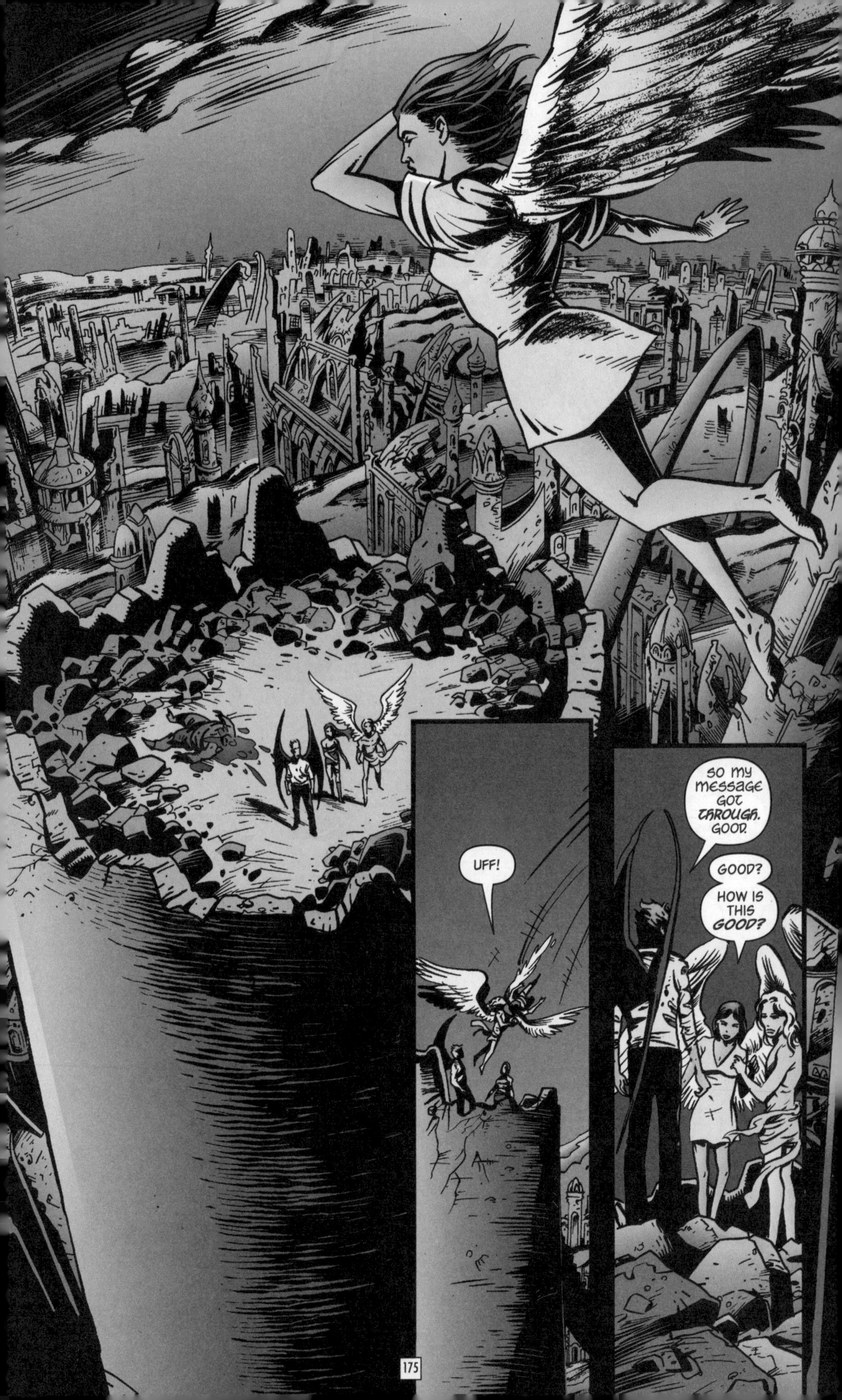
UFF!
SO MY MESSAGE GOT THROUGH. GOOD.
GOOD? HOW IS THIS GOOD?

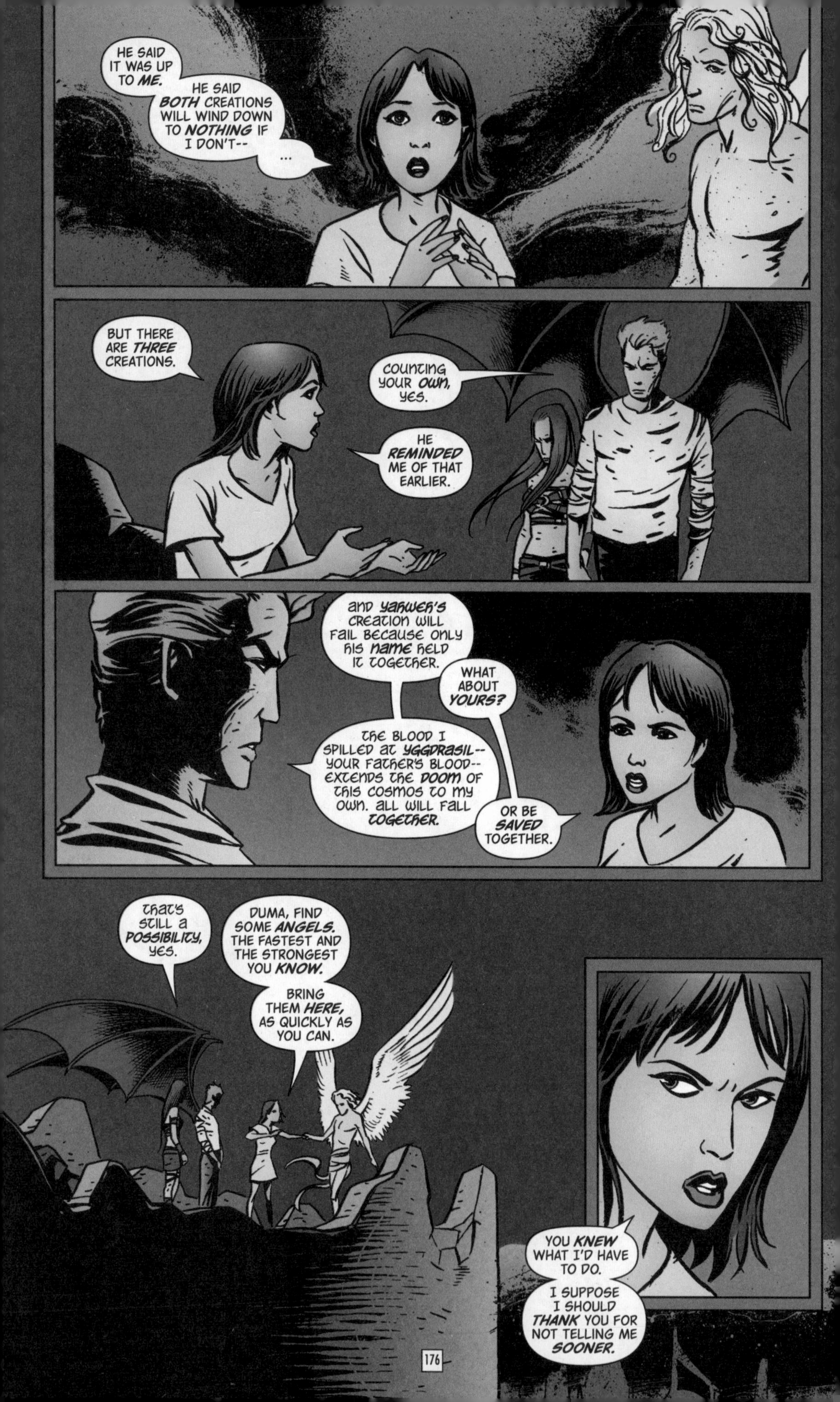
HE SAID IT WAS UP TO ME.
HE SAID BOTH CREATIONS WILL WIND DOWN TO NOTHING IF I DON'T--
...
BUT THERE ARE THREE CREATIONS.
COUNTING YOUR OWN, YES.
HE REMINDED ME OF THAT EARLIER.
AND YAHWEH'S CREATION WILL FAIL BECAUSE ONLY HIS NAME HELD IT TOGETHER.
WHAT ABOUT YOURS?
THE BLOOD I SPILLED AT YGGDRASIL-- YOUR FATHER'S BLOOD-- EXTENDS THE DOOM OF THIS COSMOS TO MY OWN. ALL WILL FALL TOGETHER.
OR BE SAVED TOGETHER.
THAT'S STILL A POSSIBILITY, YES.
DUMA, FIND SOME ANGELS. THE FASTEST AND THE STRONGEST YOU KNOW.
BRING THEM HERE, AS QUICKLY AS YOU CAN.
YOU KNEW WHAT I'D HAVE TO DO.
I SUPPOSE I SHOULD THANK YOU FOR NOT TELLING ME SOONER.

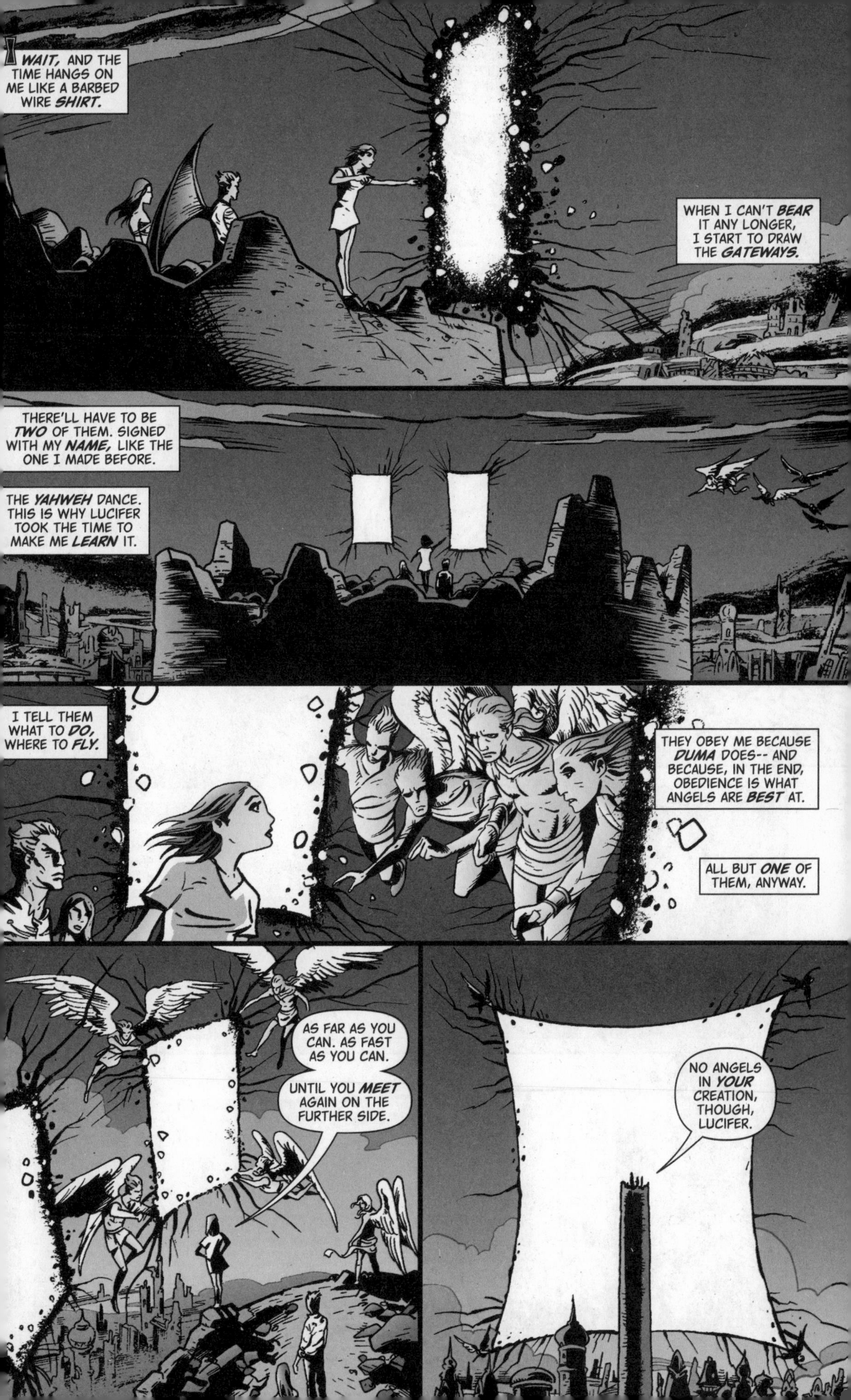
WAIT, AND THE TIME HANGS ON ME LIKE A BARBED WIRE SHIRT.
WHEN I CAN'T BEAR IT ANY LONGER, I START TO DRAW THE GATEWAYS.
THERE'LL HAVE TO BE TWO OF THEM. SIGNED WITH MY NAME, LIKE THE ONE I MADE BEFORE.
THE YAHWEH DANCE. THIS IS WHY LUCIFER TOOK THE TIME TO MAKE ME LEARN IT.
I TELL THEM WHAT TO DO, WHERE TO FLY.
THEY OBEY ME BECAUSE DUMA DOES-- AND BECAUSE, IN THE END, OBEDIENCE IS WHAT ANGELS ARE BEST AT.
ALL BUT ONE OF THEM, ANYWAY.
AS FAR AS YOU CAN. AS FAST AS YOU CAN.
UNTIL YOU MEET AGAIN ON THE FURTHER SIDE.
NO ANGELS IN YOUR CREATION, THOUGH, LUCIFER.

NO IMMORTALS AT *ALL*, ELAINE BELLOC. AND NO TIME TO *SUMMON* ANY.

IF THE FOUR OF *US* CAN'T DO THIS THING, THEN IT CAN'T BE *DONE*.

ALL RIGHT. YOU KNOW THE *RULES*. AND WHERE WE'RE *HEADED*.

I'LL SEE YOU *THERE*.

THEN WE NEED TO DECIDE WHO--

SAVE TIME BY TAKING OUR *CONSENT* FOR GRANTED.

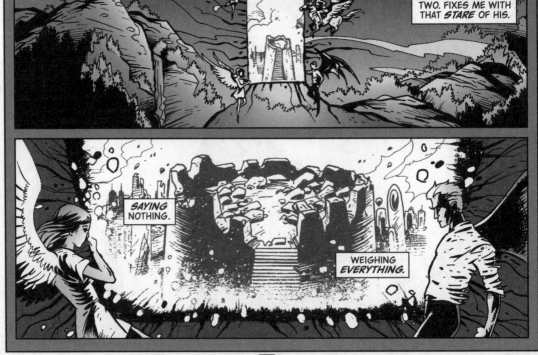

LUCIFER BACKS AIR FOR A MOMENT OR TWO. FIXES ME WITH THAT *STARE* OF HIS.

SAYING NOTHING.

WEIGHING *EVERYTHING*.

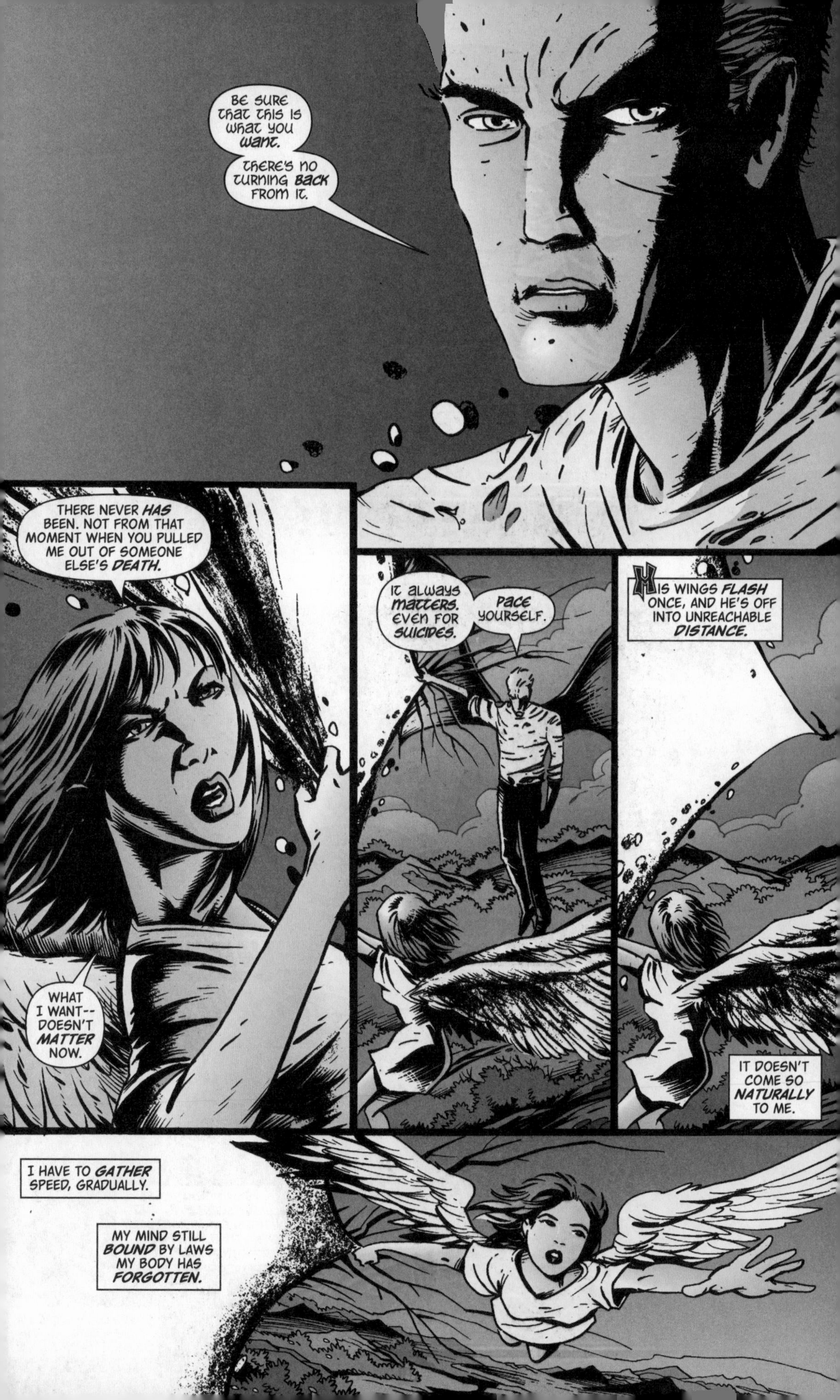
BE SURE THAT THIS IS WHAT YOU WANT.
THERE'S NO TURNING BACK FROM IT.
THERE NEVER HAS BEEN. NOT FROM THAT MOMENT WHEN YOU PULLED ME OUT OF SOMEONE ELSE'S DEATH.
WHAT I WANT-- DOESN'T MATTER NOW.
IT ALWAYS MATTERS. EVEN FOR SUICIDES.
PACE YOURSELF.
HIS WINGS FLASH ONCE, AND HE'S OFF INTO UNREACHABLE DISTANCE.
IT DOESN'T COME SO NATURALLY TO ME.
I HAVE TO GATHER SPEED, GRADUALLY.
MY MIND STILL BOUND BY LAWS MY BODY HAS FORGOTTEN.

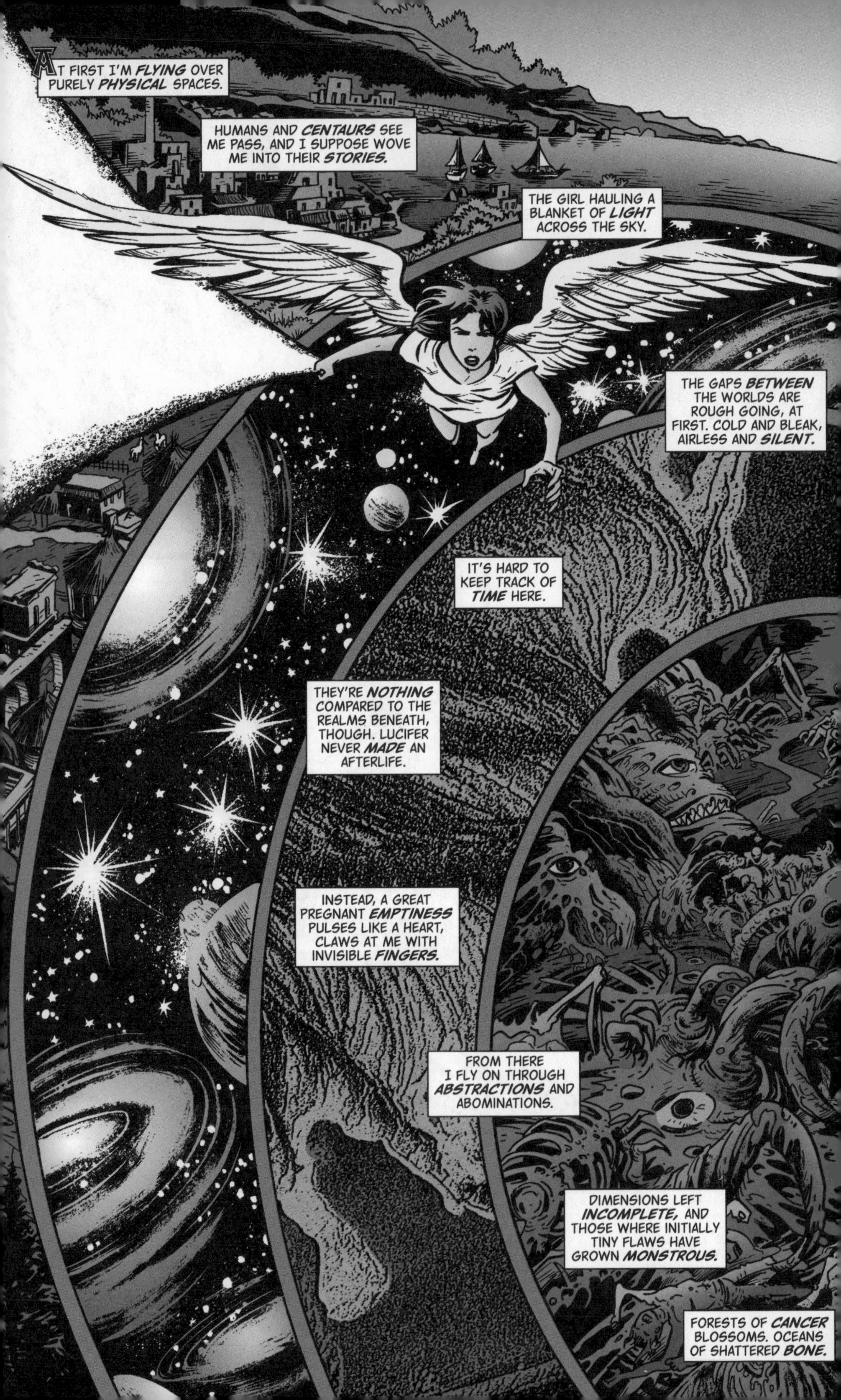
AT FIRST I'M FLYING OVER PURELY PHYSICAL SPACES.
HUMANS AND CENTAURS SEE ME PASS, AND I SUPPOSE WOVE ME INTO THEIR STORIES.
THE GIRL HAULING A BLANKET OF LIGHT ACROSS THE SKY.
THE GAPS BETWEEN THE WORLDS ARE ROUGH GOING, AT FIRST. COLD AND BLEAK, AIRLESS AND SILENT.
IT'S HARD TO KEEP TRACK OF TIME HERE.
THEY'RE NOTHING COMPARED TO THE REALMS BENEATH, THOUGH. LUCIFER NEVER MADE AN AFTERLIFE.
INSTEAD, A GREAT PREGNANT EMPTINESS PULSES LIKE A HEART, CLAWS AT ME WITH INVISIBLE FINGERS.
FROM THERE I FLY ON THROUGH ABSTRACTIONS AND ABOMINATIONS.
DIMENSIONS LEFT INCOMPLETE, AND THOSE WHERE INITIALLY TINY FLAWS HAVE GROWN MONSTROUS.
FORESTS OF CANCER BLOSSOMS. OCEANS OF SHATTERED BONE.

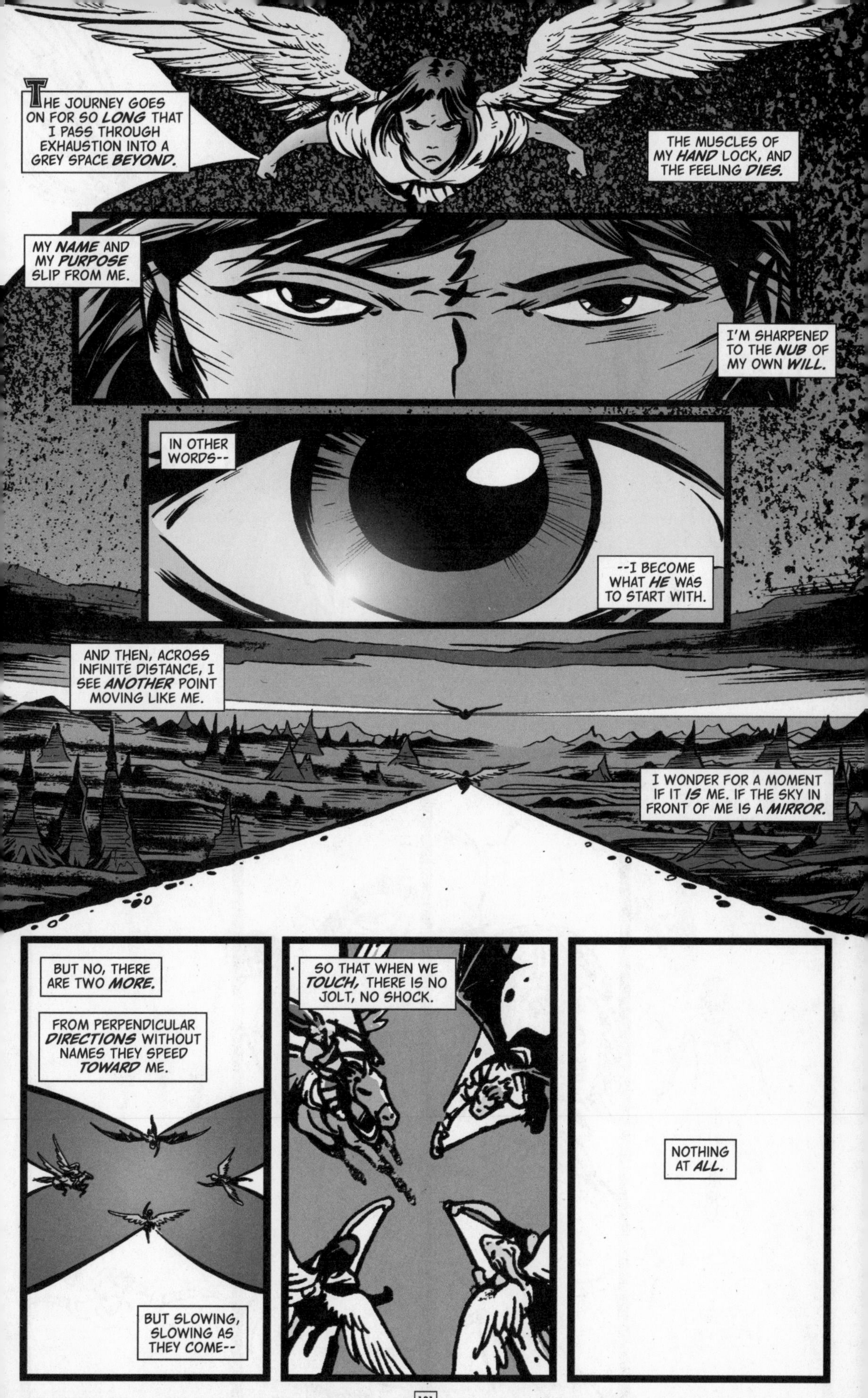
THE JOURNEY GOES ON FOR SO LONG THAT I PASS THROUGH EXHAUSTION INTO A GREY SPACE BEYOND.
THE MUSCLES OF MY HAND LOCK, AND THE FEELING DIES.
MY NAME AND MY PURPOSE SLIP FROM ME.
I'M SHARPENED TO THE NUB OF MY OWN WILL.
IN OTHER WORDS--
--I BECOME WHAT HE WAS TO START WITH.
AND THEN, ACROSS INFINITE DISTANCE, I SEE ANOTHER POINT MOVING LIKE ME.
I WONDER FOR A MOMENT IF IT IS ME. IF THE SKY IN FRONT OF ME IS A MIRROR.
BUT NO, THERE ARE TWO MORE.
FROM PERPENDICULAR DIRECTIONS WITHOUT NAMES THEY SPEED TOWARD ME.
BUT SLOWING, SLOWING AS THEY COME--
SO THAT WHEN WE TOUCH, THERE IS NO JOLT, NO SHOCK.
NOTHING AT ALL.

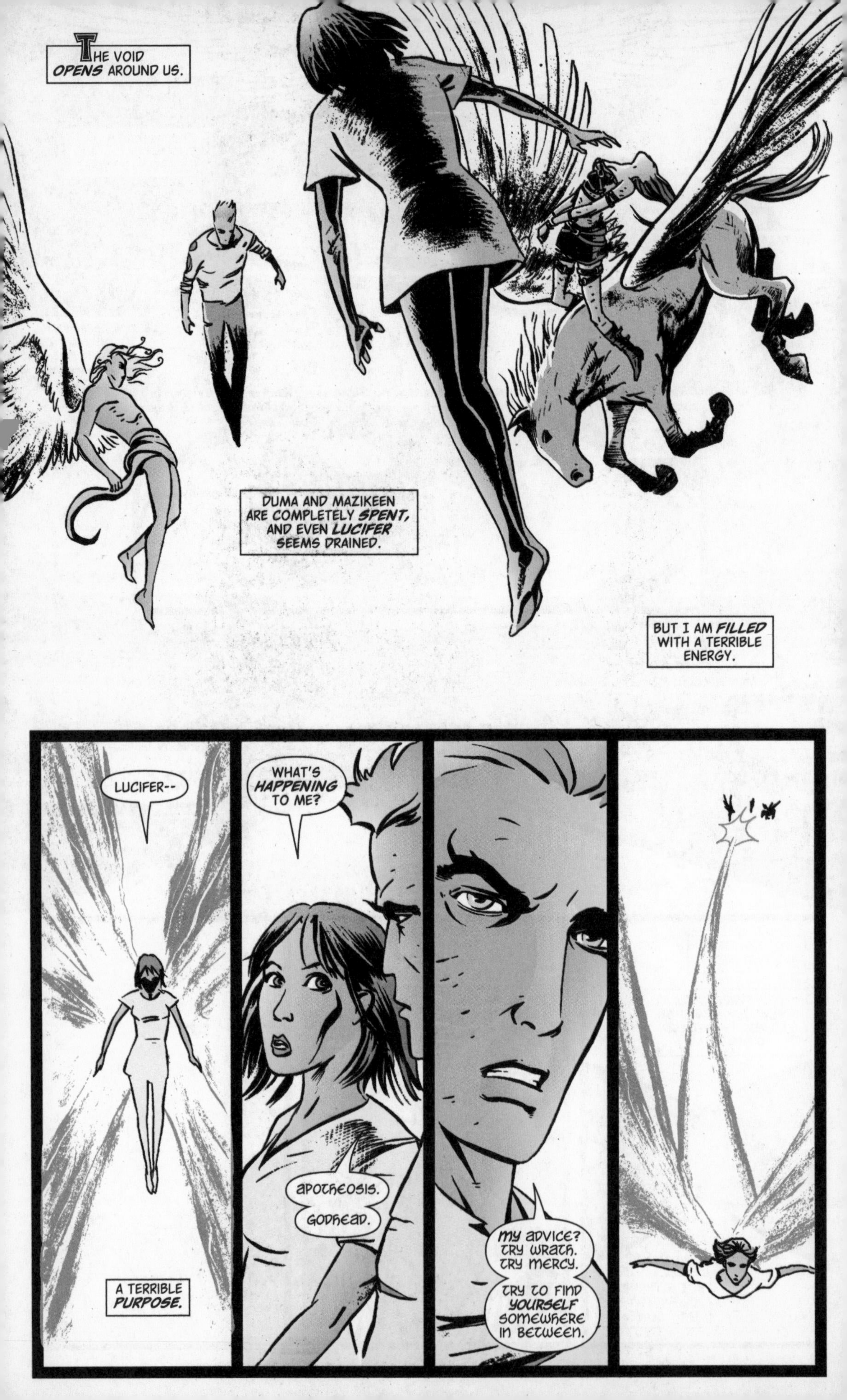
THE VOID OPENS AROUND US.
DUMA AND MAZIKEEN ARE COMPLETELY SPENT, AND EVEN LUCIFER SEEMS DRAINED.
BUT I AM FILLED WITH A TERRIBLE ENERGY.
LUCIFER--
A TERRIBLE PURPOSE.
WHAT'S HAPPENING TO ME?
APOTHEOSIS.
GODHEAD.
MY ADVICE? TRY WRATH. TRY MERCY.
TRY TO FIND YOURSELF SOMEWHERE IN BETWEEN.

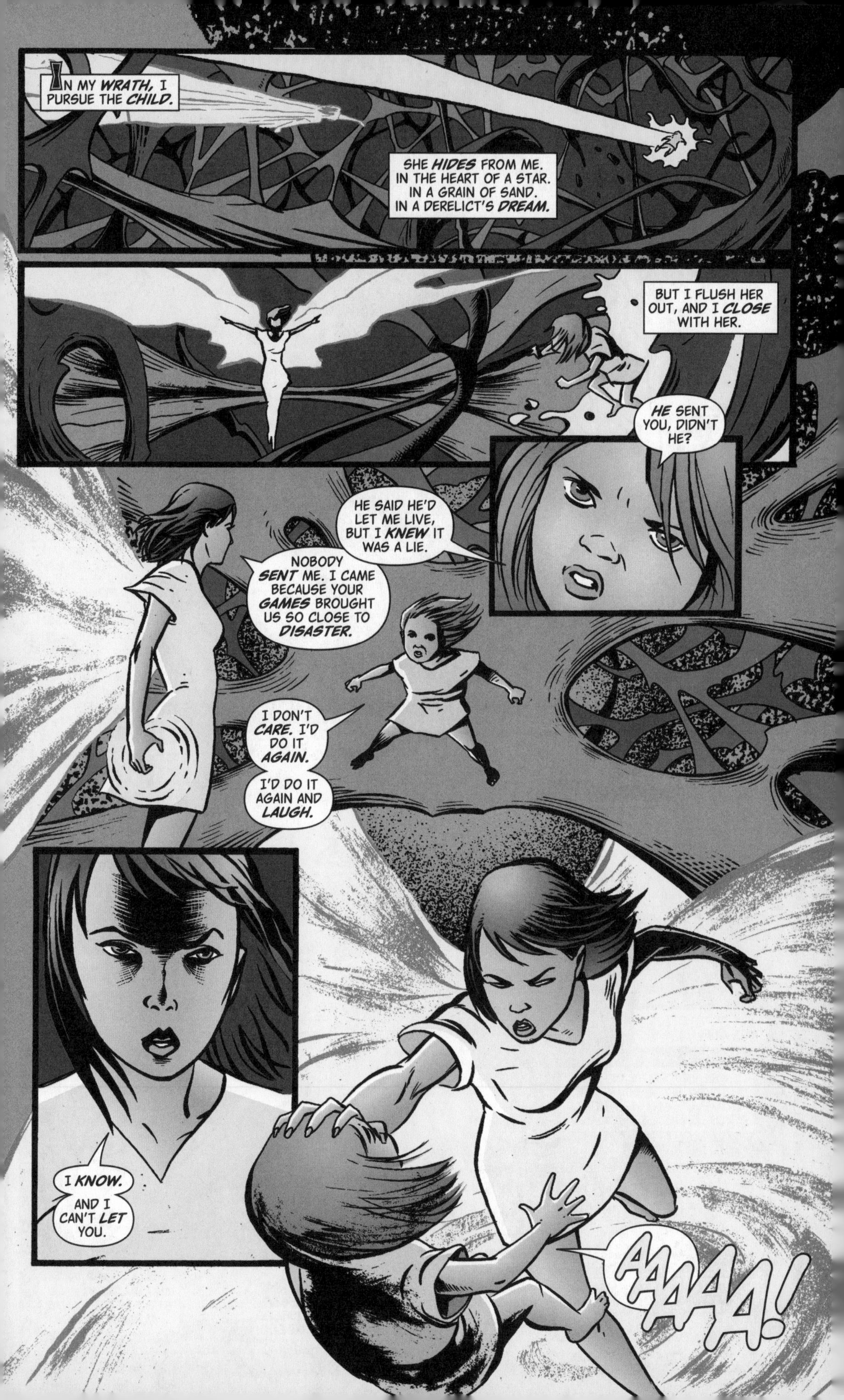
IN MY WRATH, I PURSUE THE CHILD.
SHE HIDES FROM ME. IN THE HEART OF A STAR. IN A GRAIN OF SAND. IN A DERELICT'S DREAM.
BUT I FLUSH HER OUT, AND I CLOSE WITH HER.
HE SENT YOU, DIDN'T HE?
HE SAID HE'D LET ME LIVE, BUT I KNEW IT WAS A LIE.
NOBODY SENT ME. I CAME BECAUSE YOUR GAMES BROUGHT US SO CLOSE TO DISASTER.
I DON'T CARE. I'D DO IT AGAIN.
I'D DO IT AGAIN AND LAUGH.
I KNOW.
AND I CAN'T LET YOU.
AAAAA!

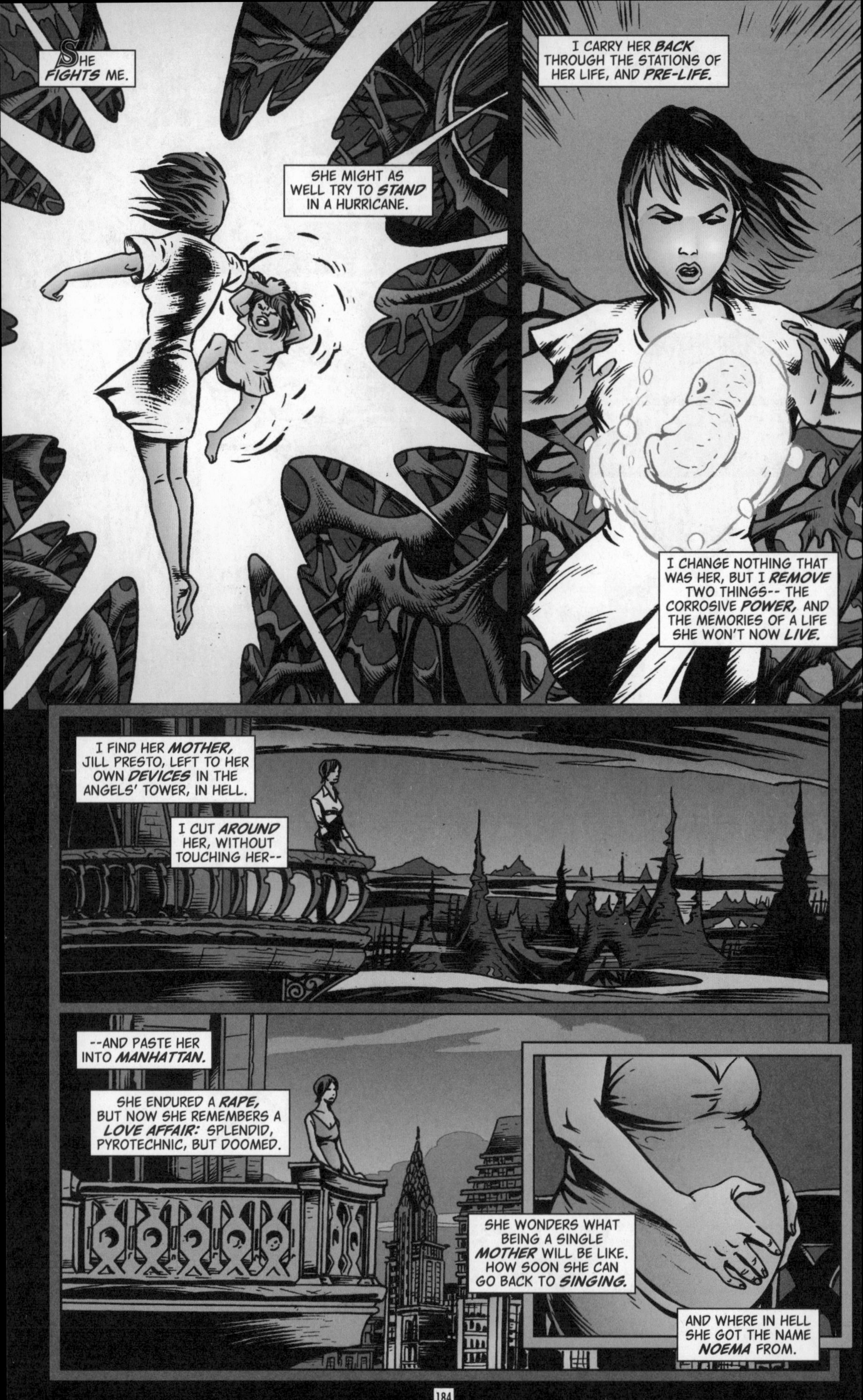
SHE FIGHTS ME.
SHE MIGHT AS WELL TRY TO STAND IN A HURRICANE.
I CARRY HER BACK THROUGH THE STATIONS OF HER LIFE, AND PRE-LIFE.
I CHANGE NOTHING THAT WAS HER, BUT I REMOVE TWO THINGS-- THE CORROSIVE POWER, AND THE MEMORIES OF A LIFE SHE WON'T NOW LIVE.
I FIND HER MOTHER, JILL PRESTO, LEFT TO HER OWN DEVICES IN THE ANGELS' TOWER, IN HELL.
I CUT AROUND HER, WITHOUT TOUCHING HER--
--AND PASTE HER INTO MANHATTAN.
SHE ENDURED A RAPE, BUT NOW SHE REMEMBERS A LOVE AFFAIR: SPLENDID, PYROTECHNIC, BUT DOOMED.
SHE WONDERS WHAT BEING A SINGLE MOTHER WILL BE LIKE. HOW SOON SHE CAN GO BACK TO SINGING.
AND WHERE IN HELL SHE GOT THE NAME NOEMA FROM.

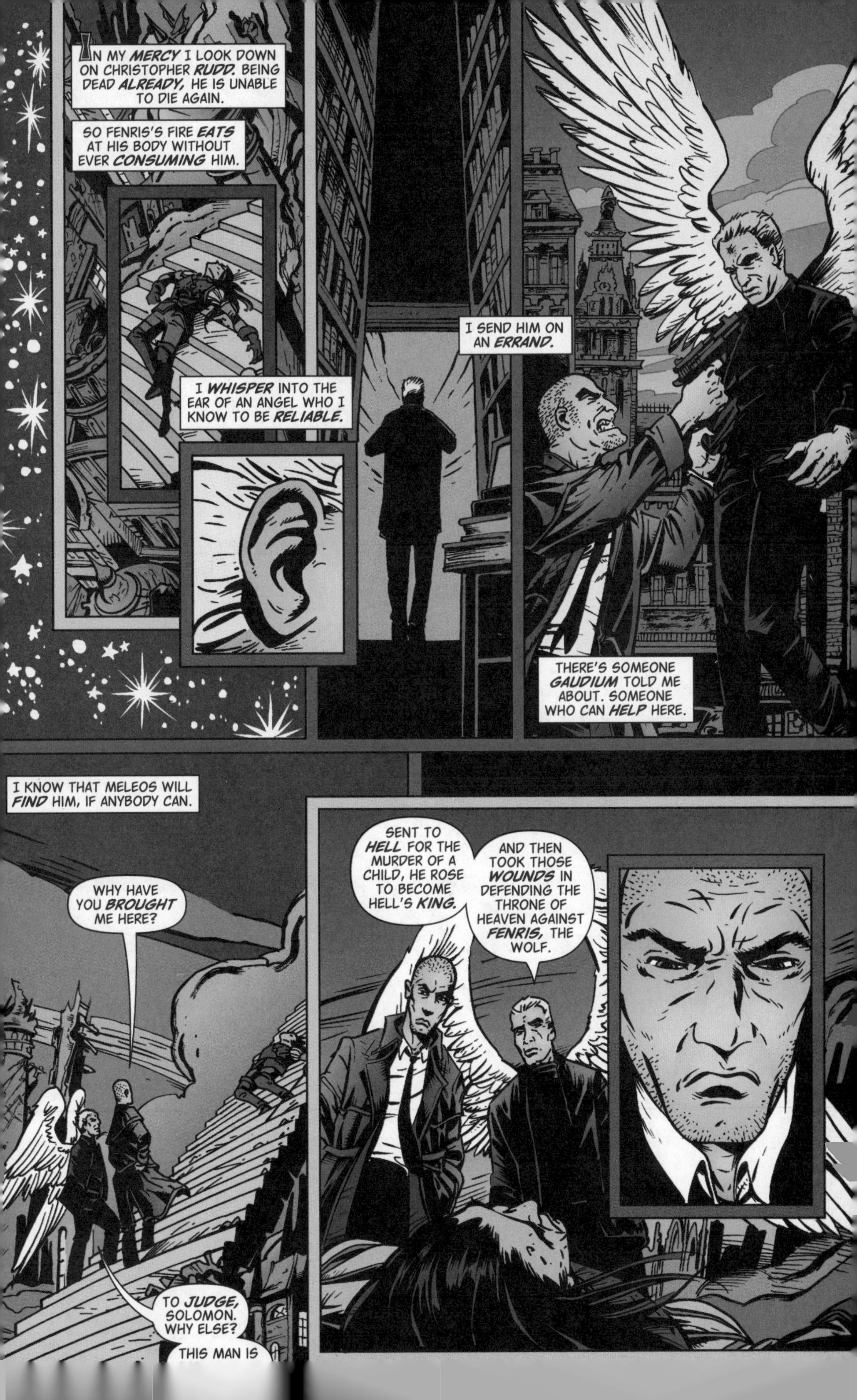
IN MY MERCY I LOOK DOWN ON CHRISTOPHER RUDD. BEING DEAD ALREADY, HE IS UNABLE TO DIE AGAIN.
SO FENRIS'S FIRE EATS AT HIS BODY WITHOUT EVER CONSUMING HIM.
I WHISPER INTO THE EAR OF AN ANGEL WHO I KNOW TO BE RELIABLE.
I SEND HIM ON AN ERRAND.
THERE'S SOMEONE GAUDIUM TOLD ME ABOUT. SOMEONE WHO CAN HELP HERE.
I KNOW THAT MELEOS WILL FIND HIM, IF ANYBODY CAN.
WHY HAVE YOU BROUGHT ME HERE?
TO JUDGE, SOLOMON. WHY ELSE?
THIS MAN IS
SENT TO HELL FOR THE MURDER OF A CHILD, HE ROSE TO BECOME HELL'S KING.
AND THEN TOOK THOSE WOUNDS IN DEFENDING THE THRONE OF HEAVEN AGAINST FENRIS, THE WOLF.

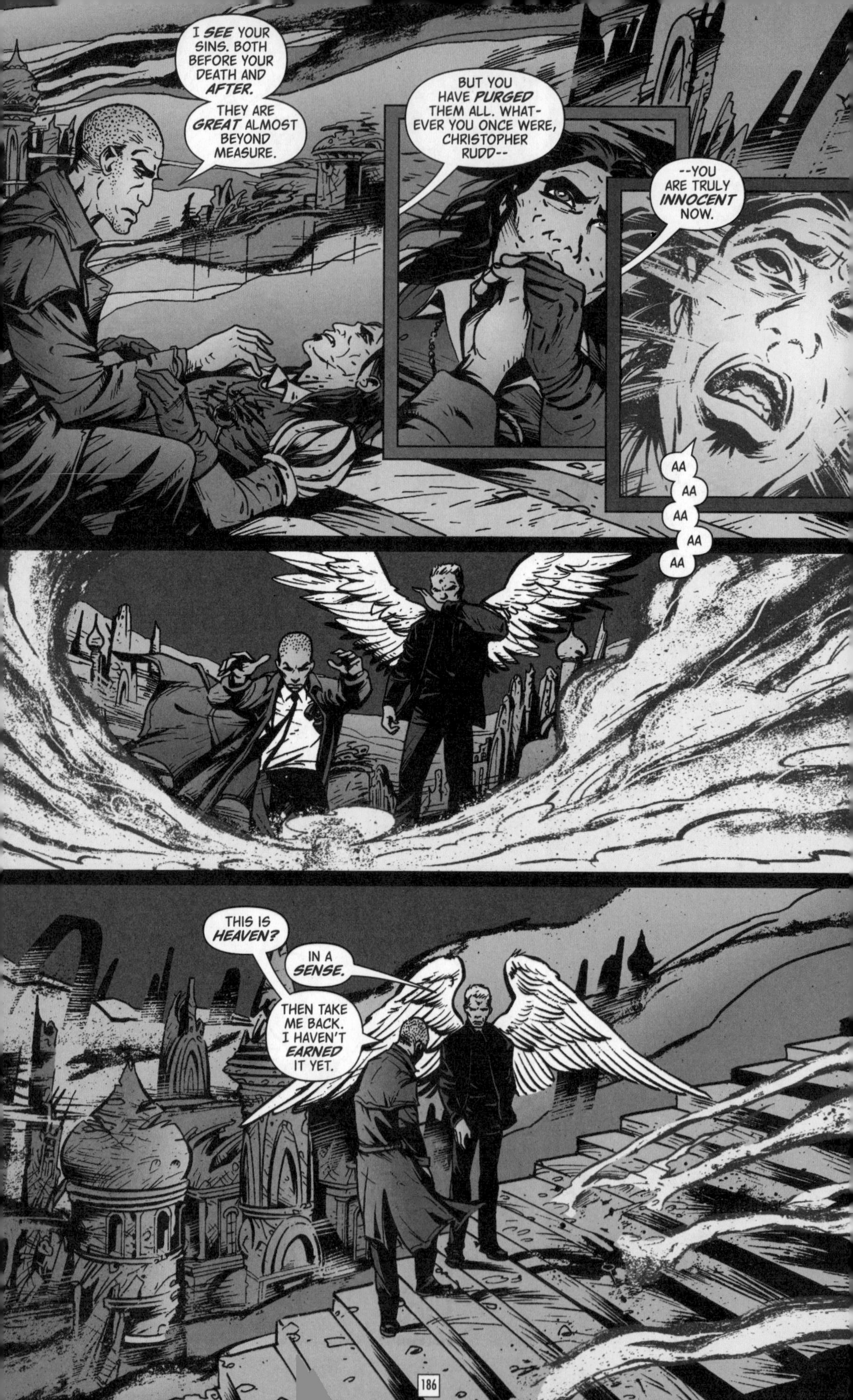
I SEE YOUR SINS. BOTH BEFORE YOUR DEATH AND AFTER.
THEY ARE GREAT ALMOST BEYOND MEASURE.
BUT YOU HAVE PURGED THEM ALL. WHAT-EVER YOU ONCE WERE, CHRISTOPHER RUDD--
--YOU ARE TRULY INNOCENT NOW.
AA AA AA AA AA
THIS IS HEAVEN?
IN A SENSE.
THEN TAKE ME BACK. I HAVEN'T EARNED IT YET.

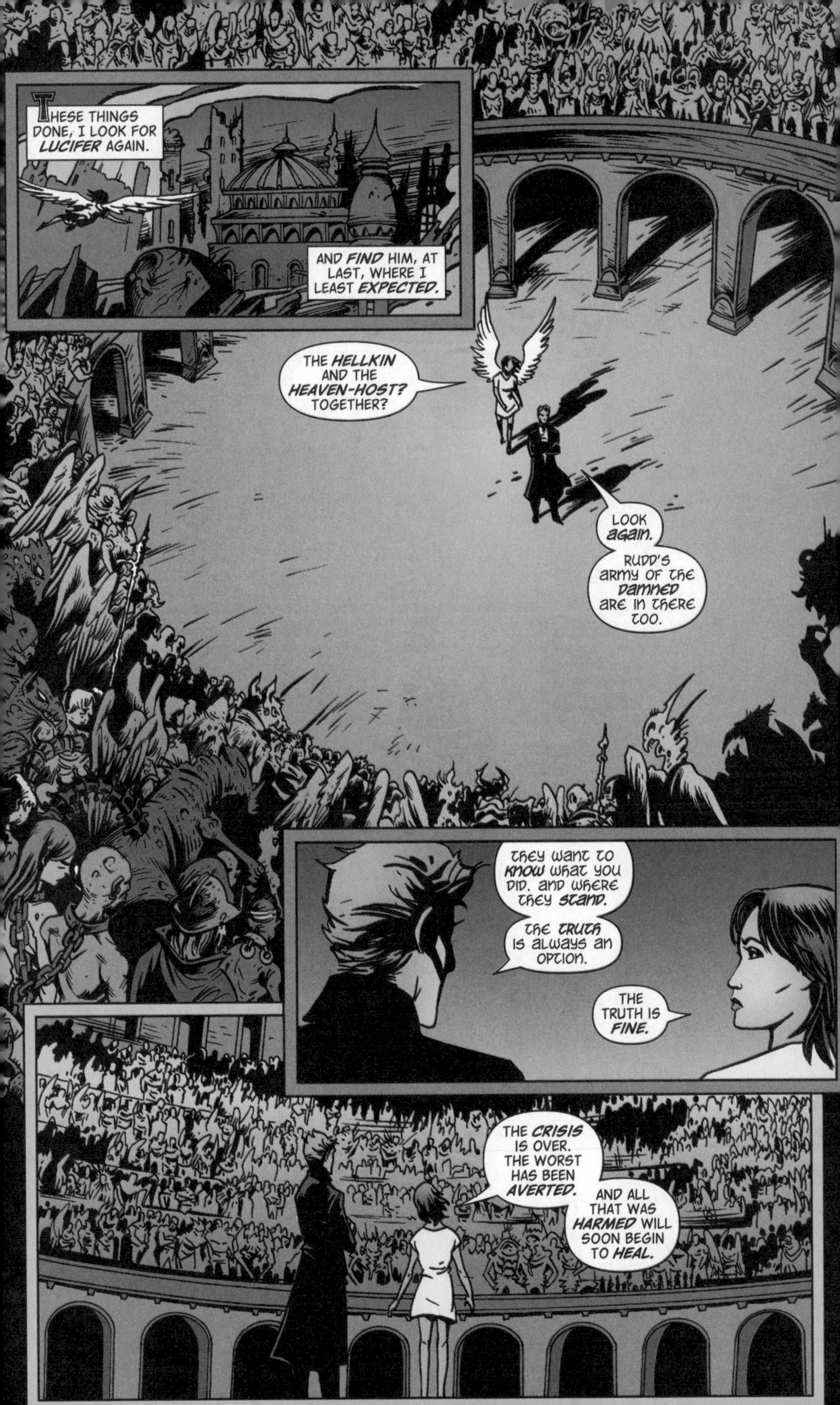
THESE THINGS DONE, I LOOK FOR LUCIFER AGAIN.
AND FIND HIM, AT LAST, WHERE I LEAST EXPECTED.
THE HELLKIN AND THE HEAVEN-HOST? TOGETHER?
LOOK AGAIN.
RUDD'S ARMY OF THE DAMNED ARE IN THERE TOO.
THEY WANT TO KNOW WHAT YOU DID. AND WHERE THEY STAND.
THE TRUTH IS ALWAYS AN OPTION.
THE TRUTH IS FINE.
THE CRISIS IS OVER. THE WORST HAS BEEN AVERTED.
AND ALL THAT WAS HARMED WILL SOON BEGIN TO HEAL.

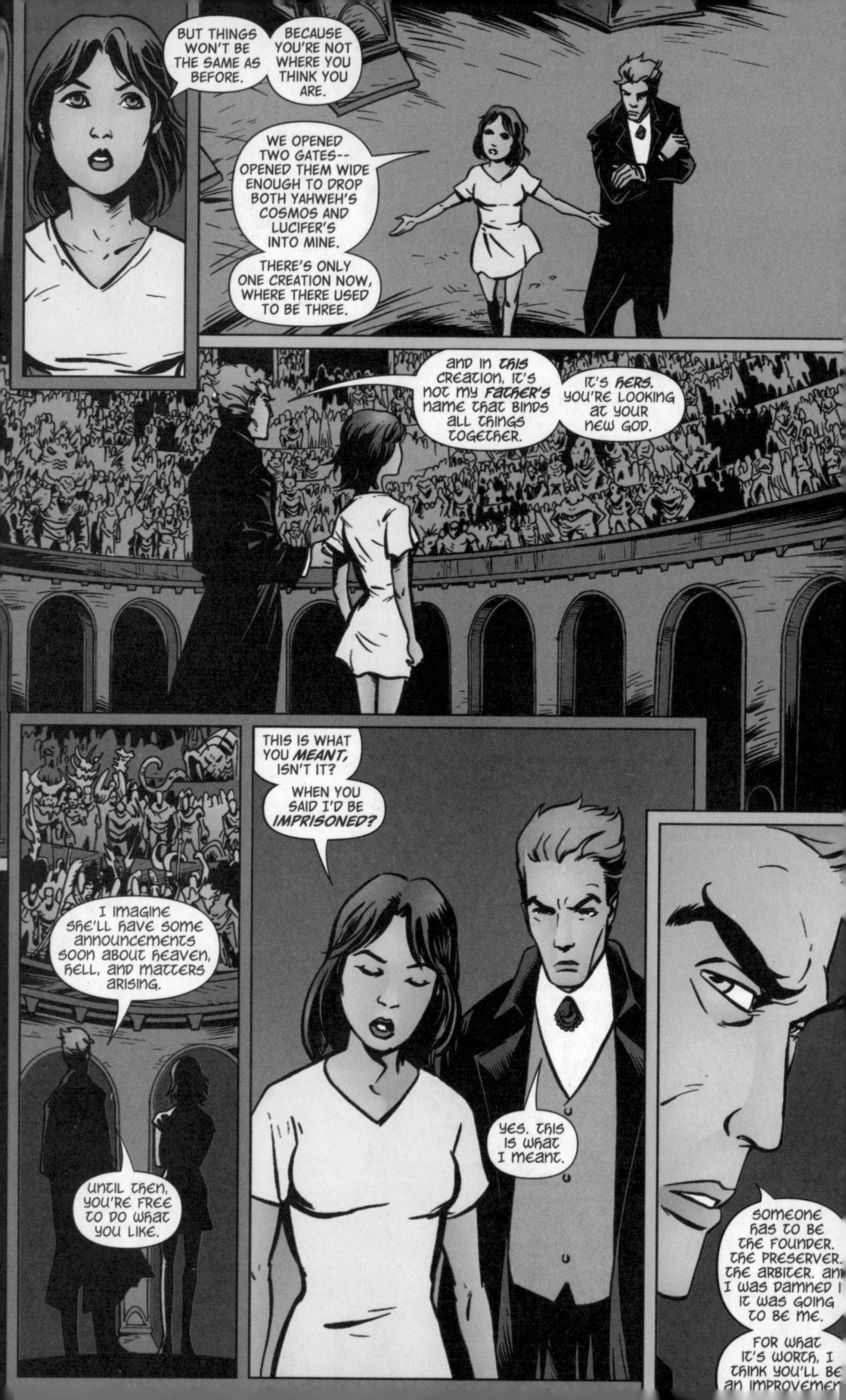

BUT THINGS WON'T BE THE SAME AS BEFORE.
BECAUSE YOU'RE NOT WHERE YOU THINK YOU ARE.
WE OPENED TWO GATES-- OPENED THEM WIDE ENOUGH TO DROP BOTH YAHWEH'S COSMOS AND LUCIFER'S INTO MINE.
THERE'S ONLY ONE CREATION NOW, WHERE THERE USED TO BE THREE.
AND IN THIS CREATION, IT'S NOT MY FATHER'S NAME THAT BINDS ALL THINGS TOGETHER.
IT'S HERS. YOU'RE LOOKING AT YOUR NEW GOD.
I IMAGINE SHE'LL HAVE SOME ANNOUNCEMENTS SOON ABOUT HEAVEN, HELL, AND MATTERS ARISING.
UNTIL THEN, YOU'RE FREE TO DO WHAT YOU LIKE.
THIS IS WHAT YOU MEANT, ISN'T IT?
WHEN YOU SAID I'D BE IMPRISONED?
YES. THIS IS WHAT I MEANT.
SOMEONE HAS TO BE THE FOUNDER. THE PRESERVER. THE ARBITER. AN I WAS DAMNED I IT WAS GOING TO BE ME.
FOR WHAT IT'S WORTH, I THINK YOU'LL BE AN IMPROVEMEN

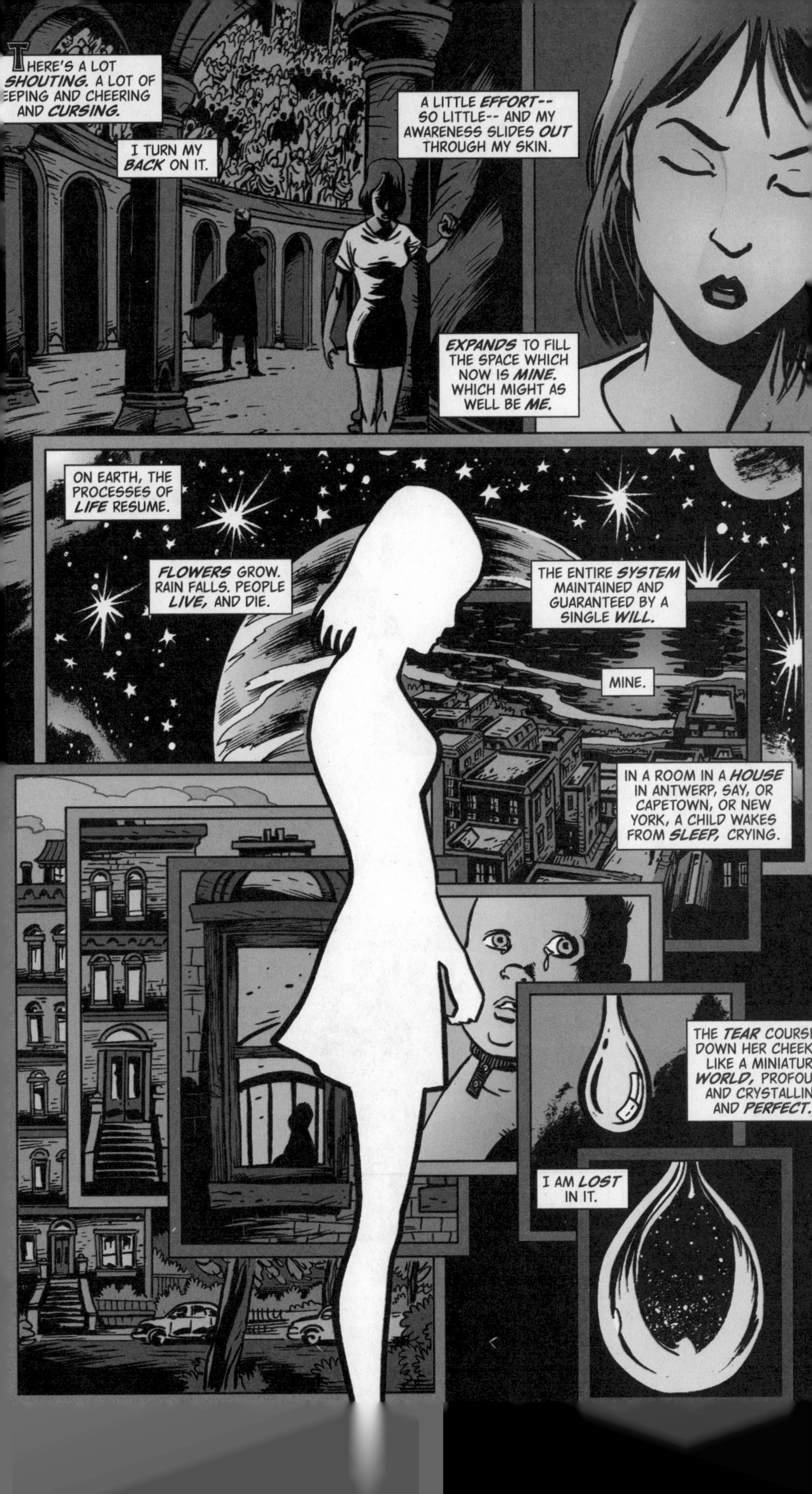
THERE'S A LOT SHOUTING. A LOT OF EEPING AND CHEERING AND CURSING.
I TURN MY BACK ON IT.
A LITTLE EFFORT-- SO LITTLE-- AND MY AWARENESS SLIDES OUT THROUGH MY SKIN.
EXPANDS TO FILL THE SPACE WHICH NOW IS MINE. WHICH MIGHT AS WELL BE ME.
ON EARTH, THE PROCESSES OF LIFE RESUME.
FLOWERS GROW. RAIN FALLS. PEOPLE LIVE, AND DIE.
THE ENTIRE SYSTEM MAINTAINED AND GUARANTEED BY A SINGLE WILL.
MINE.
IN A ROOM IN A HOUSE IN ANTWERP, SAY, OR CAPETOWN, OR NEW YORK, A CHILD WAKES FROM SLEEP, CRYING.
THE TEAR COURS DOWN HER CHEEK LIKE A MINIATUR WORLD, PROFOU AND CRYSTALLIN AND PERFECT.
I AM LOST IN IT.

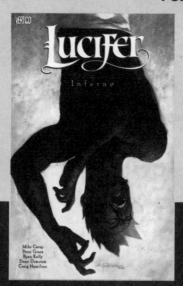
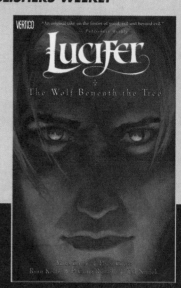

NEW YORK TIMES BEST-SELLING AUTHOR NEIL GAIMAN DELIVERS A RICH BLEND OF MODERN MYTH AND DARK FANTASY IN WHICH CONTEMPORARY FICTION, HISTORICAL DRAMA AND LEGEND ARE SEAMLESSLY INTERWOVEN.

THE SANDMAN

The New York Times best-selling author of American Gods and Coraline
NEIL GAIMAN
Volume One
THE SANDMAN
PRELUDES & NOCTURNES
Illustrated by
Sam Kieth
Mike Dringenberg
Malcolm Jones III
Introduction by
Karen Berger
FREE INSIDE!
CD-ROM Preview
with 900+ pages
from DC Comics'
best-selling books.
VERTIGO

VOLUME 1:
PRELUDES & NOCTURNES

ALSO AVAILABLE:

VOL. 2: THE DOLL'S HOUSE
VOL. 3: DREAM COUNTRY
VOL. 4: SEASON OF MISTS
VOL. 5: A GAME OF YOU
VOL. 6: FABLES & REFLECTIONS
VOL. 7: BRIEF LIVES
VOL. 8: WORLDS' END
VOL. 9: THE KINDLY ONES
VOL. 10: THE WAKE
SANDMAN: ENDLESS NIGHTS
SANDMAN: THE DREAM HUNTERS

"WHAT GAIMAN HAS WRITTEN IS A COMICS MASTERPIECE."
— *PUBLISHERS WEEKLY*

"SANDMAN JUST MIGHT BE THE SMARTEST COMIC BOOK EVER WRITTEN."
— *USA TODAY*

The New York Times best-selling author of American Gods and Coraline
NEIL GAIMAN
Volume Two
THE SANDMAN
THE DOLL'S HOUSE
VERTIGO

Neil GAIMAN
The SANDMAN
ENDLESS NIGHTS
Illustrated by
Glenn Fabry
Milo Manara
Miguelanxo Prado
Frank Quitely
P. Craig Russell
Bill Sienkiewicz
Barron Storey
VERTIGO

NEIL GAIMAN & YOSHITAKA AMANO
SANDMAN
THE DREAM HUNTERS

ALL TITLES ARE SUGGESTED FOR MATURE READERS.

SEARCH THE GRAPHIC NOVELS SECTION OF

www.VERTIGOCOMICS.com

FOR ART AND INFORMATION ON ALL OF OUR BOOKS!

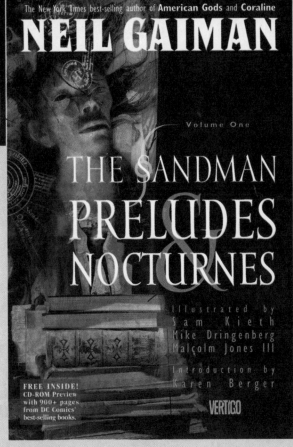

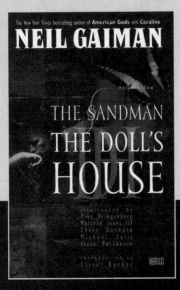